SONG MEANS: ANALYSING AND
RECORDED POPULAR SONG

Song Means:
Analysing and Interpreting
Recorded Popular Song

ALLAN F. MOORE

ASHGATE

Published by
Ashgate Publishing Limited
Wey Court East
Union Road
Farnham
Surrey, GU9 7PT
England

Ashgate Publishing Company
Suite 420
101 Cherry Street
Burlington
VT 05401-4405
USA

www.ashgate.com

British Library Cataloguing in Publication Data
Moore, Allan F.
Song means: analysing and interpreting recorded popular song. – (Ashgate popular and folk music series)
1. Songs – Analysis, appreciation. 2. Popular music – Philosophy and aesthetics. 3. Sound recordings in musicology.
I. Title II. Series
782.4'2164-dc22

Library of Congress Cataloging-in-Publication Data
Moore, Allan F.
Song means : analysing and interpreting recorded popular song / Allan F. Moore.
p. cm. – (Ashgate popular and folk music series)
Includes bibliographical references and index.
ISBN 978-1-4094-2864-0 (hardcover : alk. paper) – ISBN 978-1-4094-3802-1 (pbk. : alk. paper) – ISBN 978-1-4094-2865-7 (ebook) 1. Popular Music–Analysis, appreciation. 2. Popular music–History and criticism.
I.Title.
MT146.M66 2012
782.42164'117--dc23
2011026564

ISBN 9781409428640 (hbk)
ISBN 9781409438021 (pbk)
ISBN 9781409428657 (ebk)

Bach musicological font developed by © Yo Tomita

Printed and bound in Great Britain by the
MPG Books Group, UK.

List of Figures and Tables

Figures

Tables

List of Music Examples

General Editor's Preface

The upheaval that occurred in musicology during the last two decades of the twentieth century has created a new urgency for the study of popular music alongside the development of new critical and theoretical models. A relativistic outlook has replaced the universal perspective of modernism (the international ambitions of the 12-note style); the grand narrative of the evolution and dissolution of tonality has been challenged, and emphasis has shifted to cultural context, reception and subject position. Together, these have conspired to eat away at the status of canonical composers and categories of high and low in music. A need has arisen, also, to recognize and address the emergence of crossovers, mixed and new genres, to engage in debates concerning the vexed problem of what constitutes authenticity in music and to offer a critique of musical practice as the product of free, individual expression.

Popular musicology is now a vital and exciting area of scholarship, and the *Ashgate Popular and Folk Music Series* presents some of the best research in the field. Authors are concerned with locating musical practices, values and meanings in cultural context, and draw upon methodologies and theories developed in cultural studies, semiotics, poststructuralism, psychology and sociology. The series focuses on popular musics of the twentieth and twenty-first centuries. It is designed to embrace the world's popular musics from Acid Jazz to Zydeco, whether high tech or low tech, commercial or non-commercial, contemporary or traditional.

Professor Derek B. Scott
Professor of Critical Musicology
University of Leeds

Acknowledgements

Some of the material, particularly from Chapters 7, 8 and 9 has already appeared in different form within the following publications, but it is here pressed into the service of this larger project. 'Addressing the Persona', *Black Box Pop: Analysen populärer Music* (Beitraege zur Popularmusikforschung 38), ed. by Dietrich Helms and Thomas Phleps. Bielefeld, 2011; 'One Way of feeling: contextualising a hermeneutics of spatialization', in Stan Hawkins (ed.), *Critical Musicological Reflections*, Ashgate 2012, forthcoming; 'Beyond a musicology of production', in Simon Frith and Simon Zagorski-Thomas (eds.): *The Art of Record Production*, Ashgate, forthcoming 2012; 'Where is here? An issue of deictic projection in recorded song', *Journal of the Royal Musical Association* 135/1, 2010, 145–82; 'Configuring the sound-box, 1965–72', with Ruth Dockwray, *Popular Music* 29/2, 2010, 181–97; 'The track', in Amanda Bayley (ed.), *Recorded Music: Society, Technology and Performance*; Cambridge University Press, 2010, pp. 252–67; 'A hermeneutics of spatialization for recorded song', with Patricia Schmidt and Ruth Dockwray, *twentieth-century music* 6/1, 2009, 81–112; 'Interpretation: So what?' in Derek B. Scott (ed.), *Research Companion to Popular Musicology*, Ashgate, 2009, pp. 411–25; 'The establishment of the virtual performance space in rock', with Ruth Dockwray; *twentieth-century music* 5/2, 2008, pp. 219–41; 'The Persona/ Environment relation in recorded song', *Music Theory Online* 11/4, October 2005; 'Authenticity as authentication', *Popular Music* 21/2, May 2002, pp. 209–23. My thanks to successive cohorts of students (you know who you are!), whose deliberations have informed the interpretations developed in Chapter 6 onwards and to the many colleagues whose work I have plundered The collaborative nature of understanding is always hard to pin down, but that does not mean its existence should not be insisted upon. All I have done is to put this collection of thoughts in a particular order that suits my excessively systemic temperament. I owe particular debts of gratitude: to Nick Reyland, who has gamely used versions of this material with his own students (and to his students, who respond most generously); to Ruth Dockwray who acted as my research assistant for some of the work I have made use of here; to Patty Schmidt with whom I worked on one particular project; to Derek Scott and Heidi Bishop at Ashgate for their unfailing support; and to Charlie Ford, Tim Hughes and Dai Griffiths who, in discussing many of these ideas with me over the years have consistently, and justifiably, worried me that I wasn't making sense!

I am pleased to dedicate this work to various European colleagues who have played their own parts in its gestation: to Roberto Agostini and Luca Marconi in Bologna, to Franco Fabbri in Turin, to Stan Hawkins in Oslo and Esa Lilja in Helsinki,

Chapter 1

Methodology

Introduction

Who are you? How do you define yourself, your identity? The chances are that who you believe yourself to be is partly founded on the music you use, what you listen to, what values it has for you, what meanings you find in it. You may not at present be conscious of this (few are), you may not wish to be. If that's the case, then don't waste your time by reading any further …

So, unless you're just idly perusing, that's clearly not the case. What meanings can experiencing a song have, and how does it create those meanings? That, broadly speaking, is what this book is about. Note, though, that it's not about *what* songs 'actually' seem to mean, it's about *how* they mean, and *the means* by which they mean (which is my excuse for the strange title). And, although I would hope you find in it much that is accessible, if you find reading about musical detail difficult, then you may need to be prepared to put it down from time to time. Listening to songs is as easy as driving a car – easier, probably. Understanding how they work is as hard as being a mechanic (or so I believe – it's as much as I can do to understand how and why to check the oil in mine). The reason I focus on the 'how' is that I believe that, as a listener, you participate fundamentally in the meanings that songs have. As a listener, you're not fed these meanings on a plate, and if someone (particularly someone in a position of power, a music journalist, a musician, a teacher or parent) insists a song's meaning is such and such, you have every right to disagree (yes, even with the musicians who wrote and sang the song). Indeed, much of the book is effectively a series of arguments and demonstrations as to the value of doing this. Your disagreement will be most effective, of course, and most convincing to yourself, if you understand how it is that a song means for you, and it is particularly in order to develop those tools of understanding that this book was written. The rest of this chapter concerns its academic background and rationale. It's not essential reading – you may want to skip straight to Chapter 2 – but the context has some importance in developing more fully the necessity of the task.

Analysis

In the past 25 years, perhaps since the launch of the journal that bears the discipline's name, music analysis has taken its place at the centre of the body of techniques with which scholars of music can address their subject. And, although it may have been assailed by post-structuralists, by post-modernists, and by cultural theorists within the field, this has only served to refine the methods that music analysts employ to make them more suitable to the object at hand, or to the analytical imperative that begins the process of analysis itself. The academic study of 'popular music' is a newer phenomenon, beginning from such disciplines as sociology, literary and cultural studies, and has only far more recently been addressed within the academic field of music. Bringing these two together, 'music analysis' and 'popular music', is an undertaking that has been addressed a number of times[1] but not yet, to my mind, at sufficient length and in sufficient detail. That observation was a secondary motivation for this study. For O'Donnell, the time is not yet ripe for a thorough theoretical treatise even on the workings of rock music alone, a subset of the repertory I address here: 'we need many more close analytical readings of specific songs ... before attempting to generalize the musical properties of fifty years of rock'.[2] Because I have some sympathy with this view, I offer in this book a methodology, rather than a theory proper.[3] For all its minor uncertainties, and despite its age, Middleton's *Studying Popular Music*[4] remains the best theoretical overview of popular music we have. The theoretical pose of parts of the opening chapters (in which I have avoided the rigour of theory per se) is thus intended chiefly to support the hermeneutic[5] superstructure of the remainder, rather than to be self-sufficient. More on this relationship anon.

I begin with the two understandings of the book's title to which I have already alluded. The first is to try to lay bare the means by which popular songs are constructed. I do this from the viewpoint of the analyst, the listener with a deal of prior knowledge, but I always endeavour to bear in mind the more numerically common listener, the everyday listener, whose ears will frequently be as acute as mine, but who will not have the technical vocabulary, or will not perhaps be aware of the wealth of associations, to which I draw attention. The second, which I believe is no less pertinent, is to assert that popular songs create meanings in listeners (or perhaps the listeners create the meanings through listening to the songs, the difference being a matter of theoretical, but not practical, interest).

---

[1]   For example, John Covach, 'We won't get fooled again: rock music and musical analysis' in David Schwarz et al (eds.), *Keeping Score: Music, Disciplinarity, Culture* (Charlottesville VA, 1997), pp. 75–89 and Robert Walser, 'Popular music analysis: ten apothegms and four instances' in Allan F. Moore (ed.), *Analyzing Popular Music* (Cambridge, 2003), pp. 16–38.

[2]   Shaugn O'Donnell, Review of Stephenson, *What to listen for in rock*, *Music Theory Spectrum* 28/1 (2006), p. 139.

[3]   Alternatively, in Heideggerian terms, a ready-to-hand rather than a present-at-hand.

[4]   Richard Middleton, *Studying Popular Music* (Buckingham, 1990).

[5]   I intend this term simply as a less confusing alternative to 'interpretive', since to 'interpret' music is often felt to be what a performer does with the music presented to them. This latter meaning plays no part in what follows – I use 'hermeneutic' as synonymous with 'interpretive' rather than making any great reference to the German philosophical tradition.

Thus, I endeavour to explain the means by which songs can mean. I do this as an analyst, not a composer, nor an ethnographer, for the sounds to which we listen are the minimum of what we have in common as listeners. The book lays out the methodology which I have used, at first implicitly and subsequently explicitly, in all the interpretive work I have undertaken in the field since the early 1990s, and particularly in the interpretations I have presented in the broadcast media. Their level of reception suggests to me that what follows is of far from only academic interest and applicability, even if that is where it begins. Whereas many writers on popular music are interested in why a host of the activities connected to music are meaningful, I am concerned here with only one of those activities, the making sense of specific listening experiences.

I address popular song rather than popular music. The defining feature of popular song lies in the interaction of everyday words and music. Commentators, myself included, tend to address one at the expense of the other (often because of what they perceive as their level of expertise – does one have to be an expert to address musical details?), but it is how they interact that produces significance in the experience of song, in most cases. This also explains why I largely restrict my study to Anglophone songs. An analogy may be fruitful. The rush to interpretation that so many make, without grounding such an interpretation in the detail of the song that gives rise to it, seems to me akin to talking about the enjoyment of pancakes by focusing only on the maple syrup (which requires the pancake to carry it), and by declaring either that the size and type of egg that goes into the batter (hen, duck, goose?) is irrelevant, or that breaking the egg should be done mechanically, because it is too hard for human hands to get right every time.

Writing in 2010, the 'analysis of music' no longer requires justification. But, the 'analysis of music' is often taken (by both sympathizers and detractors) to be synonymous with the 'structural analysis of music', that is with the ascertaining of the musical relationships that obtain between different parts of a musical object (usually the score, occasionally the performance) or between parts of the object and the whole. It is a self-sufficient enterprise and it succeeds to the extent that it demonstrates those relationships. Although that may be all very well for the music of the concert tradition (I don't believe it is, but that is a separate argument), it is not adequate to the discussion of popular song: indeed, I find a more realistic (and acceptable) definition of analysis to concern the issuing of an invitation to hear a particular sample of music in a particular way. Because popular song neither exhibits stylistic complexity (on the basis of which its success can be evaluated) nor necessarily results from carefully considered, artistic creation, its analysis is often thought to require justification, perhaps along the lines I am suggesting. However, popular songs are, frequently, put together with a minimum of overt concern for aesthetics (although aesthetics are still there), and always with an ear to a particular listening public. They will only attract that public if they can resonate with potential listeners, if they can mean something to them. To analyse songs without addressing the issue of meaning is, quite simply, to evade the issue. So, in principle at least, analysis can be directed towards two different types of question: first, asking of a musical experience questions like what, how and why; and, second, asking questions of value, effectively analysing whether a particular aesthetic is achieved. Determining the aesthetic of a given item of music needs to be based on explicit criteria because we can imagine mutually exclusive criteria of value: relational richness; motivic logic; surface diversity; economy of material; breadth of reference; structural coherence; emotional impact; commercial potential (etc.). Each of these criteria may be valid, but only for particular styles. (One of the most pressing of contemporary tasks is the explication of criteria for the various musics we encounter, for we have still not escaped the academic hegemony of the European canon.)

Michael Chanan extended Roland Barthes'[6] emphasis on the importance of *musica practica*, of acknowledging that the way listeners listen is greatly determined by whatever bodily knowledge they have of producing music. This has two important consequences. First, as we now know from the discovery of the operation of motor neurons in the brain,[7] trumpeters' neurological response to trumpet music differs from her or his neurological response to piano music, a response she or he cannot control, by virtue of the fact that she or he has intimate physiological knowledge of what it takes to produce music from a trumpet. This is because the same body of neurons fires whether the action (e.g. playing the trumpet) is being undertaken, or is being perceived and hence simulated. But, second, trumpet music will forever engage him or her more completely than it will a non-trumpeter, no matter how competent at listening the latter may be, for the same reason. In terms of focusing on the details of melodic and harmonic structures, particularly if we refuse the artificial aid of visual notation, experience of producing the sounds can be crucial, and this is my second point. Across a variety of fields, we find testament to differences of mental operation in regard to these competences. From music education, Keith Swanwick[8] follows Michael Polanyi in distinguishing 'explicit' from simply 'tacit' knowledge. From music theory, Nicholas Cook[9] distinguishes 'musicological' from simply 'musical' listening. From psychology, Howard Gardner[10] distinguishes 'musical' from other forms of 'intelligence'. From pedagogy theory, David Elliott[11] distinguishes 'problem-solving' from simply 'problem-reducing' competences for music. Theodor Adorno,[12] of course, distinguished the 'expert' from the simply 'emotional'

---

[6]   Michael Chanan, *Musica practica* (London, 1994) and Roland Barthes, 'Musica practica' in *Image–Music–Text* (London, 1977).

[7]   Jerome Feldman, *From molecule to metaphor: a neural theory of language* (Cambridge MA, 2008).

[8]   Keith Swanwick, *Music, Mind and Education* (London, 1988).

[9]   Nicholas Cook, *Music, imagination, and culture* (Oxford, 1990).

[10]   Howard Gardner, *Frames of Mind* (Cambridge MA, 1985).

[11]   David Elliott, *Music Matters* (Oxford, 1995).

[12]   Theodor Adorno, *Introduction to the Sociology of Music* (New York NY, 1976).

listener, while Mark deBellis[13] combines analytic philosophy and cognitive theory to distinguish 'conceptual' from simply 'non-conceptual' listening. Despite disparities of detail, these writers are all acknowledging the same basic, structural, difference. In order to discuss how a musical experience was, we need to communicate its changing effect on us, and we therefore need to be able to identify parts of pieces precisely in order to do this. 'Popular', or 'non-conceptual' or 'problem-reducing' competences tend to have access to no such precise language.[14] In the method outlined here, then, I am not necessarily modelling the sense any particularly listener may actually make, I am modelling the sense particular listeners will have the potential to make, related to their competence in the styles that articulate the structures they are hearing. This is necessary in order to counter some of the assumptions that stand for scholarship in some circles. To take just one example somewhat at random, Sean Cubitt has argued that: 'Melody must disrupt the perfection of the tonic just as any good story has to begin with a departure, a mystery or some similar intervention ... like narrative, in its departure from the norm, melody must contain a promise to return to the narrative closure of restored order ...'.[15] Such an unnuanced view may have been adequate in 1984, when we had undertaken little research into how popular melody actually operates but, as Chapter 4 will show, such globalizing assumptions (this is how melody must work) are no longer tenable. It will be clear by now that my concern is with music as it sounds, rather than in any representation of it: as Shepherd notes: 'little work has been undertaken on issues of textuality in relation to the sounds of popular music'.[16] It is in that sphere that this book operates.

To analyse a popular song is, of its very nature, to offer an interpretation of it, to determine what range of meaning it has, to make sense of it. Such determination, such making, is an after-the-event operation. Think what happens when we encounter somebody we do not know. Frequently, after that encounter, we will find ourselves reflecting on it, thinking of alternative ways it could have gone, coming to a decision (however implicit) as to how to act should we encounter the person again. The analogy with what happens in listening to a song is, I think, a good one. While listening, we are simply experiencing the song. Afterwards, however, if we are so inclined, reflection on that experience can produce for us an understanding of ourselves within that experience, and an orientation to adopt in listening to the song again. Too often in the literature, whether academic, journalistic, fan posting, or whatever, interpretations are made without adequate anchorage in the details

---

[13]   Mark deBellis, *Music and Conceptualization* (Cambridge, 1995).

[14]   Zbikowski notes that both 'implicit' and 'explicit' knowledge are 'accessible to consciousness'. See Lawrence Zbikowski, 'Modelling the groove: conceptual structure and popular music', *Journal of the Royal Musical Association* 129/2 (2004), p. 276.

[15]   Sean Cubitt, '"Maybelline": meaning and the listening subject', *Popular Music* 4 (1984), p. 209.

[16]   John Shepherd, 'Text', in Bruce Horner and Thomas Swiss (eds.), *Key terms in popular music and culture* (Oxford, 1999), p. 171.

of an actual aural experience of a song. It is as if our determination to approach someone in a particular way on a second meeting is not actually based on what we discovered about them during the first. Journalistic and fan writing can often proceed as if the meanings of songs were determinate, as if there were 'right' and 'wrong' ways to interpret a song (whereby interpreting it 'correctly', means being 'in the know', a means by which one acquires sub-cultural capital). In so doing, this reinvents beliefs about the meanings of concert music that academic thinking has generally cast aside. There is a strong body of opinion that acknowledges the flexibility with which listeners actually approach songs and attempt to discover meaning within them. Richard Middleton writes in terms of some music being 'under-coded',[17] by which he points to the necessity of listeners' experiences being used to complete a song's meaning. I have elsewhere made use of the concept of songs 'affording' particular meanings,[18] by which I mean that although we can say what they are not about, we can only specify a range of possibilities as to what they might be thought to be about, and I return to this point later. Specification of that range requires secure purchase on the sounds, and their connotations, of which songs actually consist. Then again, for some listeners, it seems that a song means whatever they want it to mean. Again, this seems unsatisfactory, for it suggests a peculiarly hermetic, immature existence reminiscent of Humpty Dumpty.[19] To quote Mark Johnson, in a study to which I shall also return, 'we do not simply construct reality according to our subjective desires and whims ... [but neither are we] simple mirrors of a nature that determines our concepts in one and only one way ... [T]he environment is structured in ways that limit the possibilities for our categorizations of it. But the structure of the environment by no means strictly determines the structure of our experience ... .'[20] An emphasis on 'environment' will become clear in later chapters. Astute readers will have already noticed an implicit limitation I am placing on the construction of meaning. Where is that realm of concerns we might label 'socio-cultural' meanings? Bethany Klein asserts the problem clearly: 'A model of meaning that focuses only on the lyrics and instrumentation refuses to engage with another very real sense of meaning in popular music: meaning as personal and emotional significance ... Groups make use of popular music to indicate shared identifications, and to celebrate and honor shared events. Audiences ... create commonalities tied to music. Fans of sports teams use songs to distinguish themselves from fans of other teams ...' (etc., etc.).[21] While the latter chapters do address emotional significance, from a very

---

[17] Middleton, *Studying*, p. 173.

[18] Allan F. Moore, *Rock: the Primary Text* (2nd edn, Aldershot, 2001), pp. 6–7, 25.

[19] I refer, of course, to the words Lewis Carroll puts into his mouth.

[20] Mark Johnson, *The body in the mind: the bodily basis of meaning, imagination, and reason*, (Chicago IL, 1987), p. 207.

[21] Bethany Klein, *As heard on TV: popular music in advertising* (Farnham, 2009), pp. 110–13. My focus is far broader than just 'instrumentation', but I think what I offer would still come under Klein's criticism.

particular viewpoint, I do not deal with the rest. I would not wish to assert that the realm of meaning in which I am interested is necessarily more important than these others, but I do not treat them here because they are not nuanced, because the associations made cannot be predicted in advance and, indeed, because those meanings lose their grip once a listener begins to take interest in the activity of listening. In any case, these spheres are widely addressed – as I have suggested above, it is the hermeneutic approach that lags behind and my addressing of it here should be taken as a serious attempt to redress the balance.

Structure

The book is laid out in 11 chapters, for which this first lays the groundwork and provides the rationale. I try to observe a reasonably strict distinction between analysis and interpretation. Thus, in Chapter 2 I look at issues of timbre and texture, believing that it is the feel of a recorded song that first attracts or repels most listeners (not musicologists, maybe, but then they are pretty rare creatures), and that this therefore should be addressed first. Chapter 3 discusses matters of structure, rhythm and harmony, the conventional substance of most analytical discussion of music, while in Chapter 4 I look at the performing voice, together with the means a voice uses in song, namely melody and lyrics. However, it has to be said that the distinctions between these domains are artificial. They are necessary simply because in a linear medium (language), unlike the multilinear medium that is music, one cannot talk about everything at once, and some discursive order must be imposed. Constant reference forward and backward between the subjects of individual chapters will be necessary, and I hope you will have the patience to withhold judgement where necessary. In the latter part of the book, I look at issues of interpretation but, again, there is leakage not only between specific areas of interpretation, but also between interpretation and analysis. In practice, and with experience, one does not begin an encounter at the beginning (for there is no beginning – each encounter is built upon all previous encounters). Moreover, in order to get a sense that a particular musical detail may prove significant, one already has to have an intimation of how it might contribute to an interpretation – one cannot make analytic decisions without an ear to their significance. Thus, Chapter 6 looks at the issue of friction, at what happens when what happens is not what you expected to happen. Chapter 8 raises the large issue of how popular song refers to matters outside itself, focusing initially on the insights semiotics provides, but ultimately finding this unsatisfactory. Chapter 7 provides a deep discussion of the notion of the persona that a song presents, while Chapter 9 raises the twin issues of authenticity and intertextuality. In the final chapter I provide a digest of the questions that this study raises of any particular track, and that I anticipate serving as a starting-point for any study you undertake. Between these two parts of the study, in Chapter 5, I provide a brief outline of a style history of popular song, in order to situate the styles to which the rest of the book refers, and because such an outline study of Anglophone popular song (incorporating what has originated not only in North America, but also in the UK) does not at present exist.

I raised above the notion of *musica practica*. The second consequence of *musica practica* is that there is an embedded implication that all questions imply some sort of norm, deviation from which is a prime carrier of signification. This is the assumption that underpins Chapter 6 and, in starting discussions of interpretation at this point, I follow the view of systems theorist Gregory Bateson, who argued that 'information consists of differences that make a difference'.[22] Making a difference is the realm of signification, but in order to recognize that something is different, we need to have an implicit understanding of what it is different from, that is, of the norm against which we measure it. Mostly, this is implicit. Style-specific details for music are nowhere laid down, nor could they be, for musical styles are living constructs, subtly altered every time we hear something for the first time that is couched within the confines of a particular style. But norms are found within the understanding of 'style'.[23]

This is not, of course, the first book either to suggest an analytic method for recorded popular music, or to offer models for its interpretation. However, the two activities are rarely brought explicitly together. Although some of the ideas developed here first saw the light of day in my *Rock: the Primary Text*[24] (originally 1993), the link between analysis and interpretation remained, at that point, implicit. Ken Stephenson's recent introductory theory text for rock music[25] offers a fairly exhaustive treatment of certain analytic domains (although others he unfortunately leaves entirely unaddressed), but says little about the consequences of the patterns he discusses. For an earlier repertoire, Allen Forte's numerous analyses of the sheet music of American ballads,[26] for all their detail, are even less informative about the larger significance of the songs. From the opposite perspective, David Brackett's wide-ranging approach to signification[27] is rich in hermeneutics, but takes almost for granted the process of determining what it is we are hearing. I think this assumption is too risky a one to make, hence my concern to draw these two sides of the activity together. In doing so, certain specific approaches would have been possible. I have decried the formalist (Stephenson, Forte, etc.) wherein meaning is considered as an afterthought, even though the personal pleasure to be gained from such work is frequently intoxicating. In the opening chapters I steer close to this territory, but insist that this is only part of the book. An alternative

---

[22]   Gregory Bateson, *Mind and Nature: a necessary unity* (London, 1979).

[23]   Allan F. Moore, 'Categorical conventions in music-discourse: style and genre', *Music and Letters* 82/3 (2001).

[24]   Allan F. Moore, *Rock: the Primary Text* (Buckingham, 1993).

[25]   Ken Stephenson, *What to listen for in rock: a stylistic analysis* (New Haven CT, 2002).

[26]   Allen Forte, *The American Popular Ballad of the Golden Era* (Princeton NJ, 1995).

[27]   David Brackett, *Interpreting Popular Music* (2nd edn, Berkeley CA, 2000).

would be to adopt a psychoanalytic approach (Middleton's *Voicing the popular*[28] *par excellence*) but this, to me, seems to veer too far the other way, to be too hermetic in approach, too prone to flights of fancy and insufficiently grounded in the intricate details of a song. Alternatively, I might consider a semiotic approach. However, the principles of semiotics are opposed to principles I shall develop here. Recall the Saussurean insistence on the arbitrariness of the relationship between the signifier and the signified. Recall also the Derridean characterization of meaning as a system of unanchored differences. We must grant, I think, arbitrariness at the level of vocabulary, and the operation of unanchored difference in some creative fields, but semiotics has developed by promoting these levels to positions of principal significance. Thus, the arbitrariness of the signifier/ signified relationship and the system of differences have come to be assumed normative in the construction of meaning. I disagree and thus claim greater, more encompassing, significance for principles not of arbitrariness and unanchored difference, which I pursue particularly in the second half of the book. There are other, more idiosyncratic approaches that individuals have adopted,[29] but for me the explanatory basis on which an approach is developed needs to be fuller than this. The analytical approach I offer here is one that I characterize as interrogative. (Although you might be tempted to turn to Chapter 11 to discover the details of these interrogations now, I encourage you to read further before you do.) To return to an analogy I have already drawn, in order to get to know individuals, we will often ask questions both about them, and of them. The questions we ask will, of course, depend on answers to previous ones, but the interrogative approach normally results in us knowing them better than simply observing them. What is important is to have a bank of questions to employ, probably starting with the most general, and discarding those that seem irrelevant in a particular case. This was an approach I learnt to develop as an undergraduate, as a way of assuaging the fear of not knowing where to start when faced with the task of 'making an analysis' of some music new to me. The questions I use here are different, but the approach remains just as functional. It is this methodology that underlies this book. (I choose not to foreground these questions at any point in the text, which would become rather simplistic; they are nonetheless all laid out in Chapter 11 to enable you to either trace their influence, or to use them to work at your own analysis/ interpretation.) Each discussion gives rise to a series of potential questions to be levelled at whatever song you are listening to, the answers to which will help you to know the song better, and hence to understand it better. Ultimately, they will lead you to a discovery of its meaning for yourself, a meaning that will have many points of contact with what other listeners find, but that you should not expect to coincide at every point.

---

[28]   Richard Middleton, *Voicing the popular* (London, 2006).

[29]   For example Christian Kennett, 'Is anybody listening', in Allan F. Moore (ed.), *Analyzing Popular Music* (Cambridge, 2003).

Theory

The intellectual aim of this book rests ultimately on arguments that surface in two passages from Paul Ricoeur's *Interpretation theory*. He speaks of the necessity of interpretation, and of its creative cast:

> What is indeed to be understood – and consequently appropriated – in a text? Not the intention of the author, which is supposed to be hidden behind the text; not the historical situation common to the author and his original readers; not the expectations or feelings of these original readers; not even their understanding of themselves and historical and cultural phenomena. What has to be appropriated is the meaning of the text itself, conceived in a dynamic way as the direction of thought opened up by the text. In other words, what has to be appropriated is nothing other than the power of disclosing a world that constitutes the reference of the text. In this way we are as far as possible from the Romanticist ideal of coinciding with a foreign psyche. If we may be said to coincide with anything, it is not the inner life of another ego, but the disclosure of a possible way of looking at things, which is the genuine referential power of the text.[30]

The general hermeneutic programme embodied in this book seeks not only the disclosure of such (musical) worlds, but the grounding on which such opening up is performed. In other words, the *possible way of looking at things* has to be communicable, has to have its premises made explicit if it is not to reside in some hermetic space accessible only to the appropriator.

My endorsement of Ricoeur's use of the word 'text' might seem odd here, but it has become common practice in the interpretation of culture. This is not the place for a full discussion of the application of the concept to recorded song; it is sufficient that a text is something that is 'read', that is, made sense of, interpreted. I appropriate that sense here, while ignoring the assumption that a text be a visible object.[31] However, one crucial difference must be identified. The book you hold in your hand (or perhaps read on the screen) bears no physical trace of the presence of its author – that presence was lost as this document became the responsibility of the publisher. The recordings I discuss bear, for many of their listeners, the genuine aural trace of the voices (and instrumental performance) of the musicians themselves. And yet, the process of their transfer to the digital domain (for, like that of many listeners, most of my listening now takes place in this domain)

---

[30]   Paul Ricoeur, *Interpretation theory: discourse and the surplus of meaning* (Fort Worth TX, 1979), p. 92.

[31]   If you make a careful reading of Ricoeur's key analysis of textuality, you will find very little to challenge were his written, linguistic 'text' to be replaced by a recorded, musical 'text'. Paul Ricoeur, 'What is a text? Explanation and Understanding' in Ricoeur: *From text to action: Essays in Hermeneutics, II*, trans. K. Blamey & J. B. Thompson (London, 2008).

enacts a similar effacement, but it is one in which the disguise of that aural trace is ordinarily transparent. When we listen to the last 50" of Hothouse Flowers' 'Spirit of the land', the energy embodied in all those short 'oo' sounds, sung at full volume, is palpable, and is conveyed by the medium. Some of the power of this moment comes from the superimposition of a $\frac{6}{4}$ pattern over a $\frac{12}{8}$ beat, but that only increases the level of energy as these voices pull against that basic metre. Or, when we listen to Robert Plant sing the word 'gone' at 31" of his duet with Alison Krauss ('Gone, gone, gone'), as he slips from unison with her to an inflected note a third below, we can hear that the only way he can make that particular 'o' vowel is with his lips beginning to open towards a smile, and a corresponding tautening of the cheeks, and that (subtle) realization cannot help but have an impact on the sense we make of the track, notwithstanding the fact that all actual trace of that vocal movement is lost. No such equivalent information is available with regard to my hand movements in typing (and retyping) this particular word. So, acknowledgement that meaning in a recording can be seen as coinciding with disclosure of the world referenced by that recording is not the purely formalist enterprise that would deny recognition of the import of the action of Robert Plant's body, or Liam O'Maonlai's (or, by extension, mine) in its manifestation.

Ricoeur speaks also of the provisionality of interpretation, to which I have already referred in the context of Johnson and of affordance:

> if it is true that there is always more than one way of construing a text, it is not true that all interpretations are equal. The text presents a limited field of possible constructions. The logic of validation allows us to move between the two limits of dogmatism and scepticism. It is always possible to argue for or against an interpretation, to confirm interpretations, to arbitrate between them and to seek agreement, even if this agreement remains beyond our immediate reach.[32]

There are many ways to formulate this dynamic. Another comes from Theodore Gracyk, who insists that:

> different audiences approach the text in terms of their own interpretive framework. If they can make sense of it from within that framework, their reading is no better than the reading of someone employing a different framework, *even if these frameworks differ from the ones governing interpretation in the musical community of the originating musician.*[33]

Individual listeners form audiences, although I concentrate here on what is available to the former. And, although different readings are not 'better' than each

---

[32] Ricoeur, *Interpreting*, p. 79.

[33] Theodore Gracyk, *I wanna be me: rock music and the politics of identity* (Philadelphia PA, 2001), p. 38 - italics in the original.

other as Gracyk describes, interesting discussions and persuasions can take place over their relative usefulness, once the basis on which they are made is clear.

The theoretical basis of my methodology is formed from the interface of a number of positions, the majority of which will be explored during the latter stages of the book. The foundation is that of *ecological perception*. The ecological approach to perception was first developed by James J. Gibson,[34] and has been reconceived specifically with reference to music, particularly by Eric Clarke.[35] Ecological perception can be characterized most simply by the phrase *invariants afford through specifications*. An ecological approach *identifies* invariants that are perceived in the environment. In the case of music, this environment is purely sonic. Such an approach then observes what *responses* these invariants afford, and it thus promotes *action* on the basis of the source the sound is (not necessarily consciously) interpreted as specifying. That action may consist of no more than a decision to make sense of that sound in relation to others. A chief component of the ecological view is the observation that the environment limits our room for interpretation, but does not prescribe it. As a result of this foundation, this book does not accept the assumption that a song carries a message, which is communicated from a singer to a listener (or from a group of musicians to a group of listeners, etc.). I take a basic line from the ecological theory of Edward Reed, who argues that '*Language is not a means of transmitting ideas or representations; it is a means of making information available to others*',[36] and that the widely used metaphors of channels, senders and receivers, have only developed since the invention of the telegraph[37] – they thus misrepresent the normative function of language. In this limited way, and particularly because of its use of lyrics, popular song seems to me no different.

A view closely related to the ecological is that of *embodied cognition*, found in the work of a number of cognitive scientists, particularly Johnson, Lakoff, Fauconnier, Turner, Feldman and Fillmore.[38] Although a wide-ranging field, perhaps the largest single point that unites it is the theory that language usage and

---

[34]   James J. Gibson, *The senses considered as perceptual systems* (Boston MA, 1966) and *The ecological approach to visual perception* (London, 1979).

[35]   Eric F. Clarke, *Ways of listening* (Oxford, 2005).

[36]   Edward S. Reed, *Encountering the world: toward an ecological psychology* (New York NY, 1996), p. 155.

[37]   Reed, *Encountering*, p. 156.

[38]   Johnson, *The body in the mind*; Mark Johnson, *The meaning of the body* (Chicago IL, 2007); George Lakoff, *Women, fire, and dangerous things* (Chicago IL, 1987); George Lakoff and Mark Johnson, *Metaphors we live by* (Chicago IL, 1980) and *Philosophy in the flesh*, (New York NY, 1999); George Lakoff and Mark Turner, More than cool reason: a field guide to poetic metaphor (Chicago IL, 1989); Gilles Fauconnier, *Mappings in thoughts and language* (Cambridge, 1997); Gilles Fauconnier and Mark Turner, *The way we think: conceptual blending and the mind's hidden complexities* (New York NY, 2002); Mark Turner, *The literary mind: the origins of thought and language* (New York NY, 1996);

ability is integrated into the brain rather than operating in specific language areas and ways, a view dominated by the work of Noam Chomsky. I have drawn from this field some useful models, mainly those of *mental spaces* (Fauconnier), *conceptual blends* (Fauconnier and Turner) and *image schemata* (Johnson). Feldman's text is particularly valuable in that it develops a neural theory of language in which all these models are integrated in a single sweep. I argue that there is no fundamental contradiction between these ecological and embodied views in Chapter 8.

So much for foundation. The remaining theoretical positions, which are coherent with this basis, are all explicitly musical, and will develop during the course of the book. Two must be mentioned at this point, however, since their ramifications are wide. The first is the importance of style. Musical style is analogous to spoken language. Just as the sounds that make up a word mean different things in different languages (or, at least, potentially do so), so the sounds that make up music have different significances depending on the style. This is a tricky idea since, although we know implicitly the difference of sound between the blues and gospel, between swing and country, between rock and metal, those differences cannot be defined exclusively. In an earlier book (*Rock: the Primary Text*) I argued that, as far as 'rock' is concerned, rather than come up with a set of characteristics that define it such that any example can be clearly labelled as either 'rock' or not, we can better understand it 'by treating it as structured by a multiply-evolving but coherent set of rules and practices'.[39] I stick by that, but would add that other 'style' labels, cognate musical categories, are best understood in the same way. In fact, this approach is one that has become quite widespread and not only in the humanities. George Lakoff has drawn together contemporary thinking on categories, and the problems of their definition, arguing that not only are our categories partly dependent on 'the bodily nature of the people doing the categorizing' (in other words, they are not 'objective'), but that 'members of a category may be related to one another without all members having any properties in common that define the category'.[40] Thus our categories are dependent on the work we want them to do. The second is the belief that the formal elements of music do not only refer to themselves, but refer beyond themselves. Another way of saying this is to assert that elements of music all carry meaning, or signify, at the level of style – they help us determine what style we're listening to and, hence, how to 'categorize' what we're listening to, but many of those elements also signify at the level of the individual song – they carry meaning that differs from song to song within the same style. To take a simple example: when a musical process comes to an end (when a verse gives way to a chorus, for example), that can be 'read' as a feature of the realm to which the song refers coming to an end. The referential power of musical syntax implies, for example, that harmonic closure or its avoidance modifies a song's

---

Feldman, *From molecule to metaphor* and Charles J. Fillmore, 'Frame semantics', in Dirk Geeraerts (ed.), *Cognitive Linguistics: basic readings* (Berlin 2006).

[39] Moore, *Rock*, p. 7.

[40] Lakoff, *Women, fire*, pp. 371, 12.

degree of narrative closure. It is a basic factor of human perception that we transfer meaning in one domain to another, a notion that is recognized within what I have characterized as *embodied cognition* as *cross-domain mapping*. In the words of Lawrence Zbikowski, who has explored the value of this idea for the understanding of concert song: 'Cross-domain mapping is a process through which we structure our understanding of one domain (which is typically unfamiliar or abstract) in terms of another (which is most often familiar and concrete).'[41] Zbikowski illustrates the concept by suggesting we understand electrical conductance through a hydraulic model – we talk of electricity *flowing*, for example (although whether are all more familiar with hydraulic than electrical processes is perhaps a moot point). To my mind, it is only with the theoretical understanding of cross-domain mapping that we have a reliable basis for all theories of representation – we now understand the sort of operations our brains (inevitably) make to enable representation to take place. It is possible that a motive for formalism (the position that music means only itself) may be the lack of empirical evidence for theories of representation. That evidence, that justification, it seems to me, we finally have.

As consumers, we gain access to popular songs through four formats. Until the 1960s, all popular songs were performed live. Many continue to be so performed, but it is no longer the case that songs necessarily are. While for some performers the live performance is still the main focus of activity, for others (and for some genres), it represents only an approximation of what time and care in the studio was able to develop. Moreover, a live performance is an evanescent thing, where subsequent attention to detail is almost impossible, since no reference can be made to the performance (unless it was recorded, of course, but then the reference is made to the recording, not to the performance). Writers of popular songs do not create scores, in the way that classical composers do; such writers tend to work with sound and music directly, rather than through the medium of writing, of coded instructions given to others to realize. This is not to say that we cannot find song composers, whose output is given to others to sing but, in these cases, the intervention of producers, arrangers and engineers is arguably as important as the contribution of the original songwriter. Nor is it to say that we cannot find songs written down; this remains a small part of the market even today, while magazines directed towards musicians frequently employ detailed transcriptions, effectively instructing readers in exactly what actions to perform to create the sounds that will culminate in a particular song. The key word here, however, is transcription; it only represents someone else's *post hoc* view of what the song is. (I shall make use of many transcribed portions of songs in this book, but they serve only to enable writer and reader to focus, to take out-of-time, to make available for reflection, a portion of an actual recorded song.) And transcriptions can be notoriously inaccurate. Until the development of digital media, recordings were committed to analogue tape (and still sometimes are, in certain circumstances) and thence to vinyl.

---

[41]   Lawrence Zbikowski, *Conceptualising music: Cognitive Structure, Theory, and Analysis* (New York NY, 2002), p. 13.

Although sound quality deteriorated on multiple uses, many listeners gained access to material primarily through this medium. Today, of course, this has been superseded by digital recordings. And, whether we buy CDs or download material from the internet, songs are most easily accessed these days in this format. Of course, this makes the analysis of the sound constituents of a recording easier, but does nothing to improve the analysis of the music, which still has to be done by an interpretive mind.

It is for this reason that this book concerns the analysis of recorded songs. Exactly what, though, is the recorded song? I distinguish three key terms: song; performance; track. Think of (or listen to) the song 'All along the watchtower'. What does it consist of? A particular sequence of chords can be identified (in the relationship C♯ minor–B major–A major or, in shorthand, c♯–B–A[42]), as can particular lyrics, and a regularity of metre (four beats to the bar, or one emphasized beat followed by three of lesser strength). But what about its melody? What about an answer to the question 'what does it sound like?' To answer that, we have to go to a particular recording, maybe Bob Dylan's original, Jimi Hendrix's famous cover, U2's later cover, or a more recent version recorded by Richie Havens.[43] What these four hold in common we can identify as constituting the 'song'. In the case of 'All along the watchtower' (and most, but not all, other songs), these four recordings share the metric and harmonic structure. They approximately share the melody, although there are deviations (of the sort I shall address in Chapter 4). They share the lyric, although there are differences in the use of specific words, while U2 add a few lyrics, and Richie Havens reorders them. What they do not share is matters of instrumentation, speed and tone, production value or style. These matters that are not shared are the realm of the performance (and this word is worth retaining even where a 'performance' is only 'virtual', i.e. is assembled in the studio – what we are presented with stands for an ideal performance). Combining both song and performance gives us what I define as the track and, throughout this book, it is in the tracks that are developed from songs that I am interested. Of course, in this particular case, there is far more to be said. Hendrix's reworking has been received as so powerful that all subsequent covers refer more to his 'interpretation' than to Dylan's (and Dylan's own subsequent work appears to have acknowledged this[44]). This is clear in the case of U2, but perhaps Havens' recent recording might appear to redress the balance? Then again, the sheer anxiety present in most versions appears to be lost in Havens' cover. Why might that be? And what is the import of U2's interpolation of 'three chords and the truth'? These are all matters of interpretation, all matters that will concern an interested listener,

---

[42]   In discussing harmonies, upper case identifies major, lower case identifies minor.

[43]   In order not to clog up too many pages with footnoted references to recordings, full details of all recordings referred to will be found in the discography.

[44]   See Albin Zak III, 'Bob Dylan and Jimi Hendrix: juxtaposition and transformation "All along the watchtower", *Journal of the American Musicological Society* 57/3 (2005), p. 639.

but unless we recognize how these are all versions of the same song, and thereby recognize the detail of the differences inherent in the performances, we remain at the level of answering only what is happening, and cannot attempt to move on to the so what, which directs the trajectory of all critical enquiry.

Repertory

But which recorded songs? What is the repertoire covered by this book? I approach this question in the same way as definitions of categories (above). It is not possible to definitively collect together every track that falls under the methodology's purview – some are central, some are borderline, some are outside. This is one reason why I have tried to avoid offering a *theory*, but offer a *methodology* instead. As I understand the latter term, it is an approach to take without concern for what it rests on. Those theoretical principles are there, and will surface from time to time, but are never the central issue. One reason for that is historic – the methodology began at a particular point in time and has subsequently developed. I originally devised it for use with the pop/rock of the late 1950s and 1960s[45] and it has grown by accretion as I have asked questions of other areas of the repertoire. Thus it may work most effectively for that original repertoire, but it is also pretty effective elsewhere, as I shall show. It will not yield everything to be discovered about a track, but that is an unrealizable goal anyway, for part of that everything is formed from each listener's individual past history. In order to demonstrate the stylistic range of material that responds to this methodology, I have intentionally chosen my examples from a wide range of recorded song, in the hope that whoever you are, you will be familiar with at least some of my examples (which partly explains why I go so often to the Beatles). Many examples are passed over rather briefly, but some I return to more than once. This is not to suggest that these tracks should be regarded in any way as 'canonic', merely that they provide rich examples of the ways that tracks are involved in the creation of meaning. The songs I choose have a strong tendency to work as tracks and not just as songs, they have a strong tendency to have been published as recordings and (nowadays at least) those recordings take priority over live renditions, they have a strong tendency to have circulated fairly widely (although I occasionally refer to something fairly obscure simply because it is such an apposite example), they have a strong tendency to be imitative rather than 'original' (although I will return to this idea in detail subsequently). And, most importantly, they exemplify the points I am making. So, with the proviso that this is a *methodology* rather than a *theory*, I believe that what is offered here does have wide applicability, across the whole discursive field that was, is, and for some time will be, popular song. While how something operates is

---

[45]   A similar repertoire to that offered in Walter Everett, *The foundations of rock*, (New York NY, 2009).

Chapter 2
Shape

Texture: Layers

The purpose of this chapter is to discuss a range of issues focusing on instrumentation and sound-sources in general within a recording. I start here simply because it is the sound-world set up by a track that frequently forms the point of entry for a listener, that first triggers a sense of recognition. Observations focus on what instruments sound like, how they work together, where they appear to be situated within the recording. There are three broad categories I shall discuss: *functional layers*, the *soundbox* and *timbre*. All these observations should lead to a series of questions: to what extent are they encountered in the track listened to; is the track consistent in its answer, or does it change; are there moments of surprise? It is most important to recognize, however, that what I am outlining here are not prescriptive rules, but generalized descriptions. Frequently, a particular track will, in whole or in part, challenge the assumptions it seems to encourage us to make. Such a challenge is a fundamental contributor to its effect.

Among my earliest experiences of teaching in higher education was that of trying to instil in general Humanities students, most of whom had no particular musical expertise, the important structural features of the concert and chamber music of the late eighteenth century. Heavily under the sway as I was at the time of Schenkerian, structuralist approaches to this music, I was loath to revert simply to having students listen out for themes and their differences. As might be expected, I got nowhere; until, that is, I began to realize, first with the early Beethoven string quartets, and then subsequently with Mozart chamber music, that points of structural importance were frequently marked by changes of texture. This was quite a realization for me, since texture was a feature that my own undergraduate studies had barely ever even mentioned. 'Sparse', 'dense', 'busy, 'calm' were okay as handy descriptors, place-holders, until one really got into worrying about the notes. Even technical descriptors such as 'homophony', 'heterophony' and 'polyphony' had their place, but they didn't really enable much analytical purchase. No, I learnt the hard way that it was changes in the detail of texture that proved really useful. It was at that point that I realized that by dismissing matters of texture we run the risk of missing crucial details about music, and about how it relates to us, since texture is of its nature about relationships, relationships between strands in a musical fabric (note how early I have to rely on metaphors here), and in finding significance for ourselves in the music we listen to, we may find our relationships mapped in that music. This is indeed a path I shall pursue, in various ways, later in the book. In order to do that, however, I need to give a clear idea of the norms to expect. We need to know what relationships we might anticipate being put forth.

The vast field that is popular music (this is wider than simply the case of 'song') exhibits a strong tendency to display four textural layers. Not all will be present in every example, not all will remain unchanging throughout a particular example. However, while one layer may be absent, or changes in these layers may occur in the course of a track, they do so against this background assumption of their presence. It is the principal norm of popular music.[1] In some cases, the mere observation that melodies are always accompanied can be interpretively forceful, and I shall follow up some instances of this observation. For now, though, I concentrate on these four layers.

Almost all popular song employs instruments for its enactment. Although we would expect to find certain instruments (a drum kit of some composition or other, a bass guitar, string bass or equivalent, strummed instruments, perhaps piano or electronic keyboards, banks of strings or wind instruments, and voices), a range of other instruments is possible. It is more fruitful not to begin from the instruments themselves, but from the functions they perform (the 'layers' they constitute) within the musical fabric. In most cases the most obvious, that which is most aurally apparent, is what I shall term the *explicit beat layer*. It is the function of this layer to articulate an explicit pattern of beats, the major constituent of the 'groove'. Most ordinarily, it is the function of a set of drums, a drum kit, or some such. The key feature of this layer is that it is nominally unpitched. I write 'nominally' since there is of course a difference of pitch between a snare drum and a kick drum, but it is an approximate difference. None of the instruments making up a conventional drum kit has a precisely identified pitch. The very presence of this layer is crucial in that, however closely related the material of popular song may be to its forebears in the earlier concert tradition, this layer serves to distance popular styles from those of the Western concert tradition. It is as basic to the popular song of Brazil as it is to Indonesia, for example: what differs is how it is manifested.

There is another facet to the 'groove', which is provided by the rhythmic profile of the instrument that provides the *functional bass layer*. This, again, is normative. It is not new to popular song – its presence has antecedents in the baroque trio sonata, for instance. What is distinctive about it is that, in most popular styles, its pitch role is to connect root position harmonies in one or more ways.

The third function is to make explicit one or more melodies, in the *melodic layer*. We will find primary and, often, secondary melodic lines. The primary line, of course, is the tune, and its essential role is to enable the articulation of the song's lyrics. Other than voices, a whole range of instruments can be found inhabiting this layer – electric guitar, keyboard of some sort, solo instruments (saxophone, trumpet, flute, fiddle, pipes of some kind, etc.). The instrumentation here may have a strong effect on identification of the style. If listeners are asked to communicate their memory of a particular song, it is on this layer that they tend to focus, and it

---

[1]   I argued this in the first edition of *Rock: the primary text*.

is thus this layer that carries a high proportion of the identity of the song. Thereby, bass and treble are prioritized within the texture.

The fourth function is to fill the 'registral' space between these bass and treble layers. This *harmonic filler layer* will, like the previous two, be familiar to listeners aware of the trio sonata. Here is where we can find the greatest range of instruments, from rhythm guitars, organs and pianos to saxophone choirs, voices, brass sections, even entire orchestras. It is arguably the constitution of this layer, and the way it is actualized, that has the greatest impact on the attribution of a particular style by any naive listener. A majority of styles probably have a keyboard instrument somewhere dominant within this layer although certain styles (rock, for instance, or country) will replace this with a guitar, while other styles (much metal, for instance) will dispense with it.

Layers: Examples

Some very basic examples will flesh out this schema. David Bowie's 'Queen bitch' presents a clear starting-place. The track begins with a few seconds of vigorously attacked harmonic filler, played on Bowie's acoustic guitar. This layer is then doubled, by the entry of an electric guitar, played with less rhythmic freneticism. Two more layers are then made apparent, with the combined entry of bass and drums. Finally, Bowie's voice enters, with a somewhat *parlando* melody, whose tune does not become properly apparent until the chorus at the end of the verse. Even such a simple example as this demonstrates two very important points. First, the electric guitar should ordinarily swamp the acoustic – it is appreciably louder. Indeed, for most of the song, we cannot pick out the pitches Bowie is playing. What we can pick out, however, is the rhythmic enlivening – the sound of the plectrum as it is strummed across the strings at some speed. The actual performance details, then, are material to the *song* that we encounter, as a *track*. Second, the track begins with the harmonic filler. Most listeners are less aware of the details, and functions, of harmony, than they are of any other element within music. It is the least transparent. For musicians, however, it often represents the starting-point both conceptually and performatively, often preceding (in both these senses) both lyrics and melody. One can guess that that was the case with 'Queen bitch'. An equally simple textural layout underpins the Honeycombs' cult 1964 hit 'Have I the right?' The track begins with all four layers apparent – bass and drum kit, solo guitar pre-empting the very simple melody, and guitar filler. The track is bathed in echo, the work of noted producer Joe Meek, which contributed in part to its cult status. The texture changes, however, to mark the chorus (in the way I outlined at the beginning of the chapter). The whole band switches to stop time (everyone coinciding on the beat, and playing only on the beat), beneath the singer's imploring injunction to 'Come right back, I just can't bear it ...'. Change of texture, here, marks a new urgency in his delivery.

The same functions are present in rock'n'roll but, belying its connotations as a music lacking in complexity, they are not necessarily straightforward. Chuck Berry's 'Johnny B. Goode' employs two electric guitar parts, for a start. One (Berry's own) shares the melody with his voice, in a pattern which develops from blues and gospel, known as 'call and response'. The second acts as a harmonic filler, but a rhythmically active filler, playing a 'boogie' riff (Example 2.1). There is a (string) bass and a kit, although the former is felt rather than heard, partly a function of contemporary recording technology. Finally, there is also a piano. At various points in the track, the piano switches between three functions – those of harmonic filler, of supplying a bass line, and of melodic interjections (in effect, secondary melodies) at the upper extreme of the instrument.

Example 2.1   Chuck Berry: 'Johnny B. Goode'; 6''

This switching between functions on the part of a single instrument is often found. On the Who's 'My generation', for example, Pete Townshend's guitar moves occasionally from harmonic filler to secondary melody while, most notably, John Entwistle's bass moves during the instrumental section from bass function to lead melody, effectively acting as a soloist.

These examples could be multiplied *ad infinitum*, for this is the basic way of thinking about texture that underpins popular song. Even earlier examples can be understood in this way: Paul Robeson's definitive 1936 reading of the Kern/Hammerstein song 'Ol' man river', for instance. It begins without an explicit beat layer, although it has a clear bass (bass clarinet, it appears), a harmonic filler (piano doubled by strings) and melodic layer (Robeson's voice, largely doubled by violins), but in the bridge there is a clear offbeat emphasis of the harmonic pedal played by the orchestra's bass instruments. Songs of the dance band era also exemplify the pattern. Al Bowlly's recording with Ray Noble's Orchestra of 'Love is the sweetest thing' has no obvious beat layer (it was there, but the exigencies of recording in 1932 mean that it is frequently inaudible). However, its principal function (a differentiation between odd and even-numbered beats) is clear in the interplay of string bass (on first and third beats) and strummed guitar (on second and fourth beats). Hans Weisethaunet has more recently offered a more nuanced discussion of these layers, specifically in relation to how they operate for blues players.

> In performance, interplay (collaboration/communication) is based on the idea that each player finds or defines his 'space' in relation to the others. At the bottom there will be a keeper of the groove: usually the bass player and the drummer in interaction. At the next layer there will be some rhythmic 'lift-up-over-sounding' discrepancies': rhythm guitar or keyboards. On top, there will be vocals and lead guitar soloing. Together, all those layers make the 'groove', while simultaneously creating the 'texture'.[2]

He offers a table including my fourth layer, which he labels 'background'; the similarity of models is clear, and it demonstrates how it needs to be adjusted in detail for a particular style ('keeper of the groove' is sometimes a more useful construction than 'explicit beat layer'). Serge Lacasse has also made valuable contribution to this model: in a discussion of sound treatment effects, he observes the effect of *long echo* on each of these layers in turn.[3]

However, having now entered the realm of exceptions, there are a couple of obvious ones to be dealt with. A number of singers accompany themselves with a solo instrument. The function of the piano and the guitar in this role are very different, due partly to the planes in which the instruments lie relative to the body, and the fact that the piano has all its keys available at once, whereas the guitar does not. Both, however, operate against the background of these functional layers. Kate Bush accompanies 'The man with the child in his eyes' with her piano and a small string orchestra. The piano acts principally as a harmonic filler, but with a prominent descending bass line, whose importance is underlined by its being taken over by a cello pretty early into the song. In the chorus, it carries a characteristic syncopated rhythm (Example 2.2), such that it has clear aspects of both bass and beat layers. Because she is a (and presumably the) pianist, this implies a measure of self-sufficiency on Bush's part: the orchestra appears to play an ornamental, rather than a structural, role.

Example 2.2 Kate Bush: 'The man with the child in his eyes'; 49"

---

[2]   Hans Weisethaunet, 'Is there such a thing as the 'blue note'?', *Popular Music* 20/1 (2001), p. 103.

[3]   Serge Lacasse, *'Listen to my voice': the evocative power of vocal staging in recorded rock music and other forms of vocal expression* (PhD. thesis, University of Liverpool, 2000), pp. 243–6.

Her later song 'This woman's work' is again piano-led. Here, the piano marks the regular harmonic movement (changing every half bar) while the second half of each half-bar is rhythmically enriched by a pattern that mimics that of a 'normal' drum kit pattern, which I shall discuss in Chapter 3. Since, in this song, most harmonies are not in root position, the bass is very important, and is, itself, later thickened by strings. Again, the piano covers two further layers. Billy Joel's 'And so it goes' accompanies the piano only with some synthesizer hazing. Here, the piano doubles and harmonizes the melody, producing a bass line with the same rhythmic profile. In this case, there is no drum-like beat emphasis, befitting the rather confessional lyric. However, a clear rhythmic pattern is evident, together with clear melodic, bass, and harmonic functions. Elton John's 'Take me to the pilot' demonstrates the stylistic roots of this, by now mainstream, piano idiom. The track opens with John's piano alone, before the addition of strings and a full rhythm section. The piano acts as harmonic filler, with little melodic identity (that is supplied by the voice), but a strong, syncopated attack. Those syncopations continue once the rhythm section has entered, and it can therefore be heard that the piano, even when alone, is working against the assumption of a regular beat. Even in the absence of other instruments on specific layers, then, the accompanimental solo piano tends to supply them and in the case of the beat layer, either explicitly, or as an imagined layer against which to work.

The nature of the guitar makes it less easy to have all layers working simultaneously, but they nonetheless can be implied. Key early examples of this can be found in the work of Robert Johnson. A simple track such as 'Stones in my passway' uses a tonic pedal in the bass, struck at metrically strong points, while between these a rudimentary upper line is accompanied by block harmonies. The rudimentary accompaniment to his 'Me and the devil blues' is much more interested in keeping a regular beat, with only the occasional intrusion of upper strings to keep the song on track harmonically. This occasional appearance is fit for purpose, because the harmonic background of the track is a matter of shared experience, certainly among his community of players, and arguably among his (contemporary) listeners also. Woody Guthrie's 'Dust pneumonia blues', one of his 'dustbowl ballads' provides an example of a pattern that has been a staple of folk guitarists for decades – a pattern that emphasizes down and (weaker) off beats, with some rhythmic interplay, made explicit by harmonies, but with no melodic content, since that is taken entirely by the singer. This is almost a normative practice, but can be used with some sophistication, as in Elvis Costello's 'Little palaces', when the bass takes on stronger rhythmic and melodic profiles, a bluegrass technique that goes back at least as far as Maybellene Carter's playing with the Carter Family. Indeed, these songs demonstrate the fundamental division in guitar-playing – whether strings are picked (either simultaneously or successively) or strummed (i.e. providing near-simultaneities). The regular picking on Richard Thompson's paean to folk revivalist Anne Briggs, 'Beeswing', activates its basic $\frac{12}{8}$ metre – the emphasis is on providing a strong bass line to counterpoint the vocal melody, while the guitar also interjects melodically between verses. The harmonies are only sketched, but in their simplicity are easily inferred. So, even in the case of self-accompanied songs, the three non-melodic layers are present in some form or other, or are deemed to be present implicitly for the player to work against.

Layers: Guitar as Harmonic Filler

A sense of the importance of the harmonic filler layer in the attribution of style and expressive intent can be gained simply by focusing of the activity of the guitar within this layer. The most basic method of filling out harmonies is by *strumming*. A strummed acoustic guitar fills out the harmonies of Jethro Tull's 'We used to know' according to the song's regular $^6_8$ pattern. Eddie Cochran's rock'n'roll 'Three steps to heaven' fills out the harmonies with a little more variety, instantiating a habañera pattern. Example 2.3 shows the stronger down strokes marking the pattern, with the weaker up strokes filling the temporal space.

Example 2.3 Eddie Cochran: 'Three steps to heaven'; 8''

The regular offbeat strummed strokes of the Beatles' 'Taxman', in their insistence, perhaps give an air of pungency, which underpins the disillusion expressed by the lyrics. This method of playing is still the basic technique but, in the wake of punk, such a guitar is now often overdriven, resulting in a high degree of noise. On a track such as British Sea Power's 'Remember me', the heavy feedback comes across as strongly matter-of-fact and direct, while on Echobelly's 'Insomniac', guitarist Debbie Smith's decisions about where to play and where not to are less predictable, and more carefully judged, implying a greater concern for finesse. In fact, there are earlier examples of overdriven playing in what would become heavy metal – the power of this uncompromisingly unsubtle way of playing is clear on Grand Funk Railroad's 'Into the sun'.

Strumming necessarily makes a harmonic pattern explicit. Other methods of playing only sketch out the harmony, relying on the listener's understanding of harmonic conventions to 'hear' the complete harmony. I have already referred to the *boogie* pattern in 'Johnny B. Goode'. This pattern became a staple in the 1970s rock'n'roll revival associated with glam rock. The guitar plays a pattern alternating between the fifth and sixth degrees of the scale (identified as $\hat{5}$ and $\hat{6}$), above an open string root where possible. It is very clear at the beginning of Status Quo's 'Caroline', where the pattern extends to $\hat{5}$–$\hat{6}$–$\hat{7}$–$\hat{6}$ and so on. In 'Johnny B. Goode', although there is no third in the chord (which could thus be either major or minor), the fact that roots of this technique lie in the blues mean that it is ordinarily interpreted as a sequence of major chords, all other things being equal. The very repetitive nature of this pattern links to the next technique by which a harmonic pattern may be outlined, that of the *riff*.

A riff is a short monophonic melodic idea that repeats without being changed – it retains its identity in an assertive manner. Its roots lie in big band jazz – a number such as Glenn Miller's 'In the mood', whose arpeggiated repeating melody changes only minimally to accommodate its notes to the underlying harmony. From here, by way of Count Basie, it gets into rhythm'n'blues by way of jump jazz – Louis Jordan's 'Choo choo ch'boogie' is a classic example. Here, the riff appears as a vocal melody – again somewhat arpeggiated, and again minimally varied to accord with the change of harmony. An early appearance in pop is that of the legendary 'Louie Louie': in the Kingmen's version, the organ riff is even more minimal – simply a stepwise line, again according with the changes of harmony. Not only did this song become a mainstay of blues-influenced bands (even appearing in the early repertoire of Pink Floyd), but it led the riff to become the defining feature of early tracks of the Kinks. Minimal (two-note) riffs ('You really got me', 'Set me free') over a single harmony became extended ('Till the end of the day') and, as with the earlier examples, identified a harmonic pattern ('All day and all of the night'). In most of these examples, the riff is doubled by the bass, such that the underlying harmony is either inferred, or is barely present. 'Set me free' is the barest of these riffs, although clearly there is a commonly understood harmonic pattern in the song's background, over a descending chromatic bass. The rawness of tone this achieved was used to support the mild recklessness associated with the early mods, although within a decade this had developed into the power riff that would accompany the unrestrained expression associated with heavy metal.

Prominent stages in this move are represented by quintessential riffs that have, perhaps, become so commonplace as to be derided. Cream's 'Sunshine of your love' is one such, a song that begins like a twelve-bar blues where the riff is transposed up a fourth in bar five (fundamentally the same device to be heard in Status Quo's 'Caroline'). Deep Purple's Smoke on the water' is another. Here, though, because the harmony is an unchanging drone, the riff remains at its original level throughout. So, although tempo and tone may have changed markedly by the time (and stylistic development) of Metallica's 'Blackened', and harmony may have become even less important, the riff-based means of construction has not. And we should note that the riff has not simply been hijacked by heavy metal. In the wake of the re-emergence of guitar-based rock through grunge and aspects of Britpop, it remains almost a given in much popular song – the riff to the 22–20s' 'Devil in me', for instance, does exactly the same job as on those early Kinks tracks.

By the 1980s, the more flamboyant, less anarchic end of metal signalled the iron hand within the velvet glove, by combining riff-based material with the ringing *arpeggiations* of a basic harmonic sequence. In Gary Moore's 'Victims of the future', a plaintive introduction (over arpeggiations) gives way to anger in the song proper, over a riff. This song also makes use of an additional means of playing. We have already encountered overdriven guitar playing block chords, with the aim of sounding muddy. Musicians of an earlier generation (or at least of an aesthetic closer to the blues or metal than to punk) tend to use *power chords* instead. These are simply a pair of notes a bare fifth (or, less often a fourth or sixth) apart which, by control of feedback, can sustain almost unlimitedly, giving sense of a great deal of power, frequently 'held in reserve'. In 'Victims of the future', the riff does not consist simply of single notes, but of such two-part power chords. And this means of continuation is also not historically circumscribed, although by the time of Velvet Revolver's 'Fall in pieces', some two decades later, it marks a more generalized *faux* acoustic opening that gives way to a more brash, overdriven remainder of the track. An early example of this sort of distinction appears on the Pretty Things' 'Private Sorrow', where a chordally dominated acoustic guitar introduction (with a prominent lower line) gives way to an incessant riff that underpins the rest of the track. The apogee of this subtle textural thinking is perhaps found in the music of Jethro Tull, on a track such as 'Aqualung', where the two different means of articulation carry connotative consequences.[4] Thus, I have identified a number of distinct ways that a guitar can operate within this harmonic filler layer: strummed chords (with or without feedback); boogie patterns; riffs; power chords; arpeggiations. Other instruments, and operating in other layers, can be less complicated. However, as this brief survey of guitar playing suggests, the method of playing can have quite an impact on the sense of a track.

Layers and Style

The vocals–guitars–bass–drums approach to functional layers has been very much a mainstay of rock songs for some four decades. Other styles can, in part, be defined simply by how they make these layers explicit. The synthesizer rock that began in the late 1970s, for instance, replaced the guitar with one or more synthesized lines in the filler (and may even have replaced beat and bass instruments with synthesized sounds, although they did not do away with those layers). The Pet Shop Boys' 'It's a sin', for instance, opens with held synthesizer chords (equivalent to a strummed guitar), before introducing a riff (which will become a vocal line) and then, under that vocal line, adding an offbeat, quick, arpeggiated part. Producers such as Holland, Dozier & Holland, working with Tamla Motown, created for the label an identifiable sound-world that in part depends on how the functions are treated. Over a bass and kit rather lacking in prominence, the harmonic layer is often filled by an electronic organ, topped (in the upper register) by a vibraphone – it is this combination that is particularly distinctive. A horn section both provides a riff that thickens this layer and, on occasions, doubles the melody, as it had in swing. This is a clear example of instruments migrating from one layer to another. The style is notable for the absence of a prominent electric guitar, as was much of

---

[4]   Allan F. Moore, *Aqualung*. New York NY, 2004.

the pop music of the same period. Diana Ross and the Supremes' 'Stop in the name of love' is a quintessential example.

Although this set of functions is normative, some styles can be defined by specific, fairly rigid, expansions of these roles. Dixieland jazz, for example, rethinks the melodic layer. Take Louis Armstrong's 'Big butter and egg man'. Unusually for Dixieland, there are no drums on this track, both bass and filler layers are supplied by the piano, while the banjo's attack substitutes for a beat layer, also supplying harmony. The melody is taken in turn by May Alix and Louis Armstrong singing, and by Armstrong taking a related line on the cornet. The ensemble also contains clarinet and trombone, whose roles are fixed within the style. The clarinet plays generally in a slightly higher register than the cornet, normally more even notes and, as a rule, faster. This line effectively weaves arabesques around the stronger trumpet melody. The trombone provides a contrapuntal line to the cornet, in the tenor register. These roles are normative for the Dixieland.

Swing provides an alternative example. Antiphonal choirs of saxophones and brass (trumpets or cornets, and trombones) provide counter-melodies that are harmonized normally in rhythmic unison, providing the filler layer, as in the Joe Williams/Count Basie 'Thou swell'. The development of this pattern into rhythm'n'blues can be heard in Ray Charles' 'Busted'. Over a conventional rhythm section (drums, a highly prominent stand-up bass and minimal piano filler), Charles shares a call and response pattern with the horn section. This pattern is brass-dominated, contrasting with the smooth, held saxophone harmonies that accompany his sung lines. There are, of course, other examples, but these demonstrate that the instrumental line-up, and the way the instruments are disposed across the layers, provides a strong initial clue to the style of the track we hear. Far from a trivial thing to discuss then, the textural layering of the track shows great variety within a simple basic structure. This variety will have important ramifications.

There are many other ways that the normative layers are manifested across particular styles. I shall illustrate just one more, that of the gospel quartet approach. The Swan Silvertones used a variety of vocal textures, but the commonality can be very clearly heard. Right from the outset of 'What could I do?', the melody is differentiated rhythmically from what the other voices are singing. The bass is also differentiated rhythmically, but has a greater tendency to mark out the beat, while the remaining singers sing in rhythmic unison to fill out the harmony. On 'Grant it, Lord', the bass has become rhythmically wedded to the harmonic filler, while more rarely, as on 'Jesus met the woman at the well' (from 53"), it is the melody line that is rhythmically wedded to the filler. Here, the bass adopts an early 'doo-wop' approach. Other quartets went about their textural orientation slight differently. On 'Job', for instance, the Golden Gate Quartet filler line erupts from time to time in a secondary melody, while all parts share the same lively groove.

Texture: Soundbox

But there is much more to be said of the texture of a track than its functional division into four layers. It is only in very recent years that properly serious academic attention has been given to what I call the 'tactility' of sound in a recording.[5] Although a recording may be made up of instruments playing melodies, rhythms and harmonies (the stuff of conventional music theory), it will also carry a 'feel'. It is this feel that is frequently the first aspect to attract (or repel) a listener, but it is also often the hardest to discuss. Before providing a way of thinking about this, it will be worth traversing just a little of the history. Established music theory distinguishes primary from secondary domains of the musical fabric on the grounds, in Leonard B. Meyer's justification,[6] of their propensity to engage in syntactic relationships. Thus, primary domains encompass melody and harmony, metre and rhythm; secondary domains, which 'shape' the primary, encompass texture, timbre and location. The distinction, in other words, is one of supposed content versus its articulation, and the assumption that these are separable, and separable in this way, is foundational to the study. Early musicologically analytical approaches to popular music tended to observe this distinction, whether making emphasis on melodic and harmonic features of the music, or in producing structural analytical diagrams on paper.[7] A number of subsequent commentators (including Everett, it must be said) have remarked on the inadequacy of this approach, arguing that, for recorded popular music, secondary domains are able to do much more than simply 'shape' content: indeed, they frequently *constitute* content, even if they do not embody syntax. So, although journalistic and vernacular discourses pay great heed to this inversion of primary and secondary domains, there is not much academic literature dealing with it, and the notion of theorization in this area is fraught.

Theodore Gracyk, writing from outside musicology, has referred to this relationship between primary and secondary domains,[8] although he doesn't use this terminology. His discussion is particularly valuable in that, in discussing what he calls ontologically thin musics (where the primary domains are the principal carriers of affect) and ontologically thick musics (where this role is taken by the secondary domains), he makes it clear that there is no question of primacy involved. Some years ago, I proposed the model of what is now known as the

---

[5] An early identification of the importance of rock as a studio practice was made by Paul Clarke, '"A magic science": rock music as a recording art', *Popular Music* 3 (1983), pp. 195–213.

[6] Leonard B. Meyer, *Style and Music* (Philadelphia PA, 1989), pp. 14ff.

[7] As found, respectively, in Wilfrid Mellers, *Twilight of the Gods*, (London, 1973) and Walter Everett: 'Fantastic remembrance in John Lennon's "Strawberry Fields Forever" and "Julia"' (originally 1986), reprinted in Moore (ed.), *Critical essays in popular musicology*, (Aldershot, 2007), pp. 391–416.

[8] Theodore Gracyk, *Rhythm and noise*, (London, 1996), pp. 17–36.

soundbox,[9] to open up academic discussion of this topic, a model that was taken up in Richard Middleton's proposal for a theory of gesture. Middleton calls attention both to the failure of a notion of analytic detachment in theorizing gesture, since it depends on 'the experience of somatic movement' and to the existence of musical gestures 'semiotically beyond the linguistic domain',[10] which is his justification for developing a gestural diagram. Middleton is particularly interested in the connotations such gestures have, and their formation from both primary and secondary domains, again without the assignation of priority. Such gestural connotation is a driving force behind Philip Tagg's entire work. In an early and representative approach,[11] he identifies four elements of a sign typology to which I shall refer at length in Chapter 7. In both Middleton's and Tagg's writings, the connotations of sounds (the principal focus for both) frequently operate without reference to primary domains. They ask questions relating to the effect listeners perceive (either in theory or in actuality) in the uses of particular timbres, gestures, and their combination. The most recent notable contribution to the field is that of Albin Zak III,[12] who offers a poietics of the recording rather than an esthesics (in other words, he approaches it from the perspective of production, rather than reception). Zak begins from the recording studio, asking what aesthetic effects might be achieved by the manipulations that sound recordists apply in the recording process. On the basis of all this work, it seems vital, then, to take into account these 'secondary domains', however their function is conceived, and the *soundbox* provides an important means of doing so.

The soundbox[13] provides a way of conceptualizing the *textural space* that a recording inhabits, by enabling us to literally hear recordings taking space. That space can be both metaphorical, if we are listening through headphones, or actual, if we are listening through speakers (I shall return to this rather gross distinction below). This conceptualization is parallel to that outlined above in terms of functional layers, in that some layers may be unified in particular spaces, while others may in actuality become separated out. The key aspect of this space, the key domain, is that of location. Where, within the soundbox, do particular sounds or sound-complexes appear to be coming from? Appearance is crucial: William Moylan[14] describes the listening process of positioning sources within the

---

    [9]   Allan F. Moore: 'The textures of rock', in Rosanna Dalmonte and Mario Baroni (eds.), *Secondo Convegno Europeo di Analisi Musicale*, (Trento, 1992), pp. 241–4.

    [10]   Richard Middleton: 'Popular Music Analysis and Musicology: bridging the Gap', reprinted in Middleton (ed.), *Reading Pop*, (Oxford, 2000), pp. 104–21 at pp. 108, 110.

    [11]   Philip Tagg, 'Towards a sign typology of music', in Dalmonte and Baroni (1992), pp. 369–78.

    [12]   Albin Zak III, *The poetics of rock*, (Berkeley CA, 2001).

    [13]   There are competing concepts here – I discuss some of these later in this section.

    [14]   William Moylan, *The art of recording: understanding and crafting the mix*, (Boston MA, 2002).

available notional space (the *sound stage*) and *imaging*, drawing attention to the visual imagination that is brought into play when listening to the soundbox.

What is the soundbox? It is a heuristic model of the way sound-source location works in recordings, acting as a virtual spatial 'enclosure' for the mapping of sources. Within this model, location can be described in terms of four dimensions. The first, time, is obvious. The remaining three are the laterality of the stereo image, the perceived proximity of aspects of the image to (and by) a listener, and the perceived frequency characteristics of sound-sources. This means that it requires the development of stereo for its full manifestation, and more recent refinements in technology for more subtle positioning of sound-sources. This does not mean that we cannot talk of the texture of pre-stereo recordings. Peter Doyle[15] argues persuasively that two environmental aspects of the experience of listening to sound, *echo* and *reverberation*, when reproduced in recordings, enable the construction of senses of space that differ, to a certain extent, between genres. I shall focus, however, on the possibilities of full stereo and its three spatial dimensions. Human binaurality enables the perception of the first dimension, that of *laterality*, a dimension that thus takes on the appearance of being 'natural', of being readily experienced in the world beyond listening to music. As David Huron's lengthy study puts it, 'the perception of auditory location [is influenced by] ... the relative time difference between pressure fluctuations in the left and right ears [and] ... the relative difference in magnitude or amplitude of these signals.'[16] The other two dimensions, however, are less 'natural' and require interpretation in order to conceive. The second dimension, that of *prominence*, is a factor of both relative dynamic level and degree of distortion. The commonest component of such distortion is the presence (or absence) and degree of reverb. It is important to note, however, that whereas sounds are objectively present in the output from one speaker or the other, they are not objectively more (or less) distant than each other; they originate in the same plane, and we make inferences as to their 'distance' by interpreting their dynamic level and degree of distortion. This dimension, then, requires a degree of interpretation not necessary for laterality. The third dimension, that of *register*, or the 'height' of a sound again operates differently. Register describes a specifically musical distinction; it is not a distinction discussed by acousticians. Moylan addresses this: 'the perceived elevation of a sound source is not consistently reproducible in widely used playback systems and has not yet become a resource for artistic expression.'[17] This is true: musicologically, this dimension is not one of elevation of the sound, but is determined initially by its position in pitch space; how high or low its pitch is. In fact, it is a factor of two distinct characteristics. Music in the West carries with it centuries of experience

---

[15]   Peter Doyle, *Echo and reverb: fabricating space in popular music recordings 1900–1960*, (Middletown CT, 2005).

[16]   David Huron, *Sweet anticipation: music and the psychology of expectation* (Cambridge MA, 2006), p. 103.

[17]   Moylan, *The art of recording*, p. 49.

of notation, wherein the lower a pitch's fundamental (the lower the number of vibrations per second), the lower on a page it will appear. There is no causal reason for this to be the case, but it is a convention with which many become familiar. For this reason, low fundamentals appear towards the bottom end of the soundbox, and high fundamentals towards the top. However, bright sounds also appear higher than dull ones. Therefore, the higher the concentration of upper partials a particular timbre has, the higher it is likely to appear in the soundbox (for a flute and a clarinet playing the same 'actual' pitch, the flute will sound as if it is slightly higher in the soundbox). Both Moylan and Lelio Camilleri[18] prefer to talk about the two-dimensional space, treating laterality and proximity as of the same order. However, because each dimension works differently, as I have suggested, I see no reason to avoid the three spatial dimensions of the soundbox.

Through the latter 1960s, producers and engineers gradually came to adopt a normative positioning of sound-sources within the soundbox, a positioning that tends to remain stable throughout a track. I call this the *diagonal mix* in recognition of its determining factor. The operative elements in such positioning are a lead voice, a snare drum and the harmonic bass (normally a bass guitar), which are situated centrally on a (very) slight diagonal. The resultant diagonal mix tends to operate normatively for all genres from the early 1970s to the present.[19] In the very early years of stereo, however, it was by no means the norm. Two other possibilities tended to dominate, both of which can occasionally be found to this day. One of these was the *cluster* mix, whereby sounds were grouped rather tightly within the available space, such as Donovan's 'Mellow yellow' (Figure 2.1). The three-dimensional box represents the approximate positioning of sound-sources. As you can see, all are bunched together slightly left of centre (the ball represents the voice).

The other possibility was the *triangular* mix. If the diagonal mix observes a line through the lead voice, snare drum and bass, the triangular mix has these in three different positions, with two to one side of the mix, and one to the other (and of course various categorizations or possibilities could be made). One example will suffice: Sam and Dave's 'Soul man' (Figure 2.2) has the voice central in the mix, but bass and snare appear in opposite sides of the stereo space.

It may seem strange to isolate the snare drum from all other drum sounds, since the use of the term *drum kit* may encourage us to understand it as a single

---

[18]   Moylan, *The art of recording, Understanding and crafting the mix: The art of recording* (Boston MA, 2007) and 'Considering space in music', *Journal of the Art of Record Production* 4 (http://www.artofrecordproduction.com/content/view/180/109/, 2008), accessed 25 September 2010. Lelio Camilleri: *Il Peso del Suono*, (Milan, 2005) and 'Shaping sounds, shaping spaces', *Popular Music* 29/2 (2010), pp. 199–211.

[19]   See Ruth Dockwray and Allan F. Moore: 'Configuring the sound-box 1965–72', *Popular Music* 29/2, (2010), pp. 181–97 for details of this mix, and David Gibson, *The Art of Mixing*, (2nd edn, Boston MA, 2005) for arguments for the cross-genre nature of this norm. I am grateful to Ruth for these three figures, which are her own handiwork.

Figure 2.1   Donovan: 'Mellow yellow'. Soundbox transcription

instrument. Indeed, this is how it tends to function under the hands (and feet) of a competent drummer, but this is not necessarily how it is presented to a listener. The kit consists, of course, of a series of instruments, principally drums and cymbals of different kinds, plus possibly other assorted percussion (most likely cowbells, plus possibly other blocks, a tambourine, etc.). The dominant feature of this collection is that all these instruments are nominally unpitched. That is, although some sound deeper than others, none of them have a precise pitch (and some, such as cymbals hit on the rim, cover a wide range of imprecise frequencies). The drums are not, therefore, a 'deep' instrument that sits at the bottom of the soundbox. The bass (or kick) drum may sit near the bottom (but not in extreme metal), but snare drums and tomtoms will sit higher, while cymbals can appear anywhere from mid-range to the top. While drummers treat this collection of sound-sources as a single instrument (observe how careful drummers are with setting up instruments – they must be exactly where she or he want them, certainly to within the nearest centimetre, for the timbre of a drum skin changes depending on exactly where contact is made), in all but early (i.e. pre-1970s) production, individual instruments are miced up separately and can be sent to different locations within the soundbox. As it happens, this disposition often repeats, in some sense, how they would look in practice, with the cymbals at more extreme positions than the drums, for instance, and with snare and kick drums always in the centre. This normative disposition, then, sites all sound-sources around the drum kit. The reason for this, as far as

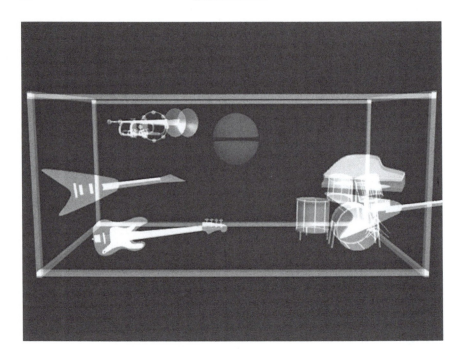

Figure 2.2   Sam and Dave: 'Soul man'. Soundbox transcription

there is a reason, is technological – when being cut to vinyl, the sharp attack of the drums necessitated them being in the centre of the groove, to avoid the problem of the needle skipping the groove (and the positioning of a deeply felt bass in the centre is for similar reasons). It has very little to do with any notion of accurately portraying live performance, for it was not until the 1970s that it became normative to situate the drummer in the centre of a live stage. It needs to remembered that the soundbox is a *virtual* textural space, which does not necessarily have anything to do with an *actual* textural space. The kick drum will be in the centre of the space towards the bottom, the snare will appear dead centre, or as near as makes little difference, with cymbals above and to the sides, and tomtoms or other drums in mid-register but also tending to the sides. Two other sound-sources are normally found towards the vertical centre of the soundbox, the bass guitar (or other bass instruments) and the lead voice, and it is because these alone are normatively positioned in the centre of the stereo image that I use them to identify the 'diagonal mix'. The angle of the diagonal is normally very slight, but can usually be spotted at least when listening over headphones. Other instruments are then deployed around this centre – a single guitar will often be double-tracked, one track to each side, two guitars will be separated, or a guitar will balance a keyboard. Argent's 'Hold your head up' (Figure 2.3) clearly identifies the diagonal mix. You will notice that voice, snare and bass are clearly positioned in the centre of the soundbox with other sound-sources around them.

In most styles, the objective appears to be to seek a balance within the soundbox – it can sound highly disorienting if everything is coming from one side, although such a disposition may be to make a point (as in the case of Jimi Hendrix' 'If six was nine', where Hendrix's off-centre voice insists on unusual attention being paid to his lyric), particularly if the other side will suddenly come into use. In addition, because the lyrics to a track are normally considered somewhat important, the lead voice is likely to be foregrounded, to stand out from the backing (this may actually be seen to follow from placing in live performance). This helps to convey the all-important illusion that we, or even I, as a member of the audience, am being directly and individually addressed. Other instruments may be brought to the fore from time to time, while harmonic pads are most likely to be deepest in the background.

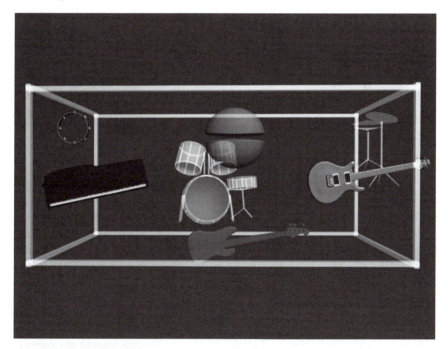

Figure 2.3   Argent: 'Hold your head up'. Soundbox transcription

The soundbox is, then, to some extent filled by sounds in various locations, around the 'foundation' of voice, snare and bass. How it is filled, though, can vary greatly. It can be filled by discrete blocks of sound in different places, it can be filled throughout by a sound (perhaps that of cymbals) that creates a haze across the entire space. It can be filled not by blocks of sound projected through time, but by points of sound, which appear to occupy smaller, but possibly more tightly defined, areas of the space. Holes can appear within this coverage, often drawing attention to what remains. Some sounds may be actually masked by others. Indeed, in thinking about how the space is occupied, again three sets of characteristics dominate: tight or loose edges; blocks or points; holes and masks. The soundbox also appears in two very different formats. Thus far, I have described it as if the listener is facing a pair of stereo speakers – a fairly normal situation, even if one is rarely seated exactly at the apex of the triangle formed by the speakers and the listener (the 'sweet spot'). Moylan[20] identifies the *perceived performance environment* as the overall space in which a 'performance' is taking place, and which is necessarily separated from the listener: sometimes the distance between this entire space and the listener is as crucial as the relative distances of sound sources within it. However, the same dimensions operate when listening through headphones, an equally likely, and far more transferable, situation. Here, the soundbox appears as if imposed on the head. Indeed, pinpointing the location of particular sounds within the space is probably easier in this arrangement. Here, of course, there is no distance between the sound stage and the listener – the listener *is* the sound stage. The two formats do have their differences, however. When listening to speakers, because sound waves have to travel through the air to reach our ears, not only do we tend to lose higher frequencies, which are absorbed in the air (in quantity proportional to the distance they travel), but as distance increases, the proportion of reflected sound to direct sound increases, changing our sense of precision. Subtle attention to potential meaning will want to take these differences into account.[21]

As far as the prominence dimension is concerned, again we can assume a norm, whereby those layers central to the song – the voice, particularly, and also the bass, perhaps guitars, will tend to be foregrounded. Drums will often be set slightly back, partly because their timbres cut through a texture so well, and 'backing' instruments (harmonic filler, often), will be still further back. Sometimes, though, the lead voice will be less foregrounded than we might expect. This is frequently the case with the Rolling Stones. If there is significance to this (rather than just creating the effect the musicians all wanted), it conveys well the democratic notion that Mick Jagger was simply another member of the band, rather than a singer accompanied by a backing band. We build this characteristic from our experience of sound in everyday perception. And yet, in real life we can distinguish between the distance of a shout and a whisper, even if both appear to be equally loud. What distinguishes a whisper from a shout in this context is the attendant features – the sound of an intake of breath, perhaps, or lips smacking, sounds that do not get louder as the voice gets louder. Therefore, we may use this sort of information in positing distance. In addition, in the studio, if a producer wishers to bring a sound

---

[20]   Moylan, *The art of recording*, p. 52.

[21]   I am grateful to Simon Zagorski-Thomas for this observation – personal communication, September 2011.

forward, to appear closer to the listener, rather than simply make it louder, they will tend to add a small amount of distortion.[22]

Before discussing a range of examples, there are a few other useful theoretical terms to bring into play. Camilleri argues that, rather than there being one 'space' that is filled, it is better to think in terms of three, which he terms *localized space*, *spectral space* and *morphological space*.[23] 'Localized space' is, effectively, the sort of space I have already been describing. 'Spectral space' is to do with timbre (which I discuss below) – it is here that we recognize the degree of saturation within a particular part of the soundbox. What Camilleri terms 'morphological space' is the sensation of change we experience as timbres subtly alter, a factor also of the register in which different instruments are playing. Francis Rumsey has offered a different way to think about notions of saturation: his *scene-based* approach[24] is concerned with the objective and environmental attributes of sound-sources. He also argues for three categories: *width*, *depth/distance* and *envelopment*. Each of these he relates to four levels: *individual sound-source*; *ensemble*; *environment*; *scene* (which in the case of envelopment, becomes the attribute he calls *presence*). Of these, the difference between environment and scene is subtle and can be ignored here, while the phenomenon of 'ensemble' (where a group of sound-sources is discreetly positioned within the scene) is comparatively rare in popular song, but might sometimes identify an orchestra or an orchestral grouping (such as 'horns'). However, the width and depth of individual sound-sources, the width and depth of the spatial environment, and the sense of envelopment remain valuable. The difference between depth and distance is subtle: *distance* is the distance between the 'front' of a sound-source and a listener, while *depth* acknowledges that there can be a 'back' to that sound-source, and the difference between front and back delivers depth. Simon Zagorski-Thomas takes a different approach, calling into play the function that a particular mix may have, by way of the concept of *staging*.[25] He draws a strong distinction between two categories: *dance music* and *rock music*, a distinction that originated in the 1970s. He argues that music that is played back in a club, through large speakers, is mixed 'dry' (that is, without the addition of reverb), in order that drum and percussion sounds remain clear. Music that tends to be played back in smaller spaces, such as home living-rooms, tends to have reverb added in order to simulate the atmosphere

---

[22]   While this level of detail is sufficient for music analytical discussion, it is of course insufficient for sound recordists: Moylan, *The art of recording*, discusses the intricacies of distance location in far greater depth (pp. 184–91).

[23]   Camilleri, 'Shaping sounds'.

[24]   Francis Rumsey, 'Spatial Quality Evaluation for Reproduced Sound: Terminology, Meaning, and a Scene-based paradigm', *Journal of the Audio Engineering Society* 50/9 (2002), pp. 651–66.

[25]   Simon Zagorski-Thomas: 'The stadium in your bedroom: functional staging, authenticity and the audience-led aesthetic in record production', *Popular Music* 29/2 (2010), pp. 251–66.

generated at the larger venues where it is played live. Thus, there is a relationship between the mix and its assumed use, and this general comment remains true for all genres. In a recent essay, Moylan[26] emphasizes the sort of interrogative approach on which this entire study is based: the series of questions he poses are invaluable in getting to grips with what a production is actually achieving. Finally, in Zak's exhaustive, production-related discussion, he adds an additional dimension to this model, that of *narrative*. This points to the vital observation that locations within the soundbox do not necessarily remain fixed throughout a track, although, interestingly, sounds move far less than the technology enables. There is perhaps something rather disorienting about sounds moving in ways of questionable significance, which presumably frequently cuts across the aesthetic that is driving a particular recording. This is particularly the case if the sound source that is moving is physically static (that of a piano, for instance).

Soundbox: Examples

A range of examples will demonstrate how this mass of theoretical ideas can help us come to terms with the textures we hear. One of the remarkable attributes of mono recordings is the impossibility of conceiving of the location of a sound-source, since, when playing a mono recording even on stereo equipment, the same signals issue from both speakers, centralizing everything. On the Beatles' early single 'She loves you', there is a sense of great density – the sound is very full – but there is correspondingly little sense of depth. There is obvious registral stratification, enabling the identification of voices, ride cymbal, snare drum, strummed guitar, bass, and there is the occasional hole in this dense texture, immediately after the line 'with a love like that'. The texture seems to consist of blocks of sound, although both voices and bass can cut through the haze provided by the cymbals, because of their marked difference of timbre. However, there is also a strong sense of saturation as individual sound-sources seem to compete for their own space. If you listen to the version issued some years later on the compilation CD, you will hear the same dense, mono texture, but the edges of the blocks of sound have been clarified. This results in a lower degree of saturation – the whole production seems slightly cleaner. This is the norm in remastering CD reissues from vinyl originals – whether it represents an improvement due to advanced technology, or a falsification of the exuberance of the original, is a matter of the aesthetics of remastering, and the presumed wishes of a contemporary audience. We are, after all, so used nowadays to cleanly reproduced sound-worlds that for a contemporary listener to hear an original production can be rather disorienting. There are, of course, mono recordings with a lower degree of saturation. The texture of Them's 'Baby please don't go', also from 1964, has six components: drum kit, bass, organ, guitar, vocal and blues harp. The organ tends to play throughout but, because of

---

[26]   Moylan, 'Considering space in music'.

the lack of differentiation within the sound space, it is generally masked by other instruments. One of the functions of stereo is to try to avoid this phenomenon. Indeed, were it not for the fact that vocal, blues harp and guitar only sound intermittently, the entire space of this track may well have sounded too crowded.

With early stereo (recorded on two- or four-channel tape or, in the USA, on three-channel tape), there is a fairly monolithic distinction between left, right and centre. Greyhound's reggae 'Black and white' from 1971 places most sound-sources right in the centre (lead voice, percussion, bass, guitar), reserving the right channel for the cor anglais melody, and the left channel for a harp and handclaps. This very straightforward simplicity remains an available aesthetic choice through subsequent decades and was particularly characteristic of the back-to-basics aesthetic of punk and new wave rock in the mid to late 1970s. The Jam's early single 'In the city' exemplifies this clearly. It opens with a guitar, alone on the right channel, playing the opening riff twice. This is joined by the bass, in the centre, for two more repeats. The upbeat to the fifth repeat is marked by the entry of the kit, in the centre, and followed by a second guitar part, together with the drummer's cymbals, on the left channel. The voice enters centre-stage, and the song is away.

By and large, producers have been unwilling to deviate too far from this normative pattern. It is true that such deviations as do exist can have a rather disorienting effect, but this does not explain why, when a disorienting effect is sought, extreme manipulation of the soundbox is not used. One exception to this is where very different instrumental takes were spliced together to create the final mix, as on the Hollies' 'King Midas in reverse'. On its (1967) release as a single, it was heard in mono – the points I am about to make emphasize the necessity of historical location, for while they are true of a 2009 listening, they would have been false for a 1967 listening. The stereo version that is that now ordinarily available opens with the band on one channel, and voices on the other. This itself is unusual, since with 40 years of listening to stereo behind us, we expect to hear the voice in the centre. The oddness of this stereo version is made even more palpable when, on the chorus, it is the tambourine that enters in the centre. Then, in the second verse, cellos muscle in on what had been the vocal territory, forcing the voices toward the centre, but still off by about 30°. Thereafter, the spatial opposition between orchestral and band instruments is maintained, somewhat mediated by the voices. Now, how might we understand this? Two points are worth noting. First, the diagonal mix convention was not yet in place in 1967, so the fact that it sounds strange to us may simply be due to our historical location. However, this track also represents the Hollies' half-hearted diversion into psychedelia, a style marked by its overturning of normal perception, which certainly stretches into some production values too. What is difficult, here, is that the achievement of stylistic norms for locational placement coincided with the efflorescence of psychedelia.[27] While the displacement of the voice from centre-stage can easily be

---

[27]   Dockwray and Moore, 'Configuring the sound-box'.

read as an analogous device to that of the Beatles' 'Strawberry Fields forever', the lyrics make such an interpretation difficult.

Rather than such gross deviations, then, intervention in this area is far more likely to be subtle. The Yes track, 'Roundabout' has a stereo texture generally dense for its time (1972). Although instruments are very much playing their own lines, rather than simply vamping chords or such like, this density makes the texture appear as blocks of sound rather than simply points. Within this, the kit is both in the centre of the stereo field and spread fairly wide, an indication of the array of instruments Bill Bruford uses. What is most remarkable is the presence of Steve Howe's nylon-strung acoustic guitar, and its relationship to Rick Wakeman's organ. At the very beginning of the track, the guitar is very much to the fore, with cleanly audible chordal harmonics (sounds that are naturally very soft). In this aural context, the entry of the band (44″) should be much louder than it actually is – clearly the guitar is brought to our attention through being 'unnaturally' loud. Later in the track, the guitar reprises its early material, but now with an organ backing (4'58″). Again, one would expect the organ to drown the guitar, but the balance is very much in the opposite direction. An over-zealous reading might suggest that nature (the 'acoustic' instrument) is being promoted here at the expense of culture (the 'electric/electronic' instrument(s)) – for now simply note that the dynamic balance we hear is not what we would expect. We should also note the way the track opens, as what appears to be the sound of an organ chord is reversed, giving way to the opening guitar chord of harmonics. The increase of volume of the reversed chord makes it appear as if the sound-source is actually approaching us (rather than simply getting louder), a factor of our real-life experience of sounds increasing in volume (and about which I shall have more to say in subsequent chapters). This energizes the 'morphological' space to which Camilleri refers.

Depth is also very much the subject of the Fleetwood Mac track, 'Little lies'. It demonstrates the degree of control of textural space available to producers by the late 1980s. Although the individual instrumental resources are far in excess of those found on Them's 'Baby please don't go', above (it is possible to identify synthesized strings and flutes, a synthesized marimba taking the role of an arpeggiating guitar, a solitary bass 'growl', three distinct timbres of synthesized oriental plucked string instrument, together with conventional kit and bass, and finally solo voice, voices in parallel harmony and voices in a responsorial relationship), they are carefully separated registrally and across the stereo space such that there is no sense of being swamped. This allows the entire texture to breathe, avoiding a sense of claustrophobia. Not all sound-sources appear at the same distance, though. As we might expect, the solo voice is to the fore, just fractionally off-centre. In the chorus, the voice appears in parallel with itself, and after singing a phrase drops from the texture. Indeed, it is almost as if it literally drops, for it reveals immediately behind (at the same point in the stereo spectrum), a synthesized oriental string instrument plucking a little pentatonic pattern (thus, stereo does not prevent the masking of sounds, but reveals it for an aesthetic device). Careful listening reveals the presence of that instrument even while the parallel voice is singing, but the sound is masked, revealed only at the point the voice drops out.

The earlier Jethro Tull track, 'Songs from the wood', is more concerned with an exploration of the laterality dimension. It opens with a solo double-tracked ('thickened') voice, just left of centre, joined speedily by a small choir to the right. Mid-way through the verse, we hear a bare fourth on a glockenspiel, far over to the left, expanding the space that had been used to this point. At the end of the verse, the instruments enter gradually, led by parallel flutes, each time expanding the space in use, until the full complement is reached. Once we are at this stage, holes do appear in the texture, again to prevent the whole from feeling too cluttered. After three verses and a chorus, we enter a central instrumental section. This begins with interplay between guitar and bass, in the centre of the field, and keyboards to left and right. The sense of competition becomes diluted towards 2'32" as the key switches from E minor directly to C minor, after which the separation resumes, now with a central flute taking the lead. Although both centre and extremes take part in this interchange, it is the melodic ideas at the centre that are clearly intended to dominate. This sense of domination is due, in part, to the fact that timbres do not change position.

As we have seen above, timbres can switch position when different takes are spliced together to create a mix. Sometimes, however, timbres switch position more gradually. A key early marker of the period of discovery was the stereo mix of *Sgt. Pepper's Lonely Hearts Club Band*, which George Martin undertook in 1967 with lack of interest (which was normal, at the time) from the Beatles themselves. 'A day in the life' begins with acoustic guitar on the right, bass in the centre and John Lennon's voice on the left. During the opening verses, the bass is joined by a kit, while a piano is heard at both right and centre. During verse 3, Lennon's voice slowly wanders from left to right, freeing the left channel for the entry of the cacophonic orchestra at the end of the verse. The interlude begins with Paul McCartney's voice on the left, again balancing prominent piano on the right, with kit and bass central. Lennon's voice replaces McCartney's for the short dream sequence, moves across to the left and back again, and then re-enters on the right for the fourth verse, finally returning to the left for the final 'I'd love to turn you on'. There is, perhaps, apparent method to this madness, which I shall discuss in Chapter 6. For now, simply note this highly unusual displacement of the voice from the very centre of our attention. Examples such as this are rare. A particularly strange one is Tractor's 'Little girl in yellow', in which the drum kit wanders constantly across the stereo space during the lengthy improvisation. This example vividly demonstrates the difference between the virtual textural space and any actual textural space – there is no way such a mix could have been reproduced live. Another can be found in the Ultravox track, 'Vienna'. The track opens with a held synthesizer note, under which a bass drum plays on three beats, and what sounds like a thunder sheet on the fourth. This sheet gradually moves across the space, before switching suddenly back to its original location, at which point the voice enters. How incidental this was to the intended meaning of the track can be gleaned from listening to the radio edit, the single release, where the move is cut drastically short.

This track exemplifies a further important feature, which is that it makes sense to think of this textural space as being consciously designed, rather than simply attempting to reproduce how a band might look live (which, as I have suggested, is by no means necessarily the case). On this track, there is clear conceptual separation between the sounds of the (synthesized) snare drum and the bass drum – the bass is foregrounded and low, the snare is high and conceivably more distant. This is not a representation of the sound of a single drummer, but of two distinct instruments. The distinction becomes conceptually possible, of course, because these are synthesized instruments that, on early drum machines, had to be programmed separately. This conceptual change, however, enables tracks such as Peter Gabriel's 'Rhythm of the heat'. Gabriel disposes of his drum sources separately within the soundbox. We begin with a resonant central hand drum, of quite high pitch. This is joined at 41" by a pair of tuned West African hand drums, fairly foreground, but well separated to left and right. These are then joined at 1'09" by a deeper, single drum, more centrally-placed. At 1'51", these are joined by drummer Jerry Marotta's beaten snare, tomtoms and kick drum, again in two different locations, and further in the foreground than the deep hand drum. This layout does not relate to any putative live layout, but is designed, literally, in the studio. Indeed, this notion of spatial layout is much more one of design than writing, actioned as it is either at a mixing desk or computer screen, but totally resistant to representation on manuscript paper.

What other aesthetic aims might producers have in designing the use of this space? There are potentially many, but I shall identify just three here. In many styles, as we have glimpsed above, it is important to fill out the soundbox. Even with the same instrumental forces, this can be done in more than one way. U2's production aesthetic has often tended to go for the big sound. On 'Where the streets have no name', as on the rest of *The Joshua Tree*, there are no obvious holes in the soundbox, and the edges of the sound-space are ragged and loose. The texture remains static throughout, beginning with an organ pad deep in the background. Edge's guitar covers a small range, in a single register, but with fast, intricate movement giving a static but busy, almost nervous feel. It encases the space from both sides, moving towards the centre a little at the ends of the verses, where it resorts to hacking. The melodically static bass provides firmness while of the kit instruments, only the ride cymbal threatens this equilibrium. This gives Bono's voice plenty of space within which to move, between the guitar and the bass, as it dominates the texture. Because of this, there is a sense of wide openness to the texture. That of the Verve's 'A northern soul' is no less full but, because it is the guitar that smothers the entire space, and that provides a backdrop, rather than a frame, for Richard Ashcroft's voice, the overall sense is much more claustrophobic. It might be added that the liner imagery for these bands reinforces their respective constructions of space.

Sometimes it is necessary to convey a sense of harshness to reinforce the tone of vocals. King Crimson's '21st century schizoid man' aimed for just that in 1969. The first verse begins at about 47" with Greg Lake's distorted vocals above an evenly struck pure guitar chord on every beat. And yet, further listening suggests that the tone doesn't sound quite as pure as at first. Close listening reveals that the guitar is panned to the right while bursts of pink noise can be heard simultaneously from the left speaker. Although they are not heard in their own right, they appear to 'colour' the pure tone of the guitar, perhaps engendering a sense of distaste, which in turn affects our response to the vocals. In 1969, this was about as far as such trickery went. The aesthetic behind Garbage's 'Push it', some three decades later, seems to me very similar, but it is achieved in a far more complex fashion. The overall dynamic level is high, while the bass and voice are pushed far forward. To begin with, all instruments appear fairly centrally, with some atmospheric noises at either side. At around 45" a rather treble-dominant kit enters to the left of the soundbox, while a scratchy guitar comes in to the centre. Within a further 15" we can hear a 'wall' guitar (so-called because it produces effectively a wall of sound) to the left, while the guitar to the right takes up a little motif. And the texture constantly changes along these lines. What sounds like just a dense texture is actually made up of highly differentiated, harsh sounds, which in appearing in different places across the stereo spectrum tend towards disorientation. These observations lead us to realize that similar effects can be achieved with markedly different methods.

As this discussion demonstrates, as soon as one considers the soundbox, it is observation of the laterality dimension that dominates, since our everyday awareness of this dimension appears stronger than that of the other two (see the latter part of Chapter 7). However, a refocusing of our attention can be instructive. The registral dimension is actually unproblematic – some instruments are simply higher than others. That is not, however, necessarily all there is to say. Compare the sound-worlds of Yes' 'I get up I get down' with Trivium's 'Pull harder on the strings of your martyr'. At around 8'30" of the Yes track, the bottom end of the texture gradually sinks away, leaving Jon Anderson's high, almost ethereal vocals, with high parallel vocal backing and mellow chords, in what we might describe as a lament for the earth mother. The 'spiritual' tone of this section is surely intensified by the lack of both bass and drums, and of any bottom end frequencies at all. 'Pull harder …' is obvious in its contrast, whereby the emphasis on bass frequencies, and a dearth of high pitches, seem to complement the lyrics' negative tone.

There is one further point worth making here. Over and above the particular aesthetic effect a producer is trying to achieve, he or she will normally have an overriding aim, either to allow separate timbral strands to stand out, or to blend them together in the service of the whole experience. The latter goes with a tendency to produce a polished artefact, which can sound flashy, or even artificial. Any rough edges on a track such as Steely Dan's 'Rikki don't lose that number' have been smoothed away. There are no harsh attacks, all instruments are at a similar dynamic level, guitar distortion is at a minimum, the drums are simply played rather than being bashed, and the soundbox is covered neatly as a jigsaw. This sound-world is unambiguously constructed. That of the Pixies' 'Wave of meditation' is at another extreme – the snare drum shoots out of the centre of the texture, the guitar and bass appear as if from different worlds (they even enter playing notes dissonant to each other) and there is so much noise attendant on the vocal (as if Black Francis is singing from the back of his throat rather than his mouth) that it is hard to pick up until your ear gets attuned to it. The sound here is made to appear more rough and ready and, although it is no less constructed, it purports to provide a more realist sound-world. This can, at its extreme, be a simple, almost undoctored, live recording. Slade's live recording of 'Hear me calling' for instance, accurately conveys the almost false start to the performance, the lack of polish in performance and the vital involvement of the audience. Note the band cannot even (or make no attempt to) maintain a steady speed. It is dangerous to assume that a 'live' recording is undoctored – few are – but as always it is the effect rather than the actuality which tends to signify. As with other norms, meaning can result from friction between what we hear and what we expect; examples of friction in terms of the soundbox will be discussed in Chapter 6.

To summarize, the textural densities of 'Little lies' or of 'A northern soul' are of an entirely different order to that of 'She loves you'. In all these cases, there is a high density of sound; but for the Beatles it is as if the entire foreground of soundbox is opaque; for the Verve it is as if the front of the soundbox is covered with muslin; while for Fleetwood Mac it is as if many small areas are covered at different depths within the soundbox. This model enables the conceptualization of varieties of density and, thus, the presence of textural holes and masks, blocks and points of sound. Thus, comparison of a range of recordings from the early 1960s through to the present suggests a clear tendency towards thinking more in terms of the virtual textural space as studio technology develops, involving the beginnings of re-thinking of the functions of instruments within this texture.

Timbre

What, though, about the actual, recognizable, quality of the sound-sources that are disposed throughout the soundbox? Identifying actual timbres can be important: as Andrew Goodwin notes, not only does timbre trigger memories acutely, but it becomes associated with its particular purveyors (his example is Phil Collins' gated snare sound of the early 1980).[28] The sound of the instruments accompanying Frank Sinatra's 'A foggy day' for instance, convey the sense of style, and thus mood, as effectively as Sinatra's laid back, conversational vocal

---

[28]   Andrew Goodwin, 'Drumming and memory: scholarship, technology, and music-making' in Thomas Swiss et al. (eds.), *Mapping the Beat* (Malden MA, 1988), pp. 121–36 at p. 129.

approach. Indeed, Paul Théberge[29] has argued that the *sound* of both particular electronic instruments, and of particular conglomerations emanating from specific studios, has become emblematic of particular identities, in a way qualitatively different from the pre-recorded era, when we had to be satisfied with the (notational) *representation* of particular sounds. And the influence is wider than specific instruments and studios; the difference between styles such as 'rock' and 'pop' are also frequently timbrally defined – overdriven electric guitars are rare in the latter (at least, until Britpop caused genre confusion), lush strings in the former (although, as symphonic metal as found in Nightwish or Rhapsody of Fire demonstrates, this is simply a norm against which to rub). What are we to make of the richness possible with contemporary recording practices? Zak's study[30] is replete with anecdotes about how particular sounds were obtained, usually as a result of accident or experimentation, to create the identities we hear. Zak suggests that for recordists, the broad range collapses to two types of function, *physical* and *rhetorical*,[31] depending on whether a sound is used for its overtone structure and envelope (for example) or for its associations. But can we do more than simply recognize the quality of a particular sound? I believe we can. The most important questions to ask of timbre, and that contribute to the way timbre signifies, again concern deviations from implicit norms. Such modifications tend to operate on various continua: from 'harsher' to 'smoother', from 'thinner' to 'thicker', from 'more distanced' (i.e. controlled) to 'more indulgent'. And there is necessarily an historical dimension to this schema, too. Early synthesizers inevitably sounded 'unnatural' to their listeners. Some 40 or more years on, the sounds of those basic machines have become naturalized, to the extent that they can in turn be subject to modification. We should note that some work has been done on timbre in relation to ecological perception and embodied cognition,[32] but, as yet, this work is insufficiently developed for me to make use of here.

So, I start with the most ostensibly natural oppositions. When Leonard Cohen begins 'Hey, that's no way to say goodbye' to the accompaniment of a simple finger-style nylon strung guitar, we are encouraged to take him at face value, as if he is sitting just before us, communicating directly with us. What is important here is that we recognize '*a* simple finger-style nylon strung guitar' rather than '*that specific* simple finger-style nylon strung guitar' for, as Gracyk reminds us, we are incapable of keeping in memory the precise sound of a particular timbre, and can recall only the way we represent it to ourselves.[33] To relive the precise timbre, we have actually to be listening. The simplicity of Cohen's guitar pattern is a part of

---

[29]   Paul Théberge, *Any sound you can imagine*, (Hanover NH, 1997), pp. 191–200.

[30]   Zak, *The poetics of rock*, pp. 60–70.

[31]   Zak, *The poetics of rock*, p. 62.

[32]   Rafael Ferre: 'Embodied Cognition Applied to Timbre and Musical Appreciation: Theoretical Foundation', *British Postgraduate Musicology* 10 (http://www.bpmonline.org.uk/bpm10/, 2009), accessed 23 March 2010.

[33]   Gracyk, *Rhythm and noise*, pp. 59–61.

the art here. And, although at a higher level of technical sophistication, Elton John's plain piano accompaniment to 'Your song' again encourages us to hear this as our song. Close listening, however, will reveal an acoustic guitar sounding along with the piano, once John's voice enters. This guitar's treble frequencies dominate – not an entirely 'natural' sound perhaps, but one whose familiarity probably causes us to hear it as a simple colouring of the texture. The same is probably best not said of Roy Harper's 'I hate the white man'; Harper's vitriol drips from his delivery. And, while his accompanying guitar remains measured almost throughout, there are points where his emotion shows here too. The performance was recorded live, and just after the end of each verse, as Harper strums in preparation for the next, he attacks the bass strings just a little too strongly – as they vibrate, the sound distorts just slightly (the same is the case of the barre chord under the line 'and the man …' at the end of the refrain). Here, then, the distortion is part of the performance, and has emotive qualities.

I have raised above questions of smoothing or roughening of sounds. Some measure of distortion has, I think, become natural, but individual cases clearly need to be historicized.[34] Take three early Kinks tracks. The slight distortion of the electric guitar in the introduction to 'Dead End Street' (1966) is probably trivial, probably does not signify any despair in the face of meaningless existence. The contrast between distorted and straight guitars on 'Tired of waiting for you' (1965) is clearly audible, but it is not obvious what it might signify. The distorted riff on 'You really got me' (1964) certainly carries at least historical import, as it marks an early disdain for a polished sound. In this context, the guitar sound on the Rolling Stones' contemporary 'Get off of my cloud' has certainly had its tone distorted – it is harsher than we might otherwise expect – and yet it seems to carry no particular affective weight other than to signal the track as by the Rolling Stones. This is a key point, to which I shall refer again, since some things signify not at the level of the individual item, but only at the level of style.

It is useful to note that certain types of distortion have themselves become normative in certain situations. Although he refers specifically to their use on the voice, Lacasse's thesis[35] is a good source. He notes a range of classes of effect. *Reverberation* and *echo* are frequently confused, although both have the effect of enlarging the virtual space we hear. The key difference is that the effect of reverberation is to *continue* a sound, echo to *repeat* it. Thus, the guitar in the Verve's 'A northern soul' is bathed in reverb, whereas the plucked banjo to the right on the Strawbs' 'Witchwood' has a very fast echo. On Quintessence's 'Dance for the one', the flute is echoed through a long passage from one side of the stereo field to the other, creating a sense of envelopment suitable to the subject matter of the song. The practice of phasing refers to the effect of delaying the sound signal in one or more ways and re-combining them. It includes effects such as electronic

---

[34]   Zak, *The poetics of rock*, pp. 64–5 contrasts Def Leppard's *Pyromania* with Nirvana's *Nevermind* in this respect, but without a historical dimension.

[35]   Lacasse, *Listen to my voice*, pp. 116–38.

double-tracking and *flanging*. Acoustic double-tracking is the practice of re-recording a textural strand and including in the mix both the original and that re-recording. Because it is impossible to repeat ourselves exactly, the overdub (whether vocal or instrumental) will be fractionally out of phase with the original, resulting in a thickening of the sound. Blur's 'Country house' is a good example: Damon Albarn's voice is single-tracked in the verse, but double-tracked in the chorus (listen to the frequent subtle misalignment on "coun-*try*", covered rather by the mass of other voices). The Groundhogs' 'Cherry Red' is an earlier example of this: Tony McPhee's voice appears on both sides of the soundbox, thickening the texture, but the alignment is not absolute – occasionally one side is fractionally ahead of the other. There is an electronic (artificial) version, first heard on the Beatles' 'Tomorrow never knows'. Double-tracking frequently conveys the illusion of greater confidence, or reliability, in the purveyor of that voice, because of its thicker qualities. It must not be confused with doubling, such as we hear on David Bowie's 'Space oddity', where a voice is doubled an octave higher – since it is the same singer we hear, this carries a rather disturbing, unearthly quality. Flanging is the whooshing sound so common as a connotator for psychedelia, one of whose first appearances was on the Small Faces' 'Itchycoo Park'. *Speed modification* is also widely practiced: in analogue contexts, this has the effect of not only altering the timbre (the faster the speed, the thinner the sound) but also pitch (the faster the speed, the higher the sound), and is frequently used for comic (and annoying) effect (think Axel F's 'Crazy frog').[36] Sometimes, changes to a 'normal' timbre can imply greater *distancing* or greater *indulgence* on the part of performers. Distancing from the emotional content of a song is often conveyed by a certain rigidity of delivery, a degree of control that implies holding emotion 'in check'. When Richard Thompson sings of going through his lover's bedroom drawers searching for evidence of her past, the tight tremolo on the guitar pitches is unnerving, in part because it does not enter into the potential emotion of the song. Indeed, 'Cold kisses' is the perfect title, specifying that they are no longer active.

At the other extreme, the issuing of live recordings has long been an important part of the marketing strategy of labels, serving sometimes to keep particular musicians in the public eye when a new studio album is a long time coming, sometimes to act as a substitute (or memory) of the sheer energy of a live performance situation. Two distinct aesthetic approaches can be observed here. Sometimes, a live recording will go through post-production in order to enhance the recording, to make it more 'acceptable' to a wider public. On other occasions, though, the documentary spirit is uppermost, and the attempt is to recreate as closely as possible the original sounds. In such cases, timbral distortion takes on a natural (because less 'artful') quality. The last three minutes of Slade's live recording of 'Born to be wild' is a case in point. Through much

---

[36] Details of many of the available effects can be found on http://www.harmony-central.com/Effects/ (accessed June 2008).

of this, it sounds as if the VU meters are going 'into the red', i.e. that the sound reaching the meters is too loud, causing cut-out and distortion. At one point Noddy Holder's noisy, unpitched strumming blots out the rest of the band, while Dave Hill's guitar employs the sort of control of feedback that Jimi Hendrix had previously perfected (to strongly emotive effect in his destruction of the 'Star spangled banner', for instance[37]). These, however, are not changes to the sound made as part of the process of production, but are made in the act of performance – a crucial difference – and their 'wildness', the indulgence in the 'over the top' characteristic of the sound for its own sake, is significant. The recording practices of an artist such as Paul Weller are important in this context, for whereas most musicians take the opportunity in the studio of post-production for purposes of enhancement, Weller's practice (on an album such as *Stanley Road*, for instance) is to get closer to the documentary spirit, to perform in the studio as closely as possible to a live context.

Two further, and perhaps ultimately more significant, sets of oppositions are often pertinent. These refer to the imagined origins of the music's constituent timbres, and to the class of gestures the music thereby suggests. Determinedly acoustic sources (such as the majority of those considered above) might be used to signify either an anti- or pre-modern world, or alternatively an intimate encounter (which itself appears to us unmediated), and thus sometimes have ideological force. This is the case with a recording such as James Taylor's 'Fire and rain' notwithstanding the use of a rhythm section, although a more conventional example might be the Askew Sisters' 'Adieu to Old England'. Metronomic regularity might equally signify a mechanistic world. This is particularly apparent in early electronic dance music, where a track such as Snap's 'The power' conjures up a clearly urban, constructed, environment, both through its undeviating metric regularity, and also through its clearly synthesized timbres. Indeed, there is a strong tendency for *naturalistic* or at least *naturalized*, sound sources and *human*, or perhaps *communitarian* gestures to co-exist in opposition to *synthesized* or *sampled* sources and *mechanical* gestures.[38] Sometimes, this is turned to notably expressive ends as in Gary Numan's 'Cars'. Numan, whose voice is deep in the mix, sings of the pleasure, the comfort of alienation from others, within a texture consisting of mechanically regular, synthesized, uninflected, rather cold timbres. The Eurythmics' 'No fear no hate no pain' is another good example, in which we hear two voices, a synthesized bass and drum machine, unearthly sounds, sampled oboe and strings, and tinny synthesizer chords. The voice is split, giving a sense of unreality. Strings provide a link between the voice's and the synthesized worlds. This is made explicit by the tinny synth chords with regular vibrato, and the unearthly sounds (again linked at the end via the oboe). Her only response is wordlessness, which suggests a momentary transcendence of the emotions of the song. The 'sound

---

[37]   See Clarke, *Ways of listening*.
[38]   Moore, *Rock* (2nd edn), pp.156–7.

Chapter 3
Form

Time: Metre

Critics of the practice of music analysis tend to make their criticism on the grounds that analysis is *formalist*, is not interested in content. Although it is my contention that form and content are far less easily separated out (as will become clear), the purpose of this chapter is to explore those elements that are normally felt to constitute music's formalist nature, that is, form itself (the order in which events happen, from small to large scale) and that peculiarly musical domain, most opaque to so many, harmony.

In order to communicate to somebody else a particular part of our experience, we need to find a way of identifying that part, in the context of other parts. In the spatial field, we can do this by pointing, or some other sort of spatial measurement. In the temporal field, we have to adopt a different strategy. In listening to a recording, for example, it would be perfectly possible to identify a particular moment by how many seconds have elapsed since the recording began. While pretty precise, this method bears no relation at all to the measurement of time the recording itself makes. Generally, therefore, I prefer another way, which uses the music itself to organize the temporal stream through which we experience it. It is that sense of organization of the time-stream that gives rise to the notion of a track as embodying some sort of narrative, whether that be static (the exploration of a particular state of affairs) or progressive (the change of one state of affairs to another). Not only is a means of measuring time necessary for musical narrative, but a means of embodying content is also indispensable. Thus, a discussion of both the rhythmic realm and the sounds that activate such rhythms, which I shall discuss in terms of harmony, is necessary.

Song (and indeed most music) is organized in terms of repeated units, of equivalent length – indeed, US English terminology is precise about the temporal function of such a unit, calling it the *measure*. *Bar*, the British term, is an acceptable equivalent, and is what I shall use here. With notated music, the length of the bar is self-evident – it is marked by bar-lines. But bar-lines themselves are inaudible; we need to be able to identify what it is that serves the aural function, what it is that marks off one bar from the next. In an aural stream of music, the problem lies in deciding the length of that 'bar' – once done, its subdivisions and multiplications follow easily. We need a rule of thumb, an initial assumption (a norm, against which we can measure deviations), and the best is the *standard rock beat*, which has the virtue of being both widespread and part of the almost innate vocabulary of most contemporary working musicians. The standard rock beat implies a bar consisting of four beats. The kick drum can be heard on the first and third of these, the snare drum on the second and fourth and, in many cases, sticks used on the the hi-hat (foot cymbal) subdivide each beat into two. Although the snare drum beat (the *backbeat*) appears most audibly apparent, the kick drum beat is normally assumed to be 'stronger'. Distinguishing between first and third beats is not always easy, but another initial assumption is that harmonies change far more often on first beats than they do on third. Also, the first beat is more likely to coincide with a melodic emphasis. So, the division of bars into four (beats) is normative. So to is the larger grouping of bars to create yet larger units – *superbars* or, more normally, *hypermeasures*. Thus, sections of songs will very frequently consist of 8, 12, perhaps 16 and sometimes 32 bars, as I discuss below.

Some initial examples are clearly in order. Although the historical roots of this pattern can be found as far back as early jazz, many early recordings either do not use such a drum kit pattern, or the drums appear inaudible. However, the pattern can often be inferred even there. Returning for a moment to Al Bowlly's 'Love is the sweetest thing'; although the drums are virtually inaudible, there is a clear timbral distinction between the rhythm section's emphasis on odd- and even-numbered beats. What can actually be heard is a textural bass line, played by the double bass, on the odd-numbered beats, and a strummed guitar on the even-numbered. Timbrally, the double bass approximates to a kick drum roughly as a strummed guitar (higher pitched, with a more prominent attack) approximates to a snare drum. A perfectly standard example of this pattern can be found in the Beatles' 'A hard day's night', a track which also distinguishes clearly between the first half and the second half of each bar, in that drummer Ringo Starr plays a little *fill* on tom-toms through the third and fourth beats of every second bar; thus the first beat is identified partly by resulting from this fill, while the third beat launches it each time. This track introduces a further key distinction. Paying attention to the hi-hat, it clearly subdivides the beat into two equal halves. If you listen to Diana Ross and the Supremes' hit 'Where did our love go?', from the same year (1964), although the hi-hat is a lot less prominent in the texture, it is clearly subdividing the beat unequally – in the ratio 2:1. These two alternatives (a *straight* rhythm in the Beatles, a *shuffle* in the Supremes) are the only alternatives commonly used – the latter tends to imply a more relaxed, more laid-back feel. The relationship between the two can be clearly heard on the Fall's 'Mr. Pharmacist', which begins at a shuffle, moves to a straight division of the beat, and then returns to the shuffle. A particularly potent example of this change occurs at the end of Tractor's 'Hope in favour', where the first pattern identified in Example 3.1 seamlessly becomes the second pattern at 2'22". The distinction between straight and shuffle is gross and, in practice, drummers can offer a range of gradations in between, particularly those drummers with a jazz pedigree. The historical relationship between the two modes is also unclear. There was a general shift from shuffle to straight rhythms in the early years of rock'n'roll (1953–54), while subsequent recourse to shuffle rhythms tends to carry connotations of the blues and historical African American

Example 3.1   Tractor: 'Hope in favour'; metric modulation

practice. Tamlyn[1] provides evidence that these straight rhythms do not migrate to rock'n'roll from rhythm'n'blues (as had previously been assumed), but appear in both styles contemporaneously. While shuffle rhythms dominated in swing and related styles, Stewart[2] notes the presence of straight rhythms in styles such as bluegrass (which influenced Chuck Berry), and suggests their possible entry into rock'n'roll via calypso and other Caribbean styles (an influence on Ray Charles). While these issues have some importance, in that a norm can always carry the sense of its originary location, straight rhythms have subsequently become so normative as, now, to seem simply 'normal' in almost all contexts.

At the level of the bar, we can observe a number of variants on the standard pattern. Starting with a simple example, the pattern on the Runrig track 'Canada' (Example 3.2) is much more to the fore than in either the Beatles' or Supremes' examples, because the improved recording technology provides more space for elements to parade, enabling us to distinguish the separate strands of the pattern more immediately. The basic pattern is the same as in 'A hard day's night', with the exception that there is an extra bass attack half-way through the second beat. (These examples shows kick and snare drum only.)

Example 3.2   Runrig: 'Canada'; drum groove

Led Zeppelin's 'When the levee breaks' (Example 3.3) is an altogether emotionally harsher track, and the powerful attack of the kit appears to leave no room for subtlety. The actual pattern, however, betrays the influence of funk, in the anticipation of the third beat (in the kick drum), and the lead into the fourth beat's snare drum. The hi-hat even carries the obligatory half-beat (i.e. regular quaver) pattern.

Example 3.3   Led Zeppelin: 'When the levee breaks'; drum groove

---

[1]   Gary Tamlyn, 'The rhythmic roots of rock'n'roll in rhythm and blues', in Tarja Hautamäki and Helmi Järviluoma (eds.), *Music on Show* (Tampere, 1998).

[2]   Alexander Stewart, '"Funky drummer": New Orleans, James Brown and the rhythmic transformation of American popular music', *Popular Music* 19/3 (2000).

The pattern to James Brown's 'Cold sweat' (Example 3.4) indicates the stylistic origin of John Bonham's development.

Example 3.4 James Brown: 'Cold sweat'; drum groove

Snap's 'The power' (Example 3.5), an early electronic dance track, is very close in pattern to the Led Zeppelin. (Bracketed notes are not always audible, while the whole groove comes from a drum machine rather than a kit. The effect of the groove, however, is comparable.)

Example 3.5 Snap: 'The power'; drum groove

In style, of course, it is utterly different, and demonstrates that a similarity of pattern does not in itself determine a similarity of style. We shall certainly observe this difference in operation later, in discussing aspects of form, harmony and melody. Indeed, the stylistic origins of this latter pattern are probably to be found within Latin patterns, particularly that of the habañera with its characteristic rhythm (Example 3.6).

Example 3.6 Basic habañera pattern

   The Radiohead track 'Street spirit (fade out)' has a very clear example of a pattern that derives ultimately from the rave/acid house music of the 1980s (where it is often less clearly articulated): from 1'50" of 'Street spirit', the pattern of Example 3.7 is particularly audible.

Example 3.7 Radiohead: 'Street spirit (fade out)'; drum groove from 1'50"

The pertinent aspect of this pattern is the subtle shift of the snare drum either side of the downbeat (it appears immediately before, and immediately after): in the example, this can be seen as the symmetrical 3:2:2:3 pattern heard as the groove repeats. In this case, the pattern does carry stylistic connotations.

So far, it appears that the assumption of the 'standard rock beat', with a strong backbeat on the second and fourth beat of the bar, is reasonable, and so it proves to be in a large majority of instances. Not all, however, and here stylistic knowledge has to come into play. The pattern beneath Black Box's 'Ride on time' alternates kick and snare drum in exactly the way I have defined for the 'standard rock beat'. The effect, however, is not for the kick to sound on the odd beats and the snare on the even, but for the kick to sound on every beat, and the snare to bisect them. In other words, hearing it as a 'standard rock beat' would be to hear the track twice as fast as it should be heard. Should? Well, that's a difficult issue – suffice it to say for now that to hear the track twice as fast would be to deviate from the way it was heard by its initial normal listening (and dancing) public, as clarified by the phrase '4 to the floor', which indicated that good dance music of the period emphasized all four beats of the bar equally. A rigorous application of the principle I took from Ricoeur (Chapter 1) would deny that reference to a track's original listeners carried any force. And, once those listeners are no longer around, the point is certainly maintainable. However, when you were one of those listeners, it is harder (and perhaps less useful) to maintain. Questions of the 'right' speed at which to hear a track can become magnified.[3] Although Goldie's track 'Dragonfly' is hardly a song, it comes out of that tradition. Should one hear the speed as fast (following the drum kit) or as slow (following the speed at which the chords change)? In practice, dancers would tend to opt for somewhere in the middle, but does that mean that is the 'best' speed at which to hear it? Perhaps the 'most effective' is what we should try for. So what about other cases where the 'speed' is problematic? The Fall's 'I am Damo Suzuki' is a rather extreme example. An initial speed is set by bass and guitar but when the kit enters (first at 43″) with a busy pattern, but at a slower pace, the pattern is entirely 'inappropriate' – nowhere do bass and kit beats coincide. A similar aesthetic may underlie the Flying Lizards' 'The flood' – although the disjunction is less overt (in that there is no regular beat pitted against the kit), the kit constantly seems to become out of focus, and fails to coincide with changes of harmony. But it is not only in 'challenging' (in these cases, post-punk) music that such difficulties occur. In crooner Tony Bennett's early 'Rags to riches', Bennett's melody line moves at the same pace throughout. The kit shifts between two patterns, an uptempo one (seemingly to tie in with the brass, who always keep to this groove) and a half-speed, laid back one used for the majority of the track. In all these examples, could we opt for hearing two superimposed tempi? This is worth trying, but is not an easy feat, and is by no

---

[3]   Zbikowski insists that 'research on temporal acuity and judgement has demonstrated a significance [for] … a range of 85–100 bpm, and whenever possible we prefer to locate the beat in this range'. Zbikowski, 'Modelling the groove', p. 279.

means an inevitable mode of listening. Finally, it would be possible to list more varieties of the standard pattern, and even to group them in a typology. However, this seems less useful than to note that the pattern is highly malleable, and to look at the consequences of any changes in their particular examples.

The other term that is frequently used to refer to drumming patterns is *groove*. I have already used this term simply to identify a pattern that is repeated. But there is no standard definition of this and, rather than see it as something that arises simply from the kit, it is often more useful to consider it as resulting from the operation of the 'rhythm section'. What constitutes a rhythm section varies from style to style, but at its minimum it will include a bass instrument and kit. At its maximum it may include a couple of keyboards, a rhythm guitar, and horns. However, a groove is perhaps best understood as an interlocking set of repeated ideas (*riffs*, even) across these various instruments, and has been fully investigated by Tim Hughes, specifically in relation to the complex grooves employed by Stevie Wonder: Hughes notes that 'the product of a repeated groove is *flow*',[4] that sense of propulsion that leads the listener inexorably forward. Zbikowski notes, and demonstrates, that 'the explicit rhythmic pattern of a groove may be framed in relation to an implicit pattern',[5] which helps explain why a good groove is as much a factor of 'feel' as being something one can notate.

Time: Hypermetre

So far, I have focused simply on what happens inside the bar, and on just a fraction of the different ways bars can be rhythmically articulated by the drummer. Hypermetre concerns the ways that bars themselves are grouped together, are felt to belong together. Some theorists maintain an often problematic distinction between hypermetre and phrasing,[6] a distinction which for popular song is confusing in practice, since phrasing is more malleable in performance due to the use of syncopation. But for our purposes, 4-bar hypermeasures and 4-bar phrases (and other lengths also) tend to coincide – this can at least be used as a basic normative assumption. The Tymes' 'You little trust maker' (Example 3.8) makes its hypermetre explicit by the drummer executing three near-identical bars, followed by a fourth that contains a fill, leading up to the next iteration of the hypermetric group. And this can stand for a host of other possible examples (the example shows kick and snare drums and regular hi-hat – the 'x' marks an open hi-hat, otherwise it is closed).

---

[4]   Timothy Hughes, *Groove and flow: six analytical essays on the music of Stevie Wonder* (PhD thesis, University of Washington, 2003), p. 16.

[5]   Zbikowski, 'Modelling the groove', p. 286.

[6]   Fred Lerdahl and Ray Jackendoff: *A generative theory of tonal music* (Cambridge MA, 1983).

Example 3.8 Tymes: 'You little trust maker'; drum groove and fill at 54" (the hook)

The melody of the Kinks' 'Waterloo sunset' (Example 3.9) presents a perfectly regular example, but now in a different domain, that of its melody. The verse is 12 bars long, leading into a 4-bar refrain. The first four bars are repeated, pretty closely, to form the second four bars. The third group of four bars provide a contrast, and the fourth group (the refrain) returns to the beginning.

Example 3.9 Kinks: 'Waterloo sunset'; outline of main melody

We might simply represent this as an AABA form. Notice that each line of the melody begins half a bar early, with an extended upbeat. This gives the track a sense of momentum, and impels us forward to the next group of four bars, whose kit pattern does not finish until after the melody line of the subsequent group has begun (with the upbeat). If we listen to the kit line, we again find a variety of fills at the end of 4-bar groups, but it is the melody line that creates sense at the larger level (that of the 16-bar verse + refrain). Note that this AABA pattern has seen good service down the years – it is, for example, very common in the American inter-war ballad, where it is the result of using four 8-bar groups (giving rise to the designation *32-bar song form*), as in the standard 'I've got you under my skin', as recorded frequently by Frank Sinatra.

The Beatles' 'A hard day's night' makes interesting use of this form. This track is based on the 12-bar blues format (which I shall discuss below), such that the verse consists of three 4-bar groups, loosely following an AAB pattern. This can be considered a dominant form for the blues. Two verses are followed, however, by a contrasting section, which for now we can call a *middle 8*, partly because it does, indeed, consist of eight bars, two 4-bar groups, and appears in the middle of various verses. This middle 8 then leads back to a third verse. This pattern, then, verse, verse, middle 8, verse, itself replays on a larger scale the AABA pattern itself. Music is very often formed from these sorts of embedded patterns; what happens on a small scale somewhere may be replicated on a much larger scale elsewhere. This itself is a norm, and we should not be any more surprised to find it in this repertory than in more 'cultured' ones.

Another example is slightly less simple. The verse of David Bowie's 'Life on Mars' (Example 3.10) consists of six 4-bar groups. The groups all have the same rhythmic outline, although the melody is nowhere precisely repeated. However, it is based on a structure whereby each group takes the same melodic outline and begins the phrase one note higher – in effect, we hear a steadily rising scale in slow motion (this pattern only breaks at the very end, in preparation for the next section of the verse, which dispenses with this section's steady rise). Again, what is familiar on a small scale is played out over a larger scale.

Example 3.10   David Bowie: 'Life on Mars'; outline of melody, first half of
              opening verse

One of the criticisms which has, over the years, been levelled at this entire repertory is that it lacks formal complexity in comparison with 'great' music. I do not intend to address the question of value here, but it is worth pointing out that one of the benefits of establishing formulaic methods of construction, where norms are easily perceptible, is that it permits a greater degree of subtlety and nuance than in an environment of formal complexity. Take Procol Harum's

'A whiter shade of pale', for example. The verse consists of 16 bars, arrayed as four groups of four. However, the parallelisms we might expect between these four groups are transformed by what actually happens. The melody of the first four bars has an a + b pattern (the 'a' and the 'b' both lasting two bars). The melody of the second four bars moves to c, but then continues with a return to a. The melody of the third 4-bar group consists of b + c, while the fourth then winds up a' + b' (i.e. variants of a and b). The overall pattern of the 16-bar verse is, then: a + b; c + a; b + c; a' + b' (see Example 3.11).

Example 3.11   Procol Harum: 'A whiter shade of pale'; outline of melody, opening verse

Only three different melodic phrases are used, cutting across the formal layout. It may well be the regularly descending bass line that makes this arrangement easy (it is, after all, this bass line that is usually the substance of most commentary on this song), and which draws attention away from what is really happening. A more precise image of the comfortable (and almost transparent) disorientation that is the topic of the song could hardly be imagined. And this track is not alone in such an approach. The chorus of Cheap Trick's 'I want you to want me' works in a very similar way. The speed is double, and the (descending) bass line moves at half the pace of that of 'A whiter shade of pale'. Thus, four bars constitute the initial 'a', and the next four 'b' (the bass line differs, giving rise to the 'b', although the melody is identical to 'a'). The next eight bars give us c + a. The third group consists of b + c, and the fourth an initial a before moving straight into the verse. This lopsidedness seems to work because of the greater length of individual units. Here, the tight groove and repetitive rhythm seem to be in the service of the obsessive nature of the song's protagonist.

Time: Phrase Structures

So far, a hypermetric norm based on units of '4' has been unproblematic. However, at the hypermetric level, we frequently find *cuts*, *elisions* and *extensions*. Because of these, hypermetric groups at the ends of sections may have 3, 3½, 4½ or even 5 bars. Identifying these is not always clear-cut, since it can be possible to hear groups in different ways. A few examples should clarify. The Who's 'Anyway anyhow anywhere' uses a pretty standard elision: the verse consists of 7 bars of ⁴₄ (where Roger Daltrey's one-bar phrase is answered by Pete Townshend's response), the title beginning with the upbeat to the seventh bar. We would perhaps expect an eighth bar of ⁴₄, but this eighth bar is elided with the first bar of the instrumental bridge between verses. This has the effect of foreshortening it, producing a bar of only ²₄. Bar 7 has '(Any-)way anyhow any-', and those two beats of bar 8 'where I'. The foreshortening allows the last word, '*choose*', to appear on a strong beat,[7] giving force to the end of the bar. This is a very common feature. From a different era, Joan Jett's 'I love rock and roll' ends its repeated chorus in the same way. Mott the Hoople's 'All the young dudes' uses an equally standard cut: the last bar of the chorus follows four bars of ⁴₄ with a bar of ³₄, which would have worked perfectly well as ⁴₄, although the ³₄ is perhaps harmonically neater (see Example 3.12).

Example 3.12   Mott the Hoople: 'All the young dudes'; outline of melody, chorus

Dionne Warwick's 'Say a little prayer' presents quite a metrical tour de force by composer Burt Bacharach. In the verse, bars are frequently extended by two beats (e.g. 'before I put *on my* makeup') and in the chorus, bars are correspondingly cut from four to three (e.g. under 'stay in my heart').

Eric Clapton's 'Let it grow' seems to have a foreshortened, 7-bar verse, the fourth bar beginning on the word '*go*'. Structurally, this appears to be a contraction of a putative 8-bar verse, whereby the fourth bar is both the last of the first four, and the first of the last four. It works this way because the harmony of that fourth bar works both as the last and the first chord of the sequence – it acts as *closure* to

---

[7]   In fact, it anticipates this beat fractionally. I shall deal with syncopation below.

one group and *initiation* to the second (as in the overlap of grouping lines, above the stave, in Example 3.13).

Example 3.13   Eric Clapton: 'Let it grow'; melodic sketch and hypermetre

(I shall return to this when discussing harmony, noting here only that it exemplifies well the fact that individual aspects of music work together to create effects, rather than separately.) And then, as if to redress the balance, the chorus does the opposite. It begins by sounding more regular – two 4-bar groups are implied, the fifth bar paralleling the first. However, the eighth bar represents a harmonic sidestep, landing on bar 9 with where bar 8 'ought to have been'. Thus, verse + chorus comes to an unproblematic 16 bars, but this is formed of an elided 3+4, then 4+5. The verse of the Casuals' 'Jesamine' does something similar, but achieved through a cut rather than an elision. The harmonic speed is double that of the Clapton, and the pattern appears over the course of half of the verse, so 1½ + 2 bars. The verse begins with an upbeat: 'When Jesamine …'. The downbeat falls on the next syllable '*goes*', and follows with 'a part of me *knows*', the last syllable again appearing on the downbeat. The line is thus *end-accented*. However, the emphasis now switches to the beginning of the line; 'I'm *not* really living', hence the ½-bar. At least, that's how I prefer to hear it – I often have students who hear the accent remaining at the end of the line: 'I'm not really *liv*-ing'. What I find key is the harmonic move, from I–IV–I to ii on 'not', a ii that last for four beats (and entire bar), followed by four beats on V. Hearing an end-accented line ignores what the harmony is doing. Why might the band go to such lengths? Well, try to imagine what the song would sound like emphasizing 'When *Jes*amine goes, a *part* of me knows ...' etc. At the speed at which the song is taken, it simply wouldn't have enough momentum to sustain its progress.

This 3:4 proportion can also carry some stylistic specificity. It marks, for example, the way that some songs from the Anglo-Celtic folk tradition have been performed over the past 40 years or so. Both Ossian and June Tabor take this approach in singing the song 'I will set my ship in order'. Each line of verse takes 1½ bars, followed by two bars of instrumental 'preparation' for the subsequent line. June Tabor does not follow this pattern in singing Eric Bogle's anti-war ballad 'No man's land', but when 'punk folk' outfit the Men They Couldn't Hang take it on (they call it 'The green fields of France'), performing for audiences unfamiliar with the genre, they impose this 3 + 4 proportional patterning. It can therefore carry some of the connotations that attach to folk song, particularly in this case of the protest song variety, together with assumptions about the political nature of the subject matter, the self-belief and ordinariness of the performers, and so on. It seems to me this is the best explanation for John Lennon's use of exactly this 'device' (this 3 + 4 structuring) for his own 'Working-class hero'. Aside from what the lyrics say, the structuring of his performance carries subtle connotations concerning the values in terms of which he would like the performance to be interpreted.

Although elisions, cuts and extensions are particularly interesting, we should take note of other, normative, types of phrase structure, which do not involve disruptions of the basic hypermetre, such as the typology offered by Ken Stephenson.[8] In addition to elisions, he identifies four models: the *2 + 2 model*; the *extension-overlap model*; the *first-downbeat model* and the *1 + 1 model*. Naming of different structures seems to me less important than observing their effects, which I shall broach while discussing Stephenson's typology. In the *2 + 2 model*, two bars of vocal activity are followed by two bars of melodic rest. This model is, as Stephenson notes, salient in the blues.[9] Indeed, in a track such as Otis Rush's notable 'I can't quit you baby', the function of the '+2' is clear – it serves a call and response function, as the singer is answered either by other voices (in much gospel) or, as here, by (often the singer's own) guitar. In this sense the model connotes this blues/gospel heritage even where nothing else points that way. This particular track is interesting because it also exemplifies Stephenson's *1 + 1 model*, where a 4-bar phrase has two vocal lines, broadly in the first and third bars. The lyric 'I can't quit you baby' lasts 2½ beats, is followed by a gap of the same length, and then the second bar is completed by 'but I've got to put you down for a while'. Note that these two lyric phrases offer different perspectives – that the second completes the first by showing the necessary consequence of Rush's inability to quit. The delivery of the lyric would be far less effective if the second line followed immediately on from the first – we would not have the opportunity for our first perception to be subsequently modified.

---

[8]   Stephenson, *What to listen for in rock*, pp. 7–19.
[9]   Stephenson, *What to listen for in rock*, p. 8.

In his *extension-overlap model*, a vocal cadence extends just beyond the four bars of the phrase. The verse of 10cc's 'Rubber bullets' exemplifies not only this, but some other categories already mentioned. Its 16 bars fall into an AABA' pattern, where the 'A' is a 4-bar extension-overlap phrase; there is a small upbeat to the first bar, and the final syllable 'jail'/'wail' appears on the downbeat of the third bar of the phrase. The B, however, splits into two shorter phrases, following the 1 + 1 model, and with their own internal rhyme ('indiscreet'/'street'). This structure (which also happens to underlie the limerick) allows a line of lyric to both begin and end in a metrically strong position, giving emphasis. Nirvana's 'Smells like teen spirit' observes the same extension-overlap structure but here, the next phrase follows on immediately from the previous strong ending, preventing the taking of a (mental) breath, and surely contributing to its sense of claustrophobia. Sometimes, the overlap is more pertinent, as in Diana Ross and the Supremes' 'Baby love'. In the second verse, Ross sings 'instead of *break*-ing up', while the Supremes sing 'don't throw our *love* away', coinciding 'don't' with 'up'. This allows a breath, but its space is taken up – perhaps a less claustrophobic space than that of Nirvana. A subtle version of this appears in Cliff Richard's 'The day I met Marie', where the title ends the refrain, but the final word also begins the chorus: 'The day I met Ma-*rie* with the laughing eyes …'.

In the *first-downbeat model*, a very short phrase simply sits on the downbeat of a hypermeasure, perhaps to be answered later in the hypermeasure, such as the Beatles' 'Hey Jude', the Platters' 'Only you' or the Archies' 'Sugar Sugar' (to choose examples from three very different styles). In these, and in the examples Stephenson gives, the single word (or name) is definitely a term of address, but it can appear in other contexts too, such as String Driven Thing's 'Heartfeeder', which opens with the bare word 'pain', or Eternal's 'Stay' in which the opening command is to do just that. Indeed, in that the individual downbeat in this model is separated from its context, it is almost impossible not to hear it as some sort of command. Gladys Knight and the Pips' 'Midnight train to Georgia' is interesting in this respect. Knight begins simply 'LA', a declaration well separated from 'proved too much for the man', as if the separation itself enacts his feelings, justifying her decision to move with him to Georgia. This degree of separation is the focus of an alternative approach to phrase structure offered by Dai Griffiths,[10] where he defines *verbal space* as 'the pop song's basic compromise: the words agree to work within the spaces of tonal music's phrases, and the potential expressive intensity of music's melody is held back for the sake of the clarity of verbal communication'.[11]

---

[10]   Dai Griffiths, 'From lyric to anti-lyric: analyzing the words in pop song', in Moore, *Analyzing Popular Music*, pp. 43–8.

[11]   Griffiths, 'From lyric to anti-lyric', p. 43. Griffiths is rare among critics in that he accords both music and lyric equivalent attention, and speaks of both with fluency and expertise. A similar concern with the notion of verbal space, but squarely from within the study of poetry (from someone who considers poetry to be spoken as much as written), can be found in Derek Attridge, *The rhythms of English poetry* (London, 1982), pp. 96–102.

To get a sense of verbal space, imagine the line of lyric progressing past a series of fence posts on the side of the road (the posts representing the beat); what matters is how words cluster around particular posts, and leave others empty. 'Sugar sugar' begins securely from a series of posts, but gradually encroaches back on the property of the previous post as its chorus grows from two, to five, to six and finally seven syllables (i.e. with longer and longer upbeats). The verse, in contrast, fills its verbal space densely such that the return of 'Sugar' acts like a shift of attention. I'm sure that what is important here is contrast between different densities. Hank Williams' 'Mind your own business' contrasts a dense verse, where he describes an unsatisfactory situation in some detail, with the bald chorus focusing on the title, where we are forced to concentrate on the instruction embodied in the title. The Madness track 'Our house' offers a particularly rich example: in the bridge ('I remember way back then ...'), the verbal space decreases – words are squashed together to a far greater extent than elsewhere. The bridge ends with the line 'nothing would come between us' – there had literally been no space for anything between the words of the bridge. But then the verbal space opens out, we get a gap, and then 'two dreamers'. The rhythmic setting seems peculiarly apt for the sentiment.

Time: Syncopation and Other Irregularities

Syncopation is so endemic to popular song that I was tempted to begin the chapter there, but it is perhaps more natural to consider it as a particular use of verbal space. This should not diminish its importance. Rather than being a surface feature, a way particular melodies are presented, as it is in the music of the concert hall tradition, popular song cannot be imagined with the syncopation 'taken out', as it were. This embeddedness is historical: it is reasonable to trace it back to West African rhythmic practices, and thence to North American and Caribbean soil with the forced migration of slaves, to surface in blues, gospel and jazz and thence into popular song. Richard Middleton[12] argues that it arises from rhythms that are (bodily) felt rather than (mentally) counted, which is to say that although what we hear may not coincide with the beat, the beat is nonetheless present, and sometimes actualized, in the dance. However, the *forms* of syncopation we encounter cannot themselves necessarily be traced back to that origin. They depend also on the interaction of such traditions with those of Anglophone folk song, and those of the concert hall, again on North American soil. But let us simply observe how syncopation operates. Its endemic nature can initially be observed in the standard rock beat. Although all four beats are made audible, the sonic stress is on the offbeats, the second and fourth, which thus receive what would be a disproportionate amount of weight if we assume syncopation to be simply a manner of presentation. On the large scale, that of the bar, this is an instance of syncopation

---

[12]   Richard Middleton, *Pop Music and the Blues* (London, 1972), pp. 39–45.

(the stress not coinciding with the pulse), of which subtler usages are normative, as in the examples given above of modifications to this standard pattern. Normally, of course, syncopation is observed at more local levels, that is, where a beat (sounded in the kit) is tinkered with either by anticipation or delay in a voice or other lead instrument. The Beatles' 'Eleanor Rigby' provides a clear example: it is riddled with syncopation. In the introduction, the objects of McCartney's gaze ('all the lonely people') come into view before the music is ready for them – can one detect an element of guilt here? In the verse, every fourth/third syllable ('Rig-', 'rice', 'church', 'wed-', 'been') anticipates the downbeat, appearing early – not always quite as early as this bald description makes it seem, though: in the first verse alone, the words 'rice' and 'wedding' are fractionally late (i.e. don't anticipate by an entire quaver), reminding us that we need to pay attention to the subtlety with which lines are actually delivered. Crosby Stills & Nash's 'Marrakesh express' is equally full of vocal anticipation – here, this seems to echo the sense of travelling forward by train. Madonna's 'Material girl' is another fine example – does this symbolize her eagerness to accept materiality? It's common practice: in Chris Farlowe's 'Handbags and gladrags' (as in many other examples), it helps the line to approximate the rhythms of speech. The verse of Black Sabbath's 'Paranoid' takes this to a further extreme; in the verse, with the exception of the downbeats to the first, third and fourth bars of the phrase, every note is anticipated. Syncopation by anticipation is thus so normative as to be expected.

Syncopation by delay is surely nowadays less common. Van Morrison's 'Tupelo honey' (like so much of his singing) is marked by vocal delay, as he holds back on initial notes of phrases in comparison to where the guitar is. The verse of the Carpenters' 'Superstar' works similarly, as a comparison of Karen Carpenter's singing of the opening melody with the preceding oboe introduction clearly demonstrates. This is, again, very much a feature of her style, particularly in her more wistful moods. This use of delay is found often among singers coming from the big band tradition: Al Martino's 'Spanish eyes' provides a number of examples, although there is a crucial point of difference here. With delay, it is less apparent that these are facets of the *song* rather than of the *track*. One could hardly perform 'Eleanor Rigby' successfully without its syncopations (singing McCartney's line *on* the beat would sound dull in the extreme), but one could so perform 'Spanish eyes'. Particularly interesting are those few singers who employ both anticipation and delay, such as Bobby Darin (anticipating in the chorus of 'Things' and delaying in the verse of 'All of you').

So what's happening, in theory, when one syncopates? How should this be understood? Middleton[13] suggests understanding syncopation as successive transformations of normative regularity, using the opening of the Rolling Stones' 'Satisfaction' to demonstrate how this can be understood. David Temperley takes this much further, extending the transformational grammar developed by Lerdahl and Jackendoff and providing a series of rules by which syncopations can be

---

[13]   Middleton, *Studying popular music*, p. 213.

generated from assumed 'correct' positions of notes on beats: Temperley talks of syncopations as 'displaced events which belong on some other beat'.[14] While there is no doubt that anticipations and delays occur ahead of, and behind, the beat, it is another matter to say that they 'belong' on the beat. We can only properly say this latter by using as a standard of reference the assumption that notes should appear on the beat, as they do in the music of Beethoven and Handel, which forms the starting-point for Temperley's essay. I believe this to be a wrong assumption, and shall argue the same point in regard to harmony (below). If we take seriously the earlier suggestion of Middleton,[15] the rhythmic position in which we find a note is the place where it 'belongs'. There is a larger debate of which this forms a part, to which I shall return in Chapter 7, which is that of the cognitive reality of the models we develop in order to explain musical surfaces. Although the issue seems to me irrelevant to the interpretation we make of a syncopated passage, the evidence of quite varied sources[16] is that transformational grammars (and other linguistically derived models) simply make a false basic assumption.

If we return to the level of the bar, that of the standard rock beat, we find other forms of metric irregularity, sufficiently common to warrant treatment. Some tracks simply change their metre, making the *cuts* and *extensions* noted above a standard means of continuing. The bridge of the Beatles' 'We can work it out', for example, seems to move from a firm ¼ to two bars of ⁶⁄₈. Their 'Lucy in the sky with diamonds' moves in the opposite direction, between the verse and the chorus, while the Turtles' 'Elenore' shifts to ⁶⁄₈ right at the very end, and Pink Floyd's 'Pigs on the wing (part two)' works similarly. But in each of these cases, I think the ⁶⁄₈ or ⁶⁄₈ interpolation can be heard as drawn out triplets (as in Example 3.14) such that what is changing is the way the basic ¼ is being articulated, a practice I call *re-grooving*.

Example 3.14   Beatles: 'We can work it out'; two alternative readings of the bridge

There are many other examples of this sort of device. The Rolling Stones' 'Paint it black' spends most of its time alternating kit patterns with no discernible

---

[14]   David Temperley: 'Syncopation in rock: a perceptual perspective', *Popular Music* 18/1 (1999), p. 39.

[15]   *Pop music and the blues* rather than *Studying popular music*.

[16]   Johnson, *The body in the mind*, or Gibson, *The ecological approach* as developed in Clarke, *Ways of listening*.

difference between beats, and with a clear standard rock beat. At around 2'20", a new pattern begins to emerge, one that drummers know as the 'classic' pattern, and that in its incessant (fast) triplets often connotes growing menace, as it seems to in this song. This device is found in a variety of styles: Girls Aloud's 'Biology' moves between a forceful, stop time opening and a much smoother, backbeat-dominated verse. Real changes of metre, though, seem far removed from dance music, since they are harder to dance to. Radiohead's 'Paranoid Android', aside from consisting of a variety of sections in different tempi, includes changes of metre within a tempo, most notably in the passage from 2'09" in which shifts between $\frac{4}{4}$ and $\frac{7}{8}$ (where it is the second half of the *third* beat which, virtuosically, has been cut). Judee Sill's impressive 'The donor' begins unambiguously in $\frac{4}{4}$ but, as the verse extends, the sense of downbeat gets lost, such that the arrival at 'Kyrie eleison' in $\frac{3}{4}$ feels like a sure point of arrival, particularly as the melody at that point has such a strong profile. Again, many examples can be found; it is a particularly common device in metal, for instance, as in Nightwish's 'Ghost love score'. In more extreme metal, metre is treated far more roughly. Although Frantic Bleep's 'But a memory' seems to be in a standard $\frac{4}{4}$, an extra semiquaver is added to the final beat. The same band's 'The expulsion' moves in regular subdivided beats (although in uneven numbers), but then occasionally adds a couple of beats at a different speed. The technical proficiency of many metal musicians is beyond doubt. In some cases, changes of time signature seem to result from fusing what begin as different tracks, as in Queen's 'Bohemian rhapsody', or the two parts to Pink Floyd's 'Money'. Some tracks alternate different time signatures. The Beatles' 'All you need is love' switches constantly between $\frac{4}{4}$ and $\frac{3}{4}$. It would be tempting to hear this as a regular $\frac{7}{4}$ were it not for the fact that the chorus actually settles down into $\frac{4}{4}$. Progressive rock tracks are adept at this sort of switching. King Crimson's 'Red', for example, opens with two bars of $\frac{5}{8}$, one of $\frac{6}{8}$, and then one of $\frac{4}{4}$, a pattern that repeats through the introduction. Once into the verse, Robert Fripp's guitar continues to play in $\frac{5}{8}$ over Bill Bruford's $\frac{4}{4}$ drumming – the very picture of precise control, as opposed to the examples from the Flying Lizards and the Fall discussed above. Genesis' 'Dance on a volcano' follows phrases of $\frac{7}{4}$ with phrases of $\frac{7}{8}$. Sometimes this is considered virtuosity for its own sake, although that is a very difficult prejudice to substantiate. In other styles, it is less a stylistic feature than aimed to make a poetic point: Gorillaz' '5/4' superimposes a $\frac{5}{8}$ pattern on a normal $\frac{4}{4}$ kit pattern, while the latter part of Tool's 'Lateralus' superimposes a $\frac{3}{2}$ vocal line on a $\frac{9}{8}$ kit pattern.

The commonest such superimposition of metres is where a $\frac{3}{8}$ melodic pattern repeats over $\frac{4}{4}$ (although patterns based on repeating $\frac{5}{8}$ over $\frac{4}{4}$ can be found, as in the chorus of Stevie Wonder's 'Happy birthday'). This is a form of syncopation, but the constant presence of the smaller pattern draws unusual attention to itself – it is a more local version of the 'We can work it out' change noted above. Forte draws attention to the pervasiveness of two figures in the American ballad, the ragtime figure and the Charleston figure,[17] both of which are forms of a *3 + 3 + 2 pattern*. The Beatles' 'Here comes the sun' exemplifies this, in the little tail to the verse, although during the bridge, the $\frac{3}{8}$ takes over entirely, losing sense of $\frac{4}{4}$ for just a moment. Successive tracks opening Porcupine Tree's *In absentia* are underpinned by different versions of the 3 + 3 + 2 pattern, demonstrating its pervasiveness. Thus, the first track, 'Blackest eyes', uses a 3 + 3 + 2 pattern in the bass and kit, spread over two beats, as an upbeat to the groove's strong downbeat. The second track, 'Trains', strums an acoustic guitar in a 3 + 3 + 2 pattern over the length of a bar. The third track, 'Lips of ashes', doubles this, based as it is on a 3 + 3 + 3 + 3 + 2 + 2 pattern over the course of a bar. Then, the fourth track, 'Sound of muzak', is founded on a 3 + 4 pattern for its verse. These sorts of alterations are fundamental to the syntax of popular song. The basic device, as Forte suggests, goes back at least to ragtime, where it is almost definitive of the style, and is common in swing. Glenn Miller's 'In the mood' is typical: four hearings of a $\frac{3}{8}$ pattern are superimposed on six beats of $\frac{4}{4}$, while in the next two beats the pattern comes to a rest (the 3 + 3 + 3 + 3 + 2 + 2 mentioned above – Example 3.15).

Example 3.15   Glen Miller: 'In the mood'; melodic grouping

(swung)

The opening to Barclay James Harvest's 'Mockingbird' also follows exactly this pattern. It is rotated in George Gershwin's 'I got rhythm' (2 + 3 + 3 + 3 + 3 + 2); Ethel Merman's recording is particularly interesting in that the triple nature of the rising motif sometimes has its syncopation removed. It appears also in metal, as in the opening of Opeth's 'The grand conjuration'. This 'reversed pattern' (where the $\frac{3}{8}$s *follow* a straight half-bar) is less used, but does appear in, for example, Jethro Tull's 'Sweet dream'. The $\frac{3}{8}$ superimposition is also a device commonly used in improvisation; Robert Plant's improvisation in the studio version of Led Zeppelin's 'Whole lotta love' contains just such a moment, at 2'09", marked as it is by the snare, cutting across John Bonham's regular hi-hat quavers, and again at 4'32", marking out the intentionality of this device. It is used again on 'Rock and Roll', where the last line of the verse (bar 9 of the 12-bar pattern) shifts to $\frac{3}{4}$ in the voice, and then to $\frac{3}{8}$. An alternative kind of triple bears a different relationship to syncopation. Slade's 'Know who you are' pits a shuffle rhythm against regular triplets in the voice, but triplets that give the effect of hemiola (three attacks across the space of two beats). Often, such triplets would appear to give the effect of relaxation, but Noddy Holder appears to be so intent on getting these 'right' that, if anything, he subtly anticipates. The pent-up energy that is thereby conveyed

---

[17]   Allen Forte, *The American Popular Ballad*, pp. 19–20.

seems to embody the aggressive self-awareness that the beginning of the song, at least, promotes.

In *Rock: the primary text*,[18] I drew attention to the presence in rock improvisation of a device that is fundamental to Hindustani improvisation practices and that, following that tradition, I called a *tihai*. Here, a short melodic fragment that does not fit into the subdivision of the beat, repeats a total of (usually) three times, the end of the last 'miraculously' coinciding with the next downbeat. In these instances of 3s against 4s, although the number of repetitions is more than three, the effect is of the same kind, and this seems to me an important feature breaking momentarily, as it does, a sense of rigidity, introducing a momentary sense that a norm is to be broken, only to reinstate it. And, because it is so widely used, it itself has acquired a certain normative status. It is an inevitable means of enlivening a line.

Harmony: Modal Theory

Of course, if this seems intricate enough, it is as nothing compared to the details not of when notes are played, but of what notes are played. I deal with harmony here not because there is an obvious link between harmony and these metrical matters, but because both intersect in the formal patterns that songs observe. To non-musicians, harmony always appears the most abstruse of musical factors. Pretty well all other features of the musical fabric can be understood, and even discussed, by those without the experience of actually making music. Harmony is resistant to this. It is hardly surprising, therefore, that the meaningfulness of harmonic patterns is so often regarded with suspicion. And yet, harmony has a profound effect on the meaning of what we listen to. The harmonic syntax of popular song is both simpler (on a large scale) and more complex (on the local level) than the harmonic syntax of other Western musics. It is therefore vital to sort out its basic attributes. Two main approaches can be taken here. Some writers regard the harmonic system of Western 'classical' tonality as providing a basic norm, a quasi-universal, psychologically or acoustically necessary, and observe that popular music deviates from this norm. Thus they account for those deviations.[19] It is conceivably possible to take exactly the opposite approach, and to assume there is no real link between the harmonic language of popular music and that of Western tonality. To take this approach, one would need to develop a theory purely from the language of the musicians involved. And, while this may

---

[18]   Moore: *Rock: the primary text* (2nd edn), p. 84.

[19]   Stephenson, *What to listen for in rock*, Walter Everett, 'Pitch down the middle', in Everett (ed.), *Expression in Pop-Rock Music* (rev. edn) (New York, 2008), and many others adopt this approach.

appear to be possible,[20] it encounters two problems: (1) that musicians' language itself is bound up with musicians' own experiences, which usually (even if only negatively) include that of Western tonality; and (2) that such language is insufficiently strong to enable the development of a robust descriptive language. The other main approach, then, is to accept the language of both musicians and Western tonality, but not to accord priority, not to regard popular harmony as a deviation from the norms of Western tonality, but as establishing norms in its own right, which may or may not accord particularly strongly with those found in the music of Bach, Beethoven, or Brahms. It is that latter approach that I adopt here. A more thorough approach along the same lines can be found in Philip Tagg's study of popular harmony;[21] my preference is to see 'tonality' as forming only one part of the musical fabric.

The popular song that we encounter today is, of its very nature, hybrid. It is the heir to different traditions that rarely present themselves in anything remotely resembling a pure form. These traditions can be loosely thought of as belonging to two groups: the traditions of African Americans (the blues, spirituals) and the traditions of Tin Pan Alley, while those of European folk song and dance play a part in both traditions. These differences are briefly explored in Chapter 5. Although these labels, which identify a historical point near the beginning of the twentieth century, are themselves the result of years of development in which they do not remain distinct, they are nonetheless useful ways of identifying two alternative ways of thinking about musical continuity that can be thought of as existing at either end of a continuum. This is a model I shall return to a number of times; my task is to develop a way of discussing the practices at opposite ends of this continuum in the same terms. After all, I am talking about songs that parade themselves as single entities, even if they split apart under analysis. Thus far, with concepts such as texture, timbre, and even basic rhythm, this has not been a problem. The realms of harmony and form are, however, not so simple. As I have suggested, many writers start from the assumption that the language of Western tonality is perfectly adequate to describe this music, treating anomalies as just that. However, this is surely not adequate: the 'anomalies' (particularly identified from the gospel/blues end of the continuum) are no less central to the repertoire than the harmonic practices that can be traced back to eighteenth-century Vienna.[22] Another way must be found, and this can be achieved by assuming a harmonic modal system. In so doing, I offer an alternative, perhaps simplified, approach to that put forward by Walter Everett,[23] but one geared towards different ends. One

---

[20]   Graeme Boone, 'Tonal and expressive ambiguity in "Dark star"', in Covach and Boone (eds.), *Understanding Rock*, (New York NY, 1997), seems to be the only really serious attempt in the literature.

[21]   Philip Tagg, *Everyday tonality* (New York NY, 2009).

[22]   I argue this more fully in 'The so-called "flattened seventh" in rock', reprinted in Moore (ed.), *Critical essays in popular musicology* (Aldershot, 2007).

[23]   Walter Everett, 'Making sense of rock's tonal systems', in *Critical essays*.

aspect of Everett's extended article is his classification of rock into six harmonic/ tonal systems. This identification does not prevent him from adopting a single methodology to enable him to discuss music that falls into different categories, and it is the singleness of a methodology that is important, for without it there can be no comparison. His classification has a great deal to recommend it, and it does not seem to me to cover only rock. The differences of system he identifies do not *in themselves* determine different spheres of meaning and, in any case, the harmonic repertoire can all be discussed modally, as I do below.

Most popular musicians conceive of harmonies as *a priori* vertical concatenations of pitches (i.e. as chords) rather than as the resultants of horizontal movements of separate contrapuntal voices. This is not to say that some aspects of tonal thinking do not find their way into their practices (a C^{sus4} chord, for example will often be followed by a C chord, the 'suspended' fourth ('F') resolving to 'E' according to traditional voice-leading), but they must not be seen as fundamental to all styles of playing, as quasi-universal, psychologically or acoustically necessary; it is for this reason that I am resistant to Everett's recourse to Schenkerian principles.[24] It is also the case that some styles (particularly in metal) avoid full chords, either utilizing bare fifths or single lines over which melodies are constructed (e.g. Evanescance's 'Sweet sacrifice'). Esa Lilja[25] explores the particularities of metal harmonic practice in great detail. Parallel chord shapes are common elsewhere (systems 5 and 6 of Everett's classification), whether in keyboard- or fretboard-led situations, and they perhaps result from ease of playing as much as from aesthetic choice. The patterns that result from sequences of chords are, I believe, best described by referring the roots of the harmonies to a *harmonic modal system*. The labels *lydian, ionian, mixolydian, dorian, aeolian, phrygian* and *locrian* will normally allow the roots of all harmonies within a pattern to be identified (this system thus subsumes the major/minor system as ionian equates to major, while an aeolian/ionian mix equates to minor). Naming is only the beginning of the process, of course, but accurate naming is a necessary starting-point. The labels themselves come from jazz theory and, further back, from nineteenth-century misunderstandings of the practices of Renaissance musicians. They are, however, enough for our purposes as they are. Many musicians are familiar with, and use, these labels.

Another important difference between this modal music and tonal music is the assumption of span – over what span of time does a particular mode operate? There seems to be no *a priori* reason why we should assume that a mode operates throughout a song. Modal change is extremely common, and

---

[24]   Everett, 'Making sense', p. 302. Although this is now perhaps a point of minor disagreement between us; a Schenkerian hearing will certainly highlight those cases that do not conform to conventional voice-leading principles. Everett: 'Schenker's methods are useful not only for showing how songs are tonally normal, but in showing precisely in what ways songs deviate from conventions' ('Making sense', p. 306). The aim is crucial, even if the nature of the deviation is contested.

[25]   Esa Lilja, *Theory and analysis of classic heavy metal harmony* (Vantaa, 2009).

a first approximation should be to assume that a mode operates only for the length of the pattern it describes.

Table 3.1   The system of seven-note modes

Mode		T		T		T		S		T		T		S		T		T		T		S		T		T	
Lydian		T		T		T		S		T		T		S													
	F		G		A		B		C		D		E		F												
Ionian										T		T		S		T		T		T		S					
									C		D		E		F		G		A		B		C				
Mixolydian				T		T		S		T		T		S		T											
			G		A		B		C		D		E		F		G										
Dorian												T		S		T		T		T		S		T			
											D		E		F		G		A		B		C		D		
Aeolian						T		S		T		T		S		T		T									
					A		B		C		D		E		F		G		A								
Phrygian														S		T		T		T		S		T		T	
													E		F		G		A		B		C		D		E
Locrian								S		T		T		S		T		T		T							
							B		C		D		E		F		G		A		B						

Table 3.1 makes clear the perfectly regular nature of this system. The pattern of tones and semitones (identified by the letters 'T' and 'S') remains constant across all modes – the determining nature of the mode is simply where one starts – which note is identified as the 'tonic'. (An example of each mode, without accidentals, is given beneath, for ease of comparison. Note, though, that each mode can, of course, begin on each of 12 semitones.) The chords that musicians use are, for the most part, tertial concatenations of these. Thus, the chord C–E–G is chord V in F lydian, chord I in C ionian, chord IV in G mixolydian, chord VII in D dorian, chord III in A aeolian, chord VI in E phrygian, and chord II in B locrian. Some characteristics of this system are worth noting. Only two modes (lydian and ionian) have a 'leading note' (a semitone from the seventh degree to the upper tonic), only three (lydian, ionian, mixolydian) have a major third above the tonic, only one (lydian) has no perfect fourth above the tonic, and only one (locrian) no perfect fifth. These characteristics may seem purely theoretical, but they do have an impact on the expressive nature of songs using these modes. Alf Bjornberg[26] pointed many years ago to both the importance and the value of using a modal description, but my classification differs from his in one important respect. For Bjornberg, to describe a track as using the aeolian mode means that all chordal pitches are derived from that mode. I prefer a more lenient description,

---

[26]   Alf Bjornberg: 'On Aeolian Harmony in Contemporary Popular Music', in Moore, *Critical essays.*

whereby the mode is identified simply by the harmonic roots. I say this because the mode is a *post hoc* description, and cannot take priority over the decisions musicians actually make. It is an approximation, which will (sometimes) require modification to make it accurate. Thus, the common aeolian pattern i–VII–VI (e.g. the sequence e–D–C) is sometimes modified to produce I'–VII–VI (e.g. the sequence E–D–C).[27] Some other examples may be in order at this point, assuming the first chord of the pattern to be the tonic. The sequence A–D–b–E is in A ionian (I–IV–ii–V); the sequence c♯–f♯–D–E is in C♯ phrygian (i–iv–II–III); the sequence E♭–F–B♭–g is in E♭ lydian (I–II–V–iii); while the sequence B–A–E is in B mixolydian (I–VII–IV). Identification of chords becomes slightly more complex when chords are not stated in their entirety, but are merely hinted at, or where the bass moves during a chord. This leads to common interchanges of chords. In any mode, III and V; V and VII; VII and II; II and VI; IV and VI are often interchanged, as are chords with roots a tritone apart in any jazz-related context.

Modifications to the unaltered use of the mode, as Bjornberg describes, are common. Madness' 'New Delhi' alternates two chords: d and E. E begins and ends the song, so it is reasonable to think of this as the tonic. We then have a vii–I sequence, one that doesn't appear in any particular mode. However, the gap between vii and I is a tone, which rules out lydian and ionian. Because I is major, mixolydian is a more preferable identification to any of the other modes. Thus, the pattern is reasonably described as mixolydian vii⁻–I. George Harrison's 'Isn't it a pity' is based on C–F–C (over a pedal bass), but introduces a diminished inflection of the opening C, thus producing an ionian I–i⁼–IV–I pattern. Motorhead's 'Damage case' uses another four-chord sequence: E–B–G–D (the first underpinning the verse, the remaining chords revolving for the chorus). This can be understood as either dorian or aeolian, which differ only in the sixth degree. In either case, chord V becomes major, thus: I–V'–III–VII. Sometimes, the quality of the tonic is modified. Thus, Jimi Hendrix's 'Ain't no telling' is a dorian pattern (because chord IV is major), described thus: I'–III–IV–VII–V'. So far, all these patterns have begun with the tonic, but this by no means has to happen. The bridge (or middle 8) of 'The In crowd', as sung by Bryan Ferry, moves round the cycle of fifths: B–E–A–D–F–G. The use of both B and F sounds a little unorthodox, since chord III is rare in a mixolydian sequence. It is the penultimate chord that identifies it as mixolydian, thus: III'–VI'–II'–V–VII–I. And, sometimes, in order to preserve the location of

---

[27] I use the following symbols to identify these modifications: ' for a triad turned to major (i.e. III'); - for a triad turned to minor (i.e. iii⁻); '' for a triad turned to augmented (i.e. II'') and = for a triad turned to diminished (i.e. iii⁼). Some writers used figured bass notation, which works equally well. We can identify sevenths in a similar way. Thus the following modifications of chord III. Allowing M = Major third, and m = minor third, then the augmented seventh (MMm) appears as III⁺, the major seventh (MmM) as III^M, the large minor seventh (mMM) as III^/, the dominant seventh (Mmm) as III^x, the small minor seventh (mMm) as III^m, the half diminished seventh (mmM) as III^Ø and the full diminished seventh as III°. This is the scheme I use in 'Patterns of harmony', *Popular Music* 11/1 (1992).

roots within a single mode, all the chords may require modification. The verse of 'The happening', by Diana Ross and the Supremes, ends with the sequence B♭–E♭–A♭–D–G. This altered cycle of fifths is most concisely described as phrygian, but with all chords modified to major, thus: III'–VI'–II'–V'–I'. One might (not unreasonably!) ask why go to such lengths of description? The answer, shortly, is consistency, which makes for easier comparison of patterns from one song to another, a vital issue that I shall take up in subsequent chapters. Occasionally, the mode remains ambiguous, as in Kate Bush's 'Wuthering heights'. This sequence uses A–F–E–C♯, which can be understood as both an ionian I–♭VI–V–III' and as an aeolian I'–VI–V'–♯III'. Both require modifications to the scale, and point to the limitations of the modal model: it captures the vast majority of patterns used, but is a descriptive rather than a prescriptive tool. Stan Hawkins' study of a Prince track[28] provides an extended discussion of the issues involved in one complex modal case.

One cannot be content with simply identifying patterns – the same pattern may appear to originate from very different impulses. Take the ionian pattern I–II'–IV–I (where chord II has been 'borrowed' from the lydian mode). This pattern underpins the melody of most of the verse of Procol Harum's 'Homburg'. Over a pedal bass F, the opening phrase of the melody sinks chromatically from C through B and B♭ (each taking a bar), to A. Now it seems as if this is the guiding idea of that sequence – the chords F, G, B♭ and again F are chosen simply to harmonize the melody and bass. But this is not the only pattern of harmonies that would do the job – the aeolian sequence I'–VI^x–V'–I would do the job equally well, but this sequence does carry a bluesier feel that might seem inappropriate in a psychedelic context. Billy Joel's 'Storm front' uses almost exactly that sequence for its chorus, except that chord i is minor – the chromatic line is hinted at in the organ, but no more.[29] Now the Beatles' 'Eight days a week' uses exactly the same harmonic pattern as 'Homburg', but here the bass is mobile and the melody has no hint of chromatic descent – the chord sequence seems to have driven this particular occurrence. And we should note that both approaches (melody-driven and chord-driven) are part of the repertory of most musicians – Procol Harum themselves covered 'Eight days a week'. A comparison of these three near-identical chord sequences enables us, then, to observe them operating in context to partake of different significances.

In order to be able to compare patterns, it is necessary to be able to identify a tonic within any sequence. This is not always self-evident, as the Kinks' 'You really got me' shows. The guitar and bass alternate pairs of chords: F and G; G and A; and C and D. The guitar gets lost within the texture, such that it is the bass notes we are probably most aware of. In each case, the first note tends to decorate the

---

[28]   Stan Hawkins, 'Prince: harmonic analysis of "Anna Stesia"', reprinted in Middleton, *Reading Pop* (Oxford, 2000),.

[29]   In jazz, of course, V[7] is frequently decorated by a preceding ♭VI[7], and this song hints also at that usage.

second, which, taking the most time, seems the most stable. Ray Davies' melody is modally unstable – over the G, for instance, he hits a B♭ as frequently as a B. What is vocally stable, though, is the backing chord – definitely an A (major) and a D (major). So, how should we hear this? If we hear the G as tonic, it's a lydian tune (because of the C♯ in the A chord). If we hear the D as tonic, it's an ionian tune. Which to choose? A tonic will normally exhibit one (or more) of three qualities: persistence, laterality and emphasis. Thus, it may be longer than adjacent chords (often twice as long), it may begin or end a repeating pattern, and it may receive an accent, or be marked by a change of timbre, perhaps, or density in some way. In this example, since the D ends the song, I prefer the ionian interpretation, but it is a close call. Sometimes these tonic qualities contradict each other. In Steeleye Span's 'Two butchers', successive halves of the verse begin with chords of D and A, while A ends the verse, but the most time is spent on an E. In this case, it is the laterality of the A that seems to take precedence, possibly because the most prominent melodic pitch is an A (which is dissonant to the E chord). Procol Harum's 'Pilgrim's progress' is unproblematically in G ionian, the G both beginning and ending verses and appearing in prominent places. However, with the song over, a closing tag repeats the sequence D–D/C (i.e. D with a C in the bass) –G/B–a⁷/C, until the track fades. This can still be heard as G ionian (although the G is now in a weak inversion), or it can be heard as a shift to a D mixolydian. Since the song is about the process of history, and the individual's small place in 'taking turns in trying to pass them [i.e.truths] on', that switch at the end suggests a strange perspective. Are these the truths that are being passed on (endlessly)? Perhaps this can be heard as a failure to get them across (the switch of mode)?

Richard Thompson's 'Calvary Cross' also exemplifies issues surrounding the tonic. The extended verse moves a–F–G–G, while the chorus has C–F–C–G. Clearly both a and C act as tonics for their respective sections, but should we hear the song as aeolian i–VI–VII … III–VI–VII or as ionian vi–IV–V … I–IV–V? Which decision we make will have a profound effect on how we interpret the song, as fundamentally optimistic (the latter) or pessimistic (the former). The reason these issues matter is that the larger the number of minor intervals the mode contains between successive scale pitches and the modal tonic, then the more depressed/emotionally negative/lacking in energy the effect of the track is likely to be, all other factors being equal. In other words, the further down the Table 3.1 (from lydian to locrian) one moves, the more negative the modal connotations. In this particular example, there is a third option, which is to hear each two tonics, one for each pattern, with a moment of ambiguity as these are exchanged. While this is perhaps theoretically unpalatable for some, in that it transgresses the assumption that a song is a unity, it certainly captures the experience of the song, particularly the wonderful lightness of the C chord after so much seeming failure to achieve it (with the G constantly going to the a). A more straightforward example of this effect is the song 'Everybody get together' – I refer to the H.P. Lovecraft original. The tonic is unambiguously A, but whereas the verse alternated a mixolydian I–VII, the chorus is based on ionian IV–V–I. It seems most sensible here to talk of two equal modes, rather than one modifying the other. The hybrid nature of the repertoire alluded to above gives rise to two very different approaches to the use of harmony, but two approaches that have interpenetrated to the extent that they can be difficult to disinter. Accordingly, I shall treat them here first at a theoretical level, as if they were distinct, and then 'in reality', analysing examples according to this assumption, in the subsequent sections. The first of these approaches relates strongly to Everett's systems 4–6 (with some presence in system 3), and the second approach to systems 1–3. However, because these approaches have interpenetrated, I would argue that Everett's systems in many cases pertain more readily to parts of songs than to complete songs.

You will note that many of these examples are from the post-rock'n'roll era. Yet, the hybridity I mentioned above relates also to the use of modes: blues and gospel traditions make full use of mixolydian, dorian and aeolian. Tin Pan Alley traditions are far more likely to use ionian and the harmonic minor. But there are exceptions even to this norm: Al Bowlly's 'Sweet and lovely' is a mixolydian tune, while Cyril Grantham's 'How beautiful you are' contains an intermediate aeolian cadence within the verse. And, to my ears, these two examples sound noticeably strange.

Harmony and Form: Loops

The first approach is fundamentally iterative. Here, a sequence of chords is simply repeated either for a section of a song, or for an entire song. The influence of sequencing technology has become so pervasive that these sequences are now most usually referred to as *loops*, initially from the practice of creating a loop of recording tape, but now from simply cutting and pasting a section of material in a programme such as Cubase. Sometimes, the harmonic structure is so minimal that we simply have a single harmony, acting effectively as a drone. The Beatles' 'Tomorrow never knows' exemplifies one approach to this. The bass and sitar sit on a tonic C pedal. Lennon's melody begins by using simply the notes of the chord of C. However, on the word 'dying' (at 19"), he rises from a G to a C through a B♭, instantiating the mixolydian mode. Although the bass stays on the tonic, a keyboard reinforces Lennon's B♭ with a B♭ chord, rising to a C. Here, then, we have a drone I, but we also have a mixolydian VII–I sequence. Blues-related jams often exemplify drones: Cream's 'Spoonful', for example, is based throughout on a dorian E, with hints at the mixolydian at some points, while Fleetwood Mac's 'Oh well' simply uses the simplified dorian that is the pentatonic blues minor. Indeed, it is the blues that most stereotypically uses this device: John Lee Hooker's 'Boogie chillun', for example, invents a simple riff that outlines a tonic chord. Z.Z. Top's 'La grange' is more equivocal, since the bass clearly outlines the common aeolian i–III–IV pattern (although the band's publisher accepted accusations of their plagiarism of the Hooker tune). Frank Zappa's parodic 'Cheap thrills' takes this to its ultimate conclusion – after an introduction that promises a stock harmonic sequence, the song sticks resolutely to the tonic thereafter. Indeed, it is perhaps best to conceive drones as existing at one extreme of the use of iterative harmonic patterns. There are many such patterns,[30] although some are far commoner than others. Following Richard Middleton, I call these *open-ended repetitive gestures*: 'open-ended' because there is no external restriction on how many times the pattern can repeat. A pattern can remain in place for a verse, for a chorus, or even for an entire song. The most common arrangements are to have:

- four equally spaced chords (each lasting for one or, less often, for two bars);
- two equally spaced chords (each lasting for two bars or, less often, for one bar); or
- three chords, one of which is twice the length of the others.

Such songs equally tend to the expression of stasis, because the open-endedness of the repetition means there is no change in the situation, no point to aim for, and thus no possibility of resolution of a situation. It is common for such songs to end with fades.[31]

Siouxsie and the Banshees' 'Hong Kong Garden' is a very good example of a two-chord oscillation, where a mixolydian I–VII pattern (equally spaced) repeats throughout the verse and chorus,[32] such that the distinction between the two can only be made on grounds of texture and the chorus' repeating lyric. Patti Smith's 'Gloria' is perhaps more extreme, since there's no sense of the imposition of a 'verse' on the pattern's open-endedness. The Deviants' 'I'm coming home' is similar, except that the singer's vocal tone makes a distinction between his coming, his being there, and the pleasant after-effects. Longer patterns often acquire a history. The ionian I–vi–IV–V pattern, for example, although found from the 1940s on, became so common in the 1950s that it is often known as the 'doo-wop' progression. In the Penguins' 'Earth angel', which may be taken as axiomatic, the progression takes four bars, and four repetitions constitute the 'A' section of what is essentially an AABA form. The 'B' section is harmonically simplified, based as it is on IV–I oscillations of the sort described above. Ben E. King's 'Stand by me' is in some senses a simpler example, since there are no modifications to the pattern (there are in the Penguins' track, which I shall discuss in Chapter 9). However, the relative lengths are changed such that the IV–V move takes only one bar, leaving a fourth bar to return to I, thus: |I–|vi–|IV–V–|I–|. Common patterns of this type often undergo modification. The chorus to U2's 'One' for instance, uses I–vi–IV–I, where the last chord replaces V. The effect of this is to close off each repetition of the pattern giving a sense of security and comfort, entirely lacking in conflict, because of the rather relaxed tempo and texture.

---

[30]   Discussed and listed in Moore, *Patterns of harmony*.

[31]   This whole topic receives extensive treatment in Tagg, *Everyday tonality*, pp. 159–240.

[32]   The bass sometimes, irregularly, sticks to the tonic, thereby reproducing the pattern of 'Tomorrow never knows'.

One of the other, common, sets of changes is the 'flamenco progression', i.e. the aeolian progression that moves i–VII–VI–V' (or v). One of the earliest appearances of this is in Ray Charles' 'Hit the road, Jack' (1961), where the harmonies remain implicit. Indeed, it may be best to conceive this pattern as originally simply a bass line, which then becomes harmonically thickened. The Animals' standard version of Nina Simone's 'Don't let me be misunderstood' repeats the pattern twice for its verse, before taking up a contrasting pattern for the refrain. The Turtles' 'Happy together' spends twice as long on each chord, repeating twice, before again switching to another pattern for the chorus. These examples seem to me to originate during a period in which this pattern was entering the repertory, so to speak. Once it is familiar, it can then be used in other ways, as exemplified by P.J. Harvey's 'The dancer', post-dating these by some 30 years. This song opens with a couple of hearings of the i–VII–VI–V' pattern as an introduction to set the scene, to remind us of the pattern, as it were. The verses are based on i–iv–V'–V': identical outer points, but a different pathway. These steadily shift toward i–ii–V+–V', where the 'ii' is closer to 'VII' than 'iv' had been, while V+ clearly prefigures VI. Then, after some almost ecstatic reaching for the top part of Polly Harvey's range, the organ finally announces i–VII–VI–V' almost as a point of arrival. The narrative direction of the song is thus reinforced by the way harmony is made to operate.

Regularity of harmonic movement is, therefore, a common norm. Even where a track appears to challenge this, that underlying regularity is likely to assert itself. Franz Ferdinand's 'This fire' opens with a pattern that seems to move at the rate of two harmonies per bar. In the chorus, this shifts to one harmony per two bars – one quarter of the speed of harmonic change. However, as the second verse recovers the opening of the first (and that speed of change), the bass (silent at the beginning) now moves at the chorus' rate, such that the guitar harmonies can now be heard as decorations of a basic 2-bar per harmony rate of change.

In each of these examples, it is the pattern of harmonies that acts as the identifying feature, rather than the relative length of them. Theorists have asked how these successions come about. Everett[33] offers a list of chord colours and how they function in the repertory of the Beatles, while the issue surfaces throughout Pedler's examination of the Beatles' idiolect.[34] Stephenson devotes two entire chapters to this topic,[35] most importantly identifying what he calls the *rock standard root movements*, arguing that movements between successive harmonic roots that fall by a second, rise by a third,[36] and fall by a fourth, constitute the commonest

---

[33]   Walter Everett, *The Beatles as Musicians*: Revolver *through the* Anthology (Oxford, 1999), pp. 309–13.

[34]   Dominic Pedler, *The Songwriting Secrets of the Beatles* (London, 2003).

[35]   Stephenson, *What to listen for in rock*, pp. 73–120.

[36]   This move is both the topic of Chris McDonald, 'Exploring modal subversions in alternative music', *Popular Music* 19/3 (2000), and the focus of Guy Capuzzo, 'Neo-Riemannian theory and the analysis of pop-rock music', *Music Theory Spectrum* 26/2 (2004).

patterns, some of which he then demonstrates. Christopher Doll[37] exhaustively treats the ways harmonic successions are derived from others. Allen Forte[38] offers a far briefer overview of harmonic succession in his repertory, where he finds root movement by fifth the only pattern necessary to summarize from the compendious analyses that follow. Guy Capuzzo's paper returns to neo-Riemannian theory (a way of modelling the relationship between chords in a succession that do not simply fall within a particular mode) to explain the logic behind some apparently haphazard sequences. One topic that such work does not address is the way certain established harmonic patterns are sometimes enriched by the interpolation of others.[39] Jethro Tull's 'We used to know' is a case in point. It utilizes the 'flamenco' changes (i–VII–VI–V) decorated (enriched) by surrounding harmonies, all a fifth away from the decorated chord. The full (aeolian) pattern is i–V–VII–IV–VI–III–II–V, i.e. i–(V–)VII–(IV–)VI–(III–)(II–)V where bracketed harmonies are seen as decorative of the basic structure. Led Zeppelin's 'Since I've been lovin' you' provides an alternative example of enrichment. Here, a 12-bar blues pattern is enriched first by decorating chord IV in bar 10, and then by replacing the firm final I with a turnaround (a pattern that leads 'inevitably' into the next hearing of the entire sequence). In both of these cases, it appears to me that for a pattern to be heard as being enriched, it needs to have an independent identity, otherwise we could make out that all patterns included such enrichment, and the rules of such enrichment are not self-evident. So, while there clearly is some value in predicting the likelihood of a particular succession, and in uncovering a logic not immediately apparent, it is hard to see how this impacts on tracks' meanings, and so I do not develop this theme here.

There are some patterns, however, where an irregular set of lengths is at least as important as the actual harmonic succession. Most of these are versions of blues sequences, such as the 12-bar blues pattern. The identifying feature here is the very presence of a 12-bar repeating unit (whether that be a 12-bar verse, or an 8-bar verse and 4-bar chorus). The simplest representation of this pattern harmonically is I–I–I–I–IV–IV–I–I–V–V–I–I and it is already common practice by the time of early recorded blues in the 1920s. Indeed, so is the practice of ornamenting these 'fundamental' harmonies, such that Bessie Smith's 'Spider man blues' of 1928 uses this sequence: |I–|IV–V–|I–|I–|IV^x–|IV^x–V–|I–|I–|V–|IV–V–|I–|V–|.[40] In the hands of a wayward bluesman such as Robert Johnson, the actual sequence remains as much implicit as explicit – in 'Crossroads blues', for example, we

---

[37] Christopher Doll, 'Transformation in rock harmony: an explanatory strategy', *Gamut* 2/1 (2009).

[38] Forte, *The American Popular Ballad*, pp. 12–17.

[39] I am explicitly referring to harmonic patterns here, rather than voice-leading, and so this is not an instance of a quasi-Schenkerian elaboration of a background contrapuntal motion.

[40] In actual fact, the sequence is even more complicated, if we take into account every ornamental harmony the pianist uses, but the point stands even with this simplification.

can hear the liberties he takes with the regularity of the metre, and also the way he plays against the harmonies running through both his and, surely, his original listeners', heads. What is unmistakeable, though, is the move to IV in bar 5. And it is this feature, more than any other, that is essential to the 12-bar blues pattern. Provided there is a sense of chord I during the first four bars, and a move to chord IV in bar 5, the allusion will be secure. It is, though, in the rock'n'roll period where the stability of the pattern becomes normative. Recorded performances of Little Richard's 'Long tall Sally', for example, deviate from the initial pattern only by a switch to IV at bar 10 (a very common amendment), although they will often start in 'stop time' (where the band plays only on the downbeat), shifting to normal on bar 5, that crucial IV chord, emphasizing its identificatory nature.

Not all regular blues conform to the 12-bar pattern. There are standard 10-bar, 8-bar and 16-bar blues, although the harmonic patterns are far more variable here. Here are two alternative 8-bar patterns, for example. 'Key to the highway', as appearing on Derek & the Dominos' *Layla*, has a sequence that moves I–V–IV^x–IV^x–I–V–I–V. Here, it is the move to IV in bar 3 that is pertinent to its identification as a blues. In Chuck Berry's 'Sweet little sixteen', however, the pattern is V–I–V–I–IV–I–V–I. The opening on V may be unorthodox, but it transmits to the song a strong sense of momentum (because verses finish and restart on different chords). Here, it is the turn to IV in bar 5 which is crucial.

Throughout this section, the harmonies I have been discussing are found within the 'harmonic filler' layer of the texture (see Chapter 2). What happens in the melody and the bass layers? As a basic norm, we can assume the bass will conform to the mode identified; after all, it is harmonic roots that identify the mode, and in most styles roots are far more likely to appear in the bass than any other pitch. The same assumption can be made for melody, if only because so many musicians derive the melody from chords already chosen, rather than vice versa. However, it does not always happen. In those cases where there is conflict, Peter Winkler[41] argues that what happens is that such a melody realizes an alternative background harmonic structure from the one actually presented. Contrarily, Peter Van der Merwe[42] argues that what happens is that melody and harmony fall out of synchronization. Since the writers address different repertories, there is no necessary reason to choose between these possibilities *a priori*. David Temperley[43] offers a more nuanced study arguing that rock often observes what he calls the *loose verse/tight chorus* model, wherein verse melodies often employ dissonant, non-stepwise-resolving strong pitches, expressive of a contrast between the chorus' expression of social unity and the verse's of individual freedom. He also notes that this pattern is not entirely restricted to rock; it can be found wherever the blues (wherein the practice seems

---

[41]   Peter Winkler, 'Toward a theory of popular harmony', in Moore, *Critical essays*.

[42]   Peter van der Merwe, *Origins of the Popular Style* (Oxford, 1989).

[43]   David Temperley, 'The melodic-harmonic "divorce" in rock'; *Popular Music* 26/2 (2007).

to originate) has had an influence. All three writers provide a range of examples, which it would be superfluous to multiply here.

Nor is it always the case that the bass follows the harmonic pattern. This issue has been less widely studied, since it tends only to be found among musicians with a prominent DIY approach – there is almost a sense in which it is by nature transgressive. It can be found in early U2, for one. The opening of 'Another time, another place' is a simple example, wherein the bass sticks solidly on the tonic while the guitar plays a series of diatonic natural harmonics that imply a changing harmonic pattern (including v and VII in an E aeolian context). On a track such as 'Wire', it hardly makes sense to talk about harmony at all – the bass has a minimal riff, the voice soars above and the guitar arpeggiates according to the same dorian scale. Big Country's 'Where the rose is sown' is similar, in that although all parts conform to the same scale, there is independence of movement that seems almost random – it makes little sense to try and identify the four chords involved. Inspiral Carpet's 'Weakness' is more extreme – over an aeolian harmonic pattern I–III–II, the track spends three bars on I before moving, but the bass uses $\hat{1}$–$\hat{2}$–$\hat{3}$–$\hat{5}$ in every bar, the aeolian third (F) sticking out against the F♯ in chord I. This false relation does not seem to generate tension that needs to be resolved (as in Temperley's model, above), but is simply manifest. 'Anthrax' by the Gang of Four is an example of something slightly different – here, the voice hovers around $\hat{6}$, $\hat{7}$ and $\hat{8}$ (F♯, G, A, which carry a sense of D ionian) as the bass plays on A, C♯ and D, with little coordination. So there are varieties of approach, although I would suggest that conformity of the bass to the dominant succession is, so far, always normative. I shall say little about bass movement at this point. I have already noted that the vast majority of harmonies appear in root position[44] – this is why I prefer an analysis in this way rather than one that suggests that bass and harmony are stratified and not necessarily related. However, as with harmony, the way the bass instrument moves can also often be described in terms of oppositional pairings. In terms of rhythm, it can tend to be rhythmically *regular* (playing on every beat or every half beat) or with a strong rhythmic profile, making for rhythmic *variety*. In terms of style, it can tend to be *static* in pitch (repeating the root of the harmony and then simply moving to the next root at a change of harmony) or *mobile* (employing inversions, and perhaps consciously stepwise movement). The playing of Adam Clayton (U2) and Paul McCartney (the Beatles) exemplify this distinction. The type of use of the bass is often highly constitutive of the track's style. Stasis and regularity are normally paired against mobility and rhythmic variety (which can lend the bass a 'melodic' quality). How the bass is moving, and whether it is consistent, are key questions to ask.

---

[44] Note that Lilja, *Theory and analysis*, argues persuasively that for some heavy metal, because of the acoustics of an overdriven electric guitar, the harmonic assumption of inversions (which dates back to Rameau) needs to be rethought. My ears remain somewhat unconvinced, but that may simply be due to my own listening habits.

Before moving on to discuss the second of the approaches to harmony I identified above, I need to broach some initial questions of a song's form since, as I suggested, the two categories are intimately related. Almost all popular song proceeds by sectional forms. By this, I mean that hypermetric groups of up to 32 bars in length (with, if necessary, elisions, extensions and cuts) are concatenated to produce conceptually separable stretches of music whose formal functions can be identified, and whose sections can be named. This process of naming is more important than it is often given credit for being, since by naming a discreet unit, we are comparing it to similar units in other songs, and thus developing the norms by which we understand how to orient ourselves temporally in relation to that to which we're listening. A standard example is given by the Amen Corner 1969 hit, 'Hello Susie', written by Roy Wood (leading light of the Move) – Wood was expert at pastiching popular styles of the period. 'Hello Susie' begins with a four-bar introduction, grouped as 2 bars + 2 bars. We then move into a 16-bar verse, four groups of 4. The first two groups are identical (a + a), while the second two begin alike but diverge toward the end (b + b'). Notice that in the last of the four bars of 'a', the brass intrude with a bluesy riff. Riff structures will become important below, but here the riff simply acts as a momentary response to the melody. This moves into a nominally 8-bar chorus. The first four bars are grouped 2 + 2, where the first '2' consists of the hook ('Hello Susie') repeated. This is then repeated, and followed by a further four bars of instrumental interlude. However, the last two beats of the chorus are elided with this interlude, such that the chorus + interlude last for 11½ bars. This whole structure (verse + chorus) is then repeated, giving way to a central, contrasting section, often called the 'bridge' or 'middle 8'. The latter term comes from 32-bar song form, where it is usually 8 bars long. I prefer to use 'bridge' because its length can actually vary widely. In this example, the bridge appears likely to fall into a 4 + 4 pattern, each four itself divisible as 2 + 2. However, the seventh and eight bars of this bridge are elided into another 4-bar group, while the last of this latter group is itself extended by a bar, giving us a structure of ((2 + 2) + (2 + 4 + 1)). This combination of elisions and extensions is pretty normative – it adds to the sense of movement, just toying slightly with the sense of absolute predictability, but does not fail to deliver the following section 'as promised'. In this sense, the formal outline acts as a sort of contract with the listener, a contract that will be delivered, but not necessarily in the simplest way. As such, these changes do not in themselves necessarily carry any expressive force – it is only if the contract were not to be delivered that a strong affective charge would ensue. After this bridge, in some songs we would get a third verse. In this one, though, we simply move into the chorus that is repeated either to fade, or in this particular performance, to close out.

This song, then, introduces many of the key formal features endemic to Anglophone popular song. We have a *verse*, which will have different lyrics each time it appears. We can expect it to last for anything up to 1 minute, and take anything from 8 to 32 bars, depending on the style. As in this example, it often falls into two distinct parts, the second of which is often termed the *pre-*

chorus. This is a common formal device in heavy metal and hard rock styles. (Some metal extends the verse into three or more distinct sections, as in the case of Dragonforce's 'Fury of the storm'.) As in this case, while the first half of the verse will contain repeating groups, the pre-chorus is highly unlikely to, for its function is to increase the sense of tension and momentum, to be released at the start of the chorus. Indeed, a *chorus* is often only distinguishable from the verse by virtue of the fact that its lyrics repeat on each occurrence. Indeed, Jocelyn Neal[45] argues that in country music at least, it is not necessarily the repetition of the lyric, but the 'rhetorical function of reflection ... supported by musical intensification and harmonic closure' that is definitional of a chorus. The chorus is usually equal to or half the length of the verse although in some styles (such as the show ballad, music hall, some metal), it can last for twice the length of the verse. Some sort of regular proportion, though (allowing for cuts and extensions) is to be expected. A *bridge* will normally be found only once in a song – this is primarily what distinguishes it from the other sections. In some songs (particularly those by Lennon & McCartney), it is distinguished harmonically, beginning on chord V or vi or, more rarely, iii or IV. In these cases, it may be repeated. It is often of the same length, or half the length, of the verse. The other common sectional terms are *refrain* (the final four bars or so of a verse, with the same lyrics on recurrence, such as Jerry Lee Lewis' Great balls of fire', or most of the tracks on Bob Dylan's *Blood on the tracks*); *introduction* (which will normally have no lyrics – the harmonic pattern of an introduction may return as refrain, bridge or playout); the *break* (an instrumental interlude, often using a sequence from one or other of the units); and the *playout* or *closing tag* (which appears at the end only – a playout will fade over a repeating sequence, a tag will come to a definite conclusion). I also use the term *tag* to cover those 2- or 4-bar short interludes between the end of a chorus and the beginning of the next verse (and for which no ready-made name exists). All of these can potentially be found in a single track, except that a refrain and a chorus are normally mutually exclusive. In this discussion, I have noted that it is the nature of the lyric (whether repeated or not) that distinguishes verse from chorus. While Stephenson[46] concurs with this, Covach[47] argues that harmony is the main determinant of form, since in some songs lyrics can appear over different stretches of music. This is true but, I would argue, comparatively rare. Forte argues that the popular ballad is dominated by the ternary AABA, although a binary AAB can also be found. He uses verse-refrain as terminology, rather than verse-chorus, suggesting that a refrain (32 bars) consists of a double period (chorus 1), bridge and repeat of the first period (chorus 2). But, he says that in this repertory: '... formal units are more appropriately regarded as convenient

---

[45]   Jocelyn Neal, 'Narrative paradigms, musical signifiers, and form as function in country music', *Music Theory Spectrum* 29/1 (2007).

[46]   Stephenson, *What to listen for in rock*.

[47]   John Covach, 'Form in rock music: a primer', in Deborah Stein (ed.), *Engaging music: essays in music analysis* (New York NY, 2005).

descriptive terms, not as analytical ends in themselves ... more often that not, harmonic progressions override ... surface groupings [at the level of the phrase]'.[48] In terms of interpretation, it seems to me that Neal's nuanced view (above) is most valuable: the distinction between a narrative-developing, or situation-exploring verse, a reflective chorus, and a bridge that offers an alternative view, may well be the most productive way to characterize these differences.

Of course, the discussion of 'Hello Susie' presented above is not particularly easy to read, and even less easy to use as the basis for an analysis. A tabular form of this information is often useful, such as Table 3.2 for the Beatles' 'Ticket to ride'.

Table 3.2   Beatles: 'Ticket to ride'; form

Section name	Abbreviation	Length	Notes
Introduction	I	4 bars	Based on opening of verse
First verse	V^1	8	Harmonically static (4 bars) then mobile
Chorus	C	8	
Second verse	V^2	8	
	C	8	
Bridge	B	7	Moves to chord IV
(rudimentary) solo over tag	S, T	2	Elided from eighth bar of bridge
Third verse	V^3	8	
	C	8	
	B	7	Note how the kit changes for B, S & P
	S, T	2	
Fourth verse	V^4	8	
	C	8	
Playout	P	2 +	

Both Stephenson and Covach[49] discuss more global formal terms, particularly varieties of binary structure. I see little to be gained from this – from an interpretive point of view, what is crucial is the difference of movement between verse, chorus and bridge. In live performance, or in covers, the order and length of these sections is subject to variety – it is fixed only for a particular track. It also implies a 'god's-eye perspective', i.e. seeing the track in one glimpse, which does not seem to be part of the popular song experience, where what matters is exactly where one is at a particular point in time. In Chapter 6, I shall raise the issue of those tracks that superimpose on a conventional formal layout a sense of growth,

---

[48]   Forte, *The American popular ballad*, p. 41.

[49]   Stephenson, *What to listen for in rock*, Covach, 'Form in rock music', and Covach, 'From "craft" to "art": formal structure in the music of the Beatles', in Kenneth Womack and Todd F. Davis (eds.), *Reading the Beatles* (New York NY, 2006).

what Mark Spicer (following Peter Burkholder) has termed 'cumulative form'.[50] What is worth noting here is that such sense of cumulation often introduces tracks: among Spicer's examples are the stereotypical 'Smoke on the water', by Deep Purple (where, in turn, we are introduced to guitar, hi-hat, snare and kick drums, bass, and finally voice and organ), New Order's 'Blue Monday', which works similarly, and Radiohead's 'Packt like sardines in a crushd tin box'. However, other than this sense of growth, descriptions of larger formal patterns do not seem to me particularly germane to the listening experience and so I shall not develop terminology, or discussion, at this level.

Harmony and Form: Periods

Where a verse breaks up into sections of regular length, these sections relate to one another in various ways. I have already discussed the situation where it is the harmonic pattern that drives the form. Sometimes, the nature of the open-ended gesture is so repetitive that we have no sense of sections, of verse, chorus, bridge or whatever. This may be thought of as one extreme point on a continuum, as in Li'l Louis' 'French kiss', where the lyric content is minimal, or in John Lee Hooker's 'Boogie chillun'. James Brown's 'Get up, I feel like being a sex machine' is near this end of the continuum, for it shifts to a bridge, but at a point whose instantiation is not predictable. At this end of the continuum we are likely to find disco and various forms of dance music. At the other end of the continuum are those forms where the regular nature of the verse and chorus itself seem to determine the harmonies that will be used. In these latter cases, we may find no repetitive harmonic pattern at all, and this is the distinctive feature. It is this class of relationships that I term *period structure*, where the word 'period' is analogous to 'sentence'. Period structures carry meaning less by what they consist of harmonically, than by way of how they end. The opening verse of Abba's 'Take a chance on me' is a blatant example. The verse has four lines of lyric. The first two stretch for four bars, harmonically |I–|I–|I–|V–|. The second four take only 3½ bars (the third bar is elided with the last), harmonically |V–|V–|V–|I|. This is a pattern familiar from earlier concert music, where the relationship between these two halves is often conceived in terms of 'question' and 'answer'. In other words, the first half is unfinished, 'open', because it ends on a chord other than the tonic. The second half is finished, 'closed', because it ends on the tonic. This open–closed relationship between pairs of a period is normative. A metrically more regular, but less well-known, example (without the elision) is Bob Seger's 'C'est la vie' (a version of Chuck Berry's 'You never can tell'). Frank Sinatra's 'Strangers in the night' has four phrases; the first moves from I at the beginning to ii at the end, while the second answers, moving from ii through V to I. The third

---

[50]   Mark Spicer, '(Ac)cumulative form in pop-rock music', *twentieth-century music* 1/1 (2004).

starts elsewhere, on iv⁻, moving through a cycle of fifths to V, such that the last can start, and end, on I. The initial question and answer, then, is extended, probed, loosened in the third phrase, such that the final phrase has to enforce I strongly in order to close the verse, and such a pattern is fairly typical of the style. This is an example of *ballad structure*, to which I shall return in a moment. An altogether different example is formed by Billy Joel's early hit 'Piano man'. The verse of this is based on a descending bass-line, moving all the way down from the tonic to the second degree, before moving up to the dominant, and then in the second half of the phrase completing that move. Harmonically (and ignoring chordal inversions for the moment), it can be described as |I–V–|IV–I–|IV–I–|II–V–| answered by |I–V–|IV–I–|IV–V–|I|. You can see why the concept of 'answer' is used here – both halves start in the same way, but whereas the first finished inconclusively, the second short-circuits that pattern (omitting the chords between IV and V) and moves swiftly to closure. Open phrases can end on chords other than V. In classical tonality, great play is made of a series of different cadences, where the differing qualities of final harmonies are considered pertinent. I am not convinced the same degree of quality is relevant in this repertory, although those differences are certainly present; the Eagles' 'Take it easy' again splits its verse in two, the first part sitting on I before moving to IV for a half-close, and the second half then using the common |I–V–|IV–I|.

Although open-closed pairings may appear the most obvious, they are by no means the only patterns encountered. The verse of the Beatles' 'Hey Jude', for example, consists of two closed pairs: |I–|V–|V–|I–| answered by |IV–|I–|V–|I–|. Note that the two are not identical. The second phrase is harmonically slightly richer than the first, by the inclusion of the chord IV. This means that we might want to use an analogy such as 'has to work harder' to mark the point of closure of this phrase. It also points to the fact that to properly understand how it works, we have to look at more than just harmony. The melodic span of the second part of the verse is larger, starting from the norm set out by the first part, extending it, and then coming back to rest. So, although the pairing is closed–closed, the second sounds a little more completely closed than did the first. Open–open pairings can also be found, although here the 'pull' of the closure is often diminished, presumably because there is no actual closure against which to measure them. Closed–open pairings, for obvious reasons, are almost unknown. To summarize, then, discreet formal divisions may well employ a period structure, where a period is two successive segments (each either one or two phrases in length) tending towards a harmonic relationship that may be characterized as question/answer. In such cases, the particular harmonic pattern is subservient to the needs of the form, and usually the melody, and will be comparatively unrepetitive.

There are more explicit structures present in popular song. Indeed, an important question is raised by the point at which a recognizable structure becomes recognized, acquires its own label, becomes a fixed entity against which new music is organized. There are two such patterns that are worth consideration through their ubiquity, the *blues* forms I have already mentioned, and *ballad* forms. Ballad forms utilize the pattern AABA, and are so common during the period of the American popular ballad that such an identification becomes trivial. The chorus (what Forte terms the refrain) of 'Somewhere over the rainbow' as sung by Judy Garland, for instance, is a typical example. The chorus consists of 32 bars, dividing into four equal parts. The melody and harmony of the first eight, the second eight, and the last eight are all but identical (each of these eight-bar sections ends on chord I). The melody of the third eight contrasts, and itself splits into two parts, where the second is a variant of the first. These two parts each close on V, helping to create the sense of inevitability in the return of the A section. This schema is so common in the 1930s and 1940s that it acquires the name '32-bar song form' (although it was known far earlier in European music). Other ballad forms, however, can be found. Chris Rea's 'Road to hell' is an interesting case in that it contains two such patterns. Part 1 of the song is based on Rea's singing over a bass drone, in a pattern represented as AA'BA" (where the closing harmonies are I; V; IV; I). The ' and " signs represent (successive) variants, and so the A sections undergo some modification, but the family resemblance is clear. Then part 2 of the song is uptempo, with the entire band, and a melody which is only tangentially related to that of part 1. This is in standard 32-bar song form (even though, stylistically, it represents British rhythm'n'blues), AABA with closing harmonies I; I; V; I.

Like the blues sequences discussed above, ballad forms have become pretty uncommon in mainstream popular song over the past couple of decades. This is less to do with a loss of influence of the practices of playing associated either with the blues or with Tin Pan Alley, than it is to do with the rise of compositional technology making the use of precisely repeating patterns both easy and sonically sophisticated, that is, sequencing. I'm referring to the iterative patterns identified in the section on loops, above, and that now dominate most mainstream styles. Occasionally, however, perhaps in a desire to sound somehow authentic, contemporary musicians will return to an earlier means of organization. The track 'Hold on' by Spiritualized is one such. The first and third phrases end IV–I, while the second phrase closes on V and the final one on I. However, the game is given away by the introduction to the track, an instrumental verse of 'Amazing grace', whose structure the remainder of the track uses. (The album contains a modified ballad structure – 'Lay it down slow' and a modified 12-bar blues – 'Cheapster'.) The verse of Steve Earle's 'John Walker's Blues' recovers this structure – although a renegade country musician in some respects, he utilizes formal patterns endemic to that genre.[51] All but the second phrase are closed.

I have already suggested that these two methods of organization (period structures and open-ended gestures) have penetrated to an extent that makes them difficult to disinter. Let me explore just a couple of examples of this. Slade's 'Thanks for the memory' uses a ballad structure for the verse: an AABA' pattern.

---

[51] See Neal, 'Narrative paradigms'.

The contour of the A section falls by one step, the B section by a full sixth, and the A' remains on the pitch on which the A section ended (see Example 3.16).

Example 3.16   Slade: 'Thanks for the memory'; formal sketch

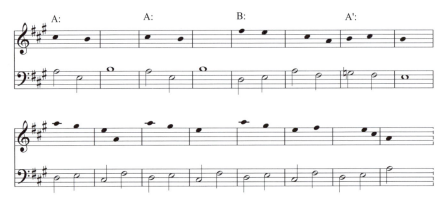

None of these phrases is closed, however: ending harmonies are II; II; VI and V. It falls to the chorus to provide closure. This uses an open-ended IV–V–iii–vi pattern, repeated three times. The fourth time, however, it is short-circuited, cutting from the IV–V– straight to I. Thus the open-ended structure has acquired a quality (the possibility of closure) from period structure. Inspiral Carpets' 'This is how it feels' moves in the opposite direction. The verse repeats an open-ended I–vi, while the chorus uses a standard I–III'–iv–VI; Ic–V–I[52] progression to conclude. This is simplicity itself, but it demonstrates the interpenetration of these two methods; I would argue that such a practice is frequent. Michelle Branch's track 'Here with me' is a little more complex. The chorus is a straight open-ended pattern, the aeolian i–VII–v–VI repeating four times. The verse alternates i–v three times, before moving on to VI. Thus the repeating pattern of the verse moves elsewhere to mark the end of the phrase, thereby nodding toward a period structure, even though all phrases in the song are open. Secret Affair's cult hit 'Time for action' melds a two-chord oscillation with clear cadences. The verse and chorus each alternate ionian I–IV chords. The verse repeats this sequence four times, before instituting a chromatically descending pattern leaving an open phrase end. The chorus repeats the sequence three times, before shifting to an aeolian VI–VII–I, closed, cadence. As we saw above, the Penguins' 'Earth angel' is an early example of the standard I–vi–IV–V sequence. It moulds this into an AA'BA' pattern. The first A repeats the pattern four times, while the A' changes the fourth of these to a I–IV–I to provide closure. The B section (from 1'05") avoids the repeating pattern, closing on II–V, moving back to A'. It then recovers the BA' to close – a common pattern for 1950s doo-wop/slow rock'n'roll.

---

[52]   In this example (and subsequently), 'c' identifies a second inversion chord.

A final example will demonstrate the importance of hybridity. The Beatles' 'Can't buy me love' represents a seamless conjoining of blues and Tin Pan Alley practices. The verse consists of a 12-bar pattern, a downward scalic melody and prominent blue thirds in that melody, exemplifying the band's blues heritage. The chorus, however, is as different as possible. It uses a cycle of fifths pattern (reminiscent of 'established' pop structures, as in the standard 'All the things you are'), an upward arpeggiated melody, and straight 'major' thirds, exemplifying another side of the band's heritage. Why is this distinction so hard to hear? Because of the Beatles' habit of smoothing such irregularities out (at least in their early career) through standard instrumentation and pacing.

This chapter has focused on matters of form rather than of process. To my mind, this is the clearest way to lay out the norms of popular song, but there is the attendant risk of distancing the discussion from what listeners actually perceive. I shall recover this approach in later chapters, but for now acknowledge Carol Vernallis' argument that music videos draw viewers in rather than allowing them to act as spectators, as in narrative films.[53] She draws attention to the notion of flow, which I have raised above in terms of Hughes' analysis of groove. Richard Middleton makes the same point: although he argues that we can avoid the 'formalist trap' by concentrating on 'process' and 'qualities of musical flow', this does not enable him to entirely ignore the categories I have discussed above.[54] We need to recall that however we choose to segment a track, it is the way it leads from beginning to end that is experientially crucial.

To conclude, I have suggested that the distinction between period and open-ended structures is foundational, has historical reasons, and becomes hybridized. We shall find it operative in the realm of melody also, as the next chapter will develop. Disinterring the different patterns, while important for comparative analytical work, must be put alongside how they actually appear in practice. Middleton, in alluding to this distinction, argues that open-ended patterns are redolent of collective participation, while period structures exist as the remnants of bourgeois song and private listening practices. And yet: 'the categories never present themselves in a pure state. They interrelate dialectically.'[55] For this reason, a consistent system of description is necessary.

---

[53]   Carol Vernallis, 'The aesthetics of music video: an analysis of Madonna's "Cherish"', in Moore, *Critical essays*, p. 445.

[54]   Richard Middleton, 'Form' in Horner and Swiss, *Key terms*, pp. 142 and 145–52.

[55]   Middleton, *Studying popular music*, p. 217.

Chapter 4
Delivery

Melody: Contour-Rich

The previous two chapters observed a common distinction in the discussion of artistic expression. Chapter 2 was concerned with the musical context for the delivery of a song without particular reference to temporal unfolding, while Chapter 3 did the same, but now with particular concern for temporal order. But these chapters skirted around the main issue, avoided the question of their purpose, for without a singer at the centre of the song, then there is nothing to shape or form. I think this order of presentation is helpful for the reasons given, but the time has now come to focus on that presence at the centre of the song: the singer. The key question, to my mind, is 'to whom are we listening?', from which arises the supplementary 'how do I make sense of what they mean?'[1] As always, the immediate answer to this question hides far more important issues, which we shall need to consider in order to make a useful interpretation. I intend this as an explicit counter to the sort of approach typified by Allen Forte,[2] who declares that singers' inability to faithfully reproduce songwriters' notated rhythms is problematic. I declare that such non-reproductions are not problematic, and the 'reinterpretation' of the songwriters' apparent 'intention' gives rise to what we are interested in, even where it is not straightforward. (Indeed, I would suggest we are more interested in the actions of the performer than the composer, at least with this repertory.) This is how we construct the persona, of which more in Chapter 7. The way that a persona becomes clear to a listener is partly, self-evidently, through the lyrics of the track but, perhaps more importantly, by means of the melody through which those lyrics are delivered, and by means of the voice through which the lyrics and melody are articulated. Accordingly, it is with those features that this chapter will concern itself.

The literature on popular music harmony is extensive indeed compared to that on melody. The most obvious reason for this is that musicologists regard melody as a function of harmony, and that harmony is therefore prior. Such an assumption leads to effective analyses of music towards the period structure end of the continuum I have already introduced, but less so towards the other end. In practice, although many musicians do seem to conceive harmonies first, and weave a melodic line over the top of such harmonies, others develop melodies initially almost without

---

[1]   Naomi Cumming, *The sonic self* (Bloomington IN, 2000) comes to a parallel conclusion from a very different starting-point (pp. 277–8).

[2]   Forte, *The American Popular Ballad*, p. 23.

reference to harmony. Accordingly, just as I have adopted a bipartite structure for the examination of harmony, I shall follow a similar approach in the examination of melody, in part responding to Stefani's call to recognize that popular melody must be regarded as a 'relatively autonomous part of a musical piece'.[3] Tracks that utilize open-ended harmonic gestures tend to employ melodies in which it is melodic contour that is expressively dominant. Tracks that utilize period structure harmonies tend to employ melodies where some sense of voice-leading is more overt (i.e. where melodies have a propensity to move by step to a concluding point), or where specific focal pitches are expressively dominant. In this chapter and subsequently I adopt the caret (^) to indicate degrees of the (seven-note) scale (even where only a pentatonic subset is in use – thus the minor pentatonic would be $\hat{1}$, $\hat{3}$, $\hat{4}$, $\hat{5}$, $\hat{7}$ and $\hat{8}$).

A convenient starting-point for this demonstration is provided by the conventional blues melody. Archetypically, this can be conceived as falling through an octave from tonic to tonic. Howlin' Wolf's 'I ain't superstitious' provides a simple norm. The melody begins on the upper tonic ($\hat{8}$), remains there for a line and a half of lyric, and then falls roughly through a minor pentatonic to the lower tonic ($\hat{1}$) during a further half-line of lyric. This pattern remains more or less constant throughout the track. 'I ain't superstitious' also exemplifies the comparative dislocation of melody from harmony, for the fall coincides with a change of harmony from IV to I, precisely as Wolf hits $\hat{4}$ (see Example 4.1: the tonic is E; the mode is mixolydian, hence the omission of the D♯ from the key-signature), which is 'dissonant' to chord I and is hardly heard as a movement toward a resolution (from the A to the G). Moreover, the third line of lyric pits a stable upper tonic note against V, before again falling, and $\hat{4}$ coinciding with I.

Example 4.1   Howlin' Wolf: 'I ain't superstitious'; melodic sketch, verse 1

Rod Stewart's later recording of the same song, with the Jeff Beck Group, demonstrates the fluidity of such a melody line. Over the same IV–I–IV–I–V–I harmonic pattern, Stewart's line focuses on $\hat{1}$ of each chord, with the exception of chord V, where he focuses on $\hat{5}$ (see Example 4.2).

Example 4.2   Rod Stewart/Jeff Beck: 'I ain't superstitious'; melodic sketch, verse 1

---

[3]   Gino Stefani, 'Melody: a popular perspective', *Popular Music* 6/1 (1987), p. 21.

The sense of fall remains (although it is sometimes reversed, as when Stewart pushes up to a blue third on some instances of chord I), but it is less structured than Wolf's pentatonic scale, ably expressing the British musician's prized individuality.

This pattern is so endemic to the blues, that further comment might seem superfluous. However, it does permit a range of flexible melodies. Blind Willie Johnson's 'Nobody's fault but mine' is melodically more complex than 'I ain't superstitious'. The song consists of a series of three-line verses, with various lyrics repeated, and occasionally using the title as a refrain for a fourth line. But each line of the verse traverses the downward movement differently, through the blues pentatonic. Line 1 drops from ♭$\hat{3}$, or sometimes from $\hat{5}$, or $\hat{8}$ (hence the bracket in Example 4.3) to $\hat{1}$. Line 2 repeatedly raises the tension, leaping to $\hat{8}$ and then dropping to $\hat{5}$. Line 3, with more syllables to cram in, falls from $\hat{8}$ to $\hat{1}$, while the refrain also drops from $\hat{8}$ to $\hat{1}$ but, on reaching ♭$\hat{3}$, rises momentarily to $\hat{5}$ to complete the downward motion.

Example 4.3 Blind Willie Johnson: 'Nobody's fault but mine'; melodic sketch

Big Bill Broonzy's 'All by myself' sets six lines of lyric over a harmonically conventional 12-bar blues pattern: the first two lines act as 'verse', and the remaining four as a chorus or refrain. The verse sticks almost monotonously on $\hat{8}$. Some verses begin with the upper blue third (♭$\hat{10}$), and all verses drop from $\hat{8}$ to $\hat{5}$ at the end. The chorus remains largely around $\hat{8}$, with intimations of fall: line 3 drops from $\hat{8}$ to $\hat{6}$, line 4 from $\hat{8}$ to $\hat{3}$ through $\hat{6}$ and $\hat{5}$, and line 5 avoids the major pentatonic dominant throughout by sticking on $\hat{7}$, so as to harmonize with chord V. Then the final line of verse recovers $\hat{8}$ and drops swiftly to $\hat{1}$ (Example 4.4). So, the downward contour is retained, but is traversed only once, and in a fashion which provides a much more obvious, 'tuneful', melody.

Example 4.4 Big Bill Broonzy: 'All by myself'; melodic sketch

A couple more examples will demonstrate more complex versions of this norm. Fleetwood Mac's 'Black magic woman' was written under the influence of US American blues, but by the (British) musicians themselves. Again, the pattern is a 12-bar blues. The first line splits in two: remaining on $\hat{8}$; and falling from $\hat{8}$ to $\hat{5}$, respectively. The second line expands the range, leaping to $\hat{10}$ and falling to $\hat{4}$, while the final line ultimately leaps to $\hat{1}\hat{2}$ before falling to $\hat{1}$ (and all using the minor pentatonic – Example 4.5[4]).

Example 4.5   Fleetwood Mac: 'Black magic woman'; melodic sketch

In Led Zeppelin's version of the J.B.Lenoir/Willie Dixon song 'You shook me', Robert Plant maintains the sense of downward motion, particularly in the last line of the verse. However, in the opening two lines, he rises each time from around $\hat{5}$ to ♭$\hat{1}\hat{0}$ before falling back to ♭$\hat{7}$ and then sliding down to $\hat{5}$ and beyond (Example 4.6).

Example 4.6   Led Zeppelin: 'You shook me'; melodic sketch

How might one hear this? Out of context, it appears like a perfectly balanced line – rising to the word 'shook' and then falling back. However, because it is a blues, I would suggest a neater way to hear it, one that preserves its history, is as a rising upbeat (which gains in prominence as the track progresses, latterly reaching $\hat{1}\hat{2}$) to a pronounced fall. This is clear in Muddy Waters' original, where the downward slide from ♭$\hat{1}\hat{0}$ falls through $\hat{5}$ to $\hat{1}$, and in the last line of the verse, where he reaches to a blue third (♭$\hat{1}\hat{7}$) before falling more than two octaves down. Willie Dixon's later recording reaches even more frequently for an upper octave from which to fall. Rod Stewart's recording with the Jeff Beck group preceded Led Zeppelin's by a matter of months; it places such great emphasis on the shape of the upbeat rise and subsequent fall that we lose all sense of any longer drop (the three phrases are sketched in Example 4.7).

Example 4.7   Rod Stewart/Jeff Beck: 'You shook me'; melodic sketch

There is clearly no necessary association between the contour and the word 'shook', since in Elvis Presley's 'All shook up', while there is a constant upbeat rise to the tonic, there is no fall from it. David Bowie's early 'She shook me cold'

---

[4]   A fuller analysis of the melody appears in Moore, 'The so-called "flattened seventh"', p. 287.

has nothing whatever to do with the blues. Bowie, however, would have known Waters' hit, and it is startling to note that the template of local fall with upbeat rise, giving way to larger falls, which we find in 'You shook me', is also present in Bowie's song (Example 4.8). Whether this counts as an example of 'borrowing' will have to await the discussion in Chapter 9.

Example 4.8 David Bowie: 'She shook me cold'; melodic sketch from 31"

approx. pitches

Before leaving the blues, note should be taken of the melody line's potential to effect closure without harmonic underpinning. Cliff Richard's first hit, 'Move it', is a slightly strange imitation blues written by his original guitarist Ian Samwell. 'Strange' because this is a 12-bar blues pattern with the first four bars doubled, producing 16 bars with the first eight on I, two bars to each line of lyric. In the first half of the 16-bar verse, odd-numbered phrases drop to either $\hat{5}$ or $\flat\hat{3}$, suggesting the necessity of completion, which is provided in the even numbered phrases, which drop to $\hat{1}$ (although they sometimes rise up thereafter in a little flick of the melody – see Example 4.9).

Example 4.9 Cliff Richard: 'Move it'; melodic sketch (first half verse)

Thus, a contour-dominant melody acquires aspects of closure: as with discussion of harmony, the two ends of the continuum are not entirely distinct.

I have emphasized the blues as a model for contour-prominent melody for both historical and presentational reasons, but example aplenty can be found in other styles. Marjorie Kingsley sang with Harry Roy's dance band: with the exception of the title itself, the melody to their 'Down Argentina way' falls throughout. It can do this because the end of every line presents a large leap up to the beginning of the next line. Despite the *parlando* style of delivery, every line of the verse of Paul Simon's 'You can call me Al' tends to drop to $\hat{1}$, the majority of lines falling from either $\hat{5}$ or $\hat{4}$ depending on the harmony at the time. The chorus, in contrast, rises to $\hat{5}$ (usually from $\hat{3}$) until the very last phrase, which drops back to $\hat{1}$ providing closure. No closure is apparent from the harmony, which is a simple I–V–IV–(or ii–)V loop. Tellingly, the song fades (remains open-ended) over a repeated chorus, while the melody line remains around $\hat{5}$. The verse of Stevie Wonder's 'Isn't she lovely' also tends to fall, with a slight rise to $1\hat{1}$ falling to $\hat{8}$ and to $\hat{5}$ (the melody has an upbeat, but the downbeat falls not on $1\hat{1}$ but on the subsequent $\hat{9}$). The chorus' third line rises to $1\hat{2}$, falling to $\hat{6}$, and the final line provides closure by recapitulating the $1\hat{1}$ to $\hat{5}$ notion and continuing on down to $\hat{1}$. Black Sabbath's early heavy metal 'Paranoid' has a very minimal melody, but even here it is driven by a sense of contour. The melody's only phrase falls from $\flat\hat{3}$ to $\hat{1}$, overshoots by a step, recovers to $\hat{2}$ and comes to rest on $\hat{1}$. However, with a melody such as this, because of the focal nature of certain pitches, it makes sense to retrieve it as part of the discussion in the next section. This melody exemplifies a feature of many contour-prominent melodies, which is that their span equates to a revolution of the harmonic pattern, rather than extending over the course of an entire verse. Examples are legion but, from very different sources, observe the melodies to Snow Patrol's 'You could be happy' and the Drive-by Truckers' 'Life in the factory', which very plainly do exactly that.

All of the contours discussed so far are falling. Indeed, in the abstract, where a contour is expressively dominant, there would seem to be four possible models: generally *falling*; generally *rising*; generally *flat*; and *undulating*, i.e. where neither direction dominates. The last two of these are best discussed below, while rising contours appear to be much rarer than falling ones, perhaps because it is so much easier to sing a downward phrase than a rising one (the latter requires much more control of the speed at which air is used, and is therefore less likely to be found among unschooled singers). Steadily rising contours appear aspirational (think Elvis Presley's 'The wonder of you', Frankie Laine's 'I believe' or Gerry and the Pacemakers' 'You'll never walk alone'). Two good examples of less obviously rising contours are Cilla Black's 'Step inside love' and the Koobas' Hollies-esque 'Where are the friends?'. In 'Step inside love', the verse rises twice, without reverse, to $\hat{8}$, before meandering down and starting another rise, but this time only to $\flat\hat{7}$. It rises again, equivocally, as far as $\hat{6}$, and then moves assertively up to $\hat{9}$, reaching further to $1\hat{1}$ before coming to rest on $\hat{8}$. There is poetic justice here – she is inviting her interlocutor in (hence the promise of the ever-rising line), and on the final, conclusive, $\hat{8}$, she insists he 'stay'; indeed, there is very often poetic rightness in the contour of a line. In 'Where are the friends?', the four lines of the verse start from the notes of an upward arpeggiated triad, but each line falls only emphasising the distance between the friends who are needed, and their absence. Unarguable rising and falling lines are equally found in what must be the most extreme example of contour dominance, Kathy Kirby's 'All of a sudden my heart sings'. The entire melody consists initially of a major scale rising by step, one note every two bars, and each separately harmonized. This is then countered by a steady fall, at exactly the same rate (although each note is now ornamented), a modulation up a semitone and then both upward and downward motion repeated, followed by a leap up a fifth for the final note. That's all.[5] Nothing could be more stark, and yet the lyrics talk of extreme abandonment to this feeling in her heart. In noting the span of the contour over which change takes place, it is worth considering whether the tessitura changes gradually ('You can call me Al') or suddenly ('Step inside, love'), radically ('Isn't she lovely') or minimally ('Move it').

What about contours whose shape is less marked? Again, four categories are useful.[6] Some melodic contours adopt the quality of *chant* in their focus on a single pitch. This represents an extreme position and is rarely maintained entire, but much of Harper's Bizarre's 'Witchi tai to' uses chant, as does John Lydon's singing on a track such as the Sex Pistols' 'Holidays in the sun'. More likely is a melody that is oriented around a single pitch, and that we can describe as *axial*, such as the Edgar Broughton Band's 'Apache dropout', or the second phrase of Led Zeppelin's 'Immigrant song'. The first phrase of this latter moves between two pitches, and is better described as *oscillating*, while the entire melody of the verse might be described as *terraced*, since it has three distinct pitch levels (we could almost talk about registers, except that these are so close, much less than an octave apart) and the melody simply jumps from one to the next. These descriptive categories are, I think, only useful insofar as they enable us to think about degrees of similarity between different melodies.

Melody: Period Structure

At the other end of the continuum from contour-rich melodies are period structure melodies, those that tend to be used in tandem with harmonic sequences avoiding internally repeating patterns. Let me begin with an unambiguous example to illustrate. The chorus of the Bee Gees' maudlin 'I've gotta get a message to you' moves from $\hat{3}$ to $\hat{2}$ over I–ii, and from $\hat{2}$ to $\hat{1}$ over (IV–)V–I (I'm hearing the melody as formed by the lower line of the chorus, which is harmonized by a slightly stronger upper line; I'll return to this issue later). And, although in a different key (a tone below), the verse makes the same move: $\hat{3}$ to $\hat{2}$ over I–ii, $\hat{2}$ to $\hat{1}$ over V–I. In order to hear it this way, certain ('ornamental') pitches need to be ignored. This ($\hat{3}$–$\hat{2}$–$\hat{1}$) is the main structural line posited by Schenker for tonal melodies, and there is much of this repertory where such a hearing makes sense. Indeed, I think this is a clearer way to hear Black Sabbath's 'Paranoid' – it is not a period structure melody, but it does move between specific pitches that carry the melody's sense. A richer example is provided by the Icicle Works' 'Don't let it rain on my parade'. The verse of this track ornaments four pitches in turn: $\hat{3}$, $\hat{4}$, $\hat{7}$ and $\hat{6}$, repeating this pattern. In this way, the line seems to circle $\hat{5}$ without coming

---

[5]   In its baldness, perhaps this is nothing more than a historical oddity, rather like (to talk about an entirely different genre), Beethoven's two little Preludes, op.39, which wander swiftly through all available major keys, through the cycle of fifths.

[6]   Middleton, *Studying Popular Music*, p. 203.

to rest on it. The chorus picks up this absent $\hat{5}$ and falls to $\hat{4}$, but seems to hang there. Simultaneously, the melody also leaps to $1\hat{0}$, falls to $\hat{9}$ and slowly, finally, to $\hat{8}$ where it comes to rest. The chorus is harmonized by an unambiguous periodic pair: a mixolydian I-IV- ... VII-V‡ is answered by I-IV- ... VII-IV-I. The $\hat{9}$ coincides with V‡, and the $\hat{8}$ with I. What has happened, though, to the $\hat{4}$? I suggest it can be felt to move, but via octave transfer to the upper $1\hat{0}$, as can be seen by recasting the melody with the upper octave transposed down (Example 4.10).

Example 4.10   Icicle Works: 'Don't let it rain on my parade'; sketch

mixolydian: I   IV VII IV   I   IV   I   VII   V   I   IV   VII IV I

This is an example of a split-voice melody (in both verse and chorus), a comparatively rare feature in popular song. A slightly richer example is 'Over the rainbow', which, like many songs of the period, added words to music rather than vice versa. The music, then, has an unusual degree of integrity, and I shall focus on the chorus. The form has a standard 32-bar pattern: AABA. The B section splits in half, the second half echoing the first, while a final codetta recalls just one half of B. The chorus opens with an octave leap, $\hat{1}$ to $\hat{8}$, while the remainder of A gradually winds down, filling in that octave gap (a motion made plain by successively smaller leaps, $\hat{1}$ to $\hat{6}$ and then $\hat{1}$ to $\hat{4}$). In contrast, B begins toward the bottom of the octave, climbs as far as $\hat{7}$ and then overshoots to $\hat{9}$. Although the final A does 'fill in' the missing $\hat{8}$ (thus acting as part of the line of both A and B, as in 'Don't let it rain on my parade'), the real culmination of the line appears in the codetta, where the line rises gracefully by step from $\hat{4}$, achieving the final $\hat{8}$ with the final note.[7] However, it is not necessary for the completion of the line to be realized. The verse of Secret Affair's 'Time for action, for instance, drops four times from $\hat{3}$ to $\hat{1}$, while the harmony shifts from I–IV, avoiding any coincidence of $\hat{1}$ and I. The pre-chorus laboriously works from $\hat{3}$ to $\hat{2}$, via $\flat\hat{3}$, as the harmony moves from I–V over a chromatically descending bass line. The chorus retrieves the verse's harmony, as the melody drops from $\hat{5}$, through $\hat{4}$, to $\hat{3}$. The final cadence, however, is an aeolian VI–VII–I, over which the melody rises from $\hat{1}$, through $\hat{2}$, to $\hat{3}$. Every opportunity to provide full closure with $\hat{1}$ over I is therefore avoided. And the track fades out (well, the original vinyl single slipped into crowd noise on the playout groove, but the effect is analogous). In John Lennon's 'Imagine', this technique is put to good effect. The melody of the first half of the verse is constantly reaching for an upper tonic (climbing from $\hat{5}$ to $\hat{7}$, but always falling back to $\hat{6}$). It reaches this point at the beginning of the second half

---

[7]   See Forte, *The American Popular Ballad*, pp. 231–6.

of the verse, but the harmony obstinately remains on IV, before rising to V. After a second verse, the chorus then takes place over a IV–V–I–III pattern. A conjunction of 8̂ and I is finally achieved here, but it's in a weak place metrically, and so with little sense of achievement. Even the very end of the chorus, where 8̂ and I coincide, is understated, since the 8̂ is preceded by the consonant 1̂0̂, which actually appears on the beat, before the melody falls to the tonic. An interpretation of the effect of this initial delay, and then weak arrival, must await Chapter 8.

I look now at a couple of slightly more complex examples, which illustrate (unsurprisingly) how, in many cases, melody can only be fully understood as it functions with harmony. 'Blue skies', although made famous by Frank Sinatra in the 1940s, originated in the show *The Jazz Singer*, from 1926, sung by Al Jolson. The form is again AABA and, again, the A is an eight-bar period, while the B is two identical four-bar periods. The opening melody is led by the strong leap from 1̂ to 5̂, answered by a fall from 5̂ to 1̂. That fall is, however, repeated and overshot (note how important such a little device can be) by a step, signalling a harmonic change from minor (E minor) to relative major (G major). The B section then rises by step from 1̂ to 5̂ (now understood as being in G), and the harmony is inflected by a I–iv motion, the iv being a C minor with a prominent E♭. In order to get back to the original key for the A section, that E♭ is reinterpreted harmonically as a D♯, as the fifth degree of V in e, and there we are (see Example 4.11).

Example 4.11   Frank Sinatra: 'Blue skies'; melodic sketch

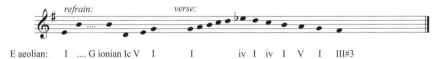

E aeolian: I   .... G ionian Ic V   I   I   iv I iv I V   I   III#3

A similar subtlety can be observed in 'Smoke gets in your eyes', recorded by the Platters in 1958. Here, as in much early rock'n'roll, a 32-bar format gets stretched to form the entire song. The B section, unusually, modulates from E to C (i.e. to ♭VI). These two chords share one note in common – an E – and around this note the melody is organized. The A section rises from 1̂ to 4̂ to 8̂, each note being decorated in turn, before falling in similar manner through 7̂, 5̂ and 3̂. The 1̂ then is reinterpreted in the B section, as 3̂ (now in C); the melody leaps to 1̂0̂ and then falls, largely by step, to 5̂. Repeated, the melody begins to shift back towards the home key, falling now to ♯5̂, which is now 3̂ in E (see Example 4.12).

Example 4.12   Platters: 'Smoke gets in your eyes'; melodic sketch

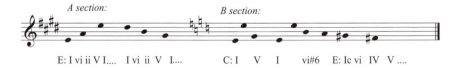

E: I vi ii V I....   I vi ii V I...   C: I   V   I   vi#6 E: Ic vi IV V ....

These sorts of harmonic reinterpretation of melodic pitches are fairly common in melodies deriving from Tin Pan Alley,[8] but are far less common in melodies deriving from the blues or gospel. This says something about the relationship of melody to harmony. In Tin Pan Alley-derived styles, there is a sense in which harmony is made to do the most work, melody acting as decoration of the underlying harmony. In blues- and gospel-derived styles, however, the relationship is rather the reverse. Here, melody dominates, and harmony serves merely to underpin this. In discussing melodies where the contour is not necessarily the dominant feature, it is useful to adapt a set of criteria developed by Allen Forte. Here, we note the *focal* pitches of the melody, i.e. those receiving particular articulative emphasis, or the highest and lowest pitches of portions of the melody. In 'Blue skies', for example, the melody hangs between its outer pitches until one is overshot. 'Over the rainbow' also negotiates its way between its outer pitches. The potential importance of such pitches will be explored later.

Solo melodies are the norm in popular song, even if such a melody may sometimes be accompanied by that of backing singers. However, on occasion, a melody appears in two parts simultaneously, in effective two-part harmony. In such circumstances, is the *real* melody of the track the upper or the lower line? H.P. Lovecraft's 'The white ship' provides an example of this, and also provides an answer: when the solo guitar takes on the tune, it is the lower line that is played. This, I believe, is the normative position, a position I would call the *tenor* principle, recognizing that it is a practice observable since the Renaissance. It is a common practice in communal folk singing (as can be heard in recordings by the Watersons, or the Young Tradition, for instance) – a solo melody will be harmonized both below (with rudimentary bass) and above and, since the bass is an ever-present feature of popular song, it makes sense to harmonize above the main line. When this two-part singing is increased to three parts, then a norm is harder to assert. The Andrews' Sisters provide an interesting case study, since they provide early examples of regular three-part vocal lines. The commonest position in their output is to place the melody in the middle of three lines, as in 'Shortenin' bread'. If we observe their stylistic debt to early jazz, and note that the melody-taking trumpet in early jazz is situated registrally between the clarinet and the trombone, then this makes some sense. Of course, jazz does not normally make use of the Andrews' Sisters' homophony, but the opening to 'Oh Johnny! Oh Johnny! Oh!', which does, demonstrates the point. Similar dispositions can be found in other genres: the chorus of 'Baby doll', by the country Sons of the Pioneers adopts the same layout. In the chorus to Journey's 'Girl can't help it', the melody is at the bottom of a block of (three, possibly four) voices, but here the upper voices are situated further from the listener, and also the lead voice has been alone throughout the verse, and so the situation is slightly different. As part of a rich discussion of the use of vocal ensembles, Walter Everett[9] argues that in the

---

[8]   See Forte, *The American Popular Ballad.*

[9]   Everett, *The foundations of rock* (New York, 2008), pp. 127–31.

1960s it was perhaps more common to hear the upper voice as the main melody, but he acknowledges exceptions: I maintain that across the entire repertory, unless a particular example clearly demonstrates otherwise, a best first assumption is that the tune is at the bottom of a two-part texture and in the middle of a three-part.

Thus far, this chapter has concentrated on the pitches that form melodies although, of course, that is only part of what a melody is. To some extent, the rhythms of melody have been covered in the previous chapter, where phrase rhythm is discussed, and in the concept of 'verbal space',[10] which may be a better way of talking about melody than focusing too closely on its rhythm. The other reason why rhythm may be of lower importance concerns the observation that a performer's role is not to reproduce rhythms with the regularity either of harmonic rhythm, or of music that is transmitted by notation. Bradley argues that, other than heightened speech, the rock'n'roll 'singer also uses the rhythms of speech, even of ordinary conversation, cutting across the musical meters in infinitely varied ways'.[11] This aspect cannot, I think, be usefully schematized, other than to note the difference (where there is one) between spoken and sung rhythm, and to attend to that difference in specific cases.

The Voice

It is more than just rhythm that differs between the spoken and sung voice, of course. For the singing voice, we need to attend as far as possible to the details of how it sounds. We do this largely unconsciously when listening to a spoken voice, and this is important for the information such a voice contains over and above its words, but with a sung voice these possibilities are magnified. At first glance, it may seem strange to include material on the voice in the midst of more conventional analytical categories: harmony, form, melody and the like. One argument for its inclusion parallels that of texture – in a recorded medium, the sounds we hear take precedence, and song depends on its actualization by means of the human voice. There is, however, a deeper reason. For some writers,[12] the understanding of a performed song equates to the working out of the subjectivity of the artist (in pop, at least), and a principal source of that subjectivity is how the artist sounds.[13] It is therefore necessary to develop a methodology for the consideration of those sounds.

---

[10] Griffiths, 'From lyric to anti-lyric'.

[11] Dick Bradley, *Understanding Rock'n'roll* (Buckingham, 1992), p. 134.

[12] For example, Stan Hawkins, *The British pop dandy* (Farnham, 2009).

[13] I have already raised this point by way of Naomi Cumming. How the artist looks is secondary for a number of reasons: initial encounters tend to be by way of sound recordings; visual image is more readily accepted as constructed than aural image; visual encounters are overtly staged (videos, magazine shots) whereas sound *appears* unmediated.

This view is not, of course, universally held. Until fairly recently, it was often considered necessary only to understand the realm of reference of lyrics that were sung in order to understand the singer's utterance. Tim Murphey, for instance, turns this to advantage by insisting on the listener's own role in the understanding of the song's 'message': 'the listener would seem able to complete the message, or make sense of the song, through using persons, times and places from their own physical and metaphysical situation'[14] because of the degree of imprecision implicit in the lyrics to most songs. However, Roland Barthes[15] has frequently been misread as opening the debate over the importance of a singer's articulation, a point developed further by Simon Frith: 'It is through the voice that star personalities are constructed ... The tone of the voice is more important in this context than the actual articulation of particular lyrics ...'[16]. The question, then, is how best to address such matters as the tone of the voice? The outline I give below does not simply address this question, but offers a range of tools to enable a closer characterization of the effect of the voice. One reason for taking this approach will become clearer in Chapter 7, where I suggest that vocal meaning is not only a factor of what is said, but of the attitude that seems to be held by the singer to what is said – questions of trust and integrity enter the fray.

A starting point is to take account of four *positional aspects* of the singer's voice. First, in what *register* is the singer singing? Normally, three registers can be conceived. There is a low register, which adds gravity, sexiness or melancholy to a singer's delivery (and, in metal, menace). This may be compounded by an apparent difficulty to reach the lowest notes. There is a comfortable register, which may be read as 'normal'. There is also a high register, whether or not this extends into falsetto, which may be read as virtuosic, as embodying physical effort, as lighthearted, etc., depending on the context. Second, in what *cavity* of the body does the singer's voice appear to resonate; where does the voice appear to begin? A nasal tone can be read as sneering, as distanced, or simply as stylized. Singing from the head often appears weak, careless, or understated. Singing from the throat again appears as 'normal'. Singing from the chest connotes greater care, presence, power. Pushing a sound from the diaphragm intensifies this. Lacasse argues that this model I use ignores variations in timbre, and outlines a model for *paralanguage*, deriving from Fernando Poyatos. He provides brief analyses that take into account: *primary qualities* (the '"biologically" predetermined' features that individuate voices, and how they are modified); *qualifiers* (effects of the breath, nasality, the tongue, lips or jaws); *alternants* (vocal noises such as hisses, moans and slurps) and *differentiators* (laughing, yawning, spitting, etc.), all of

---

[14]   Tim Murphey, 'The when, where, and who of pop lyrics: the listener's prerogative', *Popular Music* 8/2 (1989).

[15]   Roland Barthes, 'The grain of the voice', in *Image–Music–Text* (London, 1977).

[16]   Simon Frith, 'Towards an aesthetic of popular music', in Richard Leppert and Susan McClary (eds.), *Music and society* (Cambridge: Cambridge University Press, 1987), p. 143.

which can be used to specific musical effect.[17] The third positional aspect is what is the singer's *heard attitude to rhythm*? He or she may be singing ahead of the beat, behind it, or exactly on it. He or she may be singing in a rhythm that would correspond to the way those words would be spoken in ordinary conversation, or may play havoc with linguistic syntax. Finally, what is the singer's *heard attitude to pitch*. He or she may be singing precisely 'in tune', may be flat, may be sharp, only slightly, or by a greater amount. And with all these factors, but most particularly the latter two, his or her approach may vary not only from phrase to phrase, but sometimes from moment to moment. These observations can enable us to determine whether the singer is conforming to the apparent meaning of the lyrics in the way they are delivered, or is perhaps clarifying them, whether the singer is equivocal about the lyrics (or about their addressee), or is even subverting them. I think that, unless there is documentary evidence to the contrary, it is important to assume that these factors are all under control,[18] and that the sounds produced are all produced intentionally. The opposite assumption seems arrogant in the extreme, and one must start with an assumption. These sounds can suggest that the singer is in control of his or her utterance (or not), that his/her expression of emotion can be trusted (or not). They can also enable us to identify a style in which the singer is singing, and the connotations that style may have, in relation to this particular performance.

With these ideas in mind, I approach a range of voices. John Lennon and Paul McCartney, in singing the Beatles' 'She loves you' make use of two registers, a comfortable one for the majority of the song, and a high one to emphasize the particular lyric 'she loves *you*'. This register is reached again at the very end of the song – 'be *glad*' – where it sounds slightly strained, giving emphasis and conveying a sense of sincerity (in that the register cannot simply be smoothly attained). That this take was probably recorded at the end of a long session, with Lennon's voice tired, is not particularly relevant – it is how it comes across that is significant. The trademark 'ooo' just before the refrain is in falsetto, with a slight nasal edge, but in full voice – it does not sound weak. And they sing very much on the beat. Nat King Cole, on the other hand, in singing his classic 'Unforgettable' sings very far from the beat. He is late, sometimes very much so. This suggests an extremely laid back approach – he has no need to hurry, he is entirely in control of his time. The sense is partly conveyed by his register, which is very comfortable. His vocal phrases tend to end low, to fall, entirely removing any feeling of tension. Even the melodic highpoint – 'it's in-*cre*-dible' – while emphasizing his emotional state, still does not convey any sense of anxiety. He sings a number of long notes, with a strong

---

[17]   Serge Lacasse, 'The phonographic voice: paralinguistic features and phonographic staging in popular music singing', in Amanda Bayley (ed.), *Recorded music: performance, culture and technology* (Cambridge: Cambridge University Press, 2010), pp. 228–30.

[18]   As the singer Barb Jungr implies. Jungr, 'Vocal expression in the blues and gospel', in Moore (ed.), *The Cambridge Companion to Blues and Gospel Music* (Cambridge, 2002), p. 102.

sense of vibrato (again, adding to the sense of consummate ease), but with little resonance – there is a sense that his voice is to be perceived as entirely natural. Lonnie Donegan's contemporaneous voice conveys a very different sense. On 'Battle of New Orleans', a key skiffle hit, he too sings generally in a comfortable register, and takes freedom to vary the tune (of a traditional song) somewhat from verse to verse, bending a few notes. He has a strong nasal tone, which was a style-marker for the singing of traditional folk songs, certainly in the late 1950s, using vibrato on long notes, particularly in the last verse, where it perhaps carries a sense of display. However, he sings precisely on the beat, quite possibly to encourage participation, a remnant from the live performance practice of such material. What is most notable, however, is his attempt to sound North American. Although we are listening to Lonnie Donegan, his voice does not appear to give us access to the 'real' Lonnie Donegan. And the observation that 'Lonnie' was an assumed, stage, name taken by the real Tony Donegan, is germane to this sense. The *performer* (Tony Donegan) and his *persona* (Lonnie Donegan) are here clearly distinct. I return to these concepts in Chapter 7. Fred Astaire sings generally half a beat ahead in 'I'm putting all my eggs in one basket', but occasionally drifts behind the beat at the end of phrases. Muddy Waters is singing ahead of the beat (in the middle of phrases, but not generally at the beginning or end) as early as 1948's 'You're gonna miss me'. And Chuck Berry is singing ahead of the beat as late as 1964's 'You never can tell'. What all these share is a sense of excitement, which comes across no matter what the style.

Within popular song, there are some stereotypical ways of using the voice, although one has to be careful about reading meaning too straightforwardly in such cases.[19] For some writers, voices are unavoidably gendered. It is difficult to avoid essentialist positions here, but it can certainly be noted that, for instance, the ambiguity of Tori Amos' 'Hey Jupiter' arises from an excess of pronouns, which excess provides an esoteric text that her fans find pleasurable. The intimacy that this expresses, however, is always constructed as a feminine characteristic such that, in being (apparently) revelatory, she simply reinforces the divide. Hard rock and heavy metal depend on conveying a sense of power through the singer's voice. Although when singing with Led Zeppelin Robert Plant frequently uses falsetto, it is a falsetto redolent with power. On 'Immigrant song', he employs two registers, one for the majority of the verse, and the second for the end of the verse and for the bridge. He takes some freedom from the beat, but this tends to be at the end of phrases, rather than throughout like the Nat King Cole example. Because of both this factor and his registers, Plant conveys none of the security offered by Cole's voice, but rather a sense of menace, which is increased by the edge to his voice, which appears to come from the back of his hard palate and gains a nasal edge. In the context of the entire ensemble, his high voice balances the otherwise bass-heavy texture. Geddy Lee, lead singer with Rush, uses very much the same template

---

[19]   See Simon Frith and Angela McRobbie, 'Rock and sexuality', *Screen Education* 29 (1978).

(for example on 'The twilight zone'), although his voice is perhaps thinner, albeit giving the same sense of effort in its upper reaches. Robbie Williams typifies a more mainstream pop voice – singing with the same sense of force, the register is altogether lower, more comfortable. On 'Angels' he constantly anticipates the beat, lending a sense of momentum. As he reaches the chorus, he reaches for an upper register, again anticipating, but with a subtle sense of difficulty attaining the top of the range (... 'pro-*tec*-tion' ... etc.). Note how the sound of his mouth shape on the syllable 'all' ('*all* ... waterf-*all*'), as if the lower lip is tucked slightly in, and the tiny upward slide on the last syllable of 'protec-*tion*' are so reminiscent of Elton John – surely a factor in his success. This voice has its female counterpart, as in Ann Wilson, lead singer with Heart. On 'Wait for an answer', her voice is not particularly high (it only reaches an upper F♯), but gives the impression of being far higher. Her performance sets up a low tessitura for the verse, achieves a higher one for the chorus (and thus we expect this to be the climactic point), but gradually reaches for the highest register in the final chorus. This is matched by a gradual roughening of her vocal quality, connoting effort and emotional involvement. Some singers, however, achieve this sense without the same notable strain. Ian McNabb, singer with the Icicle Works, pioneered a new sense of polished vocality in the late 1980s, reminiscent of 1960s singers such as Scott Walker. On 'Hope springs eternal', he sings in a largely comfortable register with no recourse to falsetto, but a slight strain on the highest notes. His voice is resonant and full, expelled with some force right from the diaphragm. He also sings with a polished, precise sense of vibrato (to which I'll return), and is rhythmically very measured, right down to the precision of his syncopation – in other words, when a syncopated line returns, he sings it the same way. While this can connote artifice (it does not convey the illusion of being spontaneous), the sense of upper effort mitigates this. Mariah Carey typifies an approach that executes melismas at almost every opportunity (for example, on 'shows' at the end of the first verse of 'Without you') but almost without meaning. In other words, it appears to be simply a display of technical virtuosity. Why sing a particular word with such a melisma? It appears to be nothing to do with that particular word.

A way of addressing these stereotypes is offered by Barb Jungr. Although her discussion relates explicitly to blues and gospel singing, it is equally applicable to other styles. She draws together three approaches, culled from the work of Alan Lomax, Jo Estill and Alfred Wolfsohn. From Lomax she argues for attention to be paid to *embellishment*, to *vocal width* (use of changes of register) and to *melisma, rubato* and *glissando*. Some of these categories coincide with issues raised above. From Estill, she notes that singers use six discreet vocal parameters, with most voices being a combination of these six parameters, and each being defined physiologically in terms of the way the vocal folds, the thyroid and the larynx combine to produce a particular quality. Accurate usage is thus difficult for a non-practising or non-self-aware singer, but the differences between the gross qualities can clearly be heard. *Opera* concerns explicit control of the voice, frequently (but not only) associated with schooling in the classical tradition. It includes a quality of *twang*, a particularly ringing voice. *Belt* 'is a full-throttle sound and is very evident when singers seem on the edge of their voice and emotion',[20] while *speech* identifies a more conversational style of singing. *Falsetto* refers to the avoidance of vibrato associated with the 'pure' singing of some renaissance music, while *sob* is the quality most clearly associated with crooning. What is particularly interesting about Estill's approach is that it is devised in order to enable singers to achieve a particular voice – it is not intended as an analytical device, but holds promise in that respect. This is the key aspect of Wolfsohn's approach, that vocal timbre appears to be indissolubly linked to physical, psychological and emotional states and that, as Jungr insists:

> if a singer uses a vocal setting [i.e. learnt position of the vocal tract] that creates an exciting sound, the sound will be heard as such by the listener and will, more importantly, create an 'excitable' emotional state in the body and being of the singer. These 'effects' seems to be felt across cultural and aesthetic boundaries without respect to the listener's cultural competence …[21]

It is possible to devise methods to get closer to the actual manner of enunciation: Mike Daley[22] devises a method to get at the particular way Patti Smith forms her vowels, although whether this can demonstrate more than the parody, and travesty, he finds in her cover of the Them song 'Gloria' is uncertain.

In the context of reception, the risk with all these voices, considered and 'thought about' as they are, is of sounding glib, of sounding somehow 'inauthentic', of not coming 'from the heart'. For some singers, conveying this sense of immediacy is paramount. A singer such as Liam Gallagher does this particularly through absence. On Oasis' 'Rock'n'roll star', you can hear what might come across as 'carelessness' with regard to tuning (that opening word 'city' is ejected in an almost slovenly way). Gallagher's voice has no shaping vibrato and no sense of resonance – it is almost as if he's simply speaking at pitch. However, there is a certain affectedness to his vowels – the '*y*' of that 'city' again, for instance. Women are equally able to take on this sort of voice – Justine Frischmann of Elastica, for instance. The unstudied nature of her delivery of 'Annie' (no resonance, no vibrato, approximate tuning) is compounded by the minimality of the song's melodic range, consisting simply of five notes within the range of a perfect fourth (D, D♯, E, F♯, G). A fairly extreme version of this approach was that of John Lydon, singing as Johnny Rotten. The melodic range of the Sex Pistols' 'Holidays in the sun' is equally small – arguably Lydon sings only two notes, $\hat{4}$ and $\hat{5}$, in a register

[20]   Jungr, 'Vocal expression', p.107.

[21]   Jungr, 'Vocal expression', p.108. Her wide experience as a much recorded singer is important in verifying this approach. Chapter 8 will offer further general evidence in favour of the validity of this perspective.

[22]   Mike Daley, 'Patti Smith's "Gloria": intertextual play in a rock vocal performance', *Popular Music* 16/3 (1997).

close to falsetto. There is some sense of resonance, however – this is at least heightened speech, and is more stylized than Gallagher's. What is perhaps most surprising is Lydon's maintenance of the strict beat – occasionally the last syllable of a phrase is anticipated ("Now I got a rea-*son*"), but that's about all. It is as if the accompaniment has straitjacketed him, conveying a sense of claustrophobia. What is notable, however, is that any of the other singing styles mentioned would not have conveyed this sense, and the band's apparent anger, as successfully. The key thing about the use of the voice, as any other element, is its appropriateness to the expression desired. This can be observed by comparing alternative approaches taken by an individual singer. John Denver, for example, used an easy vibrato as a natural part of his approach, as can easily be heard on the easy listening classic 'Take me home country roads'. The first two long notes are the rhyming 'Virginia' and 'river' – both are given presence by the addition of vibrato. And, of course, the song has an easy nostalgia. 'Potter's wheel', however, is altogether darker, as it speaks of the way children learn to repeat the faults of their elders. And, seemingly to characterize this negativity, Denver refuses to take the option to apply vibrato to long notes – they are left plain, unadorned, a little unpleasant.

So, what can be said about the consequences of the choices singers make about how they will sing? Fuller treatment of this awaits subsequent chapters, when other elements are brought into play, but a few initial observations can be made here. Joe Cocker's performance of 'With a little help from my friends' is a fine study in wringing meaning out of a song. He sings with obvious effort, with rather wayward tuning, in an uncomfortable high register, and with a huskiness that suggests a voice raw with shouting or crying. All of these connote a personal authenticity or integrity – they signal that we should, or at least can, trust the singer's displayed emotions. Whether or not they might 'actually' be trustworthy is an entirely different matter, which I shall discuss in Chapter 8, but for now let's assume we accept the honesty of this display. Cocker takes an immense amount of time inside the beat. It is almost as if he is unaware of where the beat is. There are some similarities between this degree of freedom and that of Nat King Cole (above), but because the other elements are different, it carries a totally different connotation. During the final bridge (from 3'45"), his wordless response to 'do you need anybody?' implies that his 'friends' provide sufficient comfort to his evident distress. Style factors are important here – five years earlier, such a display would have been impossible. The style owes much to gospel singing, both in Cocker's freedom of manoeuvre, and also in the role of the backing singers. It is also indebted to the way white singers took on soul, but it was only once this style had met psychedelia in the 'spaced-out', immensely slowed pace of standard songs performed by bands such as Vanilla Fudge (e.g. their 'Eleanor Rigby') that it could become personalized in this way (a term adopted at the time was 'sanctified speed', for its relation to the sanctified gospel singing, such as in the Spirit of Memphis' 'There's no sorrow', and subsequently epitomized by Aretha Franklin's 'Never grow old'). This use of gospel-style backing singers intervenes interestingly, I would suggest, in a reading of Foreigner's 'I want to know what love is'. It is a song that has become desperately hackneyed – its emotions seem as plastic as the soundworld of its synthesized timbres. And yet, the gospel-style backing singers problematize this understanding, by the very nature of their style.

Ian Gillan's voice on any recording of Deep Purple's 'Strange kind of woman' is rich, like that of Ian McNabb, although there is no push from the diaphragm, and Gillan's high falsetto seems not to have resulted from any effort. Indeed, this is almost too easy, and this is particularly clear during the wordless bridge (c.1'30" on the *Made in Japan* recording). The smooth shifts of register and the vibrato clearly mark this out as fictional, as a dream sequence (and the use of the same harmonic sequence as in the dream sequence of the Beatles' 'A day in the life' can hardly be trivial). Billy Joel, singing 'Leningrad', is another singer who is rhythmically very late, but here, as the regularity of metre of the lyric is almost destroyed, it comes across as strongly autobiographical. The key lyric is 'eye to eye' at 2'58". Patsy Cline uses an increased level of roughness to her tone on 'Love, love, love me honey' to convey sexual excitement (particularly in the chorus at about 1'30"). This is, of course, a very common device, and I shall return to its effectiveness later. Finally here, note Bob Dylan's 'Big girl now', and his constant failure to reach the top note of the melody (the first occasion is at 55") despite the apparent effort in his voice. This conveys a sense of failure compounding that in the lyric. These are examples drawn almost at random, and I shall approach this issue systematically in Chapter 9.

There is only one further issue to be raised at this point, and that is a simple one, namely the danger inherent in too great a separation of the voice from other aspects of the musical texture. A brief comparison of Herman's Hermits' 'I'm into something good' with the Rolling Stones' 'Satisfaction' will demonstrate. At first listening, Peter Noone's and Mick Jagger's voices sound very different. Noone is singing in a comfortable register, the tone is slightly forced, the rhythm is regular if slightly 'jaunty', he sings with a slight shake to the voice rather than a vibrato, and with a wide mouth (his vowels are all open, his sibilants are slightly lisped, which sounds 'cute', and on a word like 'good' we literally get the sound of a smile). Jagger's voice is fuller, the tone is certainly forced, and the voice becomes harsher when rising in pitch. His vowels are closed, and he also sings on the beat, but with little in between. Note that 'I'm into something good' is a strict 12-bar blues, whereas 'Satisfaction is not' – a demonstration that sometimes it is valid to separate out form from content. However, close listening reveals that the tone of their relative guitarists is at least as great in conveying the differences of sense. The main distinction in their voices is surely the rhythm and the vowels, but greatly strengthened by those differences in guitar tone.

Lyrics

So; I have avoided long enough what many will consider the most important aspect of song, namely the lyrics. I am not aware of any convincing attempt at measuring their relative importance, so we must begin elsewhere. In everyday reality, the closest we come to the sung lyric is in the words of conversation. In ordinary conversation concerning feelings and attitudes (the subject matter of most song), we know that only 7 per cent of the content of a message is verbal, the remaining 93 per cent coming from vocal tone and matters of body language.[23] A starting-point, then, would be to assume a similar level of relative importance to lyrics in song (7% lyrics, 93% music). But things are perhaps not so straightforward. Very few people spend time transcribing conversation, and posting these transcriptions on the internet, and yet very many people do the same for song lyrics, so clearly for these people, those lyrics are important (and for me, as I explore at the end of Chapter 10, words are unusually important in conveying a message). There is a great deal of literature that discusses the lyrics to songs as if they were read, and that seems to me to be as useful as reading transcripts of conversations for pleasure, and I therefore entirely ignore this literature. I believe lyrics play a fairly minor role in enabling us to answer the questions 'to whom are we listening?' and 'how do I make sense of what they mean?', but they do play a role, and thus it is necessary to provide a treatment of them. So, what norms are useful? Middleton offers a 'three-pole model', distinguishing between *affect*, *story* and *gesture*. In affect, we have 'words as expression – tend to merge with melody; voice tends towards "song" (i.e. intoned feeling)'. In story, we have 'words as narrative – tend to govern rhythmic/harmonic flow; voice tends towards speech'. In gesture, we have 'words as sound – tend to be absorbed into music; voice tends towards becoming an instrument'.[24] He raises a set of connotations on this basis, a set developed by Stefani, consisting of 'intentional values [i.e. recognized connotations of formal positions] ... positional implications [i.e. connotations of the formal position in a song] ... ideological choices [i.e. preferred meanings of styles] ... emotive connotations ... links with other semiotic systems ... rhetorical connotations ... style connotations ... axiological connotations', and which may help pin down the effect of a particular lyric. But we should note that there are no recognized typologies of subject matter for popular song, and so estimating friction between norms and what is experienced here is necessarily speculative. Interpersonal relations of all sorts, from a range of perspectives, are normative. Social and political commentary, on events or situations, are by no means unknown, nor are songs simply exploring a persona's individuality, often in relation to the dance. Journeys (whether actual or metaphorical), specific places, pleasures and money, the operation of fate, these are among the more frequently encountered scenarios. The most obvious distinction to draw, and which cuts across any such typology, is whether or not things change within the course of the song. Song, after all, has to persist through time in order to be recognized as such, and the persistence (or not) through time of how we feel, of what we observe, and so on, is fundamental

---

[23]   Albert Mehrabian, *Silent messages: implicit communication of emotions and attitudes*, (Belmont, CA, 1981).

[24]   Middleton, *Studying Popular Music*, pp. 231–2.

to our existence in the world. It would be odd if a means of expression did not respond to such parallelism. The question, then, is essentially one of narrative (and I thus consider Stefani's *intentional*, *positional* and *rhetorical* passages as more important in this context).

We should expect a song to follow one of two courses. The first is where the protagonist, or the situation described, undergoes some sort of change; the second is where no such change takes place. Genesis' mammoth 'Supper's Ready' is perhaps one of the most complete examples of a transformational situation in the repertory, as the recall of the opening section at the end makes clear that the initial situation has undergone a qualitative development. Although it carries a totally different sort of narrative, Nick Cave's 'The mercy seat' observes a similar change. Here, the steady pace and the inevitability of the protagonist's execution serve only to intensify the path along which the song moves. Roy Orbison's 'Pretty woman' has a similar inevitability in its direction, but the outcome is short-circuited as the protagonist realizes the 'pretty woman' has noticed him after all. The change, then, can be found either within a protagonist or not, and it may or may not move to its predictable end. Such a narrative is not suited to a conventional verse–chorus structure. The opposite to this, and by far the more common, is the stasis found in so many verse–chorus songs. Here, while the verse may suggest some developing narrative, the role of the chorus tends to be to bring us back to the point of origin, to demonstrate that nothing has 'really' changed. In its concentration on the present moment, it is this approach that has caused particular opprobrium among the popular song's detractors. The Beatles' 'Things we said today' is such a song. The protagonist muses on what remembering 'today' might be like from a vantage point in the future and, while this is an interesting question, it changes nothing. The Archies' 'Sugar sugar' is emblematic of this position – the entire song consists of the protagonist relentlessly confirming his 'sugar' in her status. Pulp's 'Common people' is but one example of the subtlety that can be employed when formulae are so well-known: while the protagonist tries ever more outrageously to get his antagonist to see the futility of her desire to 'live like common people (like you)', she remains immovable in the second half of each verse.

In determining the import of lyrics themselves, the issue is how far we move away from conversational mode, remaining with what Frith calls 'the ordinariness of language', where what matters is 'the power to make ordinary language intense and vital'.[25] So how do we call attention to this intense ordinary? One way of doing this is by judicious reference to local history and geography. Richard Thompson's songs often make a virtue of this ('Don't sit on my Jimmy Shands', '1952 Vincent Black Lightning', 'Dead man's handle'), while it is commonplace among musicians with a strong identification with place (the southern USA for the Drive-by Truckers, London for the Kinks, New York for Paul Simon, etc. etc.). Again, there is no standard methodology, although to my mind the field of cognitive semantics offers potential. I shall briefly explore a couple of ideas in relation to

[25]   Simon Frith, *Sound effects* (London, 1983), pp. 37–8.

two tracks from the Feeling's first album. The main body of the culminating song, 'Blue Piccadilly', opens as the protagonist declares some homely things he has done for 'you'. It is at this point that we hear the key phrases 'beneath woods' and 'down where it's rumbling'. What context should we assume for these strange phrases? Charles Fillmore is a key developer of the idea of *semantic frames*: a frame provides a necessary context for understanding any word, whose meaning cannot exhaustively be given in dictionary fashion. Fillmore suggests that 'the word's meaning cannot be truly understood by someone who is unaware of those human concerns and problems that provide the reason for the category's existence'.[26] The frame that provides a context for 'beneath', for the 'rumbling' of 'it' is, perhaps, clarified by the appearance in the chorus of 'the blue Piccadilly' and, in the tail, 'twelve stops and home'. A train journey is never explicitly mentioned, but it is a train journey that the protagonist is recounting. And it is a particular sort of train journey, that on London's underground, on maps of which the Piccadilly line is conventionally coloured blue. (In case we're in any doubt, the album's cover carries a stylized passenger handle, indicative of crowded underground trains.) For so very many commuters, London's underground is the means to get to and from home and work, and is thus invested with those (positive, negative) feelings that such destinations carry: identification of the semantic frame, and the fact that it is only hinted at, as if listeners are somehow 'in the know', opens us to recognition of those feelings.

One of the four schematic systems of Leonard Talmy's conceptual structuring theory is that of attention.[27] Talmy argues that language enables the focus on 'only a certain portion or portions of the referent scene',[28] by the way in which it is used. Only partial discussion of a scene means that the attention of the listener is directed – Talmy coins the term 'windowed' – towards what is thus described. We have already seen this (although I did not comment on it) – in discussion of the previous song, where the listener's attention is drawn to the process of travelling, rather than the beginning or the end of the journey, both of which are indispensable to the actual taking of such a journey. In the Feeling's 'Kettle's on', things work differently. As with many allusive lyrics, but also with so much everyday conversational language, the listener's attention is given space to negotiate between what is actually said and what is implied; by observing the difference between what is 'windowed' and what is not, room for interpretation opens up. The song opens with the lines 'I turn on the tap and run some water/

---

[26] Fillmore, 'Frame semantics', p. 382.

[27] The others are to do with the structuring of a scene in terms of its temporal and spatial properties (the 'configurational' system); the perspective from which a scene is 'viewed' (the 'perspectival' system) and the 'force-dynamics' system, which I use in Chapter 10. See Vyvyan Evans and Melanie Green, *Cognitive linguistics: an introduction* (Edinburgh, 2006), pp. 191–200, for a concise introduction.

[28] Leonard Talmy, *Toward a cognitive semantics, vol. 1: Concept structuring systems* (Cambridge MA, 2003), p. 258.

Flick a little switch (up)on the wall'. Attention is drawn to the tap, but there is no context provided for the water. It is as if both actions were absent-minded gestures (and this is a constant feature of the album). Not only is no context provided for the water, but nor is there for the switch. We know the title, of course, but at this point it has not come into play within the drama of the song. Returning to the switch, it could be on or off, it could be an appliance or a light. Clearly, asking the purpose of these actions is the wrong question at this point – no answer is provided and we must run with the flow of the persona's thought. The next lines show that the protagonist's mind is on 'you', and on some prior conversations from a perspective where he is in the ascendancy. The tense then moves forward to the present, but a present that is clearly a repeat of past situations. He projects himself to wherever 'you' is currently situated to note the champagne is finished. Then, almost as an afterthought, the tense moves to the future, where 'you' will come home and find the kettle already on, in a setting of cosy domestic security that the protagonist clearly needs. This shifting of tense, according to Mark Turner (to whom I shall refer again in Chapter 8), is a basic facet of narrative structures where the coinciding of the viewpoint of the narrator (or here, the protagonist) with the present cannot be considered normative.[29] Now we understand the right context for the tap and the switch, but had their purpose been made clear at the beginning, there would have been no toehold for what takes place in the chorus.[30] Much work remains to be done to develop this line of approach to the meaning of lyrics, but it seems to hold great promise.

Aside from matters of content, Griffiths' concept of 'verbal space' offers a way of understanding the relationship between lyrics and the relative speed with which they are delivered, and this does impact on the meaning of the words themselves. The verses of Billy Joel's 'We didn't start the fire' effectively present a list of events and attributes outlining a chronology of some aspects of popular culture. The list is well served by its melody, a form of simple oscillation between three pitches (which, although it falls to the tonic, never coincides here with a tonic harmony), and in its crowded verbal space comes over almost like the intonation of a spell; it is the near-monotony of the delivery, combined with such a rich set of images that pass across the listener's attention so swiftly, which give it its affective power. Joni Mitchell's 'The last time I saw Richard' is rather similar on the surface, in that words are crowded together, but they appear more conversational, in that the rhythm of delivery is not uniform. And then, the length of time spent on a word such as 'café' enables us to picture Richard with a certain degree of clarity. The verbal space of Tom Petty & the Heartbreakers' 'Free fallin'' varies between squashed, active syllables, usually verbs, in the verse, and the extensive space given in the chorus to the word 'free', a space that literally illustrates the word

---

[29] Turner, *The literary mind*, pp. 149–50.

[30] I further develop the analysis of both these songs in Moore, 'One way of feeling: contextualizing a hermeneutics of spatialization', in Stan Hawkins (ed.), *Critical Musicological Reflections* (Farnham).

that animates it. Simon & Garfunkel's 'So long, Frank Lloyd Wright' exemplifies a fairly standard way of utilizing verbal space if there is no particular analogical point to be made – line lengths vary from point to point in the song in order to approximate a conversational mode of delivery that, in the absence of any other factors, is the normative position for a popular song to take.

Although lyrics are not poetry, and the two categories of expression should not be confused, some technical poetic devices can be found in lyrics, and can add a certain expressive quality. Forte[31] surveys some common devices found in the inter-war ballad, focusing on such techniques as alliteration and inner rhymes, on rhythmic niceties of word-setting, and on the appearance of triple groupings of events (rhymes, repeated words and the like). Alliteration and other *sonic parallelisms* are found throughout popular song; we can extend this category to the repetition of any particular vowel or consonant sounds within a short space of time (time, rather than space on the page). Joni Mitchell's 'Big yellow taxi' provides a good example, in the line 'They paved paradise, put up a parking lot'. The five bilabial plosives are dominant, particularly since the '-p' of 'up a' sounds more like a '-pa' in delivery. (The only other repeated phonemes are 'they pa-', 'pa- ra-' and the 'd' of 'paradise' with the 't' of 'put'. The 'd' of 'paved' is not sounded.) But note the melody line. The first five syllables move from $\hat{6}$ to $\hat{9}$; the next four extend this to a move from $\hat{5}$ to $\hat{10}$, before coming to rest on the tonic on the final syllable (see Example 4.13).

Example 4.13   Joni Mitchell: 'Big yellow taxi; final melodic line of chorus

And the 'rest' offered by this syllable is partly a factor of its consonants 'l' and 't', and its vowel 'o', novel in this situation. And of course, the installation of a 'parking lot' does indeed bring a (rather negative, from Mitchell's protagonist's perspective) conclusion to the narrative. But perhaps the previous line is more remarkable. The line splits in two: 'Don't it always seem to go that you don't know ¦ what you've got till it's gone.' The first half's long 'o' sounds ('don't', 'go', 'don't', 'know') give way to the second half's short 'o' sounds ('what', 'got', 'gone'), and the hard alveolar plosives ('don't', 'don't') give way to soft ones ('what you', 'till', 'it's' – the '-t' of 'got' is skipped). The 'n' and the 'g' remain constant across both halves of the line, but only acquire close proximity at the end of the line – 'gone'. But now observe the gradual decrease and increase in verbal space between these marked vowels, judged in terms of syllables: 'Don't ... 5 syllables ... go ... 2 ... don't ... 0 ... know ¦ what ... 1 ... got ... 2 ... gone'. This seems to mark the rightness of the handover, as what was not foreseen ('Don't

---

[31]   Forte, *The American Popular Ballad*, pp. 28–35.

it always …') becomes noticed ('… till it's gone.') While such lengthy analysis may not always prove fruitful, it is always an option, and is likely to tell us far more about the effectiveness of the lyric quality of a line than any amount of content analysis.

A second device is of course that of rhyme. As Griffiths notes: 'Rhyme appears to be so central in pop music that it is surely a surprise that there is little systematic discussion',[32] before offering the beginnings of such a discussion. Griffiths emphasizes the difference between '*full* rhyme, *near* rhyme and deliberate *non*-rhyme in a rhymed setting',[33] although the effect of such rhymes (other than being simply necessary) tends to be their cleverness. In some extreme metal, the avoidance of rhyme is studied (e.g. Frantic Bleep's 'Sins of omission'), and seems particularly due to the desire to avoid norms found widely in other styles. Internal rhymes, i.e. rhymes that do not occur at the end of a line, are also worth noting. Elvis Costello's 'This year's girl' contains a cracking example in the passage from 'hoping' to 'spoken' to 'broken' to 'open' in the song's second verse. Not only are all four words half-rhymes, but the inner and outer pairs are full rhymes (since one should allow the way Costello pronounces 'hoping' and 'open'). Note that these devices depend, in some respect, on the notion of repetition. Repetition can occur at a larger level, when the same root word can be re-used. A very interesting example is Stevie Wonder's 'Yester-me, yester-you, yester-day', where Wonder has actually coined new words to maintain the flow. And yet, in delivery, it sounds at first as if he sings 'yes to me, yes to you' – it's only with the nostalgic 'yesterday' that we realize the import of those neologisms. Note how economical Wonder's lyric is, throughout the song – short phrases pin down a particular emotive content with precision. Joni Mitchell's 'The last time I saw Richard' is very different – it almost overflows with content. Both work toward the same end, to create a very particular affect, but the difference between the two is almost categorical.

Indeed, not only rhyme, but the very sonic content of lyrics is rarely addressed; in this context the approach to *euphonics* adopted by John Michell[34] is worth developing. Although its theoretical basis is flimsy (he traces it back particularly to Socrates), its observation of practice is powerful. Michell argues that particular verbal sounds carry intrinsic connotations that modify (but cannot control) the semantic sense of poetic utterances. Michell's system is not fully adequate to a consideration of song, since it deals with written letters as much as with their sound (although it does incorporate words from outside English, suggesting a cross-cultural aspect), but my summary freely adapted and embodied in Table 4.1 provides a basis from which to work. Although Michell's full discussion includes consonants in other than terminal positions, in song this is where they seem to be most effective.

---

[32]   Griffiths, 'From lyric to anti-lyric', p. 50.

[33]   Griffiths, 'From lyric to anti-lyric', pp. 50–51.

[34]   John Michell: *Euphonics: a poet's dictionary of sounds*, (Kirstead, Norfolk, 1988).

Table 4.1   Michell's consonantal qualities

Letter/sound	Qualities	Exemplified by these words:
A	open, observant	alert, awake, attentive
B	biparity; excessive size	bluster, bulging, big, boring
C	pertaining to the centre; to cut	core, confined, concern, caution, cleave, cull
CH	brightness (of mood); irritation	cheep, chuckle, itch, catch
D	loss; darkness (of mood)	dread, dim, damp
E (long)	grief, terror	creep, scream, plead
F	frivolity; failure	fail, false, fool
FL	excessive frivolity	flippant, flutter, floss
G	stickiness; disgust	glue, grease, glob, gross
H	uplift; spirits, breath	hope, high, happy, heaven
I (short)	light affection; derision	imp, slit, thin, inward, image
I (long)	self-image, pomposity	identity, idol, didact
J	light, fun; deadening	jaunt, jerk, joy, jealous, sludge
K	careful speed; trivializing; chastisement	quick, tinkle, prickle, spank, prank
L	clarity, ease	long, limp, placid
M	maternity (in all its aspects)	home, murmur, warm, moon, gloom, dim
N	negation	no, mean, narrow
O	totality; roundness	noble, ocean, whole, pot, knoll, orb
P	paternity; perpendicularity; pride; smallness	proud, penis, power, post, pedestal, pomp, pry
QU	oddness; whimsicality	quaint, quirky, quasi, quibble
R	careless speed; hardness	run, rapid, rigid, crumble, crash
S	amiability; hostility	whistle, hiss
SL	gelatinous	sludge, slop, slough
SP	bursting forth, jumping up	spew, expel, spring, spirit, spleen
STR	strictness	strict, street, straight, strap, strike
T	slight	ditty, tune, trifle, dainty, trivial, trite, tetchy
TR	terror	trouble, twirling, terror, torrent
U	uncouth	gutter, clumsy, stumble, mug, grunt
V	lively; weak, depraved	vital, vigour, vain, vapid, venom, vile
W	evanescent, uncertain	wash, water, weak, wander
X	paradox	paradox, sex, mix, tricks
Y	coarseness; familiarity	merry, pretty, yell, yob, yid, yellow
Z	doziness; inquisitiveness	dazzle, puzzle, fizzle, quiz, zest, frenzy

In song, I simply don't think this works with individual sounds, but it can be effective when a particular sound dominates. For instance, 'They paved paradise, put up a parking lot' certainly carries a sense of the (petty?) pride of the purveyors of such a controlling scheme, while Rael's encounter with Lilywhite Lilith in Genesis' The *Lamb lies down on Broadway* certainly has a quality of liquidity, of slithering limpness. And the jauntiness of Middle of the Road's 'Chirpy chirpy cheep cheep' is not simply a matter of instrumental rhythm and drumming precision. Of course, this can be taken too far, but it is an aspect of lyric sense that is normally totally overlooked, and is worthy of development.

Another important set of devices concerns the use of puns and clichés. One of the finest occurs in David Bowie's 'Space oddity', where 'Can you *hear* me, Major Tom?' is elided with '*Here* am I floating in my tin-can.' Most importantly, both contexts have already been used before they are brought together. Shania Twain's 'Man! I feel like a woman' is obvious, but no less effective for that. The immense energy of Nick Cave's 'Supernaturally' provides a strange context for the line 'My north, my east, my south, my west; You're the girl that I love best'. This is less a pun, than the importation of an entire (stock) phrase into a new context, but its effect is similar. The familiarity of the phrase sticks out in this context, and sounds like the desperate provision of safe ground in the midst of the exploration of the new song. There are a range of other devices that may prove useful, which I only sketch here. Forte suggests attending to lyrics appearing on apex and nadir pitches (i.e. the highest and lowest pitches of a melodic phrase, or series of phrases), which are given extra weight thereby. Compare Meatloaf's 'I'll do anything for love' with Bread's 'Everything I own' (Examples 4.14 and 4.15).

Example 4.14   Meat Loaf: 'I will do anything for love'; hook

Example 4.15   Bread: 'Everything I own'; hook

Both have the same rhythm, and an equivalent word (any-*thing*/every-*thing*). Although the apex pitch is the same (G in both cases), the emphases appear on the apex for Meatloaf, but the nadir for Bread, calling attention to Meatloaf's intention to make any sacrifice, but David Gates' insistence that pauperism is okay. A similarity of setting can draw together words that are otherwise separated in the course of the song. For instance, the first verse of Procol Harum's 'A salty dog', with its strange harmony, pregnant bass and measured string attack, opens with the call 'all hands on deck'. The second verse, similarly set, opens with 'we sailed for parts unknown ...'. The implication here, not explicitly stated, is that 'we' are among the 'all hands' rather than simply observers of the action. And an emphasis on stressed nouns can suggest stasis, as in the progression from 'rain ... sun ... show', the words that open the verses of the Beatles' 'Rain'.

Although a large number of songs appear as monologues, or as discussions overheard, songs frequently address someone either within or outside the song. Songs frequently address a listener:

- in the second person singular (the all-encompassing love song);
- in the second person plural (implying general support for the position expressed);
- sometimes in conjunction with reflection in the first person (on the singer's own feelings);
- and less often in the third person.

There is no general point to be made about these different forms of address, but sensitivity to them is important, for each will affect the meaning of the track. Thus, we overhear the discussion in the Beatles' 'Michelle'; we are addressed individually by the Byrds' 'All I really want to do'; and addressed collectively by the Beatles' 'All you need is love'; we are addressed in absentia, as it were, in the Monkees' eponymous track; but we are excluded from Skunk Anansie's 'Here I stand'. Alan Durant argues that '"you" ... can engage a listener across at least four distinctions: address to one specific individual ...; address to any singular listener in an intimacy of address ...; address extending this sense to a ... 'universal' listener ...; address to an addressee determined by the listener himself or herself, upon occupying the imaginary position of the singer',[35] all of which he finds enacted by Carly Simon's 'You're so vain'. Both first- and second-person pronouns ('shifters') can appear to address different individuals, depending on the perspective taken. Durant again:

> what is most extraordinary about first- and second-person pronouns in rock songs is the possibility of identification they evidently establish: the possibility to superimpose the person of a listener on the 'I' of the singer, an identification which creates the effect of the rock singer speaking out on an audience's behalf; or alternatively, the possibility of the listener occupying the position of second-person addressee addressed by that 'I' of the singer.[36]

---

[35] Alan Durant, *Conditions of music* (London, 1984), p. 204.

[36] Durant, *Conditions of music*, p. 203.

Chapter 5
Style

Theory

In the past three chapters I have endeavoured to lay out the important musical norms within which recorded popular song operates, and to identify what assumptions are useful.[1] But before heading into the territory of interpretation, it seems wise to provide at least an outline of the way styles of popular music have changed during the era of recordings. It is quite possible, of course, to make an interpretation without any reference whatever to history, but since a dominant feature of what I have presented in the previous chapters concerns whether something is normative or not, we need to have a sense of what those norms are. And norms do not arise out of nothing – they are historically located. General histories of popular song exist[2] but their perspective is exclusively North American (dealing with non-North American artists only where they impinge on the North American market). My approach here is, necessarily, equally geographically biased, in that I am exploring styles from a British perspective, in the understanding that more styles of popular song are apparent from this perspective (not only British, but North American too). The survey that follows is not strictly chronological, but groups styles in terms of their advent.

What do I mean by the term *style*? I understand style as providing the primary condition for musical production and reception.[3] Musical styles co-exist at a variety of levels, and there are various ways of defining them, although definitions that relate strongly to internal, musical, features are most effective. They also tend to operate *prototypically*,[4] by which I mean to say that one cannot devise an exhaustive list of features that all examples of a style have, and that will enable any listener to

---

[1]   I wish to acknowledge with gratitude the strong and formative influence of Charlie Ford on this chapter, which at one time we proposed developing into a full-length study in its own right: I suspect a number of his well-chosen phrases have found their way into my writing here.

[2]   For example, Larry Starr and Christopher Waterman, *American popular music from minstrelsy to MTV* (New York NY, 2003), John Covach, *What's that sound? An introduction to rock and its history* (2nd edn, New York NY, 2009).

[3]   Lucy Green, *Music on Deaf Ears*; (Manchester, 1988), pp. 32–44; Charles Ford, 'Musical presence: towards a new philosophy of music' *Contemporary Aesthetics* 8 (http://www.contempaesthetics.org/newvolume/pages/article.php?articleID=582, 2010), accessed 11 March 2010.

[4]   Lakoff, *Women, fire, and dangerous things*.

make the same labelling decision no matter what their background. Instead, what we tend to have are 'typical' members of a style (Jerry Lee Lewis' 'Great balls of fire' typifies rock'n'roll; David Bowie's 'Jean genie' typifies glam rock; Blur's 'Parklife' typifies Britpop, etc.). These will sit in the centre of any understanding of the style, while others that do not share all of the same characteristics will be more marginal (Fats Domino's 'Blueberry Hill'; Slade's 'Coz I luv you'; Suede's 'Animal nitrate'). Consider a style to be like a constellation: it consists of individual stars, and everyone can see the same stars, but how they draw the constellation will depend on their perspective. And, unlike the sky, which we all observe from the same planet, in terms of music we can view the repertory from very different places. For some writers, *style* operates at various levels, from grouping musicians who share large geographical and historical locations (nineteenth-century Europe, for example), down to more local levels (1920s Mississippi) down to the level of individual musicians (the Beatles). I consider the last of these qualitatively different, reserving the term *idiolect*. In reasonably precise terminology, *style* for the purposes of this book 'refers to the manner of articulation of musical gestures ... [and it] operates at various hierarchical levels, from the global to the most local'.[5] In other words, it refers to a decision a band may make to play a song in, for instance, a 'rock' style rather than a 'country' style. *Idiolect* as a concept is frequently conceived[6] to be subsidiary to *style*. Thus, Glenn Miller's music (represented by his *idiolect*) is all couched within the style defined by the term 'swing'. Similarly, the idiolects of both Fats Domino and Chuck Berry carve out spaces within the *style* known as rock'n'roll. They carve out different spaces, of course – that is why we recognize their work as their work individually, and do not confuse the two – but both singers' output is subsidiary to the style known as rock'n'roll. Since I disagree, I shall return to this issue in Chapter 6.

As Ford suggests, styles change at various rates in accordance with five functionally related factors. (1) They change internally, according to 'purely musical' criteria, subject to historical dynamics, as in the growth of chromatic inflections to the standard 12-bar blues. (2) They change according to the attitudes of 'producers', typically composers and performers, such as when British blues guitarists (emblematically Eric Clapton) took space to improvise within a track. (3) They change according to the attitudes of consumers, as with the early 1990s rise of acid house. (4) They change according to circumstantial, typically technological and economic, sets of events, as with the invention and importation of the drum machine in the late 1970s. (5) And they change as a result of interventions by mediatory agencies, as in the decline of progressive rock in the 1970s due to the financial crisis in the music industry. In the early days of a style, producers (by which term I also identify, here, writers and performers) sense a need to 'explain' a style's possibilities and probabilities, either through exploring

---

[5]   Moore, 'Categorical conventions', pp. 441–2.

[6]   See Middleton, *Studying Popular Music*, p. 174 and Meyer, *Style and Music*, pp. 23–4. Meyer prefers the term 'idiom' to 'idiolect'.

them in recordings, or through other media (particularly journalism). A style that is settled, consensual, enables producers to use the 'language' creatively. As a style becomes thoroughly absorbed, producers will often seek to move away from its basic paradigms, or to leave their own idiosyncratic mark on the style. These three phases correspond to the 'preclassic ... classic ... mannerist' categories of style development introduced by Leonard B. Meyer, which he proposes in terms of relative degrees of musical redundancy, and also to Williams' emergent-dominant-residual scheme,[7] although there is *no* sense in which this tripartite scheme can be seen as operating for popular music as a whole.

Effects of the first, 'internal dynamic' model, can be viewed in what follows. As to the second factor, some producers are particularly concerned with making music purely for its own sake, others with self-expression, others with the perceived necessity to communicate to an audience, and in this sense, to re-affirm the style. Furthermore, the world of popular song production has experienced shifts in the roles of key players (composers, performers, producers, and disc-jockeys, promoters, journalists) that have themselves impacted on style change. These first two factors enter into varying relationships with audience expectations: the third category. People listen in different ways. Middleton explains this in terms of three broad attitudes: the everyday – distraction/participation/conviviality; the auratic – image/fantasy/narrative identification; the critical – shock/protest.[8] Listeners pay more-or-less close attention to music, in accordance with what the style codes of what they are hearing lead them to expect, and as determined by their own personal, and social-psychological demands for varying degrees of excitement and comfort, which will all in turn affect their musical 'competence', or understanding of styles. Fourthly, these listeners' attitudes will be affected by changing technologies, from radio to 78 rpm record, through transistor radios to CDs and mp3 files, and also by the various contexts of reception: club, car radio, cinema, personal computer, and so on. The expected attitudes and competences of listeners then feed back into compositional and performing attitudes. Fifthly and finally, all these considerations play their part in the constantly shifting styles of popular song, in conjunction with how styles are *named* as such by the agents of distribution and criticism. Issues of competence and pertinence, together with questions of value, are all inextricably bound up with one another. What this chapter sets out to do is to display the styles that have (had) the greatest impact on contemporary popular song, particularly in their 'classic' phase, observing how many of the norms that have been the subject of the first four chapters have arisen as part of the process of style change.

---

[7]   Leonard B. Meyer, *Music, the Arts and Ideas* (Chicago IL, 1967); p. 19, Raymond Williams, *Culture* (London, 1981), pp. 203–4; Vic Gammon, 'Problems of method in the historical study of popular music', in Philip Tagg and David Horn (eds.), *Popular Music Perspectives* (Gotenburg, 1982), pp. 28–9.

[8]   Middleton, *Studying Popular Music*, p. 98.

Defining the term 'popular' in the phrase 'popular song' is fraught with difficulty, a difficulty that tends to resolve into two types of definition. The first suggests that it is possible to distinguish 'popular song' from other types of song on the grounds of inherent features of various types: its use of harmony and rhythm (i.e. aspects of its style); its appearance in certain types of venue through particular processes of transmission (i.e. aspects of its genre); the motivation of its musicians (driven by commerce, or self-expression, i.e. aspects of its origination). This distinction is then definitional, in that membership by a particular song (or even performance of that song) in the class 'popular song' does not subsequently need revising. The second suggests that the category 'popular song' is inherently discursive, that is, that membership of the class 'popular song' is mutable, dependent on who is doing the categorizing, and their motives; it is thus an ideological term. While in principal most examples can be simply positioned according to the first type of definition even if we sign up to the second (most people seem to agree on their large-scale categorizations), there are nonetheless examples that demonstrate the latter approach to definition (the songs of Mikis Theodorakis or Stephen Sondheim, for instance, or songs such as 'Land of Hope & Glory', or the songs of the various folk revivals). To begin, we can note that 'popular song' can *in general* be distinguished from both 'art song' and 'folk song'. 'Popular song' has an implicit aesthetic (its distinctive features are almost never made apparent in everyday discourse, which this book certainly does not exemplify), whereas the aesthetic of 'art song' is often explicit. 'Popular song' also appears in a communal setting where the vast majority become relatively passive consumers, whereas 'folk song' is marked by engagement, by suspicion of this producer/consumer distinction. In this way, 'popular song' properly comes into being with the rise of the leisured classes in the eighteenth century; the popular song that Reginald Nettel[9] traces back at least to the thirteenth century arises under markedly different conditions.

Pre-War

Popular song first becomes an industry as early as the 1880s, in the New York street that became known as Tin Pan Alley. The very name conjures up visions of publishers' houses with tiny rooms, each containing a piano, a lyricist and a composer, each of whom was paid by the song.[10] The business was cut-throat; between 1900 and 1910, more than 100 songs sold a million copies in sheet music format, while the price dropped from 40 to 10 cents. The market for these songs consisted essentially of middle-class white women, and of course an ability not only to read music, but to play the piano and keep a tune was a necessary assumption.

---

[9]   Reginald Nettel, *Seven centuries of popular song: a social history of urban ditties* (London, 1956).

[10]   John Shepherd, *Tin Pan Alley* (London, 1982).

In this context, the sales seem huge (one might ask whether it is so much more skilful to play a simple song at the piano, perhaps with limited facility, than to download a file onto an iPod). As far as subject matter is concerned, we can find lyrical ballads, love songs, songs promoting and intended for dancing, comedic songs, sentimental songs, songs expressing the current fashion for something, all with frequent racist overtones. In other words, the subject matter seems to have remained fairly constant (although it has perhaps expanded) over the course of a century.

In the UK, there are six main performance categories prior to the 1914–18 war. Operetta and music hall were at the 'art song' end of the spectrum; both were strictly non-participative, although without the rapt, admiring, attention that we nowadays reserve for the performance of art song. The brass band movement and choral societies were partially participative, in that the performers were largely amateur, and the distinction between participant and audience was therefore fluid. Industrial/rural song (what would come to be identified as 'folk song') and home music-making were entirely participative, in that there tended to be no non-participating listeners. Music hall dominated these categories in terms of the attention given to it prior to 1914, after which it became replaced variously by music in the cinema, in 'variety' and on radio. Although only a limited amount of recorded music was broadcast on the purist BBC from its inception after the war,[11] these new media had a devastating effect both on home music-making and on instrument manufacturers. After all, who needed a piano in the home when you could hear the music played 'properly' on gramophone (on wax discs from 1887, or flat records from 1904) or radio?

The dance impulse, and hence a regular metre, was a feature of popular song from this early point at least, appearing in the output of Tin Pan Alley not only in ragtime with its associated syncopation, but in songs associated with other dance crazes (foxtrot, Charleston, etc.). As early as the turn of the century, innumerable recordings had been produced by British musicians 'in the ragtime manner', but all were orchestral. In the USA black musical idioms, developed from nineteenth-century minstrel shows and marching bands, were present in the repertory from an early age, although the black roots were usually disguised. This went for jazz too – the first so-called 'king of jazz', in the 1920s, was white bandleader Paul Whiteman. And as far as mainstream popular music was concerned, the dance bands held sway between the world wars. Their legacy, however, is minor compared to that of those black idioms on which they leant, and it is therefore on these that I initially focus.

It is important to see 'gospel' and 'blues' as two sides of the same coin;[12] respectively the sacred and the secular responses to the conditions of slavery

---

[11]   The 'needle-time' directive, an agreement with the Musicians' Union, limited the amount of recorded music to be played on the BBC to five hours per day.

[12]   Samuel A. Floyd Jr, *The Power of Black Music* (New York NY, 1993); Moore, *The Cambridge Companion to Blues and Gospel*.

in the USA. The roots of gospel are found in nineteenth-century spirituals that, themselves, often derive from early nineteenth-century Southern Baptist songs. It is therefore wrong to assume that the origins of this style lie in racial distinctiveness. The first recorded sacred songs, whether by small choirs (the Fiske Institute Singers, the Tuskagee Jubilee Singers), soloists (Rosetta Tharpe, Blind Willie Johnson), preachers (Revs McGhee, Shelton) or, often highly trained, *a capella* groups (the Birmingham Jubilee Singers, or the Heavenly Gospel Singers), show a confluence of white Christian and black Africanist practices. The first can be heard in the massed voices, developing from mass singing at Camp meetings during the early nineteenth-century religious revival, and in practices of 'lining out', whereby singers make their individual way through a melodic line, without too much concern for coinciding rhythmically. Its echoes can still be heard in contemporary performances by people such as Whitney Houston (the opening to 'I will always love you'). The second can be heard in the avoidance of 'clear', 'pure' tone (the term 'dirt' is often used to describe such tone – it refers also to the use of growls, shouts, cries and other forms of singing foreign to European practices) and in modifications to melodic scales in the form of blue notes.

That said, however, gospel has been central to African American culture. From it certainly derive two vital aspects of contemporary popular practice, i.e. styles of piano playing and of singing. In large part, these were dependent on the development of the structure of feeling[13] known as 'soul', and the modification of gospel into soul music in the early 1960s, particularly in the hands of musicians such as Sam Cooke and Ray Charles. During the 1920s, three distinct styles of gospel were being recorded. Two would not surprise us today. The first of these is the gospel quartets, which allowed rhythmic interplay but were usually without instrumental backing. Already by 1935, in recordings like the Heavenly Gospel Singers' 'Lead me to the rock', we can the hear intrusion of blue notes, a driving rhythm given by the feet, growls and hollers within the voice, and other features that would come to the fore in rhythm'n'blues. There is no harmonic elaboration (a track like this, which is based on a harmonic drone, is simpler even than many blues), placing this music at the opposite pole from where band jazz was developing. The second style is the evangelical songs of itinerant singers, who would usually have a wide repertory that would at least include the blues. Rev. Gary Davis exemplifies this movement, his 'Twelve gates to the city' played as if it were a blues, on 12-string guitar. Possibly the major style, however, is unknown today, namely the recorded sermon. The importance of this can be measured by the output of Rev. J.M. Gates. During 1926–27, he released four sermons, with total sales of nearly 80,000 records (four times as many as the major blues singer Bessie Smith could manage). And I think there are no problems in regarding his work as firmly within the orbit of popular song. His manner of heightened delivery, and his rhetorical use of repetition, are very clear precursors of contemporary rap (although without the debt to rhyme).

---

[13]   Raymond Williams, *The long revolution* (London, 1961).

The classic phase of gospel develops from about 1945, following the work of Thomas Dorsey and Sallie Martin in developing a performance circuit, which culminated in highly intense shows in large auditoria, by now thoroughly infused with elements of the blues in the singing of the Swan Silvertones, Dorothy Love Coates and the Gospel Harmonettes. It was the frenetic singing of the 'hard quartets' of the 1950s that particularly influenced soul singers with the use of free 'popping bass', with treble hollers, and with growls and yells frequently appearing as extended upbeats into new verses, which surround nervous, often highly syncopated riffs in the inner voices. A sense of drive is vital to this style: the Swan Silvertones' 'My rock', for example, contains a short repeated gesture after verse 4, which accrues tension and excitement. Aretha Franklin exemplifies how close gospel and soul singing are, if we compare 'Respect' from 1967, with her 1972 recording of 'Amazing grace'. While no longer a mainstream style in itself, gospel remains very much a valid means of contemporary expression. The Blind Boys of Alabama, for instance, have been singing since 1939. Their take on 'Amazing Grace', from 2001, sets the lyrics to the tune popularized by Bob Dylan for 'The House of the Rising Sun'. The combination is decidedly eerie, with a highly contemporary production, their free four-part harmonies redolent with experience.

The other side of the coin is represented by the blues. As a practice, the blues appears to have developed from calling between those working in the fields (the 'shouts and hollers' that Paul Oliver[14] refers to). Itinerant (generally black) musicians had a wide repertory[15] – the blues as a separate genre only developed because of the interest shown by record companies in the 1920s. What we now know as the blues appears to have been born in the Mississippi delta in the 1890s, an area that was notorious for racism and even lynchings as late as the 1960s. While these circumstances are not paraded in the blues (unlike its late-century counterpart, hip hop), they lie behind the individualist ways of dealing with the hazards of life, which make up the blues' explicit content. And, although the blues are not the first black US popular music, being the record craze to succeed ragtime in the 1930s, they frequently stand for the influence its musicians have had on the subsequent development of Anglophone popular song.

Although black idioms were highly influential in early records, it was not until 1920 that a recording by a black solo musician was released; a blues sung by vaudeville singer Mamie Smith, and backed by white musicians. Blind Lemon Jefferson, one of the first important male singers, did not record until 1926. At this point in time, segregation in much of the USA was pretty near complete. 'White' singers sold to 'white' listeners, 'black' to 'black'. African Americans were banned from white restaurants and clubs, could not play sports with whites nor, normally, work in the same music groups or even shops. To the vast majority of those of European descent, African Americans were rare and exotic creatures,

---

[14] Paul Oliver, *The story of the blues* (London, 1969).

[15] See Paul Oliver, *Songsters and saints* (Cambridge, 1984).

their culture largely fabricated in the imagination of that majority. What made the isolation worse was the categorization, the segregation of African American artists into separate categories as producers of 'race' music (which consisted largely of the blues), a practice that has echoes in the labelling of 'ethnic' music today. Many independent labels arose in order to promote and record this music for its own audience. Records were very popular, even among poor families, but companies failed during the depression of the 1930s. This is only the first of many points where we note the crucial role of music, and recorded music too, in buttressing a sense of identity.

It is a commonplace that country, or rural blues (or, to use the name its performers preferred, 'downhome' blues) pre-dated 'classic' blues, but only came to be recorded subsequently. (We still assume this to be the case, although there is little concrete evidence.) During the 1920s, 75 per cent of blues records featured 'classic blues' singers. These were all female (having developed very much out of the vaudeville circuit) and were usually accompanied by five- or six-piece jazz bands, whose musicians were almost all male: this distinction between female singers and male players can, again, be observed frequently in popular song's subsequent history, particularly in various manifestations of 'pop'. One notable difference between the classic blues and much downhome blues concerns the degree of formalization. Classic blues (and some downhome styles, for example that of Texas musicians) tends to a great deal of formalization and regularity, in contrast to the accompanimental freedom of an extreme musician such as Robert Johnson (although some singers approach his degree of irregularity in their vocal styles).

The form of the classic blues can be considered formulaic; the commonest version is the 12-bar blues pattern. As Chapter 3 notes, 8-bar and 16-bar versions exist, and there are examples that differ to a greater extent, but the starting point for a blues is the harmonic basis on chords I, IV and V. The singer usually takes the first half of each 4-bar line, calling for an instrumental response in the second half. There is scope for rhythmic and melodic embellishment with freedom of vocal timing. Indeed, it is from this distinction between harmonic regularity and melodic inventiveness that so much subsequent popular song derives a basic principle. In a 12-bar blues, the second line tends to be repeated, while the third provides a rhymed response, all of which would often be improvised on the spot from a common fund of ideas and formulaic lines. As explored in Chapter 4, the commonest melodic shape is formed by a gapped (usually pentatonic) scale moving from the top octave, $\hat{8}$, to the bottom, $\hat{1}$, with inflections and embellishments on the blue notes ($\hat{7}$, $\hat{6}$ and $\hat{3}$, and sometimes $\hat{5}$). Expressive significance is created by working within this schema. For instance, in Bessie Smith's 'Spider man blues', the rise (nearly to $\hat{8}$) in the middle of the third line creates tension by not quite achieving the upper tonic.

The 'typical' downhome blues follows the same predetermined harmonic pattern (I–I–I–I– IV–IV–I–I– V–V–I–I in its simplest form), partly due to its wholly oral nature. Melodically, it derives from the Anglo-Celtic melodic tradition with the addition of the blue notes, while performative freedom provides one of its most interesting features. Robert Johnson's 'Crossroads blues #2' uses a three-part sporadic texture (see Chapter 2): a bottleneck treble line, bass movement, and loosely attached vocal phrases. He uses irregular metre and hypermetre, with a semiquaver riff on the second beat and a pulled tenor-string note anticipating the downbeat in the middle of the last line. Although using a standard shuffle rhythm, there are points at which we can hear the shuffle being ironed out, into straight quavers, prefiguring what becomes the dominant change of rhythmic thinking of the late 1950s. The difference between Johnson's approach and the studied regularity of, say, Texan Blind Lemon Jefferson's 'Matchbox blues' is palpable. This difference is not accounted for by time (1936 as against 1927) and, while some argue for the presence of geographically located stylistic features (noting the greater regularity of many Texas players, for instance), it is most importantly a feature of their respective idiolects.[16]

The economic migration of so many African Americans northwards, from the 1920s through to the war years, brought blues styles from Mississippi, Louisiana and Georgia initially to Tennessee (and particularly to Memphis). Together with diverse approaches from Texas in the west to the Carolinas in the east, these ultimately reached Kansas and Chicago. By 1937, singers such as Bill Broonzy were recording much lighter, regular blues with small groups (tracks such as 'Hattie blues'). This 'entertainment' music, together with the boogie-woogie styles of pianists such as Jimmy Yancey or Pete Johnson developed into what we know as 'rhythm'n'blues'. Indeed, the history of the blues from the mid 1920s and early 1930s craze for both the classic blues in Chicago (Ma Rainey, Bessie Smith), using jazz musicians, and the downhome blues from the southern states (Charley Patton, Son House, Blind Willie McTell) reflected the demographic shifts of African Americans. Within the southern states, blues dialects differed in rough accord with varying social conditions. And, although the blues were dominant, other, older, styles must be accorded their place. They were visible especially in the brief efflorescence of black recorded song between 1926 and the onset of the Depression in 1932. These other styles are varied: vaudeville, medicine and tent show songs (Ethel Waters, Edna Hicks); novelty and comedy numbers; Memphis jug and string bands; domestic duets; and 'folk' forms (work songs, field hollers, some of which appear in the very wide repertoire of Huddie Leadbetter). Parallel to these, particularly in the southern states, white and 'notated' blues (W.C. Handy), string band, ragtime song and barbershop styles developed, often using many of the same musical elements. None of these, however, have impacted as strongly on the future history of popular song. Even though the blues is hardly mainstream any longer, the style has not been fully co-opted[17] and, in its raw state, is now often

---

[16]   Charles Ford, 'Robert Johnson's rhythms', *Popular Music* 17/1 (1998).

[17]   Keith Negus and Michael Pickering: *Creativity, Communication and Cultural Value* (London, 2004), pp. 100-101.

marketed as a branch of world music. R.L. Burnside's work is a case in point.[18] Well into his 70s, Burnside's 'Hard time killing floor' (released in 2000) is sparse, autobiographical and draining, but mixes prominent slide guitar with scratching and a somewhat ambient groove. Later versions of the blues also surface from time to time, as in the cult band from 2007, The Answer, whose style is clearly dependent on the 1960s British blues boom.

In terms of contemporaneous popularity, the blues succeeded ragtime as a recorded form. As formulated and reformulated by Scott Joplin in the early years of the century, ragtime provided a basic style for Joseph Lamb, for Jelly Roll Morton, The Original Dixieland Jazz Band and the white dance bands who became the principal vehicles for popular music in the 1930s and 1940s. In the UK, Mayfair became the centre for an elegant quasi-orchestral dance band style in the hands of Jack Hylton, Lew Stone, Bert Ambrose, Henry Hall and others, a style that was central to the BBC's attempt to cater to popular taste. During the 1930s, the syncopations by which jazz was identified, and which appealed to the desire for dance music, made this the only period in which 'jazz' and 'popular' became virtually synonymous. The European version of the dance band was much smoother: very little of the jazz roots were audible (with the exception of a rather half-hearted backbeat), while violins were often prominent. Ray Noble's 'Love is the sweetest thing', recorded with his vocalist Al Bowlly, is a good example. Even then, there were hot debates over the relative merits of music for 'listening' and for 'dancing', which I mention in Chapter 9. In the USA, however, dance bands (Guy Lombardo, Eddie Duchin) had a smaller consistency than the jazz-oriented swing bands, whether led by white musicians (Benny Goodman, Glenn Miller, Harry James) or black (Cab Calloway or Jimmie Lunceford in New York, Benny Moten or Mary Lou Williams in the Mafioso, criminal culture of Kansas City). Alongside these bands there were loosely associated piano styles, such as the development of 'Harlem Stride' into the virtuosic, classically inflected idiolects of Fats Waller and Art Tatum, or the less vibrant Billy Mayerl. The stylistic proximity between Basie's swing-derived small bands and the jump jive of Louis Jordan would be crucial in the development of rhythm'n'blues as, negatively, would be the cult of the singer, who gradually came to front the swing bands to provide moments of relaxation between dances (Al Bowlly, Frank Sinatra, Ella Fitzgerald). It is in some of this music that the riff first arises, whether Glenn Miller's 'In the mood' or Louis Jordan's 'Choo choo ch'boogie'.

Some of the material for these dance bands originated in the musical. The US musical had developed out of both vaudeville and operetta traditions of the late nineteenth century. By the inter-war period, this had developed the notable genre of the Broadway ballad (Cole Porter, Irving Berlin, George Gershwin) and the Broadway musical itself (Jerome Kern, Richard Rodgers). As with the blues, a particular formal pattern dominated, that of 32-bar song form, where four lines of lyric tend to take two bars each, resulting in four stanzas to create the 32 bars,

---

[18]   Burnside was marketed as 'the last of the authentic bluesmen'.

usually in the pattern AABA, as in 'Somewhere over the rainbow'. These 32 bars, though, form the refrain (what we would now call a chorus). Refrains were preceded usually by a single verse, which set the scene, and which were less and less likely to be performed as time went on. Other patterns than AABA are possible though – 'Every time we say goodbye' as sung by Ella Fitzgerald is a good example of the 32 bars falling into an ABAB pattern (although in both cases, the final 8-bar section rethinks the harmony of the earlier hearing). And, while the harmonies have developed out of the operetta tradition (with an occasional touch of Brahms, perhaps), they also become infused with the added notes, and occasionally the substitutions, of jazz. In the UK, equivalent techniques resulted first in the sentimental wartime songs of the Great War, many of which derived from music hall tunes but also, more obscurely, from the songs of the American Civil War (e.g. those of Stephen Foster). The optimistic jingoism of the early war years was soon replaced by sorrowful songs of parting and grieving (composers like Haydn Wood). The genre continued in prominence from Ivor Novello, through the inter-war years of Noel Coward (and singers like Flanagan and Allen) and the songs of the Second World War, epitomized by the voice of Vera Lynn. Note the change here from talking about composers to talking about singers, due in large part to the influence of Coward, who excelled at both.

Immediate Post-War

Communal music-making, a feature of nineteenth-century British music, remained important particularly in the north through brass bands (e.g. Black Dyke Mills) and choral societies (especially Huddersfield). Light classics (composers such as Eric Coates, excerpts from operetta, orchestrated 'National' songs) were promoted by the BBC in the 1930s as the role of radio in the transmission of popular music increased. (The nearest contemporary equivalent is probably the blockbuster film composer, such as John Williams.) The BBC also became a platform for children's and humorous songs in the 1950s and in the gradual introduction of a new wave of broadcasting (Peter Kennedy) had an important role in the second English folk revival (Ewan MacColl, Peggy Seeger, Bert Lloyd). There is an important issue here, as this revival both overturned, but also shared, the ambivalent mass culture critique embodied in the original Folk Revival (Ralph Vaughan Williams, Frank Kitson, Percy Grainger, Cecil Sharp). Radio was still the dominant means of distribution of music in the UK in the inter-war and early post-war period, the large majority of it broadcast live; those (middle-class) enthusiasts who owned the primitive record players listened largely to singers of light classics (Nellie Melba, Enrico Caruso, Paul Robeson).

US influences on UK media increased in the 1940s with the presence of GIs, and the availability of Forces Radio between 1942 and 1945, which introduced many younger UK listeners to the notable differences between US swing and UK dance bands. To this point we can date the beginnings of the globalization of the media, particularly through film heroes such as James Dean and Marlon Brando. As far as mass UK audiences were concerned, it was only these mainstream US styles that existed – swing, jazz, the Broadway musical and the ballad. Although these are separate genres in the way they operate, they share a sound-world and cultural position. Irving Berlin's 'Let's face the music and dance' typifies this, in its mild chromaticisms, its jaunty syncopations and clever lyrics, a perfect marriage of Tin Pan Alley processes with 1920s dance music. Note how the 'troubled times' are met, in Fred Astaire's rendition, almost with eagerness as the opening minor key shifts subtly to the major.

Although it is very common to think of popular song as inherently Anglophone (because of its historical origins largely in the USA), at least until the rise of 'world music', two other European languages are very important in a global context: Spanish because of Spain's colonization of much of the Americas; French because of France's colonization of much of West Africa, to which many African Americans have insisted on tracing their practices. There is no space (nor do I have the expertise) to treat either of these sets of traditions adequately here, but we must acknowledge their presence. The French tradition is particularly interesting, being so parallel to that of the UK and yet so different, itself an embodiment of the orientalism[19] that has so bedevilled 'world music'. Edith Piaf's songs about sex and drugs make much heavy metal sound almost puerile, in that her songs deal with the necessity of her own existence, rather than being a matter of choice. Songs like 'La vie en rose', with their emotionally naked delivery entirely lacking in self-pity were rarely played on UK radio, but were high in cultural capital for those 'in the know'. Indeed, the singer songwriter vogue that I shall discuss below owes much to the Francophone tradition epitomized by Jacques Brel and Georges Brassens.

In the 1950s, the singers who had achieved fame fronting swing bands were still dominant figures (Frank Sinatra, Bing Crosby, Rosemary Clooney, Patti Page, Dinah Shore, Doris Day, Perry Como) together with singers such as Louis Jordan and Nat King Cole who had begun as jazzmen, and dancer/entertainers such as Sammy Davis Jr. Sinatra was pre-eminent. He began as vocalist with the bands of Harry James and Tommy Dorsey (1939–42), gaining a celebrity matched only by Benny Goodman and, subsequently, by Elvis Presley, the Beatles, Kurt Cobain, Madonna and Michael Jackson. In becoming more important than the band in front of whom he sang (and in aiming his performances at a younger generation than did Bing Crosby), he became the first 'pop star'. But his heavy recording schedule (sometimes recording 100 songs in a day) led to a decline from 1947, and in 1952 he lost his contract. In true pop star fashion, he became the first singer properly to reinvent himself, entering films, switching in the early 1950s from singing ballads to sophisticated swing (when most pop-singers had switched to novelty records) and signing to Capitol in 1953 from whence Nelson Riddle's

---

[19]   The intoxication one feels for a foreign practice once it is domesticated. See Edward Said, *Orientalism*, (London, 1995).

arrangements rekindled his popularity, which reached new heights in the early 1960s. On Gershwin's 'A foggy day', one of Riddle's earliest arrangements for him, he sings in very close relation with the instruments. His voice is clearly studied, he is clearly 'performing' (listen to the way he sings the word 'shining'), although he conveys the illusion of being in natural conversation with his listeners. This arranger/singer relationship had precursors (Lew Stone's arrangements for Al Bowlly in the 1930s, most particularly), but Sinatra's case was special.

This brings a further important issue to the fore. Music without a foothold in the bourgeois tradition was transmitted principally by oral means. Big band numbers would have lead sheets, but usually fairly minimal notation. The music of the ballads were all fully notated in piano score, but then further arranged, again, without full parts for all performers. This tradition goes back to the nineteenth century and acts as a foil to gospel/blues practices. This oppositional pairing remains important throughout the century, such that we have very different alternatives. Nelson Riddle, in arranging 'A foggy day', controls the track's performers to a high degree. When Ella Fitzgerald approaches the same song with guitarist Joe Pass, her singing of the word 'decidedly' (for instance) signals a stylized, jazz, approach rather than Sinatra's 'conversational' one, while the lack of arrangement on her track, the gentle tone and the constant rubato all suggest she is 'singing' rather than 'performing'. Returning to Sinatra, by the time of his recording a younger generation of singers, similar in style, was arising. The growing importance of singers *per se* was founded partly on microphone technology (first capitalized upon by Bing Crosby's crooning idiolect). Singers could thereby become more intimate to fans, and radio broadcast an increasing number of singers to convey that personal touch, questioning the economic viability of larger bands, and making the ground ripe for the rise of rock'n'roll. In the UK, love songs, quasi-religious songs and novelties dominated in the early 1950s. The love songs sometimes included crude exoticisms, as in Guy Mitchell's 'She wears red feathers'. While the lyrics situate 'her' probably in Hawaii and/or Africa, the music also implies American Indian and stereotypical Chinese origins. In Frankie Laine's 'I believe', the eternally upward melodic contour and clear lack of backbeat convey the sincerity of the singer's protestation, while Lita Roza's 'How much is that doggy in the window' (all three of these, like the Sinatra, come from 1953) points to the beginning of the importance of a youth (albeit socially complicit) market.

So, when Elvis Presley burst upon the public consciousness of the western world in late 1956, it seemed for its listeners (whether European, antipodean, or even North American, in the majority) that this new, invigorating sound had come from nowhere. What was widely unrecognized at the time was its historical antecedents in that long line of development of African American musical styles, of which the most immediate root was that of rhythm'n'blues. Foreshadowings of this style can be heard in the late 1930s Chicago acoustic blues bands, such as that of Big Bill Broonzy. However, it was not until the 1940s that the style became stable. It has a number of related variants. Up-tempo shuffle blues bands, usually employing boogie-woogie patterns borrowed from Chicago pianists (Meade Lux Lewis, Bunk Johnson), emerged both in New York and Los Angeles. Here, a softer form of rhythm'n'blues for mixed-race clubs (Amos Milburn, Johnny Otis) developed alongside the high intensity of Big Jay McNeely and other 'honkers'. McNeely's '3D' (recorded around 1954) has relentless, confrontational 'bad sax' sounds, easily read as emblematic of post-war black frustrations and 'violent' LA subculture. The sax is laid over very fast 12-bar blues verses with a walking bass and quite extraordinary key changes, building into a series of riffs, honks and screams with rapid-fire exchanges between three saxes. In New York, Louis Jordan's role was crucial in the shift from big band jazz. His style was known as 'jump' – the instrumentation was a cut down big band, using brass riffs behind a honking sax solo, not that dissimilar to Count Basie's small bands. Jordan was as much an entertainer as a musician (a comparison with Louis Armstrong's various positionings is interesting); this style is the first real example of African American cross-over, full of sexual innuendo. His 'Ain't nobody here but us chickens' (1947) has 12-bar blues verses with 8-bar inserts after the first and third verses, with a boogie bass.

Another form of rhythm'n'blues grew out of the electrification of the old southern blues as singers such as Muddy Waters (McKinley Morganfield) and Howlin' Wolf (Chester Burnett) migrated northwards (as part of the general inter-war northward migration), bringing other musicians with them. Wolf, for example, moved up to Memphis in 1933, and then on to Chicago in 1952. His electric band expanded and regulated the old Delta style. In 'Moanin' at midnight' from 1951, the guitar remains central to the texture, taking a single riff through the entire song changing only when suggested in the voice. The regulation, however, comes as much from attention to the backbeat in the kit. Wolf's growling voice, the searing harmonica sound and his aggressive guitar influenced a host of musicians: Mick Jagger; Tom Waits; Captin Beefheart; Dr John. Indeed, this electrified sound (initially known as urban blues) of the 1950s became the principal origin of the following decade's rock music. The difference between the Memphis and Chicago sounds becomes replayed in subsequent decades (between the Rolling Stones and Eric Clapton in the 1960s, for instance). Whereas the Chicago bands simply electrified the older downhome blues, in Memphis, the sound tended to be clean, with comparatively little improvisation and emphasis on virtuosity. Musicians such as Bobby Bland and B.B. King synthesized these styles with the more sophisticated solo guitar style of T-Bone Walker on the West Coast, and horn arrangements from pre-war Kansas swing bands. Bland's 'Stormy Monday', with Wayne Bennett's rather jazzy added-ninth licks builds to a powerful, narrative climax with typical pleading, giving the blues an overall structure. It is in this style that the four textural layers of contemporary popular song are first indisputable.

It was the merger of rhythm'n'blues with some elements of country music that created the rock'n'roll that has been the single most dominant influence on recorded popular song. Many historians suggest that rock'n'roll is the product of the coming together around 1954 of two hitherto independent streams of North

American folk music: white country, and black blues. Bill Haley's 'Rock around the clock', from 1955, clarifies the 'country' input. It develops out of a style known as 'western swing', but contains a very rigid vocal delivery in comparison to most rock'n'rollers. Other historians[20] suggest that rock'n'roll was not really a separate development from the blues, but arose when white singers tried to sing like black blues singers. It is still a matter of some heated debate, muddied by singers such as Chuck Berry (whose 'Roll over Beethoven' was very big in 1957), who radio audiences took to be white on account of the sound of his voice. And although the vocal style of Elvis Presley (whose 'Heartbreak hotel' is usually taken to be the most prominent initial example of the style), Jerry Lee Lewis, Fats Domino or Little Richard seems to be the key marker of rock'n'roll's identity, it was important too in its effect on the music industry. Early performer/composers (such as Chuck Berry and Buddy Holly) were challenging the industrial separation of songwriting and performing and effectively claiming greater control over their material. This new style spawned imitators, of course, not only in other Anglophone countries, but also throughout Europe. Imitators they certainly were, though; against the restless energy of 'Heartbreak hotel' or 'Hound dog', Cliff Richard's efforts on his initial single ('Move it') come across as just trying too hard. Part of Presley's energy is conveyed through the use of echo and reverb to create, in the pre-stereo era, a sense of place in the recording, separating it from the acoustic of the room in which the recording was played.[21] It was during rock'n'roll that shuffle rhythmic patterns lose out to straight patterns; shuffle patterns thereafter frequently connote the blues.

A key feature of rock'n'roll was the influence of singing groups, an influence that continued into the 1960s and beyond. Doo-wop had begun in the late 1940s in urban centres when groups of black kids experimented with the use of the voice for musical creation, rather than the instruments that were too expensive (the Penguins, the Orioles, Frankie Lymon and the Teenagers). Some of these approaches were learnt from gospel groups, and the stylistic similarity can be heard in some of those groups (e.g. Spirit of Memphis' 'God save America'). The Drifters, c.1953, were probably the best rhythm'n'blues vocal group with Clyde McPhatter's highly influential, elastic voice. This style was synthesized from doo-wop, gospel and jump (the boogie bass and the tenor solo). 'Money honey' (yet again from 1953) contains 12-bar blues verses but with an 8-bar 'stop time' section in the first. And there is a line of development from this style, through the Jackson Five and the Osmonds, to Take That and the strangely-named 'boy bands' (strangely named because the term 'band' had previously been reserved for instrumentalists).

---

[20]   For instance Michael Bane, *White boy singin' the blues* (New York NY, 1992); Christopher Small, *Music of the common tongue* (Hanover NH, 1998).

[21]   Doyle, *Echo and reverb*.

The (Very) Long 60s

In the USA, the record industry maintained a policy of racial segregation in their construction of markets. Large companies in the 1950s did not want the connotations of black music (which often focused on sex and the licentious use of the body) attached to their profitable white artists, men such as Pat Boone, Andy Williams, Marty Robbins. However, when black rhythm'n'blues artists began to attract white record-buyers, these companies began the practice of 'covering'. It appeared preferable to have their white artists 'tone down' the extremes of black music in offering their own versions, than for black artists, who recorded mostly on small labels, to enter the large, white consumer market. This practice appears to have begun by accident, when the Crew Cuts covered the Chords' 'Sh'Boom' in 1954, but by the later 1950s it was common practice. Then, during 1958–59, the leading figures were, for various reasons, removed from the scene: Buddy Holly died; Elvis Presley entered military service; Little Richard entered the ministry; Chuck Berry entered jail; Jerry Lee Lewis entered just the first of his periods of absence from the public eye through scandal. This left the field open for a new product, 'rock and roll' (note the legitimization of the term through correcting its spelling), 'High School' (Paul Anka, Bobby Vee), and a new generation of insipid material. Black artists became even more marginalized, their essential contribution unrecognized. In Johnny Burnette's 'You're 16, you're beautiful and you're mine' (1960), the 32-bar song format, the formulaic cadence redolent of Tin Pan Alley, the orchestra (there is no interplay with the singer), the choral backing and the weak shuffle rhythm all typify the approach. A similar dissipation took place in the UK, as rock'n'roll and skiffle (largely originated by Lonnie Donegan, below) gave way to Tommy Steele, Adam Faith and Marty Wilde. While country music, gospel and rhythm'n'blues, and even what becomes 'easy listening' (Frank Sinatra, Bobby Darin, Tom Jones) continue their own paths through the 1960s and beyond, the most significant developments come through the music of youth culture.

Indeed, one of the most unlikely developments in post-war popular music was surely the popularity of what was called 'folk' music. Within the determinedly modernist, consumerist immediate post-war period, what was this fascination with the self-conscious archaisms of the folk movement? At the beginning of the twentieth century, in line with similar developments in Europe and North America, musicians such as Ralph Vaughan Williams, Gustav Holst and Cecil Sharp renewed the nineteenth-century practice of collecting examples of 'dying' rural music and dance, but instead merely of preserving it in library collections, they repackaged it for middle-class audiences via concert hall rewritings, or as material for schools or drawing-room performance, thus initiating the 'folk revival'. In the process, they dramatically affected the identity of what they were collecting, but that's another story.[22] Almost all of what they collected became transmitted in written form, but a few very early recordings exist (such as those of Joseph Taylor, recorded by Percy Grainger in Lincolnshire in 1908), which themselves helped to spur the 'second folk revival' of the late 1950s and 1960s.

This music doesn't become particularly relevant to this story until that second revival, initiated by the collecting and broadcasting activities organized by the BBC from the 1940s (the role of a 'national music' supporting the 'national identity' in crisis times of war is always important) and developed by musicians such as Ewan MacColl and A.L. (Bert) Lloyd. In the USA, it paralleled the beatnik movement and the acoustic, folk and protest songs of Woody Guthrie and Pete Seeger, and the 'folk blues' of Leadbelly and Brownie McGhee. On both sides of the Atlantic, they were strongly political movements, the first associated with the Campaign for Nuclear Disarmament and the second with unionization activities: the collector Alan Lomax was an important catalyst in both movements. What MacColl and Lloyd enabled was what is conventionally called 'folk', best exemplified in the work of Martin Carthy. A comparison of his 'Brigg Fair' with that originally recorded by Joseph Taylor in 1908 demonstrates a similar liking for vocal shaping, but with an additional incorporation of a rudimentary harmonic accompaniment, which actually develops by way of skiffle and some of the pre-war American country guitarists. It was only later that Carthy, particularly alongside John Renbourn and Bert Jansch, would develop the classic 'English' linear style of guitar playing (so different from the original US strumming style), which owes much to the Elizabethan style of lute playing, combined with a peculiarly English approach to the blues guitar, the brainchild of Davey Graham. Although these revivalist singers relied on traditional repertory, much of it was re-written (thus promulgating the tradition) and has a biting political edge (e.g. the songs of gender reversal, such as 'Sovay' recorded more than once by Carthy). A rich version of this guitar style is well explored by Scots singer Dick Gaughan. His 'Erin-go-bragh' is an equally political promotion of internationalism. And, like other 'old' styles, blues and gospel, 'folk' remains very much alive, in the hands of singers like Eliza Carthy, for example, whose *Angels and Cigarettes* threatened to cross over to the mainstream (although *Anglicana* is more representative of folk directions in the new century). What is particularly important here, perhaps, is the influence of music from the Celtic periphery. I shall return to this when addressing 'world music' below but, for now, I note simply the impact traditional dances and songs have always had on 'Celtic' musicians – Elvis Costello is only one of the most notable examples. Bands such as Capercaillie, Shooglenifty or Wolfstone (Scotland), Altan or Clannad (Ireland) and Fairport Convention, Steeleye Span, the Albion Band, the Oysterband and recently the Imagined Village (England)

---

[22] For very different views, see Georgina Boyes, *The imagined village: culture, ideology and the English Folk Revival* (Manchester, 1993) and Rob Young, *Electric Eden: unearthing Britain's visionary music* (London, 2010).

have all managed to combine features of mainstream rock (and sometimes even electronic dance music and other traditions) with traditional instrumentation and material in almost seamless webs. This is to move ahead of the historical account, however. Martin Carthy, like others of his generation, had been led to rediscover this British heritage through 'skiffle', a development for which we have to go back to the jazz age.

Jazz in the UK has almost as long a history as in the USA. The first US jazz recording was that by the Original Dixieland Jazz Band (whites of Italian extraction in New Orleans) in 1917. In 1919, they toured England and begat imitators. When swing became popular, the style was current also in England. Likewise in the 1940s, when the Dixieland revival took off, it was popular also in the UK. One of the major figures, Chris Barber, who led his 'Jazz & Blues Band' cut an album with 1954 with two songs by banjo player Tony Donegan (later Lonnie, after country blues singer Lonnie Johnson). These had an accompaniment only of strummed guitar, bass and washboard, and they formed a popular interlude within Barber's live shows. Due to public demand, Donegan's songs were released on singles and 'skiffle' (the first of the 'garage band' styles) was born, almost by accident.[23] 'Rock island line' made the charts in both the USA and the UK in 1956, only months before 'Heartbreak Hotel'. On his own, Donegan plundered the folk heritage of the USA, particularly that of Leadbelly and Woody Guthrie. Although short-lived, skiffle was an almost universal craze, the training ground for musicians as varied as Martin Carthy and John Lennon. 'Donegan's place with Barber was taken by the 30-year-old Alexis Korner, a musician who emphasized the 'blues' in Barber's band. Korner and Barber were responsible for bringing to the UK such singers as Muddy Waters, Bill Broonzy, Sonny Terry and Brownie McGhee, and recorded standards such as 'I got my Mojo workin' in the early 1960s. This itself is a complicated story, because in the USA, these musicians had used electric instruments for some years, but in the UK the audiences demanded acoustic guitars, corresponding to their idealized images of blues players. The tours were ignored by the British music establishment, as in the USA, but were accepted by young art-college musicians, unlike in the USA. This enabled the musicians who would form the Rolling Stones, the Beatles and the Yardbirds to hear the music at first hand. Indeed, it formed the vital feature of the style of the 'British invasion' bands of 1964. The Stones' first single ('Come on', from 1963) was actually a Chuck Berry song.

It was this first-hand (if attenuated) experience of the blues that was crucial in the establishment of what was originally known as 'beat' music, calling attention to what appeared its most prominent feature. The term 'British invasion', which is used in the USA, comes from the tours of the USA made by the Beatles, Kinks, Rolling Stones, Dave Clark Five, Herman's Hermits and other bands who swept the country in 1964 and begat US imitators. The Kinks were important for songs using

---

[23]   Young, *Electric Eden*, p. 160, argues for an equally important root in the music of John Hasted (nowadays an entirely forgotten figure).

a 'riff'; 'You really got me' (1964) set a practice that would become definitional of rock guitar by the turn of the decade. The singer/songwriter conflation of roles became particularly prominent in the 'British Invasion' bands, as the developed skiffle of Cliff Richard and the Shadows became beat (particularly in the Beatles and other Lancashire bands). In addition to acting as the impetus for skiffle, Chris Barber's 'Trad' jazz band provided the spawning ground for the British blues boom of the late 1950s (John Baldry, Graham Bond, Alexis Korner) and thence, via John Mayall, to the guitar heroes of the mid-1960s (Jimmy Page, Peter Green, Eric Clapton, Jeff Beck). This period's initial importance lies in its temporary reversal of the flow of stylistic traffic, from the UK to the USA, but it had a greater role, in that it was the route by which US Americans came to see and accept their musical heritage. After all, by the mid-1960s, African Americans had come to despise the blues and its accommodatory message in favour of soul and the protestant ethic it embodied (not only 'things will improve' but 'I can help improve them'). As an indicator of the importance of these 'British invasion' bands, there was only 1 UK hit in the US charts in 1963, but 32 in 1964.

The Beatles were certainly the most important of these bands, for three specifically musical reasons. The first was the fusion of styles they encompassed. By 1964, their range of material sets them apart both from other Liverpool 'beat' bands and from bands in other parts of the country. The early style represented an easy amalgam of the range of largely black styles they were interested in emulating (soul, Motown, pop and soul ballad, rock'n'roll, rockabilly), but 'reorchestrated' for their own forces, such that the rich range of horns, pianos, organs, orchestral strings and the like (all of which are there either to fill out harmonies or to play melodic ideas) become transposed to the guitar, either rhythm or, occasionally, lead.[24] This instrumentation (lead, rhythm and bass guitars, drum kit, lead and backing vocals but with no keyboard instrument) was derived from skiffle via the Shadows and became the bedrock of British rock until the partial demise of the rhythm guitar with the birth of heavy rock (Jimi Hendrix, Eric Clapton). The amalgam emphasized a number of elements from rock'n'roll and, ultimately, the blues: texture, melodic structure and pentatonicism, rhythm, vocal style (impersonal and using responsorial textures), combined with elements probably derived from Anglo-Celtic folk song; diatonic (and frequently modal, marked by the flattened seventh) melodies and verse-refrain form, and elements from more advanced western harmony; ornamental chromaticisms together with triadic parallelism, ostinati and modal progressions challenging any secure sense of key. The second reason was the changing relationship between songwriter and performer. Prior to the Beatles, the division of labour between songwriter and performer had been almost complete (the examples of Chuck Berry, Buddy Holly and Bobby Darin only demonstrate how rare the composer/performer was). It still remained throughout 1960s and 1970s in what tended to be labelled 'pop'. The band's experiences of playing standards in Hamburg emphasized playing as a unit:

---

[24]   Moore, *Rock*, pp. 71–2.

the raucousness and physicality (together with the cheeky irreverence, source of Beatlemania), unsullied by the British entertainment establishment, encouraged them to try their hand at writing for themselves – the first five albums have a slight majority of their own compositions. The final feature was the historical recovery of rock'n'roll. This was a style that had died as far as the public were concerned, especially in the USA. The impact of the Beatles there was thus not far short of that of Elvis Presley, felt especially strongly among musicians in New York and Los Angeles dissatisfied with the demise of the energy of rhythm'n'blues. The clearest early example is 'She loves you' (1963), containing a standard form and instrumentation, energetic performance and melody, with a blues inflection on iv⁻, although the track that initiated their North American popularity was the eager innocence of 'I want to hold your hand'.

In the UK, the Beatles and the Rolling Stones came to symbolize the distinction between 'pop' and 'rock' as separate (stylistic) categories. At this period, the Beatles were regarded largely as 'pop' – introvert, evolutionary and sensitive – while the Rolling Stones were 'rock' in their extrovert, revolutionary, macho pose. That distinction became symbolized in their repertoires' attitudes to interpersonal relations: other-centred ('All you need is love') or self-centred ('I can't get no satisfaction'). It is because this position was so ingrained that the effect of psychedelia in 1966–67 is so marked – it was the experience of LSD that led songwriters and singers to view situations from the outside, thus the Beatles' 'Penny Lane', and the Kinks' 'Waterloo sunset'. The birth of this 'new' popular music coincided with the election of Harold Wilson's Labour government, with its slogans insisting on the 'white heat of technological revolution', the popular 'I'm backing Britain' with its gently nationalistic overtones, the rise of 'swinging' Carnaby Street, together with the 'cheeky' valorization of youth, as in the Small Faces' 'Lazy Sunday'. With this, we move on to the development of 'flower power' and the hippy movement, whose other roots lie well into the past and the flowering in New York and Los Angeles of the singer-songwriter, on the back of the folk boom.

Folk music in the USA has a very long history – after all, its initial roots are in the British vernacular song that was first taken over by settlers from the 1620s onward. On more than one occasion, it has combined with other tendencies to produce new styles – most notably, and perhaps controversially, that of the blues. The modern US American folk movement dates back to the 1930s, the later war years and strong unionization activities, and is marked by singers such as Woody Guthrie and later Pete Seeger, Leadbelly, and Sonny Terry and Brownie McGhee. What was important in this genre was a song's vocal content and manner of delivery. When electric-based urban blues replaced the solo guitar country blues (of e.g. Robert Johnson), those few who retained acoustic instruments attracted an air of 'authenticity'. Add this to the realistic subject matter of songs and you have a music that attracted a mostly white, college-educated, often politically left-wing audience. Not surprisingly, someone like Guthrie was suspect in the McCarthy era with such outrageous, clearly 'communistic' notions as 'This land is your land',

and so on. Pete Seeger had even more problems with such apparent obscenities as 'We shall overcome', 'If I had a hammer', or 'Where have all the flowers gone'. That this had sown the roots for the 1960s protest movement was made clear with Bob Dylan's arrival in the popular consciousness in 1962. Here, at least, one branch of popular music was only partially intended as entertainment. The details of the words of a song like 'The times they are a-changin'' were paramount, full of social comment, and important to a degree not seen in earlier song. In the UK, this style was associated with the marches of the Campaign for Nuclear Disarmament. Songs like these early ones of Dylan's demand interpretation and mental (rather than just physical) response. Dylan was questioning, probing, requiring his audience's active participation. Bob Dylan's (and The Band's) electrification provided the impetus for the beginnings of folk-rock in the UK (Fairport Convention, Steeleye Span), frequently through Scottish musicians (Bert Jansch, Robin Williamson). Although this history is complicated, frequently such musicians considered themselves rock (Fairport Convention) or jazz (Pentangle) musicians, who happened to play some folk songs, rather than vice versa.[25] Both Dylan's influence, and that of the 'beat poets' were crucial in the development of the entire singer/songwriter genre, epitomized by Joni Mitchell, James Taylor and Paul Simon. Again, as with all these genres that typify a byegone era, there are more recent examples. One I find particularly interesting is that of Suzanne Vega, whose 1985 debut contained the song 'The Queen and the soldier', which owes much in its tone and plot (although with a stunning twist) to eighteenth-century ballads. Seth Lakeman's recent 'The charmer' exemplifies a more recent upgrade to this approach.

Within the less-politicized UK, such songs quickly turned toward the whimsy that ushered in flower power. For the Incredible String Band, on a track like 'Gently tender', this was accompanied by oriental instruments and strange syllabic stresses, giving rise to a sense of 'intimate otherness' that was crucial to the hippy experience. It reaches a powerful expression in the expatriate Hendrix, where it carries the sense of his (or his songs' protagonists) being simply uncontainable by established society: 'If 6 was 9' is the archetypal example (which I address in Chapter 10), while 'Little wing' eulogizes an aspect of his American Indian heritage. One of the most fundamental divides in popular music exists between music that invites you to think, as did early Dylan, or this Hendrix (and as will 'progressive rock' in a moment) and music that invites you to dance. This division was present in early blues performance where the singer, acting as the voice of the community, tended to be listened to by that community. It was also present in jazz in the hand-over of swing (which was danced to) to bebop (which was not). This division became hardened in the 1960s and it has remained important ever since. It was there in the British appropriation of US-American blues in an early attempt to make 'authentic' music. The fundamental problem associated with the English 'blues revival' of 1960s was an atavistic urge – the notion that US blacks lived an

---

[25]   Robert Burns, *Transforming folk* (Manchester, 2011).

ideal existence that could be appropriated by appropriating their music, illustrated in a track like Cream's 'Spoonful'.[26]

So, by the time hip white British (urban) audiences had caught on to the blues, and were listening to Cream, black US audiences had moved on. In the USA, black labels would occasionally manage to break out of the confines of the black market and cross over into the 'mainstream', although still servicing their original market. Soul really developed out of Ray Charles' 1950s synthesis of secularized gospel with rhythm'n'blues, initially in 'What'd I say' (1959), and in the work of Sam Cooke. Strangely, Charles was equally at home with country and with standards; his soul style led to the Memphis style of the 1960s, typified by Stax Records. King Curtis' 'Memphis soul stew' (1968) typifies the concise, recipe-style guide to the layered Stax sound, using 'balling Memphis guitars' and the country and western licks essential to soul. It contains a stuttering, highly syncopated sax over 12-bar verses. The Stax and Muscle Shoals soul studios of Memphis were white-dominated, but always fronted by black singers; they enjoyed the patronage of Atlantic Records as the source of an 'authentic' Southern sound, to sell as such to a 'cross-over' international market. The style depended on a home-made pasting together of various overlaid tracks – a procedure that was to prove universally highly influential. The big names – Aretha Franklin, Otis Redding, Solomon Burke – were all directly influenced by hard gospel singers. Rough and ready production could work with a good singer, such as the gospel/country mix of Shirley Brown's 'Stay with me baby', with touches of diminished chordal harmony and extended, climactic upbeats into choruses. The odd hypermetre is exacerbated by the slow § metre and second beat beginnings of vocal phrases. There are also country guitar licks and falling cadential scales with gospel hollering. With a more mainstream label (as in Lorraine Ellison's hair-raising 1966 recording), the whole production grows in size and sentimentality.

Whilst Curtis Mayfield produced a cleaned-up version of soul in Chicago, Tamla Motown, the Detroit black-owned record company, was determined to produce quick-change smash song-and-dance acts for integrated audiences (the Supremes, the Four Tops, the Temptations), whilst also enabling individual artists to develop their own, more sophisticated songwriting styles (Smokey Robinson, Stevie Wonder). Motown moved out of a 'blues' aesthetic into an era dominated by civil rights, in which black listeners sensed an empowerment through black artists taking control of mainstream styles and moulding them to their own ends. At one extreme (Diana Ross and the Supremes' 'Where did our love go' of 1964, for instance), this helped constitute mainstream pop at the time. Other writers had a harmonic palette subtly richer, from Smokey Robinson's occasional forays into jazz harmony ('Tracks of my tears') to Stevie Wonder's employment of rich chromaticisms even in his most popular material ('For once in my life') to the Four Tops' ambiguous key centres ('Reach out and I'll be there'). This brand of soul, albeit with a punchier rhythm line better geared to dancing (such as Jackie Lee's

---

[26]   Moore, *Rock*, pp. 73–5.

'The duck'), would become vital in Northern English clubs (Wigan, Manchester) throughout the later 1960s and 1970s, away from the influence of London. Things changed at Motown from the late 1960s: the Holland–Dozier–Holland songwriting and production team was largely replaced by the psychedelic-tinged sounds of Norman Whitfield; from the early 1970s Michael Jackson developed his cross-over rock style into a financially massive success; Marvin Gaye's 'social conscience' songs remained within the black market. At this other extreme, we find links with the psychedelia that had developed out of rock (and which Jimi Hendrix also exemplifies). Marvin Gaye also invokes a sense of timelessness and produces some of the 'trippiest' pop music ever, barely held together by slow string lines and a vague improvised flute and alto sax. A track like 'Wholly holy' is, however, intensely politically aware, making explicit its origins in black ghetto slang.

During the mid 1960s, another Southerner, James Brown, was leading rhythm'n'blues through soul into funk, igniting a new craze (matched by the Bar-Kays in Memphis, Sly Stone in San Francisco, the Meters in New Orleans). Brown's version of this style, often called either 'acid soul' or, later 'funk' emphasizes the rhythm that had been so much at a discount in Gaye. In Brown's 'Say it loud, I'm black and I'm proud', the politicized line, in the sense of a separatist tendency, is more apparent. The West Coast, however, influenced by the psychedelia associated with the hippies, developed a laid back version of funk. This had greater degrees of improvisation, including in the bass, and more harmonic movement. Brown's obsession with accenting the second beat is replaced, in Sly and the Family Stone's 'Luv'n'Haight', by a looser conception where anything can be accented. Other than this hippie link, black music continued very much on its own way, with other versions of funk dominant. The New Orleans-based Meters were voted the best R&B instrumental group in 1969. They revived the old polyphonic improvisation of early New Orleans jazz – 'Rigor mortis' is the extreme point. It has a 4-bar metrically indecipherable introduction. Then four two-bar 'A' riffs, one two-bar 'B', two 'A', two difficult two-bar 'C', two more 'A' then a break down into free, second-line improvisation. A softer version of this style has long been popular in the shape of the Neville Brothers. George Clinton developed in a different direction, transforming his gospel/doowop group in 1969 into two bands: Funkadelic and Parliament. The latter was the more sophisticated, with complex arrangements and extended structures, containing multiple vocal groups, keyboards and drummers in repeated but varied 8-bar blocks, with blocks of intervening material, as in 'Just one of those funky things'. He acquired the services of James Brown's highly influential bassist Bootsy Collins in 1974.

The distinction between Motown and funk parallels the distinction, in Anglophone popular music since the Beatles, between 'pop' and 'rock'. The first carries connotations of commercialism, the second of authenticity. The distinction is frequently moot, but what matters is that the music enables these senses to be constructed. 'Pop' as a term first becomes important in the 1960s, and it becomes vital to distinguish 'pop' from 'popular'. The shortened form was coined as slang, to find an apt adjective to describe music of people who were 'groovy', 'with it'.

Most writers don't problematize a term that probably originated from 'pop art', originally coined in 1954. The songs and vocal styles of a previous generation of singers (Alma Cogan and Dinah Shore, Guy Mitchell and Dean Martin, Bing Crosby and Louis Armstrong) changed little as a new generation (Petula Clark, Engelbert Humperdinck) came to prominence. TV variety shows (Cliff Richard in the UK, Andy Williams in the USA) provided an important, parent-oriented outlet linking 'music' to 'entertainment' via 'humour'. In the UK, the Light Programme and then BBC Radio 2 was precisely marketed to this audience: *Music While You Work*; *Two-way Family Favourites*; *The Billy Cotton Band Show*. Acker Bilk cunningly combined 'Trad' jazz with the Edwardian fashions of the Teddy Boys and the growing mass popularity of TV, as UK popular musicians' allegiances shifted from Equity (the actors' union) to the Musicians' Union, in parallel with a shift of capital from music publishers to record companies.

Prior to the hippies (c.1967), and with a long hangover after, we can distinguish at least four broad categories of British pop. First, there is the continuation of the mainstream pre-rock'n'roll, which includes show tunes and updated versions of the Tin Pan Alley system. Ballads remained very popular, aimed at an older demographic, and dominated by a particular orchestration: strings, choir, an occasional 'wild' muted trumpet, gospel piano, careful voice. Henry Mancini and Burt Bacharach were key composers (and the distinct roles of composer, lyricist and singer were maintained). Even by 1964, the influence of black US music as filtered through singers like Doris Day can be heard. Each verse of Petula Clark's 'Downtown' (1964) rises to a climax – a little drama. It is clearly mainstream, containing an approving reference to 'bossa nova'. Second, there is music that, instrumentally, has borrowed from rock'n'roll (an emphasis on guitars, bass, drums, often with piano, but sometimes with an orchestra in attendance), and is harmonically and melodically uncomplicated. The Four Pennies' 'Juliet', also from 1964, is very underplayed. The fragile voice and accompaniment, the strange use of the word 'reminiscent', and the careful positioning of backing vocals create an insipid version of what the Beatles were doing. The verse has three strains; chromaticisms at the beginning of the third point away from black music towards light music, with links back to music hall. Mainstream pop ballad singers like Elton John develop in large part from these two roots, although often with a hint of gospel in their makeup. Third, there is music that incorporates US forms (either from soul or country), but whose sensibility is pop. Amen Corner were a Welsh band with strong soul influences on horns and organ. 'Bend me shape me', from 1968, contains a prominent and mobile bass, a fluid vocal with tiny anticipations and syncopation, frequently anticipating the third beat of the bar. The fourth category will prove to be particularly influential. Again the instrumental basis is rock'n'roll, but the pose is not the macho one of rock. Although the Kinks began as a 'beat' band, by 1967 they had begun singing songs focused very much on everyday, but 'altered' reality (a frequent experience under LSD was that the 'ordinary' tended to become 'marvellous'). 'Waterloo sunset' can be seen as a forerunner of that hippy aesthetic. Note that the subject matter is 'realist' (describing the sky over

London, and the rush-hour crowd) rather than the 'fantasy' of personal emotion. In addition, it is self-penned (the influence of the Beatles); the song's fragility has a solid core because of the 'realism'. The Jam and, later, Blur and Pulp offered a continuation of this aesthetic, albeit within different sound-worlds.

Psychedelia in the UK was divided between the acoustic (Incredible String Band, Tyrannosaurus Rex, Donovan), and the electric (Pink Floyd, Jimi Hendrix, Tomorrow). In the USA, psychedelic bands tended to combine electric and acoustic instruments (Love, the Doors, the Grateful Dead). Musically, key was an emphasis on strange and distorted sounds and sound-worlds, and on (now rather crude) technological sound manipulation, from guitar feedback through to phasing. On both sides of the Atlantic this music was crucial in the development of the free festival, and was often determinedly strange in terms of exotic instrumentation, obscure words and shifting metres. It was this seriousness, this apparent refusal of overt commercial strategies, which was first clearly identified by the term 'rock'. Psychedelia largely paved the way for progressive rock, which developed technologically, conceptually and stylistically on both sides of the Atlantic from its roots in British 'progressive pop' (the Beatles, Procol Harum) through to a range of mature exponents (Captain Beefheart, Frank Zappa, Genesis, Gentle Giant, Caravan, King Crimson, Focus). There are links to hard rock on the one hand (Deep Purple, Led Zeppelin), to art rock on another (Yes, Emerson, Lake and Palmer (ELP), National Health) and also to both a more radical, partially improvised music that was barely 'popular' at all (Henry Cow, Soft Machine, Faust, Can, Gong), and a new aggressive, mainstream genre – heavy metal – which became popular in the extreme (Black Sabbath, Steppenwolf).

Within the popular song of the last six decades, innovation has tended to come from two alternating tendencies. The first is greater simplification ('folk' was musically simple, 'hit parade pop' is lyrically simple, 'punk' was technologically simple). The second is greater sophistication (e.g. Dylan again, but in the realm of lyrics). From the late 1960s, technological sophistication (and arguably musical sophistication) becomes common. This came first and most notably to the fore in Beatles' album *Sgt. Pepper's Lonely Hearts Club Band* of 1967, which marks the first time that popular music built a unity greater than that of the individual, self-contained, utterance, and also the first time that live performance became irrelevant to the experience of music. This was music which only existed on record, and therefore required a whole new listening experience. The drive to 'unity' was a development that has had a limited life-span, as the growth of internet downloads has encouraged a return to concern with the individual track. But let us see briefly how *Sgt. Pepper* marked this change. The album's 13 songs are 'set' within a non-musical context, i.e. an artificial (and intentionally so) attempt to create a live club setting. There is a bridge between the first two songs, challenging us not to perceive them as separate. There is also the reprise of the opening song as the penultimate song, thus creating a satisfying completion and possibly resolution of the album's dissonant ideas, and in the context of which the final song, 'A day in the life', operates outside the setting.[27] Even though previous albums had set a unified mood (notably Sinatra's *Songs for Swinging Lovers*), it was on the basis of the influence of *Sgt. Pepper* that the penchant for the concept album was born. Things might have looked very different had Brian Wilson and the Beach Boys managed to complete the album *Smile* at the time. Judging by its eventual appearance, it would have suggested an entirely different possible line of development for the concept album, wherein parts of tracks reappeared in others producing a form frankly far more sophisticated than any of its contemporaries.

It should be clear by now that, although this history appears to offer a roughly chronological succession of styles, there is no single, linear history to that thing we call *popular song*. Different publics coexist in the same time and place. The confusion surrounding these parallel developments (so many musics co-existing in the same geographical and historical locations) is brilliantly addressed by David Clarke,[28] where he argues that there are no easy responses to this situation. We can talk in terms of pairings of cultural positions: mainstream/margin; centre/periphery; established/underground. Sometimes it appears that there are only peripheries. Sometimes, audiences gravitate towards a centre. The most prominent period when this happened was in the early to mid 1960s when it seems that almost everyone, irrespective of age, class or cultural background, listened to the Beatles. But by 1970 this monolithic position had again broken down. Both the Edgar Broughton Band's 'Apache dropout' and Edison Lighthouse's 'Love grows' were released in 1970, with strong Midlands/London connections, and both were audible on the same radio stations, but were operating according to very different aesthetics. Both the 'underground' and the 'establishment' intersect their listening publics; this was made particularly clear in the career of Marc Bolan, originator of key underground band Tyrannosaurus Rex, who later became key teenybopper T.Rex.

By this year, 1970, the stage had been set for the possibility of a move for popular song from the self-contained, three-minute love song, produced for purposes of entertainment alone, into new means of expression. Parallel developments had appeared earlier; when jazz began to take itself seriously (as swing gave way to bop), much of the audience failed to move with the musicians, and critical reaction to 'progressive rock' has, until the last few years, certainly been ambivalent. Nonetheless, by 1970, it had become a major force. A number of factors contributed to its acquiring the 'progressive' label. Lyrics endeavoured in some cases to approach poetry, containing layers of meaning not immediately self-evident. Technology was used to harness new sounds (some originating with the

---

[27]   See Allan F. Moore, *The Beatles: Sgt. Pepper's Lonely Hearts Club Band* (Cambridge, 1997) and Allan F. Moore, 'The act you've known for all these years : a re-encounter with Sgt. Pepper', in Olivier Julien (ed.), *Sgt. Pepper: it was forty years ago today* (Farnham, 2008).

[28]   David Clarke, 'Elvis and Darmstadt, or: Twentieth-Century Music and the politics of cultural pluralism', *twentieth-century music* 4/1 (2007).

European avant garde), suggesting alternate realities (derived from psychedelia), and moving the music out of the reach of amateur and semi-professional performers. The music approached the condition of 'art': three-minute song structures were replaced by longer tracks and concept albums; some harmonic languages were imported from jazz and late nineteenth-century classical musics. The studio, rather than the stage, was beginning to act as a focus for musical activity, as albums began to replace singles as a focus for musicians, coinciding with a change of use from dancing to listening as middle-class markets were opened up. Studio sophistication and the apparent audience demand for 'radicalism' inherent in the protest movement allowed musicians space to develop an ideology of artistic freedom and self-expression, with freedom from the constraint of an immediate, dancing, audience. The musicians' ideology thus became integrated into the new youth ideology where 'doing your own thing' became the operative phrase. This pleased the major record labels – the term 'progressive' (connoting a concern with aesthetic rather than immediate qualities) helped them differentiate this product from 'commercial' pop, and service the very fast growing student market with their own separate 'progressive' labels. But none of this would have been possible were it not for the economic circumstances. The economic boom from the mid-1960s meant labels could afford to 'invest' in artists, giving them freedom to experiment, and assume limited control over their product and marketing, a situation that fell into abeyance between the late 1970s and the birth of internet stars. It is the end of the boom that makes progressive rock unfeasible, rather than the counteractive force of punk. The Beatles were vital in all this – they spread rock from its working-class roots to a college-base, helping the development of a college/university circuit that labels cashed in on. There are many examples of this apparent progress, from the Beatles' 'Revolution 9', Yes' Brahms arrangement ('Cans and Brahms'), King Crimson's avant garde improvisatory explorations ('Fracture'), Genesis' surreal narratives ('The musical box'), ELP's arrangements of Bartok, Moussorgsky, Copland, Janacek and, in 'Toccata', Ginastera. One of the most notable features is the disintegration of black US stylistic forebears; notwithstanding the 'British invasion', this is the first time since music hall that English popular music does begin to take on peculiarly English characteristics.

While progressive rock pursued an somewhat intellectualized course, there remained a large listening space between this and the 'pop' identified above. 'Pop' became a stylistic term that takes a number of routes, whether adventurous in terms of construction (the Beach Boys) or in terms of production (Phil Spector), or more 'conservative' (Barry Mann and Cynthia Weil and the development of Brill Building techniques), from which develops the 'manufactured' pop group (the Monkees) and the solo singer/songwriters not wedded to a 'contemporary folk' aesthetic (Elton John, Carole King). These styles were treated with irony by the British art school movement in the early 1970s in glam rock (Roxy Music, David Bowie, Queen), partly through over-emphasis of its distinctive features, in particular its focus on rich instrumental timbres. This began a period that saw: the centralization of production companies and conservatism in the face of the 1970s industrial crisis; the birth of Euro-Pop (Abba, Demis Roussos), and; a renewed interest in the 'teenybopper' (Gary Glitter, Bay City Rollers, the Osmonds) whose tastes were indulged by so many parents. For, if progressive rock was music for the middle class and the burgeoning student base (the period saw a dramatic increase in access to higher education across the UK), the working classes were often listening to pop in its form as 'glam rock' (Gary Glitter, Slade, the Sweet, initially David Bowie and even Queen), which in turn gave rise to a new set of standard tunes. Slade's 'Merry Christmas everybody', originally released in 1973, is still heard across the land every Christmas and has charted a number of times.

David Bowie's influence here was crucial. For him, 'changes' of image have been common, the notion that it is never the 'real' Bowie that we see and hear, but some particular persona he has adopted. At its time, this foregrounding of the persona (see Chapters 4 and 7) was a new development. Singers had always presented personae (think only of the debunking of 'nice man' Bing Crosby), but Bowie made this process explicit, in order to be able to play with it. Simon Frith insists:

> Bowie defined for a British pop generation what it means to be an artist. Previously, rock-and-roll fans admired honesty, direct passion, suffering, the ability to transmute feeling into a sort of misty imagery that hints at things that can be known but never said. Bowie's message, by contrast, was that what really mattered was complete control – control of the means of artistic production, control of the means of emotional production, too. Bowie had invented himself, so his 'honesty' was not an issue.[29]

This is a fundamental point in popular culture generally. In 'Kooks', his cultivated strangeness (the couple and their kid against normality), his evident being 'not in control' (of everybody else in the scenario) but the necessity to carry on anyway, marks the willing 'outsider'. The style is country (which has always connoted 'real life' even if it doesn't live it) plus honky tonk piano and strings. 'The Jean Genie', a song of transgression, is couched as a talking blues (again, 'real life'), complete with blues harp, boogie guitar and stomping beat (cf. 'glitter rock'). Note the final phrase 'loves to belong' – Bowie's wilfully obscure sexuality added to his notoriety.

Two other styles, however, grew as important alternatives to progressive rock. The first, disco, was roundly condemned by the next 'big thing', punk, while the second, heavy metal, provided important influences. The term 'disco' develops from French 'discothèque', a common enough venue in the 1960s, but it underwent a boom in New York in the mid-1970s; the emphases on the body, on display (with heavy sexual connotations), and on democratized spectacle (anyone could be a 'Saturday night hero') are particularly important. The style marked a recovery of

---

[29]   Simon Frith, 'Popular music 1950–1980', in George Martin (ed.), *Making music* (London, 1988), p. 42.

the notion of dancing rather than listening, and a corresponding importance on the quality of the groove, its regularity and the subtlety of its execution. And it is in disco that open-ended repetitive gestures come into their own, where divisions into discreet sections (verse, chorus) begin to become irrelevant.

Tamla Motown's success had inspired a white-owned copy-company, Philadelphia ('Philly') Records, who foregrounded black artists (the Three Degrees, the Ojays, Harold Melvin and the Blue Notes) for an integrated market. In the mid-1970s, disco took off from the commercial orientations of both Motown and Philly, but combined these with the bass-heavy dance rhythms of soul and early funk (George McCrae, Gloria Gaynor, Donna Summer) and Latin rhythms originally from Cuba and Puerto Rico, while the repetitive structures of James Brown are also vital. This was very much part of the gay scene in the USA until the film *Saturday Night Fever* (1977) made it commercially viable and reproducible by artists in Europe. Producers (e.g. Giorgio Moroder) were very much to the fore, but this has always been a fairly common feature of black US musics anyway. George McCrae's 'Rock your baby' has a syncopated kit, 'sexy' high voice (connoting virility in black US music), light tone, strings, and a repetitive, funky high guitar comparable with West African playing. Even five years later, Anita Ward's 'Ring my bell' was very similar, with syncopation passed to guitar and with no strings.

Profusion

In many ways, the 1960s divide between pop and rock seems to have been played out yet again in the 1980s between the largely black music originating in disco, and heavy metal. The former is best exemplified by Michael Jackson, whose 40-million selling *Thriller* (1982) set new standards, not least in terms of the length and sophistication of the accompanying video. The notion of music for dance (even if vicarious) is uppermost. However, the development of heavy metal from hard rock since the early 1970s operates almost without reference to other moves in popular music, and spawns such signifiers as Soft Metal (Guns'n'Roses), Gothic (Mission), Thrash (Motorhead), Death Metal (Metallica), nu-metal (Limp Bizkit, Korn), symphonic metal (Nightwish, Rhapsody of Fire), progressive metal (Dream Theater, Amorphis) and a host of other insider categories where spectacle in performance practice is important, and where Anglophone lyrics are by no means the norm. The emphasis on big venues at the 'hard rock' end of the spectrum (Heart, Van Halen, Magnum) provides a point of contact with the Adult Oriented Rock (Foreigner, Kansas), and Classic Rock (the Eagles, Queen, Steely Dan) marketing tags. Investigation of these two categories (acknowledging that 'Classic Rock' means different things to UK and US readers) will argue that style definitions are more problematic, as idiolects tend to cross style boundaries.

Heavy metal developed particularly from working-class roots through the US Midwest and acted as a voice of teenage rebellion. By the 1980s, it had become the centre of rock culture. It had its origin in the initial fall-out from the counter-culture, taking its Romanticism towards an undisguised misogyny and 'cock rock'. The musical sources were already present in 1967/68 in some early Pink Floyd and Cream, in the blues roots of early Jimi Hendrix, Jethro Tull and Led Zeppelin, and also in the discursive structures of bands such as the Small Faces and the Rolling Stones. Indeed, Mick Jagger (following Muddy Waters) is almost the originator of 'cock rock'. But there are other important sources. The phrase 'heavy metal' comes from Steppenwolf's 'Born to be wild', made famous in Peter Fonda's cult film, *Easy Rider*.[30] The connotations of rootlessness and individual autonomy are crucial, especially to misogynism. In the UK, earlier to emerge was a curious kind of doom-laden, alienated, almost gothic music, which for a while was called 'heavy rock' – typified by early King Crimson and Van der Graaf Generator – which became absorbed under the 'progressive' tag. Another source originally came out of soul-based bands, but combined the organ with this type of virtuosic guitar, and often acquired the sense of doom too, as in Deep Purple. There were frequent detractors, often on grounds of the mindlessness associated with 'headbanging'. Metal is still an intensely formulaic style group, but this hides the immense subtlety possible, and is what makes it so musicologically interesting. The 'mindless' roots are typified in Black Sabbath's 'Paranoid' – an immobile bass, near-monotone of strained vocal, lack of subtlety, and infatuation with madness. Deep Purple's 'Smoke on the water' contains the archetypal 'riff', together with a heavy Hammond organ. Saxon's music is so chock-full of heavy metal formulae it can only be taken as irony. 'Midas touch' alternates a 16-bar intro/refrain/riff (in a aeolian) with an 8-bar half speed verse/riff (in e aeolian). The high strained voice has heavy vibrato implying 'drama', and supporting tongue-in-cheek lyrics: hackneyed words such as 'sentinel, Hades, final conflict, Armageddon' etc. 'Metal' has now become a rich meta-genre, as large and differentiated as 'rock' or 'dance'; the mainstream breakthrough for 'thrash metal' (and other types of 'speed' metal) was Metallica's *Master of puppets* (1986). Metal is highly influential on other genres – spectacular live shows made it a natural spectacle for television and MTV: Eddie Van Halen worked with Michael Jackson; Run-DMC brought metal guitar into hip-hop; pop singer Robert Palmer used the sound; even US army advertising used it when they claimed (I paraphrase slightly): 'Rebel, escape, become powerful: join the army!' By the turn of the century, metal had become a dominant form in many parts of the world, as it intersected with industrial, goth, hip-hop and other forms (nu-metal becomes a catch-all to describe much of this). As such, it has become a mobile style ideal for the expression of the negative emotions of late adolescence. That such a style remains popular with some older listeners may be read as a comment on their relation to the operation of late capitalist society.

What we now know as 'corporate rock' very much developed stylistically out of early metal – bands such as Boston, Foreigner, later Aerosmith, the recent Rolling Stones, Guns'n'Roses or Scorpions. Survivor's 'The eye of the tiger' is a

---

[30]   This is but one version of the term's source, but it is an effective one.

standard example, the theme song to Sylvester Stallone's *Rocky* movies. The song carries connotations of success against the odds, but achieved at a price (hence the aeolian mode): the unerring determination, the sense of not knowing when you're beaten, typical of Rocky. Formally we have two verses before the first chorus, interpolated pairs of bars, the rise to the climax, three types of material (an introduction and playout, a verse, and a chorus) all pretty standard for this style group. The kit playing is equally unsubtle.

It should be apparent from 'Paranoid' (above) that 'punk' did not arise out of nothing, any more than had rock'n'roll. Punk was, of course, the 1970s' next 'big thing', arising out of the distrust some musicians felt with both art rock and disco. Like both psychedelia and rock'n'roll, its initial public life was short, but, in its nihilism, it has been hugely influential. In both the UK and the USA, it originally represented a controversial, reductionist, 'anti-musical' backlash against disco, centralized Europop (and its unrelenting disco beat), and the more escapist side of progressive rock. In the USA, punk grew somewhat seamlessly from the decadent/ libertarian music of earlier, generally New York artists (Velvet Underground, Lou Reed, MC5) via newer acts (Iggy Pop, New York Dolls). To some extent these groups inspired the London scene, through the medium of Malcolm McLaren. Punk then caught fire in the UK in 1976, with additional influences including David Bowie and even the early Kinks (on the Sex Pistols, the Clash, the Damned). By mid 1976, the Sex Pistols had come out as clearly anti- art rock and disco, while we also saw pogoing and confrontational dressing, ultimately leading EMI to cancel the band's contract. As the movement went underground, it gave rise to a variety of experimental groups (Public Image Limited, the Fall, the Gang of Four) and a new 'folk' generation (the Pogues, the Men they Couldn't Hang). Meanwhile Stiff Records, though sharing certain punk features, employed far higher production values (Ian Dury, Nick Lowe, Elvis Costello). These latter groups shared Rock Against Racism platforms with British reggae and dub reggae artists (Linton Kwesi Johnson), and 2-Tone bands (Specials). From all these changes developed a new, supposedly working-class rock known as New Wave (the Jam), similar in style at least to contemporary US punk (Blondie, Jonathan Richman). The influence of both UK punk and thrash metal can be found in later post-punk outfits (the Dead Kennedys, Rancid, Garbage), and subsequently resurfaced in the 1990s (Green Day, Nirvana and the grunge movement) from which point it has become an easy style to appropriate, but without its original historical connotations.

The Sex Pistols are reckoned by some to be the only 'authentic' punk band. Here, the 'back to basics' slogan should be apparent, but what we get is a strange amalgam. 'Anarchy in the UK' has a normative ($\frac{4}{4}$) metre, a simple riff reaching the dominant at the mid-way point of the verse, a standard form and instrumentation, all of which are clearly rehearsed, denying the critical pose that wished to see them as somehow revolutionary, and that Dick Hebdige's tone so epitomized:

> There was a homological relation between the trashy cut-up clothes and spiky hair, the pogo and amphetamines, the spitting, the vomiting, the format of the

fanzines, the insurrectionary poses and the 'soulless', frantically driven music ...
they produced Noise in the calmly orchestrated Crisis of everyday life in the late
1970s – a noise which made (no)sense in exactly the same way and to exactly
the same extent as a piece of avant garde music ... more concisely: the forbidden
is permitted ... .[31]

The first successful single was the Damned's 'New Rose' (October 1977), a band
who typify the style's reckless humour (and also its contradictions). 'There ain't no
sanity clause' is notable for its speed, its catchy hook somehow ejected, its ringing
guitar and great harmonic sequence, and its topic (borrowed from Groucho Marx).

There are two important legacies from the age of punk. First is the rise of
independent labels, fanzines and distribution mechanisms. Second is the
reintroduction of overt radical politics into popular music, re-running beginnings
of the earlier folk revival. At its best, the energy of punk was still vital 20 years
on, even if it began as a 'get rich quick and anger a lot of people' ploy by Malcolm
McLaren. Note, for example, the way Elvis Costello harnesses the energy of the
style to the very clever lyrics of his 'No action', while After the Fire's 'Laser love'
exemplifies the mainstream new wave style, in its speed, use of synthesized sounds
that will become so important, the backing voices a seeming parody of 1960s
West Coast pop, the powerful chord sequence, and the strong guitar. And yet, we
are presented with a further problem in the relation between the message of the
lyrics and the connotations of the musical style. The new wave anti-establishment
message is found not only in its lyrics, but in the music – the raw energy, insistent
lack of sophistication and even technique. And in such things as Paul Weller's 'In
the city', recorded by his band The Jam, the message (both musically and lyrically)
is very clear and unadulterated. But then what do we make of Weller in later guise?
Sure, the message of the Style Council's 'Walls come tumbling down' is as clear
as ever, but what do we make of the musical style? The delineations of this (soul)
style include having fun, being unconcerned with everyday reality, working within
the system to improve oneself, and yet the lyrics talk of overthrowing the system
and everyday (in this case Thatcherite) reality.

In the wake of punk we come, I think, to perhaps the most fundamental
historical dividing line in recorded popular music. I mentioned earlier the lack of a
single, linear history. Nonetheless, as far as the end of punk in c.1978, it is possible
to construe things in the UK in more or less linear terms, as styles succeed each
other. Since then, it has become harder, and we have to realize that although we can
date the beginning of a particular style, we cannot date its end – there are places
in the UK, at least, where everything we have so far encountered is still being
played, live, in some venue or other, either by reconstituted or tribute bands, as a
style's *mannerist* phases elongate and sometimes petrify. This relates to the shift I
want to focus on. It is, ultimately, concerned with the rebirth of dance music and
'rave', to which I shall return. Musically, it concerns a rethinking of the way that

---

[31] Dick Hebdige, *Subculture*, (London, 1985), pp. 114–15.

composers, songwriters, inventors of music, conceive their music. Hiding behind this are a couple of useful labels to which I return in later chapters: 'authenticity' and the 'post-modern'. In order to underpin this pair, we need first to focus on the development of synthesizer rock and the 'techno' that developed from it.

For some critics, the rock era was effectively over with the death of punk and, throughout the earlier 1980s with the speedy development of the synthesizer, the electric guitar was clearly seen as an anachronism. Let Gary Numan's 'Cars' (of 1979) set the context. Note the thin texture, the flat vocal delivery, the valorization of alienation (cars as artificial and not made by human hands), the very sectional construction. This had been preceded by developments abroad, particularly in Germany. Tangerine Dream, a 'progressive' band, had pioneered the use of synthesizers live and with the 1974 release of *Autobahn* by Kraftwerk, techno appeared on the scene. As a forerunner to Gary Numan, the role of 'The robots' is clear. By this time, the synthesizer had become a staple of both disco, particularly in the work of producer Giorgio Moroder and hits such as Donna Summer's 'I feel love', and the post-new wave face of pop, bands such as Depeche Mode, the Eurythmics and the Human League. It had also penetrated straight pop, as I suggested with 'Laser love' earlier. However, by the mid-1980s, the combination of disco's syncopated beat, synthesizer and soul-ridden mobile bass were becoming basic to pop. Nik Kershaw was the best exponent (as on *The Riddle*), but Level 42's 'Physical presence' is a more typical example. By the early 1980s, the recourse to technology symbolized by the synthesizer had spread to the practice of 'scratching' (to use the original Jamaican term) and a re-positioning of the role of producer (as moulder of sounds) to DJ (as moulder of sounds). Alongside this development, the late 1980s saw the origination in two US cities of new styles: 'house' in Chicago and 'techno' in Detroit. The latter was industry-driven, while the dominant term 'house' came to be used as a replacement for 'acid house' once that term became unusable due to over-exposure in the media. Voices were very much at a discount, the emphasis was on the totally regular, if subtly inflected, beat. As it became transplanted onto British soil, 'Stakker Humanoid' by Humanoid (later Future Sound of London), underpinned by the particular timbral capabilities of the Roland-TR303, became the soundtrack to the 1988 second 'summer of love'. Black Box's 'Ride on time' (1989) stresses the more 'mainstream' (less exclusive) face of this style, and the stuttering quality of the vocal makes its treatment (through sequencing) highly audible (although to counter contemporaneous claims of plagiarism, which were becoming a new problem with the use of samplers, the band's 'singer' was reputed to have sung the part live, strange vocal mannerisms and all, a claim that is barely credible.) Aside from the influence of Kraftwerk, these electronic dance styles using synthesizers developed also from Giorgio Moroder's Europop (coming from Detroit techno), from the influence of Jamaican DJs on New York club culture (DJ Herc, Afrika Bambaataa), and were later influenced by practices at Mediterranean resorts. This international, racially opaque product has now attracted a plethora of labels or sub-styles: house, acid house, techno, hard-core, ambient, trance, trip-hop, gabba, jungle, drum & bass, with both 'populist' (Prodigy, Coldcut) and 'underground' (KLF, Tricky) faces. Distinctions among these depend on such features as the presence or absence of the $\frac{4}{4}$ kick drum, the transposition of normal kit patterns across other percussive sounds, particular models of synthesizer, and the explicit use of samples. Its mediation in the UK through club culture DJs (Carl Cox, Paul Oakenfold, Danny Rampling), has involved the emergence of a new indigenous black music scene.

The development of the sampler during the later 1980s continued to restore control to the 'composer' – even less was one dependent on instrumentalists and singers to interpret one's ideas (something that had come through the classical avant garde more than 30 years earlier). A good example of the full exploitation of this is the work of Prodigy, often hailed as combining the techniques of techno with the attitude of punk. 'No good (start the dance)' from 1994 samples a vocal hook from an old disco track, takes instrumental sounds from old analog synthesizers, uses a Roland drum machine and aesthetically seems to hint at 'trance'. Goldie has been widely recognized as among the most creative in the field. On 'Crystal clear', at least a dozen different lines (notably two bass lines, two keyboards, trumpet, kit, two voices) are dropped out at will, a device that is made easy structurally by the track being based on one repeating idea. At first, though, but for the kit, it sounds like standard pop soul. Goldie himself masterminds/produces the crossover between techno, jazz-funk, soul and is technically highly proficient, but at the computer rather than a conventional instrument.

For some audiences, and particularly for those attracted to early punk, both disco and some parts of progressive rock were marked by a distancing of the performer from concerns for self-expression. The duality *pop* and *rock* had been erected during the 1960s (but with roots traceable far earlier) on this distinction between those who were musicians from a sense of personal commitment, and those who were musicians for commercial reasons. However false this duality is under examination, it remains an assumption brought to listening by each generation of listeners. *Punk* brought this duality into a new focus, in that musicians felt bound to express their (and others') poor social situations and chose music to do so. And the legacy of punk diverged, moving in separate directions. One outflow was the rise of synthesizer pop (Human League, Eurythmics) and the brief flowering of the New Romantics (Boy George, Spandau Ballet, Adam and the Ants), which combined punk's nihilism with an irony inherited from glam. In the 1980s (Madonna, Wham!, Pet Shop Boys), this combined with earlier teeny-bopper styles to produce (in the 1990s) a range of 'bands' (effectively, singers) aimed at a junior (female) market, whether boy bands (Boyzone, Take That, Five), girl groups (Spice Girls, All Saints, Eternal, B*witched) and even mixed (S Club 7, Steps). Frequently an individual singer, rather than a group of musicians, became the focus of adulation, particularly where idiosyncratic vocal techniques were exploitable (Mariah Carey, Britney Spears, Macy Gray). The crucial issue here is the potential for cross-over into an adult market, successfully negotiated by Madonna, and more equivocally by George Michael or Robbie Williams. The other notable outflow was the rise of 'indie' and 'alternative' musics (usually labelled 'rock', but sometimes avoiding this label), which took their legitimacy from punk institutions and attitudes (the Happy Mondays), through to non-commodified music associated with UK free festivals (Crass, Ozric Tentacles) and busking. The US alternative scene moved from punk to the Pixies to R.E.M. and back (Dead Kennedys) through to grunge (Nirvana), which spawned Britpop (below). The 'alternative' scene incorporated something of a revitalization for progressive rock (Dream Theater, Flower Kings, Kaipa, Big Big Train, Thieves' Kitchen) and for 'interesting' bands who avoided the label (Radiohead, Spiritualized), and Contemporary Christian Music impacts from time to time on the mainstream (Iona, Delirious?).

And again, there was a middle path, as (those who began as) punk musicians attained a certain maturity. Although heavy metal had been around since the late 1960s, its stylistic rules were very tightly defined (and so close to self-parody), such that the rebirth of rock (in opposition to synthesizer-dominated popular music) was left to those bands who reinvented the electric guitar and wedded it to an ideal of authenticity, where music was produced by physical contact with a real instrument, as against the emotional sterility of the little 'black box', the synthesizer and sampler. For white urban bourgeois youth, the music of bands nominally from the Celtic periphery (U2, Big Country, The Alarm, Simple Minds, Matmatah) or socially disadvantaged areas of the USA (Bruce Springsteen) created a space within which escape to a pre-modern communitarian ideal became possible. This was achieved not only through guitar techniques, but through pentatonic formations, open-ended harmonic sequences and a sound-box full of sonic potential. In the work of (Irish) U2 until the turn of the decade, this was enhanced by lyrics that spoke of personal struggle, and by iconography concentrating on natural spaces and human scales. 'Where the streets have no name' exemplifies this. Within the work of Big Country (who were Scottish), there is an equivalent sense of space (e.g. 'I walk the hill'), lyrics talking of remotely inhabited landscapes, simple harmonic construction (I, IV, V), and a guitar riff apparently reminiscent of bagpipes.[32] Within the context of 'authenticity' in general, we must acknowledge that constructions of authenticity (of which this is only one, for white urban bourgeois youth) are socially made (see Chapter 9). A black, working-class US audience finds its authenticities elsewhere, for example, principally in rap. With the release of U2's *Zooropa* and *Pop*, of course, it appeared that the high ground of authentic rock had been relinquished and passed to the total nihilism of Seattle grunge (e.g. Nirvana's 'Lithium'), which in turn owed a great deal to punk in its attitude, as well as in the anger of its vocals and guitar playing. And by this time, the 'indie' roots of bands like U2 had been long forgotten, such that the authenticity they originally represented (and which has always underpinned their music) was being read as its very opposite.

---

[32]   Allan F. Moore, 'In a big country: the portrayal of wide open spaces in the music of Big Country', in Raymond Monelle (ed.), *Musica Significans: Proceedings of the 3rd International Congress on Musical Signification* (Chur, 1998).

Recent Times

There is another site within the music industry where values of 'authenticity' seem to be important, and that is 'world music'. The term itself is a new one, having been coined in 1987 by a group of UK record companies distributing 'ethnic' musics, in order to better define and therefore market their product by making it easier for record stores (for example) to categorize it.[33] A recent, rather effective definition notes its incorporation of both the local and the global, ideally pleasing all, defining 'world music' as 'local music from somewhere else'.[34] The emphasis is on opposition to 'corporate rock' or 'commercial pap' or whatever. One clear benefit is that it foregrounds the realization that popular music doesn't only come from the USA and the UK, although to be 'popular' it is necessary to be mass-mediated and, hence, to make use of the necessary recording and distribution technology, far less of which existed, until very recently, in advanced forms in the less developed southern continents.

Latin American rhythms have been familiar in the pop world at least since Ray Charles' 'What'd I say', and the I–IV–V–IV ('La Bamba') pattern which became ubiquitous. From the late 1950s, Trinidadian and Jamaican musics entered the style mix. The Beatles picked up on the Latin influences in the late 1950s and this had stretched to Indian music, particularly the use of the sitar, by the mid-1960s (as on 'Norwegian wood'[35]). Another way that non-Western musics entered popular music was through the exploitation of little-known musicians. Paul Simon's *Graceland* is the *sine qua non* of this, even though it is a very complex case.[36] An earlier example appears on 'The jungle line' (1975) by ex-counter-cultural folkie Joni Mitchell, who employs a backing track of drum music recorded by Burundi musicians in the 1960s. A third entry-point was provided by ethnic songs as a form of 'exotica'. 'Wimoweh', for example, written by Solomon Linda on the basis of a Zulu chant, was originally in the repertoire of US radical folk group the Weavers in the early 1950s, and was picked up by British heart-throb country-style singer Karl Denver, and recorded in 1961.

An important factor in the UK was the mass emigration from the Caribbean in the late 1940s for economic reasons. West Indians brought with them their own styles – initially most important was Trinidadian calypso but by the late 1950s, Jamaican styles took over. These reportedly developed from Jamaicans listening to US East Coast hard rhythm'n'blues on radios with very poor reception, and trying to copy what they (thought they) heard. Reggae, in particular, is important

---

[33]   Jan Fairley, 'The "local" and "global" in popular music', in Simon Frith et al. (eds.), *The Cambridge Companion to Pop and Rock* (Cambridge, 2001).

[34]   Based on the tag line for the magazine *fRoots*.

[35]   I recently heard, in the muzak in a local Indian restaurant, this song being played by an 'authentic' Hindustani ensemble …

[36]   Louise Gray, *The no-nonsense guide to world music* (London, 2009) offers a balanced analysis.

for its double backbeat, even in Bob Marley and the Wailers' somewhat sanitized 'No woman no cry'. Idiosyncratic Jamaican R&B was first named ska (Prince Buster, the Skatellites), then rock steady (Ken Boothe, Phyllis Dillon), then reggae (Bob Marley and The Wailers, Toots and the Maytals, Big Youth), in response to shifts of tempo, metric accent, texture and Rastafarian, pan-Africanist sympathies. The contributions of particular producers (e.g. Lee Perry) and session musicians (Sly Dunbar, Robbie Shakespeare) was vital. The style had widespread appeal to a partially integrated British audience and, although its creation of an identity for racist skinhead youth was ideologically problematic, it has continued to be appropriated as an oppositional genre in many parts of the world.

All these, however, merely paved the way. In 1983, Nigerian singer King Sunny Ade was signed to record label Island (already well-known for their roster of reggae musicians) and the world music explosion began. Later attempts to bring the music of developing countries into the mainstream have, however, been less successful. These began from the revitalization of 'folk' by punk input (the Pogues) in the late 1970s, its drift into a Celtic netherworld strongly associated with New Age ideologies (Enya, Clannad) and its subsequent mutation into World Music (what in the USA was termed 'World Beat'). Although starting simply as a marketing label, creating a small but determined Anglophone audience for non-Anglophone (initially typically African) musics, this has now taken on the characteristics of a genre. Particular communities intent on preserving a distinct ethnicity have occasionally generated styles that often promise to cross over into the mainstream, but without achieving massive exposure (bhangra in the UK, salsa and zydeco in the USA).

There are many issues of both cultural and political importance concerning world music, as well as the purely musical issues. Perhaps the most noteworthy feature is the range of what is covered, and the varying degrees of accommodation to Anglophone interests.[37] Some Asian music, for example, retains an orientalist quaintness. Sainkho's 'eerie' *Out of Tuva*, for instance, was a politically important (European/Belgian) release, for Tuva is a nation (although not a state) between Siberia and Mongolia, fighting for its own identity. African music is also vital, although this is largely a Francophone tradition, and France (the original colonial power in West Africa) has been its biggest market. Musically, however, Salif Keita's 'Mandjou' (1984) bears strong resemblance to some 1960s London R&B. The music of the Celtic world is both politically and musically interesting, partly in its role in the development of 'ambient' music. Enya's 'Orinoco flow' almost qualifies as 'New Age', but Celtic music can be extremely lively. The release that was no.1 in France during the summer of 1998 (Manau's 'Panique Celtique') is overtly and proudly Breton, and raps over samples of traditional Breton folk music, using the traditional instrumentation of biniou (a high-pitched bagpipe) and bombarde (a piercing, primitive oboe) together with an accordion. It demonstrates how 'impure' styles must be recognized as being nowadays. Even the most

---

[37]   Timothy Taylor, *Global Pop* (New York NY, 1997).

popular current 'authentic' recording of the old tune used by Manau (recorded by Ar Re Yaouank around 1996) supports these instruments with acoustic guitar and electric bass. In this context, we should note the popularity of recordings like the 1995 *Adiemus*. It is sung by a clearly South African singer (Miriam Stockley), in an invented language, and has New Age referents in its texture and harmonic language. It has been received as a classical cross-over, heavily promoted by UK independent classical station Classic FM (and perhaps this is because it is identified with its composer rather than its performers), although the musicians chiefly involved (Karl Jenkins and Mike Ratledge) led avant garde rockers Soft Machine in the 1970s.

By the early 1960s, a vital industrial shift had taken place, as commercial revenue from publishing sheet music was being replaced by revenue from selling recordings. This means that the 'product' rather than the 'idea' was what was becoming important, which in turn means that 'technology' gained a new prominence that remains to this day. It initially became important with the use of multi-track recording (which begins with Les Paul's experiments in the 1950s, becoming commercially viable in the later 1960s). Stereophonic reproduction in the 1960s led to the establishment of the 'diagonal mix' by the early 1970s, and the most important subsequent innovation has been that of digital recording (in the late 1970s, resulting in the first CDs in 1982) and sequencers. Conventionally, in popular music, although instruments may be recorded one at a time, a musical texture is 'composed' in its entirety. Working with sequencers, individual layers can be invented one at a time and then superimposed, as in Peter Gabriel's 'Rhythm of the heat' (see Chapter 2). His approach is to treat each percussion instrument separately rather than as a whole pattern conceived as a unity. It is a complex, layering technique rather than, as normal, conceiving the kit as a single instrument. The percussion texture is effectively *designed* at the sequencer rather than *written*. The notion of designing rather than writing can be traced back to Bowie's seminal influence when, through the 1970s particularly, he constantly redesigned himself as an artist, helping us to recognize the difference between a 'real artist' and the artist's 'persona' (of which more subsequently). The notion of designing texture a layer at a time is of course linked to the notion of designing the sound space. Multi-tracking and sophisticated access to stereophonic space allow sound to be placed precisely in depth and breadth – allowing complete separation of sound sources within a 'thick' texture, such as in Fleetwood Mac's 'Little lies' (see Chapter 2).

One of the most important aspects of this new aesthetic is that it crosses genre lines. 1980s metal band Def Leppard (and, more importantly, producer Mutt Lange) show the same sort of concern for textural placing on 'Love bites' (also from 1987). The space is 'designed'. The kit is central, the voice to one side balanced by the bass (with some special gaps at the bass end). The kit sounds very full, with audible lower harmonics. The guitars are positioned midway, tending to the top, encasing the whole texture. The cymbal chorus shifts sides. Heavy reverb prevents holes, even when we hear single guitar lines. Yet, fourth beats, ignored by all except snare, shoot like a bullet through texture, emphasizing the whole's potential emptiness. The same band's 'Animal' represents a real *tour de force* of guitar placements. As we come closer to the present, with the growth of sampling technology, what seems to be happening is that not only are musical elements 'designed' clearly in place (as I pointed out with Goldie), but references, meanings, are also potentially layered through virtuoso parodies, pastiches and quotations, as in Malcolm McLaren's 'House of the blue Danube', a usage commonly identified as 'post-modern'. This is also one way, I think, to make sense of techno (and jungle, drum'n'bass etc.). Such an understanding may also be important for rap, in its frequent usage of sampled backgrounds.

Two further black US groups of styles became important in the 1980s: rap and quiet storm. Both have had large influences on mainstream popular music (many 'pop' singles now include rapping), while quiet storm, which was basically a radio playlist term, rekindled the close relationship between pop and outgrowths of soul. As it became enriched and glamourized, hip-hop claimed close allegiance to ghetto streets.[38] Rap, from New York Sugar Hill (Grandmaster Flash, L.L. Cool J.) to Los Angeles Gangsta (Niggers with Attitude, Ice-T), eschews the vocal black US-American popular music tradition, and indeed most melody, in favour of electronic drum tracks, and samples from earlier styles (which, in the case of artists like Dr Dre, are always recorded anew). As for punks, street realities seemed too urgent for aestheticization. Rap has reincorporated melody in Garage and other hip-hop styles (Me'shell Ndegé Ocello, Mary J. Blige, Erykah Badu), although its earliest refusal of singing is confrontational, like that of punk and early rhythm'n'blues. Hip-hop represented the 'truth' not the 'art' of US ghettoes (where infant mortality has been worse than in Bangladesh). In 1986, 49 per cent of African Americans were on or below the poverty line, and comprised 28 per cent of all criminal arrests. The simple drumming of Public Enemy's 'Public Enemy no.1' (1987), with heavy backbeat and synthetic squeaky sounds, does not divert attention from the lyrics that develop from this reality. Whilst hip-hop intended to give voice to the urgent realities of the African American majority, other, more conventionally 'musical' styles served the interests of the black minority who had reaped the benefits of the Civil Rights and Black Power movements. P-Funk (George Clinton's Parliament and Funkadelic), acid-jazz (Miles Davis, Donald Byrd, Herbie Hancock) and black rock (Living Colour, Fishbone) combined diverse style traits to appeal to middle-class, integrated (typically student) audiences. Meanwhile, up-market soul or Quiet Storm (Luther van Dross, Anita Baker, David Peaston) cultivated the more obviously sophisticated tendencies of older, specifically black styles, restoring a link with developments from hip-hop (Lauryn Hill) and contemporary pop. A sophisticated culmination of these developments, Prince has been a highly prolific songwriter and performer since the late 1970s, synthesizing a wide variety of black and white styles for an international market. Ballads had been an essential component of African American popular music since the so-called 'sepia Sinatras'

---

[38]   Adam Krims, *Music and Urban Geography* (New York NY, 2007).

of the rhythm'n'blues era (Cecil Gant, Nat King Cole), but they had been largely ignored by white UK audiences. In David Peaston's 'Luxury of love', we find a 'cool' bass, a kit and hand-drums with female backing singers and foregrounded vocal virtuosity. This example has a fluid structure – a 15-bar verse (4 + 4 + 4 + 3) with an undivided 7-bar vocal phrase leading into an oboe improvisation. The extent to which this style still lies at the root of contemporary pop can be judged on Eternal's 'Angel of mine' (1997), not so much in the vocal characteristics as in the backing. (Britney Spears, Mariah Carey, Christina Aguilera all operate from a similar style base.)

Despite the presence of styles like this, it is difficult to avoid the association of development in popular song with popular culture as youth culture. After all, styles aimed at older demographics (whether recycling back catalogue, or new product) tend to stay conventional in order to meet the apparent needs of that market. But even here, the notion of development can be valid. Take the case of 'country' music, whose history barely interacts with the constant succession of styles I have given here. In its early years, represented by the Grand Ol' Opry and singers like Hank Williams, it had roots in genres as diverse as Appalachian folk, old-time, hillbilly (Riley Puckett, Jimmie Rodgers), bluegrass and western swing (Bill Monroe). Even at this point, key techniques (such as the guitar style of Maybelle Carter, with its bass melody and strummed upper strings) remain a part of the contemporary stock. The style developed through to the Country & Western of Tammy Wynette, Dolly Parton, Johnny Cash, and the more rock-influenced Glen Campbell, Garth Brooks and Emmylou Harris. For a brief moment, it appeared that, via Country Rock (Allman Brothers Band, Creedence Clearwater Revival) and incursions into 1960/70s pop (Kenny Rodgers, Emmylou Harris), it would lose its peripheral status, but this was not to be. Country, as a style, has held appeal for artists as diverse as Elvis Costello, Robert Plant and Ray Charles. Indeed, it is a much larger genre than the limited space I give it here would suggest. And, like rock or dance, it has its 'alternatives'. In recent years, debates have surrounded names such as Sparklehorse and musicians such as Steve Earle. Lambchop, doyens of 'alt.country', provide both a near-reverential approach to the Nashville sound, and also a darker, unsentimentalized reality. Their *Is a woman* (2002) switches again, to a very bare, laid-back, almost late-night balladic texture with minimal kit. 'The daily growl' sends me back to trying to find the Tom Waits track it reminds me of. There are no overt references to country themes or sounds here, so it raises the question of what defines the genre. Steve Earle, on the other hand, still produces music whose sound-world recalls red-necked Southerners, but has run into much trouble for his opposition to contemporary US imperialism disguised as the 'war on terror' and adventures in Iraq. 'John Walker's Blues' dramatizes the life of the infamous individual apprehended by US troops in Afghanistan in 2002. No instrumental virtuosity here, just sufficient to provide a backdrop to Earle's voice. Neil Young is perhaps the clearest, best known, model.

If we deny the post-war equation of 'popular culture' with 'youth culture', we note there are a host of styles, listened to by many people, that have never been associated with revolt, but which nonetheless contribute greatly to the contemporary popular soundscape. Alongside the country styles I have already mentioned, these move from Burt Bacharach and Karl Jenkins to the determined marketing of 'light classical' music: Gorécki, Tavener and Einaudi, Nigel Kennedy, Lionel Bart, Andrew Lloyd Webber, The Three Tenors, Kiri Te Kanawa, Lesley Garrett, that very last popular Imperial institution the Last Night of the Proms, and, most incredibly, Gregorian chant. We cannot understand 'popular song' without at least having a nodding acquaintance with the importance of these, although, as song, they seem to owe little to the dramatic changes introduced by rock'n'roll and samplers.

Although 'pop' continues unabated, as do many of the styles I have been discussing, the most recent unambiguous development was that of 'Britpop'. In retrospect, I think, it signalled two very important things, both ultimately cultural. It began as a new nationalist response to grunge, and had various roots in styles from New Wave and the Jam, rave and the Stone Roses, through to Blur, Pulp and Oasis. Fortunately the label is now dead, but for an extended period it served to revitalize guitar music in the UK, from Thee More Shallows through to the Doves through to the Feeling (and is at least partly responsible for the somewhat bland, paceless style represented by Coldplay, Embrace and numerous other bands whose names are a single word). The first important point is, finally, the rehabilitation of the Beatles. It has probably been a matter of envy but, over the years, it has been difficult to parade any love of the Beatles – they have been easier to hate. New Wave band XTC succeeded, on the stunning *Skylarking* from 1986. Soul-influenced pop superstars Tears for Fears tried on 'Sowing the seeds of love' three years later. These were isolated experiments. With Britpop, however, everybody was doing it, along with recalling the Byrds, the Rolling Stones, the Kinks and the Who (again), but with a 'knowing', self-conscious air (as on the Boo Radleys' 'Joel'). Oasis went all the way, making their debt explicit. The style identified with 'Britpop' grows out of the 'indie' (independent label) bands from the early 1980s and is already firmly in place by the time of the Stone Roses' psychedelic rave-inspired debut in 1989. Returning to Oasis, we can notice the studied avoidance of a 'singing' voice (as on 'Rock'n'roll star', Chapter 4), the voice's depth in the mix, and the emphasis on the noise of guitar-work, which also shows the influence of grunge. The second, and surely more important, point is the emphasis on re-living the 1960s culturally – the return of pride in Britain, the 'New Labour' government initially so reminiscent of Harold Wilson's, the lionization of pop stars thereby (and the cheeky disdain with which bands like Pulp greeted such attitudes). Some of this is made particularly clear by Mono's 'Life in Mono'; not exactly Britpop (more 'lounge') but with such loving references to the tacky 1960s (Henry Mancini, the exoticism of French cinema tracks, etc.).

A number of stylistic directions have threatened to dominate in the period since Britpop. For a long while after Britpop, indie guitar music was in the ascendancy, but in the last few years of the 2000s, 'urban' music (both hip-hop, e.g. Dizzee Rascal, and R&B, e.g. Leona Lewis) and a revitalized largely electronic pop (e.g. Lady Gaga) have taken centre stage. The immense influence on contemporary popular taste of the aesthetics of Simon Cowell, as demonstrated in the unarguably successful *X factor* format has had a strong causative role here but, rather than uniting the musical market, this dominance appears to have led to greater segmentation. As a result, anything seems stylistically possible these days (although if your main aim is making money, the current fad, whatever it is, must remain in your sights. Aesthetic success and commercial success maintain an uneasy relationship). At the turn of the new millennium, garage promised the rehabilitation of dance music with the voice (Craig David's 'Fill me in'). The combination of some form of rock together with a child-like simplicity and love of the obscure (Simian's 'One dimension', Circulus' 'Song of our despair') constantly promises to represent a return to some New Age-related hippy consciousness, but without dominating. One might posit that the determined anti-rock evolution of Radiohead suggested for a while a renewed interest in the difficult, in music which needs working at (as did most of *Kid A* and only a little less of *Amnesiac)*, even in music whose ultimate rewards will outlast initial incomprehension (and if this sounds like a return to the avant garde aesthetics of 1910 or 1950, maybe that's food for thought), were it not for the comparative safety of *Hail to the thief.* Then again, largely beyond the reach of the myopic mainstream media, there's the strange revitalization of progressive rock, due at least in part to the celebratory virtuosity of musicians growing out of metal (Dream Theater, Angra, Opeth). But then, how do we understand Toploader, Tram, Travis, Turin Brakes (simply to reel off a few British flashes in the pan) in this landscape, or the refusal of Mick Jagger, King Crimson or Elton John to retire (and we can multiply these names many-fold)? Perhaps what we need to notice is that stability no longer rests in styles, but conceivably rests in practice. One illustration will suggest what I mean. For the past decade and more, the use of open-ended patterns and harmonic loops has become entirely normative, whether one is a metal band (Trivium's 'Suffocating sight', where the harmonies remain implicit), mainstream rock (Coldplay's 'Clocks', where the middle two chords of a four-chord loop are the same), R&B (Beverley Knight's 'Shoulda woulda coulda' alternates two loops), or pretty well anything else. Against this background, the variety available on the Kaiser Chiefs' *Yours truly, angry mob* or TransAtlantic's *The whirlwind* should be remarkable, but attracts no comment. The transparency of harmonic practice remains paramount.

What continues to strike me strongly is the renewed energy with which the newest great band is greeted. In turn the Coral, the Thrills, Franz Ferdinand, Keane, Razorlight, the Magic Numbers, the Hoosiers (etc. etc.) offered something truly novel (although the Magic Numbers' attention to detail stood out for me). The Coral (earliest of these) soon vanished back into obscurity and the same seems to have happened with the rest's second albums, and beyond. Perhaps this only replays the pattern of the last 40 years anyway. If so, then we are still operating within a modernist aesthetic that expects artists to mature, to recognize a vocation. However, if you prefer a post-modern reading (or even a late capitalist one), then you must celebrate these momentary explosions of energy, for we should expect no

Chapter 6
Friction

Interpretive Assumptions

The focus of the book's remaining chapters is more deeply on the process of making sense. In this chapter, I shall focus on the notion of the friction that can operate between the expectations listeners may bring to a track, on the basis of normative assumptions, and a track's frequent refusal to conform to those assumptions. Prior to addressing this, however, I need to make some preparatory remarks on interpretation itself, and on the assumptions it is necessary to bring to the act of listening.

I assume that not only is the act of listening to a song meaningful in itself, but that we care about distinguishing between different songs, and indeed tracks; the difference between these terms was addressed in Chapter 1. This may seem a trivial assertion, but the import of some writings is to doubt this basic assumption.[1] If we make a distinction between tracks, if we care to distinguish one from another, this implies that the meaning of one track is not the same as the meaning of another (even if both tracks develop from the same song and, perhaps, are sung by the same singer). If we can be sure that the meaning of listening to one has the potential to differ from the meaning of listening to another, we can approach the question of what they might mean individually. There is more than one argument to bring to bear here. Mass market theorists tend to argue that the meaning of a track is imposed on the listener, that the power to determine its meaning resides with the industry and with its gatekeepers (journalists, DJs, etc.); that the meaning equates perhaps simply to the act of listening, and the use of the music this entails. Subculture theorists have tended to argue that meanings are constructed within the subculture using a particular track. In this sense, a listener has a determining role to play in deciding its meaning. This distinction parallels that between over-coding and under-coding, between tracks whose meaning appears so obvious that no alternative is possible, and tracks whose meaning is entirely open to appropriation (the difference between Donny Osmond's 'Puppy love' and Peter Gabriel's 'Here comes the flood', for instance). There is merit in both these historically determined theoretical positions; neither are wilful. Neither, however, seem fully to explain the process of developing meaning from a track, and accordingly I adopt a position some way between the two. It is the act of listening that dominates, in which meaning is created, but that act is merely one in a long

---

[1]   I have in mind work like Lawrence Grossberg, *We gotta get out of this place* (New York NY, 1992) and some other writing of a determinedly sociological cast.

series of acts of listening.[2] In this way, a listener relates the current experience to past experiences, develops meaning from meanings already understood. And since no two listeners' experiences are identical, even if they inhabit the same subculture, the meanings they find in their listening cannot be predetermined; as Bradley notes of the individual's 'musical experience', its 'resemblance ... to some objectively defined sonic object, "the music", is of course unmeasurable'.[3] These meanings can, however, be chosen. What the remaining chapters of the book endeavour to do is to make available for explicit use those processes that develop out of an encounter with the music by which a track's meaning can be addressed, by which its enlivening of our experience can be focused on, in order to show what effect musical detail has on that enlivening, why it is important that it sound just like *this* rather than like *that*. Exactly what meaning a track has is only for an individual listener to determine, but how meaning can be created from it is explored here.

Of course, I have in mind a particular meaning of the word 'meaning'. Patel's recent study identifies at least eleven 'types of musical meaning that have been discussed by scholars of music'[4]. This is a resonably comprehensive list, although exemplification through popular music of any kind doesn't really appear. However, the construal I am putting on 'meaning' crosses all of these categories at some point: structures are the focus of the material in Chapters 2–4, for instance, while ideas of motion, tone painting, narrative and life experience relate to my discussion of the persona in Chapter 7. I think, though, that a focus on 'meaning' is perhaps less frutiful that a focus on 'interpretation' (although I will continue to keep both terms in play). A key point is to determine the level at which you make an interpretation. Are you responding directly to the track or to some discourse surrounding it? I find the most persuasive interpretations to be first-order interpretations, that is, interpretations made directly in relation to a listening to the track. Many listeners will make an interpretation on the basis of a video which has been shot for the track, but such an interpretation is normally a second-order interpretation. The video itself is an interpretation (normally first-order) of the track, normally suggesting an interpretation to which the listener can then respond, that is, offering (and sometimes strongly) a particular subject position. (It is rare that a video either precedes, or is developed exactly concurrently with the recording and production of a track.) If listeners determine the meaning of a track for themselves on the basis of reading someone else's (a blogger, a journalist, an academic even), then that, too, is a second-order interpretation. And, if you

---

[2]   The parallel with Solomon's insistence that emotions '*bestow*' value as well as appraise it' is striking. Robert C. Solomon, *True to our feelings* (New York NY, 2007), p. 162.

[3]   Bradley, *Understanding Rock'n'roll*, p. 21.

[4]   Aniruddh D. Patel, *Music, language and the brain* (Oxford, 2008), pp.305-26. He gives these as: the Structural interconnection of musical elements; the Expression of emotion; the Experience of emotion; Motion; Tone painting; Musical topics; Social associations; Imagery and narrative; Association with life experience; Creating or transforming the self; Musical structure and cultural concepts.

are working from someone else's understanding of the video to a track, then your room for manoeuvre is even more constricted, you will be making a third-order interpretation. Of course there is nothing wrong with such an interpretation, unless you mistakenly believe you are interpreting the track directly.

Aside from these basic positions, interpretations are made with reference to a host of other discourses, but in the literature (both academic and journalistic), these are frequently made without explicit reference to any recognition of music as sound. In observing how sound affects the meaning we regard a track as having, there are five key factors to take into account. The first factor is the *inherent meaning* of the track. In this sense, 'inherent' refers to the tendencies of one sound to be related to, to be followed by, to coexist with (etc.) any other particular sound. Inherent meanings are style-specific,[5] but may be shared between related styles. This category includes such observations as the tendency of blues melodies to fall, the tendency of beats to be grouped in 4s, the tendency of chords to conform to a particular (nameable) mode, the tendency of the bass layer to construct a line around harmonic roots, the tendency of the soundbox to be balanced, the tendency of a particular vocal approach to remain constant throughout a performance, and so on. (For some writers, such as Walter Everett,[6] that degree of sharing is extreme, such that there are musical quasi-universals that can be said to underlie all styles, such as the pull that chord I exerts on chord V. Debate over the extent of such 'universality' remains ongoing.) Broadly speaking, it is this realm of 'inherent meaning' that was explored in Chapters 2–4 of this book. While those chapters lay out a series of norms, a more nuanced view needs to take into account the second factor, which is the *style* and *genre* of the track. Although 'style' and 'genre' (with which I am not concerned here) are shared characteristics, individual styles and genres are not rigidly definable. The rules for how one recognizes *disco* are not written anywhere, they have no objective existence; they exist only in our heads, and our experiences. The reasons for this are complex (why would one bother to specify them in all their fullness, for instance?) and in any case, as I argued in Chapter 1, it is not possible to be definitive. Styles shade into one another, and it is only when one is clearly on one side of the divide or the other, that we can identify a style unproblematically. Because these categories are not fixed, and arise in the process of making and promoting music, it is better to regard them as *intersubjective* (i.e. as matters of shared subjectivity) rather than objective descriptions of how closely one track resembles a host of others.

Many ascriptions of style are unproblematic; there is widespread agreement over whether a particular track is country, or rhythm'n'blues, or punk. However, what might be 'easy listening' for one listener may be '1960s pop' for another, while the presence of rapping in both contemporary R&B and in nu-metal can make it hard to fit such tracks into rigid categories. Rather than accept the rigidity offered by Amazon, iTunes or HMV, a more realistic option is to recognize that

---

[5]   Green, *Music on Deaf Ears*, pp. 12–44.

[6]   Everett, *The foundations of rock*.

these are means of categorization present only as they are employed, that they are resident in the listeners and not in the track itself. They thus relate to the *track* rather than to the *song*. And it is important to note that a listener's *competence*[7] with the style is relevant; listeners with a high degree of competence or experience will tend to agree on the specifics of the style (and even substyle) of a particular track (or at least will have the experience to debate its positioning), while those with less familiarity will identify a style less precisely. Definitions of style and genre are problematic (and are outside the scope of this particular chapter).[8] The third factor is to recognize the context vital to any sense of shared meaning. This context is listener determined, but is frequently shared, and can be social, stylistic, historical, and so on. No generalizations to be made here, but any sharing of meaning has to take account of the relationship we have with whomever we are sharing meaning with.

The fourth factor concerns the delineations of the style and the range of subject-positions called forth by both the style and the track. 'Delineation' is a concept developed in Green's theory of style.[9] It refers to the connotations and denotations that a sequence of sounds has for listeners familiar with the style, a familiarity that is in turn measured by their type of competence in music, that is, whether they play it, listen to it, study it, write it, and so on. Green notes that our taste for a particular style is as often a feature of its delineations for us as it is simply the sounds of the style. And our taste is also subject to our response to the subject-position of a track. Subject-position, a key concept in Clarke's theory of listening,[10] refers to the attitude a track can appear to encourage us as listeners to take in respect of what it says to us. Although I do not make specific use of the concept, in Chapter 8 I argue a related point, that the music to a track does not necessarily encourage us to agree with the track's lyrics. This leads to the final factor, the relationship between the *style* of the track and the *idiolect* of the performers. If *style* is the manner of articulation of musical content, then *idiolect* refers to the individual stylistic fingerprints (perhaps the tone of the voice, perhaps the way the kit and bass interlock, perhaps the particular guitar tone) of a performer or group of performers. It is defined by what appears typical of a particular combination of performers, as made explicit within a given track. The entire output of a large number of performers can be categorized within one particular style label, due both to the innate flexibility of musicians and their frequent desire to remain 'true' to their audiences, and to the pressures enforced by musicians' management, in order to retain a level of commercial success. But although for this reason idiolect

---

    [7]   Gino Stefani, 'A theory of musical competence' (1987), reprinted in Moore (ed.), *Critical essays in popular musicology*, (Aldershot, 2007): pp. 19–34.

    [8]   Particular explorations can be found in Moore, 'Categorical conventions' and in Franco Fabbri, 'Browsing music spaces: categories and the musical mind', reprinted in Moore (ed.), *Critical essays in popular musicology*, (Aldershot, 2007), pp. 49–62.

    [9]   Green, *Music on Deaf Ears*.

    [10]   Clarke, *Ways of listening*.

is frequently subsidiary to style, it is not necessarily confined to a particular style, as the careers of Bobby Darin, David Bowie, Elvis Costello, Karl Jenkins or Annie Lennox (or a number of progressive rock musicians) attest; indeed it is harder to define the idiolect of Bowie, say, than that of Oasis, or of Tony Bennett.[11] Beyond these five key factors, there are two overriding presences in popular song that require fuller treatment, and that I shall here call those of *authenticity* and *intertextuality*. I address them in Chapter 9.

Key to the identification of *idiolect* is recognition of the normative practices of one or more musicians. It is on the basis of amassed idiolects that we recognize the norms of style. It is a commonplace in the study of musical style that musical decisions are based on the assumption of operative rules, and that these rules can be broken. These rules can be found in all musical domains – rhythm, harmony, melody, production, instrumentation – even if they cannot be fully specified. Sometimes the reasons for these rules are purely practical (e.g. all instruments are limited in the range of sounds they can produce; to try to exceed this range may result from either an experimental urge or from sheer incompetence). Sometimes they are more clearly aesthetic (e.g. the vocal growl in death metal, or the centrality of the snare drum in the soundbox in rock styles). One thing that close study of popular song has taught me is that particular 'rules' are not supra-stylistic, and any claim that they have some sort of universal validity, that they mark some notion of aesthetic excellence, is better resisted. Such rules only govern particular styles. It is for this reason that the notion of 'breaking' rules seems to me problematic; I prefer to think in terms of 'norms' than 'rules'. The notion of 'breaking' such rules is then replaced by the concept of the creation of friction between the accepted norms of a style and what actually happens in a particular track. The norms (however poorly explicated) are in place both before and after the track comes into existence (in the experience of its musicians and its listeners), but they create an additional realm of meaning, for once we notice such friction, any enquiring mind will try to observe what effect that friction may have. This has to remain imprecise, for at what point does repeated friction become a new available norm? For example, in Chapter 3, I called attention to the appearance of momentary changes of metre (moving from $\frac{4}{4}$ to $\frac{12}{8}$). I do not know the first recorded example to employ such a change, but it clearly must have appeared to be novel. Even now it is hardly common, but seems to have appeared frequently enough to no longer cause surprise to a competent listener. Thus its degree of friction is very low. This is, though, a matter of interpretive judgement and where an interpretation becomes communicated, will need to be justified. What I point to in this chapter is more extreme, or rare, examples of friction between norms and appearances, to demonstrate the range within which the concept operates. For

---

[11]   A fuller discussion of idiolect, and its operation in the case of Radiohead, can be found in Allan F. Moore and Anwar Ibrahim, 'Sounds like Teen Spirit: identifying Radiohead's idiolect', in Joseph Tate (ed.), *Strobe-Lights and Blown Speakers: essays on the music and art of Radiohead*, (Aldershot, 2005), pp. 139–58.

the classical style, rigorous demonstration of some of its rules exists, an extreme perhaps represented by Narmour's explication of the 'expectation–realisation' model.[12] It is not my intention to attempt anything more prescriptive than already discussed in Chapters 2-4. The notion of friction operates across all domains, and at varying levels of specificity – after all, fundamentally, what matters is a particular listener's configuration of the style that is performed by a particular track, and that cannot be exhaustively determined. It is the principle of friction that is paramount here, and that should be substantiated by the examples given.

Textural Friction

It appears that all interpretation works partly on the basis of comparison, between what we might expect to happen within a track (given our degree of competence with the style or with the genre of which it forms a part), and what we find actually does happen during its course. Any difference that we find creates a friction, and that friction will always carry an affective value, whether or not it is allied to something specific within the lyrics. This starts from the outset – at the very least, the instrumentation we hear at the opening, and the manner in which it is deployed, will set the style, the genre, and the tone of the track. One of the most basic norms of popular song is that of the instrumental functions discussed in Chapter 2. When we notice that the relationship between instruments is sundered, even if only for a moment, some sort of affective charge results. When John Bonham's drums thunder out the opening to Led Zeppelin's 'When the levee breaks', we await the introduction of the band, and their entry affirms that the track is under way, that the stage is set for Robert Plant's voice. (The opening to the Feeling's 'I want you now' is comparable, and there are a host of similar examples.) The rich 12-string texture of the opening of Genesis' 'Can-utility and the coastliners' means that the introduction of bass and kit can be left for the beginning of the song's drama: 'Far from the north'. We miss these instruments at first, because we expect them. Their absence on Billy Joel's 'And so it goes' contributes to the song's sense of intimacy (since he frequently uses a rhythm section), but there remains the possibility of a dramatic intervention right to the last. This is an option very effectively taken by Supertramp's 'Crime of the century', where the power of the full band is used with some care, and is dropped more than once.

Once we get into a track, refusal to continue with the opening texture set is often very effective. Take the Boomtown Rats' 'I never loved Eva Braun'. This is a fast track, although an intimation of things to come is signalled by the entry of the first verse, where the kit moves at half the pace it had taken in the introduction. Two verses and choruses are followed by another chorus whose role is to gradually increase the speed of the beat from that of the verse to that of the introduction.

---

[12]   Eugene Narmour, *The analysis and cognition of basic melodic structures*, (Chicago IL, 1990) and *The analysis and cognition of melodic complexity*, (Chicago IL, 1992).

This itself is unusual in popular song, and the contradiction between this growing tension and the stock harmonic loop (I–V–ii–IV) is palpable. That recovered introduction leads us into a third verse. But at this point, a return to the I–V–ii–IV pattern remains at the original speed, and the conventional relationship between the kit and bass is sundered. It is this friction that signals a change of meaning in the track. The drummer resorts simply to side drum flurries, while the bassist sits on open fifths on each downbeat. The increase of tempo that we have already encountered gradually repeats, but the extended time implies that something has been achieved (this is particularly marked by Bob Geldof's 'Woh yeah' at 3'43"). This is not all there is to be said about this remarkable track, and I shall return to it in Chapter 8. Nik Kershaw's 'The riddle' uses a similar device. After three verses and choruses, the key shifts up a semitone, the drummer shifts to a snare pattern, and the bass drops out of the texture. The effect is akin to that of a change of film shot, as the focus lengthens, enabling the viewer to see that there is much more going on. A third version of this same device, a sundering of the relationship between kit and bass, occurs in Elvis Costello's 'Lipstick vogue'. An instrumental break after the third verse is involved in an increase of speed, like with 'Eva Braun' (as the upward scale in the bass repeats over ever shorter spans of time). Having achieved an intense climax (at 2'3"), it is as if the drums spin off, losing the bass end of the texture, and almost hysterically concentrating on just the snare and hi-hat. With no kick drum to lock into, the bass seems lost, clinging on to harmonic roots and downbeats for dear life. And then over this strange texture, held together by an organ pad, Costello's angry voice returns, almost gasping for air, and gains a far more pointed entry than if it had returned over the very fast beat of the earlier part of the track. Björk's 'Army of me' also transgresses a norm in terms of instrumental function, but here it concerns the harmonic filler. The absence of this layer means the introduction of a bareness to the texture, a bareness not normally apparent in song. However, the sense of menace this provides (particularly in the context of the locrian mode apparent in the bass) suits the meaning of the lyrics, which explore the inadequacy of Björk's presumably male interlocutor.[13]

Changes of texture at the other end of a track are also effective. Fades are ubiquitous, and simply carry the connotation that the situation is continuing – the track continues, but out of our hearing. In George Harrison's 'The art of dying', the fade is complex. Not only can we hear the track's end (it closes just within our hearing), but not all instruments fade at the same rate. The temptation to read this as a comment of the song's lyric is powerful: in Hindu thought, rebirth necessitates a clear end of life, which is what the track's audible end provides, and it is an end we have to experience individually, hence the (slight) communal disjuncture. The end of David Bowie's 'Five years' perhaps carries two meanings simultaneously. First, the remaining presence of the kit once everything else has left the texture mirrors the track's opening, carrying the sense that the kit has been there all along,

---

[13]   Anecdote identifies this individual as Björk's brother.

simply going on its way. But second, the aridity of the kit in the pitch realm acts as a neat expression of what the end of those five years may be like.

Sometimes friction results from contrast. Most styles employ contrast within tracks, but this can sometimes appear at unusual places, for example the sudden (and unexpected) lightening of texture at 1'54" of System of a Down's 'Prison song' – a moment of tenderness ('baby, you and me') in the midst of a diatribe against US drug policy. Friction is not restricted to simply rubbing up against norms, but can also be found in how those norms are instantiated. Honeybus' 'I can't let Maggie go' now sounds quite extreme in the way it fills the normal functions, although as faux-psychedelia, perhaps the unexpected should be expected. In addition to an unproblematic bass and kit, the harmonic layer is filled simply with a strummed guitar. However, the layer is thickened by reed instruments (oboe, cor anglais, bassoon) and backing voices, which approximate a secondary melody at the top of the harmony. The oboe also moves to share the melodic layer with the voice. For a more recent example, drum'n'bass tends to dispense with a harmonic filler layer, but there is often some sort of filler occupying the notional space between the bass and the melodic layer. On a track such as Roni Size's 'New forms', this space is filled by an atmospheric layer of indiscriminate pitch, which matches the rapped vocal line (which does have often a sense of melodic contour, even if it is not actually sung).

Friction can also be observed within the soundbox. To contemporary ears, any placing of the lead voice, the drum kit, or the bass to one side of the stereo spectrum can sound disorienting. Donovan's 'Mellow yellow' is one such example – on the stereo mix all the sound-sources are clustered to one side of the centre. On Manfred Mann's 'Pretty flamingo', the drum kit and bass are found on the right, and the voice (and other sources) on the left. Simon & Garfunkel's 'Homeward bound' is a little less unusual – the voices are at least in the centre of the soundbox here, but bass and kit sit on opposite sides. Grand Funk Railroad's 'Paranoid' provides a rather interesting example of friction. A live recording was released in 1970, mixed as we would expect. The studio version had been released the previous year; the voice is central and, although the kit moves position a little, it is basically to the left, with the bass to the right.[14] This difference alone demonstrates that the soundbox norm was not yet in place and, to competent ears, the studio recording now sounds unbalanced. 'Historical ears' then can suggest to us a meaning for the friction engendered here, and indeed this is probably the most effective way to hear these two tracks. What happens, though, with an unusual soundbox placement with more recent music, that is, once the norm of the diagonal mix was established? Let me provide a couple of examples. The textures of Muse's album *Absolution* are very rich, but on 'Stockholm syndrome' and 'Falling away with you' at least, the kit is clearly slightly to the right of centre, as is the bass, matching the voice, which is slightly to left of centre. Thus the notion of balance is still achieved, but

---

[14]   Much of the band's early work is mixed this way – the entire album *On time*, for instance.

in a different way from normal. My Chemical Romance's exhilarating 'Dead!' (like much of the album) also places the kit slightly to right of centre, although the reason for this appears to be to create space for interplay between guitar lines to mid-left, mid-right and centre. The effect is not marked, but can be noticed. These are hardly instances of extreme friction, and attest to how rigid the norm of the diagonal mix is in most popular song, which makes examples of its transgression the more powerful. It could be argued that those instances where sound-sources appear closer (the acoustic guitar in Yes' 'Roundabout') or further away (Mick Jagger's voice in early Rolling Stones mixes) than we might otherwise expect are instances of locational friction, were it not that these norms appear to operate less strongly for many listeners.

If friction can be found in the textural domain, it is also present in the way timbres appear. The dominant distinction to be made here is between timbres that appear *natural*, that is, as they would when played 'acoustically' in a clear space, immediately before you, such that they can be clearly heard, and timbres that are in some way overtly *modified*. Now this is a tricky issue, because all sounds are modified by the environment in which they are heard – the *natural* pole is itself a construction but, as with other manifestations of meaning, it is the appearance that signifies. So, what is at issue here is whether the modification itself is audible, that is, whether some threshold has been crossed that allows us to say 'that's not a normal trumpet, voice, piano' and so on ... . In a discussion of the Beatles' track 'I'm only sleeping', Albin Zak III suggests the distortion on the acoustic guitar sound acts as a subtext to the dreaminess of Lennon's voice, accentuating its 'veiled desperation',[15] which might otherwise pass us by. What matters here is that the sound is harsher than we might expect it to be, and this harshness signifies. A similar instance occurs in Natalie Merchant's track 'The ballad of Henry Darger', although what is at issue is not the harshness of the timbre, but its flaccidity. I shall return to this song in Chapter 8, but for now, I just call attention to the clarinet introduction. The sound is very thin and lacking in tone, the sort of sound that no competent clarinettist ought to be producing, and it therefore signifies, possibly to prepare us for the naivety that is one important pole of the song. On the other hand, on occasions, a timbre will be thickened slightly beyond what we might otherwise expect. When the Byrds begin Bob Dylan's 'All I really want to do', the guitar sound is thicker than a conventional guitar, since it is based on Roger McGuinn's 12-string guitar, specifically used for its more resonant properties, and not exactly a conventional sound for its time.

Formal Friction

Departures from rhythmic and metrical norms are easier to identify. As Chapter 3 noted, occasional departures from groupings of events in 4s are so common as to

---

[15]   Zak, *The poetics of rock*, p. 191.

become unexceptional (groupings in 5s are rarer, and multiple groupings in 5s remarkable). But other departures in the realm of rhythm are notable. For example, Ted Gracyk points out that there are many tracks that do not use a backbeat.[16] This is true, but I would qualify it with two observations. First, when measured against the patterns used by drummers of average competence (i.e. to try to take into account full usage, rather than that on a limited number of tracks that are widely familiar), I would suggest the backbeat has now a high degree of normativity, and this even in the case where the style has no other connection to rock. Second, it is because it acts as a norm that these other examples are noteworthy. Take one of Gracyk's examples, Buddy Holly's 'Peggy Sue', a quite extreme case since the guitar strums on every quaver, the drums (a deep tom-tom) play on every semiquaver, and all we have left is the lead guitar break and Holly's voice. A couple of times, the lead guitar offers a speedy upbeat of the sort that might elsewhere be taken by a drummer (such as at 1'28"), but the key factor is Holly's articulation. When singing the title, his rhythm (see Example 6.1) emphasizes the second beat ('-*gy*'), giving that syllable a level of stress that the spoken name 'Peggy' would not receive. The anticipation of the third beat ('*Sue*') draws emphasis away from this beat.

Example 6.1 Buddy Holly: 'Peggy Sue'; vocal rhythm

Thus, it serves the same function that the standard rock beat would serve, although differently delivered. Not all such examples can be explained thus, but it seems that the absence of the audible pattern intensifies its potentiality. Did Holly have it in mind to work against? I suspect he did, although of course that is but speculation. So why do without the backbeat? Perhaps, simply, the rather intimate enthusiasm expressed by the protagonist, mirrored by the guitar and kit (particularly as it appears to approach us and then retreat), would be overpowered by the full pattern.

A different unexpected relationship between the voice and kit can be heard in the Troggs' 'Gonna make you'. The kit is playing in double tempo, that is, with snare on every half beat, a pattern much more reminiscent of rockabilly, starting as it does with the Bo Diddley beat. The voice, however, has been displaced by half a beat, such that weak points in the melody coincide with the snare. The effect is sustained, which suggests it is not accidental – exerting control over the melody in such a way perhaps illustrates the control the protagonist wants to exert over his silent other. There is, of course, a second way to hear this track, which is with the inversion of the normal snare-kick pattern, such that the snare appears on the downbeat. This destroys the effect I have mentioned and, indeed, it may be the

---

[16]   Gracyk, *Rhythm and noise*, pp. 134–7.

more 'normal' way to hear it. If that is so, it acts as a warning that the standard beat acts only as a norm. (It is not, though, such an interesting way to hear it!) A good demonstration of just how necessary to our listening is the assumption of a regular kit pattern can be found in J. J. Cale's 'Don't go to strangers'. Although the beat is clearly articulated, there is no regular pattern made by snare, kick, hi-hat or any combination of these – a tour de force by drummer Chuck Browning. It is almost as if we are to be confounded. Michael Chapman's blues 'No-one left to care' is even more extreme: within a context of a regular 12-bar blues, every so often it is as if his emotion gets the better of him, as his guitar simply breaks away from any regularity, with quite devastating effect. The opening to the Artwoods' 'I keep forgettin'' shows that a momentary avoidance of both a backbeat and a regular metre can be effective (particularly in a rhythm'n'blues style in which they are mandatory) when measured against their subsequent employment. And while the presence of a backbeat is constant in Living Colour's 'Mind your own business', the dislocation of Corey Glover's persona from the worldview of his interlocutor is powerfully dramatized by the virtuosic changes of tempo in the different choruses.

An example that combines friction in two areas is the Beatles' 'A day in the life'; this requires more complicated exegesis. In three distinct ways, the song displays tentativeness. First, the harmonic language of the verses avoids the dominant chord. Second, while the tonic harmony appears to be the opening G, the melody is clearly in the aeolian mode on E. Third, and this is the aspect most often commented upon, Lennon's voice is made to wander, in George Martin's stereo mix, from one side of the space to the other, and back, acting very much as a metaphor for uncertainty of direction. Then, in three separate ways, the song avoids normative groupings in 4s: the opening verse consists of five groups of four bars; McCartney's interpolation is phrased in groups of five bars; Lennon's subsequent vocalise (at 2'49"), during which his voice wanders again, consists of two groups of five bars. One group of 5 within groups of 4 is trivial. Three, and in each of the song's most significant places, is not. How do we understand both this tentativeness and the avoidance of normal temporal pacing? The use of '5' rather than '4' easily acts as a metaphor for the alternative time-sense championed by hippy culture, but the tentative aspects of the song imply a failure fully to sign up to this alternative, symbolising the Beatles' dalliance with, but retreat from, the mores of hippy culture (and, subsequently, the failure of the counter-culture in the UK). Of course this does not explain why the track was created as it is, nor does it seek to suggest any degree of precognition on the part of the musicians, but it is a reading that finds significance in the decisions made, and that enables the track to stand for the larger historical truth in which it played a part.[17] The Raconteurs' 'Consoler of the lonely' is equally interesting. The track is framed by a slow riff that reappears under a verse in the centre of the song, but it is overlaid at the beginning with a kit pattern at an entirely different speed, and that forms the

---

[17]   See Allan F. Moore, 'The act you've known for all these years'.

basis for the majority of the song's quasi-blues nature, of which the singer's being 'bored to tears' is the clearest aspect. The recovery of the faster tempo after the slower verse at 1'55" is breath-taking. And then the tag provides a series of texture changes – the bass sets up a new pattern, the guitar then replaces this before the bass recovers. The contradiction between these changes and the song's dominant expression sets up interesting possibilities for interpretation.

Friction can also occur in the realms of harmony and melody (which, as discussed earlier, often work in tandem). Take the Bacharach/David classic 'Alfie', as sung by Cilla Black. The track moves through two verses and a bridge, before starting the third verse. That verse, however, gets hijacked and moves off into a different direction, beginning with a new chromaticism in the bass (at 1'41"). This is significant for the course of the song, for reasons I shall address in Chapter 8. Diana Ross' recording of 'Ain't no mountain high enough' alters the straightforward two verse/chorus–bridge–verse/chorus pattern of Marvin Gaye & Tammi Terrell's earlier recording. In her version, we open with a wordless chorus, an entreating verse (where she sings '*if* you need me') and another chorus. We then reach a bridge, notable for its ascending bass (which implies reaching upwards and, because of its chromaticisms, reaching upwards against all the odds). This leads to the song's climax in which she declares she will make contact, in which her initial entreaty becomes action, before recovering the chorus. The form is thus transgressive (only one verse), the 'change' marked by a chromatic bass, and conveying in the lyrics a sense of her change of position. I do not think that we need to know the Gaye/Terrell version for the import of Ross' to come across. It is enough that Ross transgresses norms of popular song in general, although the difference between these two versions does add an additional level of meaning better understood as an aspect of intertextuality, to be discussed in Chapter 9. Other examples exist, all with formal units that are more than simple contrasting bridges, but are not always tied to this type of strong harmony, such as Ike and Tina Turner's 'River deep mountain high' (the Phil Spector production), Barry Ryan's 'Eloise', Richard Harris's recording of Jimmy Webb's 'Macarthur Park', or the Walker Brothers' 'The sun ain't gonna shine any more'. All of these examples emanate from the 1960s, and more recent examples seem rare, although Arcade Fire's 'Crown of love' qualifies. A succession of standard verses and choruses is succeeded (at about 2'45") by a sense of growing desperation in the voice. A notable chromatic rising note in the bass leads to a dramatic change of tempo that seems to compound this desperation, particularly when the harmony simply recycles. A diatonicization of that chromatic bass note appears just as the track begins to fade, promising a possible resolution, but this is not achieved. If such features really are rarer in more recent songs, then the reason is most likely due to the prevalence in recent years of harmonic loops, and the simpler structures these often entail, as noted at the end of Chapter 5.

The formal approach outlined in Chapter 3, whereby a succession of well-defined sections follow each other, is well-suited to the subject matter of so much popular song, which focuses on a static situation, describes it and often offers justification of, or explanation for it, perhaps views it from different perspectives, and maybe suggests a subsequent course of action. But what of songs that want to adopt a different approach? What of songs that actually explore a change of situation? Here, there are two formal approaches that are more likely to be taken, the 'arch' form and the 'cumulative' form, which is sometimes called the 'bolero' form. Here, the sense of overall form is important because we are offered a distinct narrative of change. I treat them here, though, because verse–chorus structures are so ubiquitous that any deviation from them carries a strong affective charge.

An arch form presents a secure place to start from, moves away, and then returns. An archetypal example is Li'l Louis' 'French kiss'. Although no words are exchanged, a persona is definitely present in the simulation of a female orgasm. The form is presented almost entirely in terms of tempo. A standard dance tempo gradually slows as we become aware of the woman's moans, the tempo effectively halts as the groove stops, and then it regathers pace eventually reaching the original speed. Forms of this nature were not uncommon features of progressive rock. King Crimson's '21st-century schizoid man' is a rich example, moving through five linked sections. The outer pair are sung, initially two verses with refrain, finally one verse with refrain. The second and fourth sections feature a faster variant of the opening riff, while the central sections is itself a three-part set of improvisations moving between saxophone and guitar. The 1970s practice of long improvisations particularly in live performance led to a profusion of arch forms from what began as simple songs. Alvin Lee and Ten Years After's performance at the Woodstock Festival of 'I'm going home' is only a particularly clear example of this. The full version of New Order's 'Blue Monday' represents the polar opposite in terms of extending a song into an arch form. Rather than expanding the centre so that an improvisation is enclosed between verses, 'Blue Monday' expands the introduction and final tag, to cover more than half the length of the track, leaving the verses to develop a narrative within this. (What is particularly interesting about this track is that the verse itself has an arch structure – the outer lines move from $\hat{3}$ to $\hat{2}$ to $\hat{1}$, while the inner lines move from $\hat{5}$ to $\hat{4}$ to $\hat{3}$.) This practice seems to be commonest in tracks that show the influence of electronic dance music, for probably obvious reasons.

What I mean by bolero form is exemplified by Doves' 'Satellites' (or, indeed, by Colosseum's cover of Ravel's *Bolero*). The key feature is a sense of growth either throughout a track, or with a momentary cessation, which is then picked up again. 'Satellites' consists of a succession of four verses and choruses, the third being instrumental (and without a chorus). The texture grows to this point, although not consistently (the second verse is marked by a lessening of activity in the kit, but the introduction of a guitar). For the final verse, everything falls away except the voice, and then during the final chorus the texture grows towards a maximum climax in that the sound gets louder, richer, denser and gains a sense of increasing reverb. For a bolero form, then, what matters is less that sections get repeated (verses, choruses), than that the overall sense is of being gradually swept away. Changes of texture are definitional (as above), but are directed towards this larger whole. Much mid-period U2 is organized in this way, particularly a track like 'With or without you'.[18] Deep Purple's 'Child in time' combines both of these formal features. An opening succession of verses grows to a climax both in texture and in the reach of singer Ian Gillan's voice, a central improvisatory section ensues, before giving way to a repeat of the opening section with its directed growth.

There is one other formal strategy worth mentioning here, which is the concatenation of different material that sometimes goes under the name of *medley*. In live performance, musicians will often lead from one track straight into another, but in the studio this is less common. Sometimes we find medleys proper, as in Mickey Newbury's 'American trilogy', which simply combines verses from 'Dixie', 'The battle hymn of the republic' and 'All my trials'. Sometimes extended medleys create the concept albums common in progressive rock – Jethro Tull's *A passion play*, for instance, which (fairly) artfully strings together a dozen cuts. Sometimes, a track is simply put together from what appear to be incomplete songs. The Beatles' 'A day in the life' can be understood this way, as can Queen's 'Bohemian rhapsody'. In extreme metal particularly, often unrelated stretches of music are put together, as in Metallica's 'Blackened'. In all these cases (even usually in metal), note that something from the beginning of the track is normally recalled at the end, in order to provide a sense of completion (I shall return to this issue later). Where the tracks cause friction is in the employment of very different stretches of music that do not fall into a verse–chorus pattern. This is a point that requires proper historicization, which I do not have space to undertake here, for in a dominant song form of the 1930s, for instance, that of the ballad, a single (often unperformed) verse tended to be followed by repeated refrains (what we would now call choruses), and so one must also be sensitive to stylistic norms.

Friction with regard to lyrics is less easy to assess. Since there are no recognized typologies of subject matter for popular song, estimating friction between norms and what is experienced here is necessarily speculative. Songs developing a deep philosophical position, or songs delving into fantasy, may be regarded as generating friction. This, I suspect, is one reason behind the denigration of much progressive rock (although it is no more escapist than a great deal of straight pop). Songs exploring deeply held beliefs, especially if unfashionable, are unlikely to enter the public consciousness unless from a singer who has already gained public acclaim (Cliff Richard, for instance). Songs that observe a change of situation, while not unknown, are sufficiently rare to be notable. The Beach Boys' 'Good vibrations', which I treat in the next chapter, is one such, while I have also noted songs like 'Alfie' and 'River deep, mountain high' that do this. One particularly remarkable example is Mike Skinner and the Streets' 'Empty cans'. The culmination to a strictly narrative concept album, the track offers two possible denouements to the narrative, first a negative one, and second a positive one, the difference hingeing on a split-second decision made by Skinner (and thus reminiscent of Heinrich Böll's

---

[18]   See Allan F. Moore, 'U2 and the myth of authenticity in rock', *Popular Musicology* 3 (1998) (http://www.allanfmoore.org.uk).

philosophy) from which the rest follows. That moment at which the alternative ending begins is thus remarkable.

With regard to local lyric detail, it is again difficult to talk about friction with any conviction, since there is very little in the way of lyric practice that is not used. From rich poetry to banal speech, all are found (although this says nothing about the quality of such examples). One feature that most lyrics are expected to have, however, is rhyme, and so I focus on a few instances where a sense of rhyme is toyed with. Elvis Costello is a master at this. 'No action' I have written about before.[19] In the very first verse, 'touch' is made to rhyme with 'much', but they don't coincide in their placement within their respective lines – 'much' is on a downbeat, 'touch' precedes its downbeat. This is a very subtle point, but the delay of 'much' behind 'that' adds to the negative quality of the sentiment expressed. Sometimes, an obvious rhyme is refused. Nick Cave's 'The lyre of Orpheus' rhymes alternate lines, but in the third verse he sidesteps the obvious rhyme for "pluck", which is strange since he uses the word later in the song. What is the effect of such word play? In most cases, it seems to me simply a display of cleverness – it is hard to hear such events without a small smile. Context is important, though. Extreme metal normally refuses rhyme, as a norm (examples are legion, but Frantic Bleep's 'Sins of omission' exemplifies this well). In most other styles, rhymes are to be assumed, such that their absence in many of the Manic Street Preachers' lyrics is more meaningful, presumably a refusal of the 'easy' position offered by rhymes, which may also be at the root of metal's refusal of them. In Pete Morton's 'Rachel', however, the casual sidestepping of many (but not all) rhymes seems to reinforce the *reportage*, and the powerful drive of the devastating narrative.

Sometimes, friction is engendered between the norms of a track's (apparent) style, and what it actually does. This is most obvious where particular readings of styles are culturally sanctioned, have become normative. The Rev. Gary Davis' 'Twelve gates to the city', for example, takes a gospel song, but performs is as a blues. Janis Joplin's versions of 'Piece of my heart' do the opposite – she takes a blues, but applies to it the vocal space, interjections and slides learnt from gospel singing. Indeed, a prime example of such friction is probably Elvis Presley's appropriation of gospel and blues techniques applied to country music. At the very least, such stylistic friction begins by sounding incongruous, but does not remain so if there is a point being made: the potential sanctity of everyday life represented by the blues, in Davis' case; the potentially transcendent power of music, in Joplin's; the power of appropriation, in Presley's. Thus, punk tracks begin from a basic reading of them as angry and nihilistic (which is why the wry humour of the Damned's 'There ain't so sanity clause', or the Rezillos' 'Glad all over' is so effective), and country tracks often appear nostalgic and supportive of old-fashioned values (the hardness of tone of Tammy Wynette's 'Stand by your

---

[19]   *Rock: the primary text*, p. 208. See Griffiths, 'From lyric to anti-lyric', pp. 48–9 for a valuable alternative perspective.

man' seen not as a paean to such values, but as recognition that her man, in his weakness, needs such solidarity[20]).

What is perhaps problematic about all these examples is that the styles are not entirely entrenched anyway, but have all learnt from each other. What is perhaps more significant in this line of thought is the interjection not only of rapping, but ultimately of ballad piano, into metal in a track such as Faith No More's 'Epic'. Here, distinct styles are brought together in a way that gives birth to a new style in its own right ('nu-metal'). Clannad's 'Theme from Harry's Game'[21] is a similar case, in that the heavy string pads and lack of any percussive element were notable against the style the band had already developed – more a case of idiolectal friction – that itself helped to give birth to the recent version (the 'New Age' version) of that mystical notion of Celtic music. Such meaning must have been developed in the early work of Bobby Darin, rare among contemporaneous performers in his brilliant ability to switch styles ('Mack the knife', 'Dream lover', 'Won't you come home, Bill Bailey'), while it was intrinsic to the stylistic cross-over that developed into progressive rock.

---

[20]   See Roy Shuker, *Understanding popular music*, (London, 1994), pp. 138–9.

[21]   This was commissioned theme music for the television drama of the same name.

Chapter 7
Persona

Theory

We come now to what seems to me the central aspect of the interpretive process. How do we interact with the track? Although it is quite possible, and quite acceptable, to be barely aware of what we are listening to, if we choose to interact with it, we give it our attention. What does it give in return? The situation is expressed very well, I think, by the novelist Michael Frayn. He is talking of the experience of reading stories, and playing games, but his comments apply equally to listening to songs: In hearing a story, he says:

> What I suspend is not disbelief but something more like any propensity I might have to divide the world into the believable and the unbelievable. What I accept, provisionally, is an alternative world … . The storyteller, in other words, creates by fiat, or web of fiats, an alternative world that I agree to inhabit for a while … . It's like a social relationship: a story entertains you – *you* entertain the *story*. You invite it in, pour it a drink, and let it talk to you without interrupting.[1]

And how does the track make itself known to us? Through the identity of the singer. With but few exceptions, it seems to me that when we listen to a track, our attention is focused particularly on the identity of the singer. It is, indeed, to the singer that we give our attention. I have raised the analogy with conversation before. In conversing, we are primarily interested in the person we are conversing with; what else may be going on becomes secondary. And we get to know that person through the interaction. I think something similar is going on in listening to songs: the principal gain is one of feeling that we better understand the 'personality' to whom we are listening, and we do this through bearing in mind the questions upon which this book is based, and which we pose to the singer.

But rather than imagine that we are listening to an individual singing to us, an individual able to express himself or herself directly, and through whose expression we understand his or her subjectivity, it is usually more helpful to recognize that we are listening to a persona, projected by a singer, in other words to an artificial construction that may, or may not, be identical with the person(ality) of the singer, as outlined at the beginning of Chapter 4. Indeed, deciding whether or not the persona is identical to the personality of the singer underpins much of the entire discourse around authenticity, a topic of Chapter 9. But even in cases

---

[1]   Michael Frayn, *The human touch* (London, 2006), p. 245.

where such identification appears to be the case, we still have to construct the persona of the individual to whom we are listening, on the basis of the track we are listening to (together with whatever other additional information we may have encountered). The first part of this chapter will address ways in which this persona operates. It is vital to remember, further, that in almost all popular song, the singer is accompanied. In practice, we construct the persona partly on the basis of clues given by the accompaniment, and there may be friction between the two. The relationship between the persona and everything else going on within the musical texture will be addressed in the second part of this chapter. Finally, I shall address some other matters linked, though more tangentially, to the issue of the persona.[2]

The identity of the singing voice that delivers the song operates at three distinct levels. At least, these levels can be made distinct through analysis, but they are not always self-evident. Indeed, that observation, and the discovery of reasons why they may not be self-evident, is itself an important part of understanding the song. It is not novel to develop such a tripartite theorization: Philip Auslander builds on work by Simon Frith[3] in distinguishing between 'the *real person* (the performer as human being), the *performance persona* (the performer as social being) and the *character* (Frith's song personality)'.[4] However, perhaps because I am less interested in musicians than I am in music, I tend to conflate the first two of these, while I further subdivide the third. My first level is comparatively unproblematic. A song is performed by a particular individual, who is normally named, an individual who has an observable historical position and identity, the song's *performer*. Thus, when we listen to the Who, we listen to the voice of Roger Daltrey. Roger Daltrey has an identity outside his existence with the Who – he has appeared in films, he is known as a keen angler, and so on. These details pertain to Daltrey as performer, and are aspects of his identity we can become cognizant of should we choose. And the same can be said of Buddy Holly, for instance, although the details will differ. In analysing the music of Buddy Holly, Dave Laing distinguishes between two approaches to a song that a performer can take, borrowing from film theory the concepts of *auteur* and *metteur en scène*: 'whereas the latter does no more than faithfully transfer [a] text to the screen, the auteur gives it certain emphases which change its meaning'.[5] When we hear Holly sing 'Every day', we create in

---

[2]   In a strong sense, what I develop here is a grossly simplified theory of narrative, but relevant to the song rather than to other spheres of narrative. It is quite possible to bring into play more complex theories of narrative (as explored, for instance, in Luc Herman and Bart Vervaeck, *Handbook of narrative analaysis* (Lincoln NE, 2005), but it seems to me that no greater complexity is *generally* necessary than what I have here.

[3]   Simon Frith, *Performing rites* (New York NY, 1998), pp. 196–9.

[4]   Philip Auslander, 'Musical persona: the physical performance of popular music', in Derek B. Scott (ed.), *The Ashgate Research Companion to Popular Musicology* (Farnham, 2009), p. 305.

[5]   Dave Laing: 'Listen to me', in Simon Frith and Andrew Goodwin (London, 1990), p. 327.

our minds an identity for that singing voice that is not identical with the identity of Buddy Holly – all performers assume a *persona* when singing and, however close that persona is to the identity of the performer, it can always be distinguished from it. Naomi Cumming notes that recording engineers modify the sound created by a particular performer: 'By altering the balance, dynamic level, and quality of her sounds, the engineers have effectively created for her a musical "body" and identity … They are able to effect this illusion because the characteristics of sounds are the aural "marks" of bodily actions'.[6] It is this 'illusion' I am calling the 'persona'. What is true of Holly is also true of, for instance, Robert Plant. But when he sings the Jimi Hendrix classic 'Hey Joe', the individual who is addressing 'Joe' is neither the actual Robert Plant (the individual who used to sing with Led Zeppelin and would go on to sing with Alison Krauss), nor is he 'Robert Plant', the persona associated with the powerful voice in those two particular situations. He is instead a figure inside the song, who has no identity outside it – he is a *protagonist* within the song. These three levels, of *performer*, *persona* and *protagonist*, are always identifiable, although the relationship between them is not necessarily self-evident.

At one extreme musicians may work to make these three categories co-extensive; at the other they may be utterly distinct. Take David Bowie's track 'Five years'. We know this as the work of Bowie the performer, a Bowie whose performance history includes such varied tracks as 'The gospel according to Tony Day' and 'Hallo Spaceboy'. However, we also know this track as the work of Bowie inhabiting the persona of Ziggy Stardust, a persona he would make explicit in performance situations, extending to some aspects of his own personal life. Who, though, is the protagonist of the song? We hear a rather didactic, despairing individual declaring that 'the end of the world is nigh' (we have only five years left …). This protagonist cannot easily be identified with either Bowie or Ziggy, although the identity of Ziggy provides a useful context for the song. Here, then, the three levels of identity are clearly distinguishable. When we hear John Lennon sing the Beatles' 'All you need is love', the situation is very different. The identity of Lennon as performer is unmistakeable, especially since the original recording was televised. It is not open to serious doubt. The characteristics of the persona Lennon adopts for the track are commensurate with the characteristics of Lennon the individual, the performer, especially since Lennon had worked so hard over the preceding years to ensure that the persona he presented was the individual he was trying to be. The song's protagonist is someone who declares that provided one loves, nothing else is necessary. Again, this appears to be the position Lennon tried to adopt in his real life, at least during this mid-1960s period. Here, then, in distinction to the Bowie example, performer, persona and protagonist appear to be identical. All tracks will exhibit degrees of relationship between these, and that degree needs to be noted. Matt Gelbart offers a thoroughgoing, perceptive and historicized analysis of the concept in particular relation to the work of the Kinks,

---

[6]   Cumming, *The sonic self*, pp. 21–2.

particularly in the subtle way that *persona* and *protagonist* are divorced.[7] He notes that in the rock'n'roll era, the *persona* was regarded as the 'genuine' voice of the *performer* and that, even after the intervention of Bowie and others 'the illusion of spontaneous composition by a protagonist–composer remains one important ingredient in rock reception'.[8] In so doing, he points to an important overlap between the *persona* and *authenticity*, which I shall address at the beginning of Chapter 9.

The identity of the protagonist is usually unproblematic – it seems to be a norm in song for the narrative to principally involve a single actor. Occasionally, there may be two equally important actors, and thus we have two protagonists. A good model for this pattern is perhaps provided by Danny Kaye and Jane Wyman's 'No two people', where the level of interchange in relation to the principal melody is very high and duties are equally shared. There is another possible actor in many tracks, a secondary protagonist. This seems to be the best way to identify those situations where some sort of conversation is going on between the protagonist and a more minor figure, as in the conversation between Ian Hunter and his backing singers ('Thunderthighs') in Mott the Hoople's 'Roll away the stone'. It can also be the best way to identify the relationship between a protagonist and an instrument, particularly if that instrument is in some way personified. This, for example, is how I hear Leadbelly's 'New Orleans' (a version of the 'House of the Rising Sun'). He takes a guitar solo (in which he's actually only repeating the line he has used under the verses), but addresses his playing of the guitar at this point: 'go ahead 'n' tell 'em' (at 1'54"), as if the guitar was an independent entity, and an independent actor.

So, what should we expect of the persona? It may be of use to impose some limits on the range of options. Three questions are useful here. The first comes from asking whether the persona appears to be *realistic*, or whether it is overtly *fictional*. A realistic persona is one that requests that we interpret it as coming directly from the singer, as a vocalized version of a direct address, through conversation or similar means (and whether or not we choose to believe that it does seem to come directly); a fictional persona is where the singer is unambiguously taking on a particular character, much as an actor does. Of course, in many cases the distinction between these two possibilities may not be immediately apparent. The second comes from asking whether the situation described, the narrative of the track, is itself *realistic*, everyday, likely to be encountered by members of the imagined community addressed by the singer, or of which the singer forms a part, or is *fictional*, perhaps with an imagined historical, or mythological, quality. The third comes from asking whether the singer is personally *involved* in the situation described, is singing from reputed experience affected by the situation, or is acting as an *observer* of the situation, external to it, and simply reporting on it. Some

7   Matthew Gelbart, 'Persona and Voice in the Kinks' Songs of the Late 1960s', *Journal of the Royal Musical Association* 128 (2003).

8   Gelbart: 'Persona and Voice in the Kinks', p. 213.

examples will explain. Billy J. Kramer and the Dakotas' 'Do you want to know a secret' is pretty unproblematic in terms of understanding the persona. 'Billy' is singing to his sweetheart in a realistic manner, duplicating the experience of thousands of contemporary men, and is clearly involved in the situation he is describing. Even in such a simple example, though, note the effect of the remainder of the texture – the punch line ('I'm in love with you') is prepared by a dramatic shift to minor vi, and by an increase in density (particularly in the kit), before the word 'you' is sung virtually unaccompanied, set apart. This example also presents answers to two further questions that help to characterize the narrative, and that I shall define as those of temporality and timespan. The time is the present (of the song), and it describes a momentary sensation (that of sharing with his sweetheart the secret that perhaps they have both felt for 'a week or two') and we are left to guess at what the future may hold. This is such a normative position for songs (whether the felt expression is positive or negative), that I shall call this combination of:

- realistic persona;
- everyday situation;
- involved stance;
- present time; and
- exploration of the moment

the 'bedrock' position of the persona. It was under the influence of psychedelia in the mid 1960s that alternative positions were first consistently explored. Foremost among these was the Kinks' 'Waterloo sunset'. This exhibits a psychedelic consciousness principally in that a very mundane experience (seeing the sun set over a metropolitan Waterloo station) is transformed into something wonderful (hinted at by the angelic choir behind the opening 'dirty old river'). The 'authentic' experience (the meeting of 'Terry and Julie'[9] who themselves gaze on the sunset) is reported from the outside by Ray Davies, whose experience of simply seeing the sunset is paradisiacal. His stance, then, is uninvolved, although his position is clearly positive towards what he describes. Note that, just because we encounter this change in the mid-1960s does not mean that the bedrock persona now becomes unattainable. One very potent example is Madness' 'Our house', from 1982. Here, the realistic/everyday/involved triad obtains, but the temporality switches rather unsystematically from the present ('father wears his Sunday best') to a future which looks back nostalgically ('she's the one they're going to miss in lots of ways', and the bridge at 2'). Kate Bush's 'There goes a tenner' comes from the same year, but its persona is rather more complicated. Kate Bush takes on the role of at least three different protagonists within the song, differentiated by vocal tone, by register and by different pronunciation, in addition to singing wordlessly

---

[9]   The names apparently taken from contemporary film stars Terence Stamp and Julie Christie.

as part of the musical texture. The plot, that of a failed bank robbery, is almost like an Ealing comedy, perhaps indicated by the tokenistic synthesized silver band. The exploration is very much of the moment, the situation is plausibly everyday (if not one many listeners will have actually experienced) and Bush's personae are clearly involved, but there is no suggestion that one (or more of them) represents 'Kate Bush' herself. The personae are unmistakably fictional. So too is the protagonist of Genesis' 'Watcher of the skies', only here, not only is the situation unrealistic (it partakes of the allegorical tone quite common in progressive rock), but the stance is again external. Indeed, the persona is almost transparent here – we're aware of the narrative being told, but we're barely aware of Peter Gabriel's individuality in telling it. Roy Harper's 'When an old cricketer leaves the crease' is sung from a similar position of detachment, and the plot is only as real as that of Kate Bush (and although the cricketers could easily be identified with various 'old masters' – Geoffrey Boycott, John Snow – since Harper's fascination with the game is easily accessible information, the description seems to be of a village cricket match). The added 'real' silver band, however, together with Harper's slow delivery, adds a mythological quality similar to that of 'Waterloo sunset'. Far from being transparent, Harper becomes the repository of arcane, or transcendental, knowledge. With some problematic tracks, we may need to think carefully about the title. It is hard to hear Fleet Foxes' 'Helpless Blues' as if the protagonist is in the midst of them, is experiencing those blues. However, if we regard the track as commenting on the 'Helplessness Blues', sung from a point of detachment or memory, then it makes rather more sense. So, the title indicates not that this track *is* those blues, but that it is *about* those blues.[10] While this basic five-part schema (persona, situation, stance, timespan and temporality) acts adequately to begin the process of constructing an identity for the persona to whom we are listening, we need to note that many concrete cases are more complex; as Umberto Fiori's analysis of Peter Gabriel's 'I have the touch'[11] argues, the immediate trust we offer to this persona is compromised by a knowingness only apparent in comparing two versions of the same song. This schema does, though, represent a basic starting-point, to be qualified by actual situations.

Address

So, the concept of the persona is not as simple as it might seem, and it combines with basic details of the setting of a track's plot to provide quite a complex set of parameters to bear in mind. The other side of the communicative relationship, that of the listener, is less complex, but is still not unitary. Who is being addressed, and how? As listener, it seems there are (again) three positions we can take up.

[10]   My thanks to Sam Englander for this stunningly important observation.

[11]   Umberto Fiori, 'Listening to Peter Gabriel's "I have the touch"', in Richard Middleton (ed.), *Reading Pop* (Oxford, 2000).

Discussions of the sense of 'musical motion' in the literature make it clear that sometimes one can seem to be part of the music that is moving (the music perhaps sweeps you up and carries you along – you seem to own the senses of feeling the music calls forth), and sometimes you can observe the music in motion, as it were from the outside.[12] Clarke suggests the former is more common with homophonic textures, and the latter more common with polyphony. These two basic positions, that we become the *protagonist*, or that we become an *observer*, are both possible in listening to song, but there is also a third position available, that of the *antagonist*. Which of these positions we take up will depend on our own sense of identity vis-à-vis that of the persona. I take Billy Joel's 'And so it goes' as an example. If I have experienced the sense of helpless infatuation that may have a frustrating outcome, which I take to be the topic of the song, then I can feel the song as an expression of myself – it is as if the Billy Joel persona becomes superimposed on me. This is equally possible if I have not had such an experience but want to feel what it might be like to have done so. If I have been on the other side of such a relationship, my identity can become superimposed on that of the antagonist (addressed by Joel as 'you'), or again, I can try on this identity. In order to do so, I may have to construe the track's persona as female, or likewise myself, and this may require some internal negotiation. If I don't wish to do this, or if I have not had such an experience, or if I don't wish to try out such an experience, the third position, that of observer, is still open to me. This one is frequently more comfortable (and certainly so in the case of this track), but enables less involvement in the narrative. All three positions are available only if the track specifies an antagonist. As a listener to the Kinks' 'Waterloo sunset', for example, the only effective options are to identify with Ray Davies' persona, or to observe his observations, standing behind his shoulder, as it were. (Were we to try to take on the position of Terry or Julie, for instance, what we experience, our perspective, is simply not covered by the song.)

Even in the case where we identify as the protagonist,[13] we are still being addressed by the persona, and it is the relationship between that persona and listener that I now turn to in more detail. In everyday encounters between individuals, recognition of the distance between a speaker and a listener is crucial in determining the type of relationship they manifest during the course of their interaction, and is particularly determined by both olfactory and visual signals. This cannot be directly transferred to the purely aural realm, of course, but it can

---

[12]   Clarke, *Ways of listening*, pp. 71–6; Mark Johnson and Steve Larson, '"Something in the way she moves" – metaphors of musical motion', *Metaphor and symbol* 18/2 (2003).

[13]   Note Raymond Gibbs on research into reading: 'Readers construct mental models for narrative by adopting the perspective of the protagonist'; we seem to identify similar positions by the term 'protagonist'. Raymond W. Gibbs Jr., *Embodiment and cognitive science* (Cambridge, 2006), p. 201.

be addressed through a modification of *proxemics*[14] to refer to recorded presences. Proxemics describes and analyses the distances (social, public, private, intimate) between individuals-in-interaction. These are a factor, on recordings, not only of the audible distance of a persona from the listener's position (i.e. loudness and degree of reverberation), but of the degree of congruence between a persona and the personic environment.[15] Doyle points to the crucial importance, in pre-stereo recordings at least, of the difference between what he calls a *realist* recording aesthetic and a *romanticist* aesthetic. By 'realist', he refers to the practice of recording 'dry', i.e. incorporating as little room ambience as possible. By 'romanticist', he refers to the practice of including room ambience. The former tended initially to be used for popular music, the latter for classical: 'the realist approach ... provided "an effect of intimacy ... the singer or soloist singing just for you" ... Romanticism conversely had the effect of seemingly "bringing the listener into the studio or auditorium"'.[16] (This is a related formulation to that of Zagorski-Thomas' *staging* (Chapter 2.)

I explore this idea through two examples: one simple, the other more complex. Leona Lewis' 'Run' utilizes a growth of texture, fairly stereotypical for the impassioned love song. In the course of the track, she moves through all four proxemic zones. The track begins with Lewis in an intimate zone, backed by a resonant piano very much in the background. The piano is joined at 45" by mid-range sustained strings, providing a carpet of sound. At 1'08", both strings and Lewis achieve an upper range: while the degree of reverb has not altered, it is as if she has stepped back, as the greater range opens her words to a wider audience; she has moved to the personal zone. By 1'38", she is no longer foregrounded by her environment, but the whole texture has receded into a social zone, or rather the environment has moved towards us. At 2', into the second verse, the drumkit (which had previously consisted simply of on-beat ride cymbals, which had been crucial in bringing the environment to the fore) falls into a conventional pattern, and any remaining illusion of intimacy is lost (she now seems proud of her profession of constancy). By 3'20", both she and the strings appear with full force, and are subsequently joined by a full gospel choir. Any sense of restraint is lost, as if she no longer cares who hears. Lewis' persona is now fully enveloped by the environment and is situated in the public zone. Table 7.1 summarizes the musical features of these four zones in terms of:

---

[14]   Edward T. Hall, *The hidden dimension* (London, 1969), pp. 110–19. The term 'interpersonal distance' is currently more commonly found in the psychology literature to refer to this conceptual area.

[15]   Maasø employs proxemics in order to investigate the viewer's perspective on the spoken voice in film and other mediated contexts, and develops his argument in a different (but not contradictory) direction from that taken here. Aarnt Maasø, 'The proxemics of the mediated voice', in Jay Beck and Tony Grajeda (eds.), *Lowering the boom: critical studies in film sound* (Urbana IL, 2008).

[16]   Doyle, *Echo and reverb*, p. 57.

- the perceived distance between persona and listener, modified by the intervention in this space of any other musical material sources;
- the relationship between the persona and the personic environment (this will be defined and developed in the subsequent section);
- the way the persona is articulated.

Table 7.1   Proxemic zones

Zones	Distance: persona/listener Degrees of intervention	Persona/environment	Articulation of persona
Intimate	- Very close to listener (i.e. touching distance) - No intervening musical material	- Persona set in front of environment - Normally high degree of separation between persona and environment - Vocal placed at front of soundbox and abuts the boundary of the soundbox	- Close range whisper - Clarity of vocal sounds (coughs, breath intake) - Lyrical content suggests intimacy/potential physical contact and addresses interpersonal relationship between two people
Personal	- Close to listener (within arm's length) - Possibility of intervening musical material	- Persona in front of environment - Still a certain degree of separation but less than in intimate zone - Vocal not at forefront of soundbox, set back from boundary	- Soft to medium vocals - Less clarity of vocal sounds - Lyrical content addresses two or three people
Social	- Medium distance from listener - Intervening musical material	- Persona within the environment - Little separation and more integration - Vocal placed within the centre of soundbox	- Medium to loud vocals - Few, if any, vocal sounds heard - Lyrical content addresses small/medium group of people
Public	- Large distance from listener - High degree of intervening musical material	- Persona engulfed and towards rear boundaries of the environment - High degree of integration - Vocal towards rear of soundbox	- Full, loud vocals, shout/semi-shout - No vocal sounds heard - Vocals address large group

The Foo Fighters' 'All my life' is a rather more complex example.[17] At the opening, Dave Grohl's vocals appear very much in focus, since they form a larger block of sound than the more elongated positioning of the accompanying guitar. This sense of focus allows us to sense the distance between our listening selves and Grohl's persona. The guitar uses the sort of fast reiterated rhythmic pattern of which Camilleri writes,[18] whereby the very speed of the pattern contributes to the sense of spatial saturation (a sense that would be magnified were it more heavily distorted). The lower dynamic serves to give it less focus than Grohl's voice, but its repeated pitches give it stability. Grohl begins in the intimate zone (his semi-whisper and audible vocal breaths). At 35", as the rest of the band enters, group width is increased, seeming to cover the entire scene width. Grohl's persona is no longer focused and detached from the environment, but has become enveloped by it, reducing its definition. Guitars panned to each side, but particularly on the right, have encroached on the persona's personal space. As a result, Grohl's persona has changed its mode of delivery – he is now shouting – in order to make himself heard over the rest of the band.[19]

Persona/Personic Environment

The expression of all singers in popular music is mediated.[20] It has for long been mediated by individuals working in the music industry, whose combined action determines just whose expression reaches us. The advent of phenomena such as MySpace and YouTube changes the detail, and the scope, of such mediation, but not the fact of it. Musicians are still prevented from reaching us simply because the amount of material available prevents us as listeners from accessing all of it, and thus any specifiable item. Singers' expression is mediated by the act of recording. Producers and engineers (and even the individual musician acting as producer or engineer) alter the sound that they hear in order to create the sound they believe listeners will accept (no matter how close these may be, they are not identical). And, it is even mediated by the act of singing – how many of us, in order to communicate with another, will preferentially choose to sing? Song is clearly a heightened situation, a situation designed to emphasize certain features and to play down others, and thus to assume that a singer communicates directly with an audience, singly or as an entity, is simply unrealistic. But singing the popular song is a situation that nonetheless has to deal with its 'unnaturalness' carefully,

---

[17]   I am very grateful to Patty Schmidt for this example, and for her and Ruth Dockwray's work on it, some of which I make use of here.

[18]   Camilleri, 'Shaping sounds, shaping spaces', p. 203.

[19]   This work on proxemics is more fully developed in Allan F. Moore, Patricia Schmidt and Ruth Dockwray, 'The hermeneutics of spatialization in recorded song', *twentieth-century music* 6/1 (2009).

[20]   I develop this argument in detail in *Rock: the primary text*, pp. 181–91.

depending on how the singer (or the singer's management) wants to appear. Simon Frith argues that one means for doing this is through the sonic elements that we would not necessarily call to mind when thinking of the musical content of a song:

> Pop songs celebrate not the articulate but the inarticulate, and the evaluation of pop singers depends not on words but on sounds – on the noises around the words. In daily life, the most directly intense statements of feeling involve just such noises: people gasp, moan, laugh, cry ... people distrust the silver-tongued, the seducers, politicians, salesmen, who've got the gift of the gab. Inarticulateness, not poetry, is the popular songwriter's conventional sign of sincerity.[21]

Meaning is thus not dependent simply on what is sung, but also how, hence my focus in Chapter 4 on taking into account a range of factors in the voice.

But the voice is mediated also by what accompanies it. The word 'accompany' indicates being in the company of something else, with an implied hierarchy of perceptual pertinence, although not necessarily one of significance. Musically, what accompanies forms the substance of the environment for what is accompanied. Philip Tagg's semiotic method (see Chapter 8) reads this implied relationship (between what accompanies and what is accompanied) as the embodiment in music of the relationship between an individual and that individual's environment.[22] He observes the normative underpinning of a melody–accompaniment dualism for all popular song, insisting that this textural structure is 'what Haydn and AC/DC share in common';[23] he argues that it is as pervasive a musical feature as its visual equivalent, the figure/ground dualism of post-Renaissance European painting. So, if accompaniment equates, at first approximation, to environment, then melody, in Tagg's understanding, equates to persona. The term 'persona' is in wide, if loose, usage;[24] I actually derive it from the writings of Edward T. Cone,[25] but in the first part of this chapter I have already departed from him in how I observe it to be constituted. Indeed, I depart also from Tagg in that for the analysis of popular song, it is less the melody *per se* that is subject to accompaniment, than 'the result of the activity of singing', and that thus encompasses lyrics and vocality in addition; Tagg's work concerns itself only little with lyrics. Eric Clarke's adoption of a theory of subject position does concern itself with lyrics, and also with accompaniment.[26] He argues that for a song to imply a subject position, for it to encourage a listener to prefer one reading to others, it must be possible to

---

[21] Frith, *Sound effects*, p. 35.

[22] As paraphrased in Middleton, *Studying popular music*, p.28.

[23] Philip Tagg, *Introductory notes to the semiotics of music* (http://www.tagg.org/xpdfs/semiotug.pdf, no date), p. 38.

[24] For example in Brackett, *Interpreting Popular Music*, p. 186.

[25] Particularly Edward T. Cone, *The composer's voice* (Berkeley CA, 1974).

[26] Eric Clarke, 'Subject-Position and the Specification of Invariants in music by Frank Zappa and P.J.Harvey', *Music Analysis* 18/3 (1999).

distinguish analytically between what he terms 'content' and 'technique', such that the 'technique' narrows the possible interpretations a listener may make of the 'content'. For Clarke, 'content' refers particularly to the realm of the lyrics, while 'technique' in principle refers to all other constitutive aspects of a song. Neither Clarke nor Tagg use the term 'persona' – Clarke prefers 'subject',[27] while Tagg uses 'individual'. Both of these, however, refer to an equivalent identity. I prefer the term 'persona' for a number of reasons. First, as explored in Chapter 4, it reminds us that this identity is fictional (and, frequently, it is passive), a characteristic that is not brought out by the competing terms. Second, it suggests comparison with the persona adopted by an actor in a drama, which is helpful in its relation to the Frayn quote at the beginning of this chapter.

I shall be defining a number of potential relationships obtaining between persona and environment in this section, and shall adopt a position that makes use of both Clarke and Tagg. Both lyric, its manner of articulation, and its shaping melody *can* conspire to create the persona, which is inhabited by the individual (or sometimes individuals) who sing to us. The environment within which (or against which) that persona operates is represented by the music that accompanies them, and that therefore includes three distinct elements:

- the textural matters normally considered under the heading 'accompaniment';
- the harmonic setting, including the modal/tonal vocabulary;
- the formal setting or narrative structure, i.e. the order in which its events take place, and the patterns of repetition within this order.

In so discussing, it is important to bring together the factors discussed in Chapters 2–4. My recourse to the notion of *environment* is deliberate here, in the context of ecological perception, which I raised in the introduction and will return to in Chapter 8. But, to necessarily complicate matters further, because as individuals we are always part of the environment against which we view others, on occasion the melody can, in theory at least, be argued to operate as if it were part of the environment rather than the persona. Elsewhere I have noted that the accompaniment can support, or even amplify, the signification of the voice.[28] This is what is generally considered the 'normal' role of the accompaniment, to such an extent that an accompaniment that does not do this is sometimes considered faulty or inept. But an accompaniment can do more. It can explain why the persona is acting in the way the song reports, even to the extent that the persona may be hiding this from themselves. And an accompaniment can go further, undermining

---

[27]   Eero Tarasti uses both 'subject' and 'actor' in his semiotic scheme, tracing the rise of the former in the late-eighteenth-century development of periodized melody in instrumental music. Eero Tarasti, *A theory of musical semiotics* (Bloomington IN, 1994), p. 104.

[28]   Allan F. Moore, 'The Persona/Environment relation in recorded song'; *Music Theory Online*   11/4   (http:www.music-theory.org/mto/issues/mto.05.11.4/mto.05.11.4.moore_frames.html, 2005).

the persona, and thus encouraging listeners into distrust. How we read what the environment may be representing in these cases is, of course, flexible. In the last of these, and potentially in the second, it acts as another site of friction that generates significance. One possible line of development of these thoughts would be through the notion of narrativity, into focusing on the relationship between the persona and the accompaniment in developing a narrative. Indeed, David Nicholls has done just that, in the process outlining a typology with clear parallels to the one I develop below.[29] However, what I have called (above) the 'formal setting' is only one aspect that contributes to the sense we make of a persona – I thus subsume it within my discussion here, acknowledging as I do the richness of Nicholls' own theoretical position.

Viewed systematically, then, the potential relationship between the persona and the environment can be described by observing the environment as occupying one of five positions:

- the environment is *inert*, contributing nothing specific to the meaning of the song;
- the environment is *quiescent*, merely setting up the (largely attitudinal) expectations through which a listener may listen;
- the environment is *active*, and supports the position of the persona, frequently through devices related to word-painting;
- the environment is *interventionist*, going further than what is specified in the lyric by amplifying what it signifies, or even by enacting the lyric;
- the environment is *oppositional*.

The following exploration follows the structure of my earlier article,[30] but exemplifies some of these environmental roles differently.

The impact an environment can have on the persona can range from the significant to the trivial, as accompanimental textures, harmonies and forms serve both subtle and blatant functions. The latter are easily discussed. The need for a singer to orient himself or herself in terms of precise metre and stable pitch is endemic to anglophone popular musics and, probably, to most European popular music. I am not convinced that the ability to retain metre and pitch can be considered normative even amongst highly respected interpreters. Producer Bernard Krause wrote of singer Patrice Holloway: 'So perfect was her pitch [on an unaccompanied track] that Paul [Beaver] was able to lay a piano track ... some weeks later without altering the speed of the tape to change the pitch'.[31] There would have been no need to make such a point were this a skill more widely exercised in practice. We can therefore cite the provision of a stable metrical and harmonic backdrop as

---

[29] David Nicholls, 'Narrative theory as an analytical tool in the study of popular music texts', *Music and Letters* 88/2 (2007).

[30] Allan F. Moore, 'The Persona/Environment relation in recorded song'.

[31] Bernard Krause: Sleevenote to Beaver and Krause: *Gandharva* (1971).

simultaneously the most necessary, most basic, and least interesting, purpose of an accompaniment. Whatever else it does, it is almost certain to function in this way. Some accompaniments do no more. A related reason is hardly more interesting. Accompaniments frequently set the genre of a track, laying out the normative environmental conditions, together with all the expectation-related baggage that a theory of genre carries.[32] Thus, a heavy metal track, a country track, a punk track, an R&B track, an adult-oriented rock (AOR) track, are in large part defined by the instrumentation and sound-sources used to accompany the singer and, in some cases (a key difference between metal and AOR, for instance), the style and manner of performance of those instruments, individually or collectively. Key here is a basic distinction between accompaniments that signify only at the level of *style* (Jacobson's metalingual function, as in the opening of Chapter 6), and those that signify at the more particularised level of the individual *track*.[33]

All tracks operate at this level and, if it does no more, in both of these senses (stable backdrop and genre-setting), the track's personic environment is inert. Thus, when Dorothy Carless sings 'I'd know you anywhere', the alternation of sax and brass choirs in Geraldo's accompanying orchestra situates us unambiguously in the swing era. Patsy Cline's 'I'm blue again' is a similarly clear example. The song is in 32-bar form, in $\frac{12}{8}$. In the first half of the verse, the kit and piano have a regular triplet pattern, which is broken for bars 17–24 (see Example 7.1). There seems to be no particularized expressive content in either this basic groove, or in the change of articulation at that point. It simply marks a formal break, the shift to the middle 8 section.

Example 7.1   Patsy Cline: 'I'm blue again'; kit patterns

In saying it has no expressive role, I mean simply that these elements could perfectly well be transferred to another song performed by Patsy Cline within the same style – and indeed they are (analogous textural changes are found, for example, in 'Today, tomorrow and forever' and 'Never no more'). So, in this example, the role of the accompanimental environment is simply to situate this song in terms of chronology and genre as an example of immediately post-rock'n'roll country music. All tracks operate at this level.

Accompanimental textures can also set the attitudinal tone of a song, laying out a particular manner of approach to which the singer then conforms, as in Bob Dylan's 'Just like a woman', in so doing moving from inertia to quiescence. The

---

[32]   Moore, 'Categorical conventions in music-discourse'.

[33]   Allan F. Moore, 'The track' in Amanda Bayley (ed.), *Recorded Music: Society, Technology and Performance* (Cambridge, 2010).

accompanying band has a certain rhythmic looseness, most identifiable in very subtle delays of the guitar behind the kit. This comes across most typically as relaxed, but it might be read as hedonistic, as hippy, or even as sloppy, depending on the listener and his or her relationship with Dylan's persona. Whichever hearing one makes, the accompanimental environment could be argued to act as a neat metaphor for the falling to pieces of the 'little girl' who, with all her insecurities, hides behind the song's title. If the reliance on generic convention in 'I'm blue again' leads any genre-competent listener to expect to hear nothing new in the song, the (relatively) unusual 'loose' introduction to 'Just like a woman' will probably create in a genre-competent listener an expectation of an idiosyncratic lyric content, and one of a potentially personal nature.[34]

In other examples of such tone-setting, the accompaniment can function inter-stylistically, to signal that a song will depart somewhat from the style normally associated with a particular band.[35] I have in mind the string quartet in the Beatles' 'Yesterday', for instance, or the prominent Hammond organ at the beginning of Led Zeppelin's 'Thank you'. This tells us we are in for an early rock ballad rather than a track in blues-rock, or proto-heavy-metal, idiom (which the name 'Led Zeppelin' might indicate), a promise redeemed by the earnestness of Robert Plant's expressions of constancy. In Roy Harper's 'When an old cricketer leaves the crease', which I addressed above, the function of the accompanimental silver band is rather more specific: it encourages a culturally competent listener to hear the song as nostalgic, in its evocation of a no longer communal, rural English, late summer twilight, echoing the familiar conceit equating the passage of a year to the course of a life.

So, the function of tone-setting acts to prepare the listener for how to respond to the style, probably from the outset of a song. As far as this function is concerned, the accompaniment will not necessarily intervene thereafter in the expressive meaning of the song. Recall that this is what the majority of accompaniments simply do.[36] And it is here, we may suppose, that a large number of listeners 'switch off'. It seems to me that all will be, on some level, aware of these lower levels of functionality of accompaniments; as Nick Cook argues, the music of Madonna's 'Material Girl' 'essentially amplifies that of the words'.[37] I assume this is a major structural cut-off point because, for so many listeners, music seems to act as a reflection and confirmation of their (or others') lives, rather than an active constituent of them (or maybe it is their desire that music should so function). However, to note the functions that follow, active listening is definitely required. Other than making this simple distinction, I would not suggest that the functions I

---

[34] My thanks for Anwar Ibrahim for this point.

[35] This just about qualifies as a *genre synecdoche* (see Chapter 8).

[36] Some genres have a greater degree of stereotypicality than others: Motown; old skool hip-hop; early 1970s Status Quo exemplify this at various levels (those of label roster; subculturally delimited style; idiolect).

[37] Nicholas Cook, *Analysing Musical Multimedia* (Oxford, 1998), pp. 151–9.

outline are hierarchically related in terms of 'importance' – what is important for
a listener is for that listener to determine. Nonetheless, a degree of active listening
is required in order to achieve the greatest richness from the listening experience.

As with so many expressive features, we become alert to them when faced with
their subversion. ''T smidje', by Flemish vocal trio Laïs, begins with the sort of §
clod-hopping accompaniment that was the bane of 1970s folk rock (see. Example
7.2) – examples such as Fairport Convention's 'Lark in the morning' or Steeleye
Span's 'The mooncoin jig' come to mind.

Example 7.2 Laïs: ''T smidje'; opening

However, as soon as the vocals enter, with what is initially an offbeat subsidiary
figure (Example 7.3), doubts are raised as to the provenance of the accompaniment.

Example 7.3 Laïs: ''T smidje'; from 12"

I would suggest that, by the time the exquisite upper dominant pedal, in the voice,
makes itself felt in the second half of the verse, over the increased rate of harmonic
movement there (Example 7.4), we have been lifted well out of the putative world
of the introduction.

Example 7.4 Laïs: ''T smidje'; from 46"

The fact that the vast majority of listeners to this track will not understand the
(Flemish) lyrics does not obscure the way the texture overcomes its initial hindrance.

(In any case, Kadril, the band who accompany Laïs on this track, acknowledge Fairport Convention unproblematically within their stylistic heritage.) In these examples, then, the accompanimental texture gives us information about how to situate a particular track against its stylistic background, but without necessarily relating to the signification of the song as represented by the lyric.

It is with this function, as the environment becomes active, that we begin to tread interesting ground. We begin to approach that realm where some attention to the *detail* of the environment is necessary in order to apprehend the expressive richness of the virtual performances of particular personae. Here we have the received view of the role of an accompaniment, which is to conform to the ostensible meaning of the lyrics and, in doing so, to support, or perhaps illustrate, the meaning of the song. Forms of word-painting are the most obvious devices here, but it is important to avoid seeking the sort of notationally based word-painting techniques familiar from notated music. In a recorded genre, word-painting works by reference to the sounds heard, not to their visual representation. Iggy Pop's track 'Whatever' (from 2003) exemplifies this clearly. The song originates on a lacklustre album, and is ironic in its consistent recourse to the kind of adolescent disdain indicated by the title (Iggy Pop was born in 1947). The stylistically conventional overdriven guitar that forms part of the accompaniment simply drops from the texture on the words 'her voice just fades away'. It is not a true fade, but the parallel is strong enough – by dropping away, the texture literally illustrates the content of, actually energizes, the lyric. Indeed, the very obviousness of the device adds to the rather tongue-in-cheek subject position the song adopts. An analogous, although not ironic, situation can be found in Joe Cocker's cover of 'With a little help from my friends', discussed in Chapter 4. A similar situation occurs in Razorlight's 'In the city' and other songs with a form of call-and-response between voices – the backing voices here simply promote the lead singer, responding to him – they do not represent the 'you' he was 'looking for', but are almost looking over his shoulder, amplifying his anger. There is no doubt that he is in charge. Buddy Holly's 'Raining in my heart' contains some conventional string writing supporting the lyric – the pizzicati, particularly as they appear immediately after the 'raining', act as a sonic anaphone for drops of water, followed by the downward string glissando, as if rain is cascading down, emphasizing how deeply his sorrow is felt. However, the accompaniment perhaps goes too far, in emphasizing 'misery, misery' with repeated blue thirds, to which the violins slide. A string orchestra resorting to blue notes is rather arch. In the chorus to Eric Clapton's 'Let it grow', it is the pattern of bass and melody that supports the lyric – the growth is literally enacted by contrary motion in these outer parts, extending (growing) the pitch range. A similar degree of accompanimental support is offered to John Lennon's 'Imagine' by the production qualities particularly of Lennon's accompanying piano. Here, the sonically unfocused quality of the production of the instrument's sound supports a similar fuzziness in the singer's ideology, which has contributed to the debates about both the degree of realism, and the self-delusion, that may surround Lennon's song.[38]

We don't have to wait for the rise of rock to find such examples. Nat King Cole's recorded performances of 'When I fall in love' spend most of their course promising how he will behave when that eventuality comes about. Unexceptionally, the song matches turns to the minor with recollections of sadness but, at the last, as his falling in love becomes directed ('when I fall in love ... with you'), the final 'you' is marked by an unexpected chromaticism. Here, it is not the accompanimental textures, but the harmonic environment that supports the lyric. A rather different example appears in the Yes song 'Heart of the sunrise'. According to the lyrics printed on the album sleeve, the word 'sharp' is clearly marked for attention, being capitalized. Almost without exception, each appearance of the word is immediately followed by a 'sharp' sound, i.e. one with a notably crisper attack than its surrounding sounds – on its second appearance (at 4'26") by a most pointed kick drum, at its third (at 5'43") by the entire band. By enacting the lyric, these examples seem closer to what I would describe as 'amplifying' the meaning, rather than simply 'supporting' it, suggesting that 'supporting' and 'amplifying' be seen as two stages on a continuum.

Enactment of a lyric will often take place by means of a track's form. The lack of final closure embodied in Janis Joplin's live performance of 'Ball and chain'[39] serves to prevent the listener from treating the performance as simply a performance of the song. Here, the accompanying musicians vanish (in the actual performance, they most likely left the stage) while Joplin delivers an extempore solo but, in a departure from contemporary practice, they fail to return to round off the song. The device is derived from earlier US pentecostal preachers, and we would expect the band to return to complete the song with another chorus, resolving the tension caused by her words, distancing us from what she has said, restoring our comfort, in effect saying: I don't really mean it, it's just a fiction. The solo serves to enact the lyrics by blurring the boundary between a (fictionalized) performance and a diatribe on the nature of contemporary society. The device ensures we know she means it far more incontrovertibly than words could have managed; while the message is in the words, their import is given by a musical device. In Sonny and Cher's love song 'I got you babe', the 'us against the world' position that the lyrics promote is maintained musically by a monotone $\hat{5}$ over I–IV–I – the sense is of maintaining the melodic pitch (and thus their stance) 'in spite of' the shift to a dissonant IV. After a series of verses/choruses (none of which comes to rest on I), a final playout continues, before fading, over a I–IV–I–V–(I–IV–I–V...) pattern. This is the first time in the song that I is approached directly from a strong V, rather than from IV or an imperfect cadence. And, for the first time, the emphasis in the relationship changes, from 'I got *you*' to '*I* got you'. This change, formally specific, is thus enacted in the harmony. A more complex

[38]   Keith Negus, *Popular Music in Theory* (Cambridge, 1996), pp. 102–6.

[39]   Explored in Moore, *Rock: the primary text*, p. 96.

example appears in Ashford & Simpson's 'Ain't no mountain high enough', as sung by Diana Ross and discussed in Chapter 6. The single verse, and a bridge that marks a change of relational position, is highly unusual. But this transgressive nature of the form, marked by the chromatic bass, supports the lyrics. These tracks, in moving from uncertainty to certainty, also flout the norm whereby most popular songs explore a static position. Analogously, Cilla Black's singing of the Bacharach/David classic 'Alfie' subverts expectations of the form of the song. In the first two verses, the singer is bemused by her lover 'Alfie' (she always stresses the first syllable of the name) who holds it 'wise to be cruel'. At the beginning of the third verse, her enquiries become an assertion: 'I believe in love', after which she insists that 'without true love we just exist, Alfie', stressing for the first time the last syllable of his name. This alteration marks a change in her emotional position. I shall argue in Chapter 8 that her self-discovery coincides with both a shift in harmonic language and transgression of normal formal practice; in this way harmony and form work together to mark her moment of self-awareness.

Three further examples will demonstrate the variety of ways simple accompanimental textures are involved in such enactment. As discussed in Chapter 6, Björk's 'Army of me' overturns established gender stereotypes in angrily addressing a weak protagonist: the absence of a harmonic filler layer within the texture (i.e. the sparsity of the accompanimental strands) removes an element that distances the listener, making palpable the menace expressed. The Beach Boys' 'God only knows' leaves the answer to 'what I'd be without you' unanswered in the lyric. However, the song's conclusion provides an answer, in the three-part quasi-quodlibet, which literally enacts the breaking up that the persona would otherwise endure. In a final example, the persona's environment is formed by a combination of form and accompaniment, but which seems to go beyond both – this environment for the song 'John Gaudie', by English folk outfit Whippersnapper, clearly 'amplifies' the signification – it makes it larger, sets it on a wider stage. The song concerns our John who breaks out of gaol to go off and write a fiddle tune, which the band then go on to play. We might assume the song to be traditional, and the subsequent tune newly invented. In fact, what happens is a reversal of this – the final tune is traditional, while the song itself is credited to fiddler Chris Leslie. This variety of examples attests to the wide presence of this function.

So, we move from simply supporting the meaning of the song, to amplifying it, to providing more information than is present in the lyric. There are other ways of amplifying the song's meaning than this. One concerns lyrics of ambiguous meaning. The issue of ambiguity is problematic because, with many songs, ambiguity is only the result of unfamiliarity with idiom, and is thus dependent on the nature of listeners' competence. Traffic's 'Hole in my shoe', though, provides a case that may be more universally valid. It causes trouble to anyone who simply tries to interpret the lyrics at face value – 'an elephant's eye was looking at me from a bubblegum tree' for instance. The accompanimental texture, however, situates the song very clearly within the psychedelic movement, indicating that the lyrics are not to be taken at face value, that the environment is not a realist one.

Thus the 'tin soldiers' do not literally 'stand at my shoulder'. Indeed, the prominent psychedelic coding[40] may even imply that the texture, rather than the lyric itself, be the prime carrier of meaning. This coding is provided primarily by instrumentation (sitar, flute, mellotron) and production techniques (slow chord bending, reverse recording, phasing). Thus we are reassured that the song's ambiguity is inherent, and is not a feature of our possible lack of competence. In this way its meaning is clarified.

Meaning is also amplified when an environment provides information more deeply encoded than that of the lyrics, most particularly by its harmonic underpinning, for harmonic setting often implies very particular readings of lyrics. Simple examples are provided by Slade's 'Coz I luv you', by Jimi Hendrix' 'Hey Joe' and by the Beatles' 'I want you (she's so heavy)'. The first two songs concern troublesome interpersonal relationships, and both are set to open-ended harmonic loops. While the relationship in the Beatles' track is less troublesome, it appears (as yet) to be unrequited, and the open-ended nature of the playout (half the length of the song) underpins the not-yet nature of the expression. And perhaps the delay is part of the pleasure, since the 'heavy' nature of the playout riff[41] is not something they wish to escape from. It is the circular nature of the patterns that illuminates the obsessive nature of all three songs, something that is not fully explicit in the lyrics themselves. On 'The way that it shows', Richard Thompson uses harmony to amplify the similar disintegration of a relationship, below the surface, in the obsessive repetition of the sequence d–b–g–E. A sensible sequence in terms of root motion becomes nonsensical (in relation to assumptions about harmonic norms in his repertoire) through its chromaticisms. Slightly more complex examples are given by the Beach Boys' 'Good vibrations' and by Coverdale Page's 'Take me for a little while', both of which will be discussed in Chapter 8.

We can move further, from support, through amplification, to explanation. The environment now becomes interventionist. The harmonic underpinning to the Rolling Stones' 'Satisfaction' explains the state Mick Jagger describes. This is a constant state, one of being unable to achieve satisfaction, to achieve closure. Musically, closure is unattainable here because the constant repeated sequence of the open-ended verse is simply a mixolydian I–IV; the I is so familiar that the closure otherwise attendant on achieving it is impossible here. The melody, too, is insistent upon its reiterated tonics. No wonder he can't get no satisfaction – he has nowhere else to go. From a very different genre, Vanessa Carlton's 'Ordinary day' uses harmony and texture to explain the lyric. The song concerns an encounter with first love, energized from the outset by Carlton's breathy delivery and an insecure bass that consistently sounds the tonic third rather than the root, providing a picture of (pleasant) insecurity or anticipation (Example 7.5).

---

[40]   Sheila Whiteley, *The space between the notes* (London, 1992).

[41]   'Heavy' in the sense of 'deep', 'profound' - an overused descriptor of contemporary experience under LSD that became transferred to that borderline between nascent progressive rock and heavy metal.

Example 7.5 Vanessa Carlton: 'Ordinary day'; opening

After two verses, at 1'46", the imaginary 'ordinary boy' is providing security (she's 'in the palm of your hand') as the tonic harmony achieves its affirmatory root (Example 7.6).

Example 7.6 Vanessa Carlton: 'Ordinary day'; from 1'46"

To mark this coming together, at 2'1", the two independent parts move in both rhythmic and partial melodic unison (Example 7.7).

Example 7.7 Vanessa Carlton: 'Ordinary day'; from 2'1"

Subsequently, she exits what was 'just a dream' and we move back to separation and insecurity marked by absence of the harmonic root. However, as she recalls the experience out of the dream world, at 3'20", she recovers her security. The song thus provides a model of a girl overcoming insecurity through learning to trust a 'significant other', dramatized by the difference between 'dream' and 'reality' and the transfer of something understood while in the 'dream' state into reality. This model cannot be inferred from the lyrics alone, but requires close attention to both the texture and harmonies of her accompaniment.

In suggesting that an environment may explain the actions of a persona, Clarke argues that it is through the detail of the environments of particular songs that the potential range of listener responses to the issues presented by the persona is limited. He focuses on identification with the singer and protagonist, a rather direct confrontation with P.J. Harvey and John Parish's potent 'Taut', a song that, he argues, 'draws the listener in to a close mixture of infatuation and terrified submission that can turn people into victims'.[42] He demonstrates this most particularly through close attention to the song's introduction, its combination of particular sounds, their predictability and their connotations, and the way these set up the lyric. However, it is not only the listener who can be disposed to take up a particular reading of a song. In some instances, the persona represented by the singer can be predisposed to take up a particular reading, with that predisposition being apparent to the listener. In this sort of case, the environment is partially described as the singer's confidante. The backing singers in Joe Cocker's 'With a little help from my friends' take on this role, as they supply the support he craves. In this role, the environment effectively provides advice to the persona inhabited by the singer, about how to act in response to the situation that is the subject of the song. And this is nowhere more telling than in cases where alternative versions of the same song exist, as exemplified by a comparison of the accompaniments to Lorraine Ellison's, Bette Midler's and Shirley Brown's recorded performances of the soul classic 'Stay with me (baby)'. In Shirley Brown's rather standard performance, the tempo remains constant as her situation is left unproblematized. In Lorraine Ellison's performance, she seems almost unconcerned for herself. She is simply pleading for the continuance of a relationship. She needs to deliver the lyrics with such force, though, that we might be moved to ask whether such a continuation is in her own best interests. She points out in the song that she has always been around for 'him', she has proved her devotion, which she now desperately implores him to reciprocate. The key moment occurs in the chorus, with the way the accompaniment operates. The $\frac{12}{8}$ feel, with pronounced upbeat, seems to push the song forward rather roughly. The rallentando of the previous bar is very localized, and the chorus picks up with quite a lilt. The difference between this feel, and that of the comparable portion of Bette Midler's later cover, is striking. Midler is performing even further over the top than did Ellison (in comparison to Brown's restraint). The accompaniment then drags Midler's 'cries', giving her space to fully indulge herself. In the chorus, in opposition to Ellison's version, the accompaniment (most particularly the bass and kit) provides constant movement throughout the second half of the bar, a feel that is much closer to $\frac{6}{8}$ than $\frac{12}{8}$. This seems to support her plea for the continuation of a static situation (compare Examples 7.8 and 7.9). In Bette Midler's performance, then, the music is not pushed forward. It seems to me that for Lorraine Ellison, the accompanimental environment, which is acting as her confidante, is saying 'move to the future', which will be a better situation for her, since staying with 'him' will result in a difficult relationship. For Bette Midler, again acting as her confidante, the accompaniment, in indulging her, is saying 'stay with it', 'stay with him', 'stay with the situation', oblivious to the difficulties which a good confidante should foresee.

---

[42]   Clarke, 'Subject-Position and the Specification of Invariants', p. 371.

Example 7.8   Lorraine Ellison: 'Stay with me baby'; end of verse

Example 7.9   Bette Midler: 'Stay with me baby'; end of verse

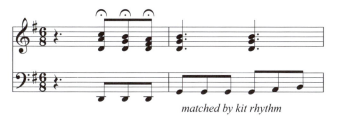

matched by kit rhythm

What is happening here, then, is that the environment provides us with information which is over and above what we get not only from the lyrics, but from the persona too. Indeed, it implies different readings of different performances. Moreover, it is information that the singer is probably only party to if she is sufficiently aware (we can only guess whether the 'Lorraine Ellison' persona will actually heed the accompaniment's advice). An analogy I have in mind here is that of the everyday understanding of 'body language'. When watching others speak, we can tell how committed they are to what they are saying, we can tell whether to risk trusting in them, by how they express themselves, how they accompany their words with posture and gesture. A very different example of the same process, of the 'reality' of a situation being available to the perception of an audience but not to the persona, is given by the Beach Boys' 'Surfin' USA'. This is an example of a different order, since the song is based, both harmonically and melodically, on Chuck Berry's 'Sweet little sixteen'.[43] There is little doubt that, when writing the Beach Boys' song, Brian Wilson was aware of the similarity (the song is nowadays credited to 'C.Berry/B.Wilson') but the change of location, and the brash innocence in which it is sung, imply that the Beach Boys personae are unaware of a link contemporary listeners inevitably made.

Philip Tagg, in his lengthy deconstruction of the Abba hit 'Fernando',[44] argues that certain features of the song – melodic intervals, instrumental setting – warn us not to trust the singer's expression of commitment to the 'revolutionary cause',

---

[43]   Of course, many other examples of this same process exist.

[44]   Philip Tagg, *Fernando the Flute* (Liverpool, 1991).

nostalgic reflection on which is the subject of the song. In such a case, where the persona and the environment are at odds, we are urged to trust the latter, in the same way that we would trust body language over direct speech. This example is by no means alone. Andy Stewart's self-penned 'Donald, where's your troosers?' is normally taken as a piece of nostalgic whimsy. The song sets up three positions, those of the Scottish yokel (who always wears a kilt), of polite (Edinburgh?) society, and (more hidden) of the (BBC) establishment of which Stewart was himself a part. Polite society is lampooned, and the yokel seems to come off best. However, the expressed distaste of rock'n'roll (the recording of the song itself contains a delightful pastiche of Elvis Presley himself singing the chorus) is voiced on the part of the establishment, with a Scots accent. The song is harmonically accompanied by a 'double tonic' (i.e. aeolian i–VII–i) pattern, which sounds authentically 'Scottish'. However, the end of each verse replaces the 'expected' VII–i cadence with the V–i of the concert hall – a subtle, but nonetheless forceful, trouncing of the Scottish vernacular with that of high culture. The harmonic environment, then, if we can hear it, tells us not to take the lyrics at face value. In the Boomtown Rats' 'I never loved Eva Braun', the protagonist is more obviously culpable. He (who can only be identified as Adolf Hitler) brazenly declares that he wasn't responsible for the results of his actions, but the breakdown and nonchalant whistling (of the sort you might have indulged in as a kid, hands behind your back, head in the air as your misdemeanour is discovered – Who? Me?)[45] that precede the final chorus (at c.3'15") give the lie to that. (Theoretical justification for this kind of reading will have to await Chapter 8.) And there are other types of example too. The position set up by the Sex Pistols' 'Holidays in the Sun' is also not to be believed. Here is a song that purports to anarchism, a line totally belied by its formulaic rhythmic, harmonic and articulative approach. Punk is good hunting ground for this sort of move, aiming as it did to destabilize accepted positions. Dave Laing offers a number of examples where contradiction can be heard between, as he puts it, the performance and the lyric: where transgression (friction) is employed between a unified position and one that shifts; where the subject of the lyric is presented as contradictory; and where that subject itself shifts 'in an unsignalled way'.[46]

So, we can declare that the environment sometimes suggests the listener occupy a subject position that disbelieves the persona, reminding us that all may not be as it seems. At this point, the environment has become oppositional. This I relate to one part of a schema put forward by Nicholas Cook, who identifies what he calls modes of media pairing – the relationships obtaining between separate media in an artwork. Cook argues that two concurrent media can inhabit one of three relationships: *conformity*, *complementation* and *contest*.[47] The views given by the two textural strands (persona/melody and environment/ accompaniment)

---

[45]   Peter Gabriel's 'Intruder' provides a similar example of this topic.

[46]   Dave Laing, *One chord wonders: power and meaning in punk rock* (Buckingham, 1985), p. 67.

[47]   Cook, *Analysing Musical Multimedia*, p. 99.

here contest each other, and in such cases I think it is always better to trust the latter. Perhaps because the accompaniment is wordless and therefore not possibly subject to Frith's 'silver tongue', the analogy with 'body language' seems to me quite fruitful.

Hitherto, my attention has been focused on the way that the environment may modify our conception of the persona. The environment has always been secondary. What, though, if the two appear more equal? After all, we are all perceived by others as actors within an environment, as well as perceiving ourselves as acting upon it. The second of Cook's terms describes the situation where the two elements are in an equal, complementary, relationship. The verb to 'accompany' implies a hierarchical relationship; it suggests that what is accompanied has a greater role in the identification of what is going on, in the sense of giving identity to it. In complementation, though, this hierarchical relationship comes into question, potentially resulting in an ecologically more sound relationship (see Chapter 8). The hierarchy may survive, if only because of the distinction between lyric and not-lyric, but it may be somewhat tenuous. In the verse of Jethro Tull's 'Fylingdale flyer', the rhythmic profile of the accompaniment is unitary, and constantly rubs against that of the parallel multi-tracked voice. The relationship here is complementary, akin to that of a couple dancing, where one (the melody) leads, but leads only because of the presence of the lyrics (Example 7.10).

Example 7.10   Jethro Tull: 'Fylingdale flyer'; opening of verse (29")

I shall deal finally with two instances where, again, the simple identification of accompaniment is problematized. In the Jethro Tull example, although there are two identifiable strands, the relationship between them is complementary. Within this broad repertory of song, can we always posit two strands, can we always distinguish between a persona and its environment (the latter identified as accompanimental)? I think so, but sometimes the voice is far less prominent than we might normally expect. This can happen in terms of production values, as in much of the Rolling Stones' early material, where what is presented to us is not so much an accompanied lead singer, but almost a communal effort, one facet of which happens to be vocal, such as in 'Sympathy for the devil'. Even here, though, I think the voice perceptually dominates simply because of the presence of the verbal strand. In proxemic terms, Jagger generally appears in a public zone. A very good test of the dominance of the voice is provided by the very end of King Crimson's 'Larks' Tongues in Aspic, Part One' in which instrumental interplay covers what appears to be a heated argument. This appears in the distance, and the words cannot be made out and yet, in the simple fact that they are words, they call for our attention (I return to this point in Chapter 10). A more common case occurs where a vocal line gets taken over by part of the accompaniment. This is common in examples of 'call and response' textures as they develop from African American genres.[48] It also happens in mainstream rock and pop, as in Wishbone Ash's 'Throw down the sword', where a bifurcated melody leads into a two-part guitar line. Indeed, perhaps this is potentially what always happens when a solo enters: if we read this solo as a continuation of the vocal melody, at the point of interchange, the expression can be seen as becoming more eloquent, as it moves beyond words. The Carpenters' 'Goodbye to love' exemplifies this more overtly, as the guitar solo actually picks up Karen Carpenter's phrasing and literally takes her expression up to new heights (Example 7.11). Notwithstanding the fact that Carpenters fans disliked the intrusion of the guitar as stylistically foreign,[49] this reading is certainly available to non-fans.

There seems to me a clear difference between this sort of case, where a melody line moves to an instrument for a solo, and the sharing of material between two forces, simply because in this former case, the melody is firmly identified with the persona before the instrument ever gets near it. But does this mean we can have a persona without a lyric? In the sense in which *persona* is understood here, I think not. On Steve Vai's 'Oooo', his guitar 'takes the part' of two vocalists, clearly differentiated in terms of tone and register, with singable lines and evident expression. However, we're unable to judge whether the singer is distant or involved, realistic or not (etc.). On this basis, I cannot see how we can hear this as a *persona*. And it's an established part of Vai's technique, as the subsequent track ('Frank'), which works similarly, demonstrates. Normatively a *persona*, then, minimally requires a *song* to receive expression.

There is an obvious question I have not yet addressed: is it right to call all the non-melodic parts of a texture 'accompaniment'? In other words, is the assumption of a melody/ accompaniment dualism sufficient? As an assumption, it appears a reasonable one within most popular song, but there is certainly one significant repertoire where it falls down. This repertoire is formed by instances where, along with a band, the persona of the singer self-accompanies themselves on a guitar (self-accompaniment on a keyboard is a different issue, if only because the performer

---

48   The chorus to Chuck Berry's 'Johnny B. Goode', for example.

49   Kevin J. Holm-Hudson: 'Your guitar, it sounds so sweet and clear: semiosis in two versions of "Superstar"'; *Music Theory Online* (http://www.societymusictheory.org/mto/ issues/mto.02.8.4/mto.02.8.4.holm-hudson_frames.html, 2002).

Example 7.11   Carpenters: 'Goodbye to love'; vocal and guitar melodies

is then normally side on to the audience, rather than facing). On Lindisfarne's 'Good to be here', we simply hear singer Alan Hull, an acoustic guitar (which Hull plays) and an orchestra. The orchestra forms an accompanimental environment that really only supports the persona from the outset, reacting expressively at the 'right' points. The guitar is sounded in conjunction with the orchestra, such that its role seems to be accompanimental. However, at the moment at which the singer becomes no longer separated from what he's describing, the moment when he wakes from what we come to realize is a dream of a ghostly nature, when he comes to describe his wife addressing him in bed, the guitar drops away from the texture. It is away only momentarily, but its absence clearly marks that moment of change. If only at this point, the guitar function is clearly separate from that of the remainder of the accompaniment, which does not mark this moment. This usage develops from the singer/songwriter genre, and was taken up by heavy rock in the late 1960s/early 1970s where the guitar, when pitted against the rest of the accompaniment, represents the individual battling against some sort of social norm, or a body of undifferentiated 'others'.[50] As this example demonstrates, in this repertoire, the guitar might more usefully be read as part of the persona.

One further question needs to be briefly addressed. I have assumed throughout that the persona is coherent, that it can be recognized through the course of a track and that it retains its identity. In the wake of the postmodern 'decentring' of the subject, there may be room for arguing against the *necessary* assumption of a unified subjectivity for the persona. This chapter is already long enough without any such diversion. But in any case, as I shall further explore in Chapter 8, I have to recognize that I write from within my own experience. And, while the idea of a fragmented subject may have intellectual credibility, if it cannot be experienced, there seems little sense in talking about it. Judith Becker's recounting of her own subjectivity is valuable[51] in that it removes the issue from one of purely intellectual consideration. I suspect, too, that if you share the experience she describes, you will expect to find this reflected in the personae you encounter in song. I, however, cannot claim that this reflects my own experience, and so I continue with an assumption of coherent subjectivity in the personae I hear.

Even with this, the persona is not simply an individual matter. The guiding import of the book thus far has been that, in order to develop the relationship between the listener and the meaning that listener observes in the tracks to which they are listening, what must be taken into account, what can be externally observed, are features of the track. Because all listeners are different, 'the listener' cannot be observed, and thus determinate meaning cannot be posed. This position is not universally accepted. It is surely true that listeners cannot, in their entirety, be substituted one for another, since listeners' experiences are not interchangeable. Theories of culture have however been proposed on the basis that, in some degree, listeners can be regarded as interchangeable. Over the course of its history, the sociological field that studies music audiences has moved from the consideration of audiences as *undifferentiated consumers of a culture industry*,[52] through an awareness of *cultural differences*,[53] to the adhesive role of musical style in the constitution of *sub-cultural groupings*.[54] The most recent step recognizes that music does not necessarily play an organizing role in such formations, that individuals may inhabit one or more *musical scenes*[55] that (in the wake of the internet) may not

---

[50]   Earlier examples include the Strawbs: 'New world' (1972); Van der Graaf: 'Lemmings' (1971); King Crimson: 'Epitaph' (1969); and the Beatles: 'A day in the life' (1967).

[51]   Judith Becker, *Deep listeners* (Bloomington IN, 2004), p. 38.

[52]   Adorno, *Introduction to the Sociology of Music*.

[53]   Paul Willis, *Profane culture* (London, 1978).

[54]   Hebdige, *Subculture*.

[55]   Will Straw, 'Systems of articulation, logics of change: communities and scenes in popular music', *Cultural Studies* 5/3 (1991).

only be physically located, be actual, but may operate only in virtual space.[56] As a result of this legacy, many writers do write on the basis that people who share (for example) a particular gender, race, or set of political beliefs will have a response to particular material that can be assumed to be identical to each other, and not necessarily to conform to the gender, race or political beliefs of the originators of that material. The degree of validity that can be found in answers to this latter question is vital for popular music studies in general, of course, but is intentionally outside of the scope of this particular project. What is within its scope is the stance available to a listener. I maintain that we cannot generalize sufficiently to explain what a particular group of listeners will understand of the meaning of a particular track, and that it is therefore obfuscatory to pretend that we can (not least, within a group, any such meaning will be negotiated, will in part depend on the power relations in that group, and may not receive universal acclaim). Theodore Gracyk emphasizes the role of gender in the way that rock music enables the creation of audience identities.[57] In the process, he observes that empirical studies of music use demonstrate that men and women tend to use music differently. As a result of this, I may assume that a reader who has progressed this far through my book is more likely to be male than female.[58] But Gracyk also demonstrates, as his discourse shifts from discussing listeners to discussing performers (always more easy because of their undisputed individuality, and presumably more rewarding judging by the space it is accorded in most of those texts that do not explicitly describe themselves as concerned with the production of musical texts), that gender identity is not fixed, and that the pleasures to be acquired from texts are not simply to be identified along the lines of one's gender. Writing from a perspective that addresses politics rather than gender, Robin Ballinger argues that listeners' use of music can quite simply have nothing to do with the intention of those who have made it available. Speaking of the popularity of US American R&B ballads among young Trinidadian women, he argues that although the music has developed within a different culture, these ballads speak to these women in terms of 'empowerment at a time of heightened socio-economic and gender oppression for women',[59] and that this is as much about the sonic qualities of these songs as about their lyrics. Any suggestion of monolithic audiences is therefore suspect.

---

[56]   Andy Bennett and Richard A. Peterson (eds.), *Music scenes: local, translocal, and virtual* (Nashville TN, 2004).

[57]   Gracyk, *I wanna be me*.

[58]   But only 'more likely', and such probabilistic thinking does not get us very far.

[59]   Robin Ballinger, 'Politics' in Bruce Horner and Thomas Swiss (eds.), *Key terms in popular music and culture* (Oxford, 1999), p. 67.

Intention

I have used Ballinger here to support my contention throughout that intention and reception are not coextensive. This is a quite extreme position, and you may prefer a more moderated one (as, indeed, does Gracyk) in which a listener may wish to take into account what can be known of, or reasonably guessed about, that intention. In such a case, though, to return to my reliance on Ricoeur (Chapter 1), the 'what can be known' has to come from outside the track to which we are listening – it cannot be discerned simply from the track. So, while this is an option that must remain potentially open, I think it important to acknowledge the barriers between our assumption of what that intention might be, and what that intention actually might be (assuming that it is possible to talk about the actuality of such an intention). Initially, we should note that the assumption that writers, performers and producers (I shall use the term 'originators' to cover this entire conglomeration of activities) determine the meaning of a track is problematic, if only because it appears that such meaning can only be transmitted extra-musically, by the originators discussing it in print, for instance, or on internet sites, or even occasionally in sleeve-notes. Moreover, if we wish to accept that a meaning is determined by the originator, then *all* aspects of the track must be explicable in these terms. The problems associated with this have been addressed by many critics – a clear exposition is Wimsatt and Beardsley's *intentional fallacy*,[60] which reminds us not to confuse what authors say they intend by what they do with what they actually produce. But what authors say they intend is, itself, problematic, since we cannot access the intention of musicians, we can only access their reports of those intentions (I shall discuss the inappropriateness of talk of 'meaning as explanation' at the beginning of Chapter 8). Recall an experience of asking someone why they undertook a particular act. You will have measured the answer they gave you against what you know of that person already, what you know of your own motives, and those of reported others, in order to help you gauge how to take that person's report of their intentions. While we make use of informal tests for the veracity of what others say: consistency; plausibility; correspondence with our prior knowledge, and so on, it seems we can never know for sure. Explanation, then, where others' activities are concerned, seems to me a problematic quest. A particular case will dramatize the issue.

Amy Winehouse's drug and alcohol problems were widely reported, and it would appear to be perverse to doubt their veracity (although, of course, their reporting acted also as publicity, which possibly had a positive, if unmeasurable, impact on her sales figures). They were tested in the courts, and her entering

---

[60]   William K. Wimsatt and Monroe Beardsley, 'The intentional fallacy', in Wimsatt, *The verbal icon: studies in the meaning of poetry* (Lexington KY, 1954).

rehab was widely reported in the press.[61] An unnamed source was reported on one website as declaring:

> Amy is stubborn but her people, as well as her friends, are keen to get her on the mend. She has already tried rehab in the UK but the problem is that when she comes out it's hard to protect her. Arizona is far away enough for her to get her head together and really focus on her career. She has been working on her album, which is brilliant, but it wouldn't take much for her to get distracted by bad influences.[62]

The same site declared Winehouse's intention in the track 'Rehab': 'According to Amy Winehouse its lyrics are factual after she refused to attend rehab for her alcohol fuelled ways.'

Such background information informed Joe Queenan's glowing interpretation of the track. Queenan argued that Winehouse combined the superficiality of the 1960s girl-group approach with lyrics more relevant to contemporary concerns, particularly 'therapy and abuse': 'The music of the Sixties was fine, Winehouse seems to be saying, but the lyrics were inane and the age of innocence is over.' Queenan points to the irony inherent in Winehouse's 'ability to predict her own future, but the inability to do anything about it'.[63] This view makes sense of a range of attributes of the track, founded on Winehouse's assumed personal encounter with the passing of the age of innocence. Note the circumspect avoidance of divining her intention. Queenan nonetheless insists she 'seems to be saying' and gently refuses to equate 'a person who does not want to go back into rehab' with Winehouse herself. Mark Ronson, the track's producer, has since been quoted on its invention and, again, there is no obvious reason not to trust the quotation. According to Ronson, the track was written quickly and its inception was a casual comment made by Winehouse during a break from recording:

> We were walking down the street and she's telling me a story about her family or something coming over ... to kind of talk some sense into her. And she was like, 'They tried to make me go to rehab, and I told them no, no, no,' and she put her hand up. I guess, as a friend, I should have been like, 'Oh my God, that

---

[61]   For instance, the anonymous article 'Amy Winehouses' rehab advice' (http://www. femalefirst.co.uk/celebrity/Amy+Winehouse-20753.html, 2008) reported her checking into a US rehab facility and confirms she had already booked in twice during the previous eight months.

[62]   Anon (http://www.mp3-easy.com/mp3blog/2006/11/watch-amy-winehouse-rehab-music-video.html, 2006).

[63]   Joe Queenan: 'Rehab is one great song'; *The Guardian*, 8 February (http://music. guardian.co.uk/vinylword/story/0,2254844,00.html, 2008).

must have been hard for you.' But as a producer, I was just like, 'That sounds hooky — you should go back to the studio and we should turn that into a song.'[64]

On this report, the song was therefore not an attempt to express frustration, but was simply triggered by a minor experience, which then developed into something else. It is worth recalling Negus and Pickering's trenchant comments on the activity of turning experience into song:

> It is of course a mistake to think that an artwork or cultural product is the expression of certain feelings, ideas or values which exist independently of the creative product and which simply result from the intention to communicate them ... What is felt is mediated by the lyrics, rhythm or beat as a form of creative expression ... we do not have a fully formed, reflexively comprehended experience which we then reproduce in verbal or sonic form. What this experience means to us, and how we may value it, is usually only discovered in the form of utterance or figuration that is given to it. The expression not only forms the experience but also transforms it, makes it into something whose meaning changes our understanding of it.[65]

So, this is as much as any interested listener could ascertain, could discover that according to probably trustworthy reports, the song had its root in Winehouse's own experience, but is not a simple recounting of that actual experience (indeed, Nicola Dibben argues that in live performances of the track, Winehouse successfully blurred the distinction between performer and persona[66]). It is contextualised, ironised, indeed it is made into an art object fit for interpretation. What effect might, or even should, this knowledge have on the sense we make of the song? If we have experienced similar drug or alcohol problems, then we might test her veracity against our own experience, and we might appreciate her irony rather keenly. If we have not had such experiences, then what would be our motive for spending time with the track? We might be satisfied with an encounter with the imagined persona of someone put in that position, and if in a foreign position would be none the wiser for any inaccuracies. If we wish to learn how it felt, then we would presumably also be willing to accept Winehouse's own interpretation. So, as it relates to real experience, we may feel enriched by the knowledge that this is not pure invention, but we need to retain that distance between the experience and its recounting – there is no way of saying that the experience of our listening

---

[64]   Chris Harris, 'Amy Winehouse's "Rehab", the theme song of modern-day celebrity trash culture: behind the Grammys' (http://www.mtv.com/news/articles/1580806/20080201/winehouse_amy.jhtml, 2008).

[65]   Keith Negus and Michael Pickering, 'Creativity and musical experience' in David Hesmondhalgh and Keith Negus (eds.), *Popular Music Studies* (London, 2002), p. 184.

[66]   Nicola Dibben, 'Vocal performance and the projection of emotional authenticity', in Derek B. Scott, *Research Companion to Popular Musicology* (Farnham, 2009), pp. 328–30.

to Winehouse's recounting is in any way equivalent to (one might even say related to) Winehouse's own experience. For my own part, I find Ronson's account reassuring, for there is something vaguely distasteful about deciding to reinterpret oneself for others – having an outsider's encouragement somehow makes it more acceptable.

One could refer to a range of other examples of the gap between experience and its informing of a song. I'll take just one other, from a very different genre, Genesis' 'Supper's ready'. Gabriel recounted to a biographer an incident with his then wife Jill and a 'psychic phenomenon', which appears to have been a frightening and threatening experience – the line 'I swear I saw your face change' is particularly chilling if regarded as an accurate account.[67] This disturbing encounter then became the basis of the track, in which the experience appears to be exorcised, in that melody's triumphant return at the denouement. What is different here is that, bearing in mind the genre's penchant for fantasy, it would have been an extreme listener who would have heard that line as part of an authentic recounting of experience.

Other Issues

In Chapter 9, I shall take up the issue of 'authenticity', one of the major interpretive schemas that people make use of in understanding the popular song. One understanding of authenticity can be approached by way of the persona, and the relation of the persona to the performer, and to the protagonist. It seems that when listeners want to regard a performance as authentic, one clear justification for this is an argument that sees no distance between a performer and the particular persona and protagonist they take on during the course of a track. Just occasionally, we encounter a song in which, irrespective of how it is performed, that distance is suddenly destroyed. Matching Mole's 'Signed curtain' is the *sine qua non* – a song whose lyrics exist almost entirely of declaring which part of the song we're in ('this is the chorus – or maybe the bridge' etc.). The persona must come out of the song in order to make such comment, thus becoming a second persona or, as I suspect it is always read, the performer himself. A similar reading seems likely in the case of the Animals' early 'The story of Bo Diddley'. Rather than sing, Eric Burdon speaks through the track, which consists of a brief history of aspects of rock'n'roll, from Bo Diddley through Johnny Otis to the Beatles, and then to the Animals' own encounter with Bo Diddley. Another example of this rare genre is Mansun's 'An open letter to the lyrical trainspotter'. The lyrics to the track make plain that they exist simply to provide material to sing – they have no other meaning. The implication is that this is how all songs work. And yet, to accept that this is the case is to accept that the lyrics do have meaning, after all, for to be entirely functional is still to have meaning (and to be successfully functional is more than many artists could ever hope for).

---

[67]   Spencer Bright, *Peter Gabriel* (London, 1990), pp. 50–52.

Occasionally, one finds a simple comment through which the performer steps out from the persona, before returning. At 3'18" of The New Radicals' strangely unfocused 'I hope I didn't just give away the ending', Gregg Alexander steps out of character momentarily to declare to his antagonist, having made a comment: 'That may not be true, but I said it so you'd feel involved with the song.' Robbie Williams makes a similar shift in 'Strong', as after the penultimate line of the first verse, he declares: 'and that's a good line to take it to the bridge' (42"). In 'School's out', at 1'53", after lines that have ended with 'class', 'principles' and 'innocence', Alice Cooper finishes the verse with 'can't think of a word that rhymes'. Finally, Leonard Cohen's 'Hallelujah' contains a small piece of theory as he sings 'it goes like this, the fourth, the fifth, the minor fall and the major lift', actually explaining what is going on in the music at that point. A small number of examples (there are many more, not least among James Brown's recordings, and particularly when comparing a live and studio recording of the same song by the same performer), but in each case the momentary movement of the persona 'out of character' immediately throws new light on the meaning of the song.

In the book so far, I have limited the notion of persona to individual tracks, suggesting that we respond to a persona as found therein. In practice, however, our sense of persona is generated from a wider encounter than just with the individual track (as is implicit in the notion of meaning generated through friction, to which I return here). If our purchasing and listening practice is principally that of albums, our sense of the persona of an individual track will be informed by this larger experience. The somewhat fey, *faux* vulnerable persona presented by Kate Bush in 'Wuthering heights' is effective because of its development across *The kick inside*. If we are fans, and follow the output of a particular band across a series of releases, then our sense of persona will have a historical dimension. The aggressive pose of an early single such as 'Shape of things to come' combines with the good-time hell-raising of 'Get down and get with it' to create the self-mocking Noddy Holder persona familiar from 'Cum on feel the noize' and other Slade singles of the time. It became a matter of speculation as to how the band could begin to take themselves seriously again (which, with 'Wheels ain't coming down' and a storming performance at the Reading Festival, they succeeded). With some artists, we may measure a persona against their entire output. Thus we can note how personae develop and change. David Bowie is an obvious example, where the changes have been overt – the androgynous Ziggy Stardust, the cocaine-raddled Thin White Duke, the intense Berliner – while Elvis Costello and Madonna also present good examples. Other personae don't develop, of course – those of Mick Jagger, of Paul McCartney, or Bruce Dickinson – while others simply become more extreme or refined, perhaps a logical development of their starting-point – Michael Jackson, Marilyn Manson, Björk. In this way, friction will necessarily arise between the persona we have observed in its process of development and that present in a particular track (David Bowie's cover of Nina Simone's 'Wild is the wind', Björk's 'It's oh so quiet', the Beatles' magnificently syrupy 'Good night'), at least until we are able to encompass that friction within our concept of the persona the artist presents. That friction can on occasion be particularly extreme, as with Paul Weller's institution of Style Council, or Radiohead's change of direction after *OK computer*.

Although when we respond to a persona we are responding to what emanates from the performer, we should be aware that it is not solely the creation of the performer. All who have had a hand in moulding the sound to which we respond have had a role. Thus musicians (not simply the singer) and engineers, and most certainly the producer, manager and a label's marketing people, are all implicated in the work that has issued in the identity on the basis of which we create the persona to which we listen. It is rarely possible to analyse this in further depth, without intimate knowledge of a particular recording process, and it is of questionable value to do so. Will Straw points to the difficulty of determining precise details of authorship in popular music because of the complexity of the relationships involved in bringing a track to completion.[68] If the musicians involved are a regular band, if the producer is the band's regular producer, who works regularly with a particular engineer, then the dynamic is established. If not, the individual expressive identity of those involved will affect the persona (were it not so, we would have difficulty understanding why particular musicians were booked, rather than others). Some key examples of the importance here would include the change of direction Eno enabled U2 to develop (and that had its impact on the persona presented by Bono, one of greater seriousness, troubled maturity and distance), or the voice that producer Mutt Lange gave Def Leppard. For this reason, while it is worthwhile to identify the other key creative forces behind a particular track, it is equally important to identify how regularly a team works together, and what idiolectal features individual musicians might be assumed to be bringing to a project.

In these larger wholes, relationships must be developed by the people concerned. Again, friction here can be productive, but this is friction as more conventionally understood. Are the musicians of the same age? Do they share class credentials? Are there differences of gender, of ethnicity, of training? The more experienced the musicians to whom we listen, the more likely we will be able to observe differences in these areas. What effect might they have on the interpretation we make? The impact of John Cale's training in the avant garde on his fellow members of the Velvet Underground had a crucial effect on the sound they developed. The keyboard training of John Evan and David Palmer had a crucial effect on the sound of mid-period Jethro Tull. The working-class credentials (however accurate) of the Sex Pistols, the Streets or the Beatles have been instrumental in affecting the sort of identity listeners were able to make with them. And so on. If we wish to probe behind what we hear, any of these relationships can be effective, the issue is the degree to which we choose to bear them in mind.

Behind these final questions is the notion of the *market*, the understanding that a track is not simply released or made available, but is directed in some way,

---

[68] Will Straw, 'Authorship' in Horner and Swiss, *Key terms*.

is made more available to certain listeners than others, is released with a view to maximizing sales through consideration of its likely market. If nowhere else, the focus of this book will be clear by how little space I accord to this term, in contrast to so many studies of popular music, and how much to other factors. It seems to me that the market operates before we get access to what we hear – it intervenes strongly between musicians and listeners. I do believe the market to be pretty irrelevant in terms of the interpretations we make, but it is not entirely negligible. It is worth noting for a particular track whether a particular market can be assumed. Again, there is difficulty in determining whether one was actually intended, although since the results of any apparent intention here are frequently made concrete by the evidence of decisions made as to how something is promoted and distributed, how many pressings are made, what label it is issued on, and so forth, then intention on the part of those who take control once the musicians have finished is perhaps more transparent here. This still does not address any intentional position on the part of the initial musicians in relation to any particular track or even, possibly, entire album. So, it is useful to be aware of a release's label, and of how it relates (stylistically) to other items on that label, indeed, whether it is an expected or unusual choice for that label. And then it is worth noting whether it crossed over, whether it exceeded the apparent boundaries of the market it was initially positioned for. Such knowledge can particularly help if we are unsure of our own taste in respect of a track, or if we are interested in why and whether our interpretation may seem transgressive. Finally, in order to do this, we need to determine whether a particular recording is 'owned' by a particular social group and, if so, how are they defined? This is easy in the case of music that, in Green's terms, acts between poles of affirmation and aggravation.[69] Familiarity tends to produce affirmative responses, unfamiliarity (or refusal of familiarity) tends to produce aggravated responses. Many styles, in the meanings that become attached to them, have done this regularly over the years – easy listening, punk, progressive, disco, electronica – all have their adherents and their detractors, and they do sometimes conform to norms. Class, age, gender, ethnicity, political allegiance can all form positions around which listeners can congregate – by having certain allegiances, as we have seen, it may be assumed that you will have a particular taste, will understand particular art objects in particular ways. And, if you don't fit that group, do you interpret a track as an outsider, or can you appropriate it for some other reason?

---

[69]   Green, *Music on Deaf Ears*, pp. 35–6.

Chapter 8
Reference

The Verbal Imperative

I have argued throughout that songs mean. In many spheres of understanding the meaning of 'mean' is to point elsewhere – we may say that seeing smoke means that there's a fire, that failing an exam means insufficient work was done, that the use of a particular word means that I had some idea in mind when I chose to use that word. A meaning that is not open to communication, that is not available to be made available to others, seems incomplete. Sometimes, we don't know 'what we mean' until we try to express it. I want to argue here that if we find some music meaningful, if we find meaning in a song, that finding is incomplete until we have passed it on.

I start by taking entirely out of context a comment of Albin Zak's in grappling with this very issue. In his *Poetics of rock*, he refers to the distorted acoustic guitar sound on the Beatles' 'I'm only sleeping', a typical Beatles sound. He says of it 'that this is not your average guitar sound … and [I] take my delight from its unusual sonic texture … By its raw, harsh tone it has gotten my attention, and even if I cannot put it into words, I know that it is saying *something*.'[1] In one very important sense, Zak is absolutely right. It is not possible simply to translate into words the meaning of music, and this observation is behind the urge so many feel that music is not to be tampered with, that the process of trying to put things into words is a waste of time, and might even damage the experience. However, avoiding doing so is equally problematic. Zak's satisfaction with privileging the identification of that sound's meaningfulness over the reason for its meaningfulness (and despite the fact that he does actually offer a powerful interpretation) reminds me of what positivist musicology has long held: the recognition that something significant is happening (in this case, the guitar tone, which can be identified analytically in terms of its departure from a norm), but whose significance doesn't need to be articulated (verbalized) in anything other than internal, formally relational, terms.[2] In this chapter, I want to suggest that the process of discovering that something matters, and then identifying what it is, is insufficient. I believe we must endeavour to identify why it matters, for communicating our understanding,

---

[1] Zak, *Poetics of rock*, pp. 191–2.

[2] I have elsewhere critiqued this comment of Zak's (Moore, 'The act you've known'). My harking back to it is not intended personally; I simply use the quote because it is such a clear example of a tendency to which so many of us (myself included) have been prone.

rather than allowing ourselves to inhabit a hermetic aestheticized space, carries a morally imperative charge.

Therefore, I insist, the search for significance should issue in its expression. An initial demonstration of what I mean here begins with the Beach Boys' hit 'Heroes and villains', of 1967, particularly the short segment that begins at 45". Many years later, Brian Wilson re-recorded this song as part of the *Smile* project, an endeavour to bring before public ears the album he had intended to complete as a response to the Beatles' *Sgt. Pepper*, but was prevented by his breakdown. A comparison of the two yields interesting results. To my ears at least, the *Smile* version is the same song, as far as pacing, harmony, groove, melody, and even arrangement are concerned. It is not the same track, though. For one thing, it seems Wilson takes lead vocal on the latter version. I want to focus, though, on something rather more subtle. In the latter version, the snare drum is altogether more prominent than in the former; it has been brought forward as a feature of the production. As a result, it seems to me to signal *something*, even if that something may be hard to verbalize. What might that something be? Remember, my concern is to articulate a reason for this difference. If we move forward to the subsequent track, 'Roll Plymouth Rock', we discover an unusual emphasis on drums (unusual with reference to the sort of style with which Brian Wilson normally works). This is not an emphasis on the snare drum particularly, but it is an emphasis on drums (as a class of instrument) nonetheless. 'Roll Plymouth Rock' itself contains an internal reference to 'Heroes and villains' in that it offers a quotation of it. Now I move forward to track 13, 'On a holiday'. This track also has an unusually prominent kit and, from 32", it re-runs the lyric hook to 'Roll Plymouth Rock'. Now of course, we do not know what *Smile* would have sounded like had it seen the light of day in 1967. We might assume from Wilson's commitment to releasing it even at such a late date that it would have sounded rather like it now does (accepting the intervening development of technological possibility, and the greater maturity of our own ears). And I propose that, if it had sounded like this, it would have had a more profound effect on the history of popular music than did *Sgt. Pepper*, for it offers a far more thoroughgoing means of overcoming the limitations of the 3' single (perhaps the most important ingredient in the ensuing progressive rock) than the simple notion of the 'concept album', in its constant intra-textual references. All I have done here is to concentrate on the most obvious, as 'Heroes and villains' becomes incorporated within 'Roll Plymouth Rock', which in turn becomes incorporated in 'On a holiday'. It is the unusually prominent drums that call attention to these embedded references, and which might convince us of some intentionality behind them (although I am not convinced that this is material to my interpretation). In this particular example, then, I can find a satisfactory interpretation of this *something* signalled, namely that the drums have a structural function, whatever else they may be felt to do. Of course, the significance *Smile* would have had in 1967 is entirely different to the one it has on its authorized release now, much of which seems to relate to a renewed evaluation of the importance of Wilson's body of work, notwithstanding that various versions and part-versions have circulated for decades.

Semiotics

Perhaps the dominant theoretical position underpinning hermeneutic work in popular music is that of psychoanalysis. It is not possible to summarize briefly all the assumptions this brings to an interpretation, but they are assumptions that develop most particularly not from Freud himself, but by some of those who claim indebtedness to him: Lacan particularly, Kristeva as a dominant feminist scholar, and more recently Žižek. While it is surely possible to pick and choose aspects of these writers' various positions, working in this way would certainly weaken one's theoretical foundation. Bradley[3] is just one writer who uses the psychoanalytic term *jouissance* to describe (at least, I think that is his intention) that very 'beyond verbalization' aspect of the musical experience I am concerned to try to get closer to, but how thoroughly such terminology has percolated through his basic perspective is open to doubt. A more thoroughgoing approach can be found in chapter 5 of David Schwarz's *Listening subjects*.[4] I have previously offered a critique of this,[5] and propose to add nothing further here. Richard Middleton's recent study exemplifies a complete orientation to the work particularly of Žižek.[6] As is right and proper, understanding these writings necessitates understanding the theoretical principles on which they are based. I note these, because this is an important field of work. I do not pursue this line of thought at all partly due to my scepticism over Freud's contribution[7] but also because I find it low in real explanatory power of the musical experience.

Instead, I focus back on music,[8] and note that music refers in three fundamentally different ways: within itself; to itself; outside itself. Semiotics, a field of study I

---

[3]   Bradley, *Understanding rock'n'roll*.

[4]   David Schwarz, *Listening Subjects: Music, Psychoanalysis, Culture* (Durham NC, 1997).

[5]   Moore, 'The track'.

[6]   Middleton, *Voicing the popular*.

[7]   See, for instance, Ernest Gellner, *The psychoanalytic movement* (London, 1985) and Adolf Grünbaum, *The foundations of psychoanalysis: a philosophical critique* (Berkeley CA, 1985). While I enjoy Peter Medawar's possibly apocryphal comment on psychoanalysis as a 'massive intellectual confidence trick', I acknowledge that my suspicions cannot be said to based on extensive knowledge of the field.

[8]   My aim in this chapter is to focus on the ways that music *refers*, and I shall find semiotics to be of limited value. Before I approach this topic, it should be noted that my focus on *friction* in Chapter 6 could, strictly, be viewed as a semiotic method, since there I call attention to the *difference* between the norms about which a listener has developed assumptions, and what actually happens within a track. I would argue, however, that in

shall address in a moment, normally claims purview over all three of these ways but, in practice, it is only in the last that it is useful. Later in the chapter, I shall find that even here, it is less useful than is often made out. The first two of these ways are encompassed in Green's concept of the *inherent* meaning of music, while the latter conforms to her *delineated* meanings.[9] When music refers *within* itself, one part of a track refers to another part. For example, the opening of a second verse will always refer to the opening of the first verse; that is, it will enable/suggest/require the calling-to-mind of its previous occurrence. Thus, all reference within music depends on repetition, or on some form of transformation. The beginning of a path to a climax (in the verse of Deep Purple's 'Child in time', let's say) refers forward to the achievement of that climax. We normally reserve the word repetition for the repeating of stretches of music (sections, melodic phrases, riffs, grooves, harmonic sequences) – lower levels of repetition, while inevitable, are usually trivial. Transformations are more debateable, since some measure of similarity must be retained (in 'Child in time', it's the repetition of the beat and maintenance of the texture, while the melody moves upward in terms of pitch, traversed by means of a unified gesture). Conventional music theory (which forms the basis for my explorations in Chapters 2–4) represents a far more powerful set of tools for this form of reference than anything in semiotics. When music refers *to* itself, it makes reference to a separate instance of music. This works in two very different kinds of way. The first we may crudely call the realm of *covers*. Thus, a cover will refer to the track being covered. The vocal identity of a particular singer will refer to other examples of that singer's work (whether or not a listener chooses to notice the recurrence). The timbre of a guitar will refer to other examples of that timbre – here, transformation is again important, for what might be found significant will be a subtle modification of that timbre (it might be less, or more, sophisticated; less, or more, proficiently handled). Music theory is again useful here, although this form of reference is far less often addressed than either of the other two. It is best considered in terms of *intertextuality*, addressed in Chapter 9.

The second kind of way is in relation to a lyric. The Beach Boys' original recording of 'Good vibrations' employs a striking double transformation. The track opens with a stepwise harmonic descent from E minor, and repeats this move, before shifting to the relative major for the chorus. The protagonist sings of being *in receipt* of 'good vibrations', over a harmonic pattern that moves upward, from G,[10] to A, to B, in readiness for the second verse. The vector is clear: gradual upward motion of harmonic roots coincides with activity in the relationship by his

---

avoiding any assumption about the *inherent* nature of such a difference, in calling attention to the necessarily experiential nature of any recognition of difference, in its lack of fixity, such a method should not be thought of as semiotic at all.

[9]   Green, *Music on Deaf Ears*.

[10]   Some listeners hear the track as based in G, others as G♭. The actual pitch is between the two, and the difference is not material to my argument – I refer to G simply for ease of presentation.

partner, towards him. This link is merely associative, but once made, it becomes an operative force (but only within this single track). In the centre of the song, the texture slims remarkably, down to organ and shakers, a change that coincides with the protagonist's dawning realization of his culpability – he's 'gotta keep those … vibrations happening with her', that is, he has to become active in the relationship himself. Thereafter, the 'good vibrations' hook is sung over the same pattern, but now transposed in the reverse direction, from B, to A, to G. Now that 'he' has become active in the relationship a new, smoother, coda melody enters, is repeated transposed from G, to A, to B, and finally back to A, thereby finishing mid-way between the outer reaches of this pattern. The original G–A–B sequential motion is thus first reversed, and then combined with its reversal to provide a conclusion. This transformation thus enables a reading of the future history of the protagonist, himself identified through his lyric, as one in which he will enjoy a probably successful relationship, resultant from the 'emotional work' he has implicitly agreed to undertake.[11] This realm of meaning is semiotic in that the direction of the transposition (upward or downward) is arbitrary (I shall discuss the importance of this in a moment) – the directions could have been reversed. What matters is simply the *difference* between them. The *meaning* of the direction is anchored only in the lyric. For this sort of internal reference, semiotics has something to say but, I would stress, only in tandem with a theory of the persona.

For the third relation, when music refers *outside* itself, it acts as a sign of something that is not music, and it is here particularly that semiotics is worth considering. Answers to questions of signification, across all fields of human experience, are considered within the domain of the discipline, concerned as it is with the relationship between human signs and what they signify (and, one should say, to whom, but by no means all semioticians are interested in this addendum). In the discussion of music, semiotics becomes a way of discussing how certain features of the track point outside the track, to the external world, how they *represent* things outside music.[12] The relationship of some features may be so common as to become conventional – distorted sounds appearing ugly, for example, or high pure sounds appearing ethereal – and I shall return to this conventionality later. A (for me, the) key feature of semiotics as practised in the field of language (and, following that, of other fields of culture) is that of *arbitrariness*, the notion that the relationship between what semioticians, following Saussure, call the *signifier* and the *signified* is not causal. The *signifier* here is a particular linguistic concatenation of sounds ('dog', for example) and the *signified* is the concept that this concatenation calls to

---

[11]   I develop this reading in 'Interpretation: so what?', in Derek B. Scott (ed.), *Ashgate Research Companion to Popular Musicology* (Farnham, 2009).

[12]   Although there are studies of the use of semiotics in the discussion of music, such as Raymond Monelle, *Linguistics and semiotics in music* (Chur, 1992) (and Monelle's rather ascetic perspective would certainly problematize my characterization), I am aware only of Giles Hooper whose work-in-progress looks at its operation across an extensive range of music.

mind (the mental image of a 'dog', in this case). Arbitrariness as a principle is built into the system because, for a Francophone speaker, the *signifier* 'chien', which is wholly different from 'dog', carries the same meaning. For some critics, this emphasis on arbitrariness is not particularly satisfactory,[13] not least because it is so far in the past (the branching of a language family into what became respectively English and French, for instance), as to be literally useless, but also because new meanings (what Sless calls 'stand-for relations') are created all the time. It certainly seems unsatisfactory in the discussion of music, as will become apparent throughout this chapter. Perhaps because of unease amongst musicologists with this brand of semiotics, which develops from the work of the Swiss linguist Ferdinand de Saussure, more attention has been given to that which developed from the thinking of US philosopher Charles Sanders Peirce, and which was subsequently developed by Umberto Eco and others. Peirce's scheme is complex and unstable, although it has been solidified for the study of (some) music by Naomi Cumming.[14] One dominant thought in Peirce's work is that rather than the simple signified/signifier relation, there are three basic types of sign: icons, which bear a relation of resemblance to what they signify; indices, which bear a relation of experiential proximity (which might or might not be causal); and symbols, which require the intervention of conceptualization and which, therefore, are frequently arbitrary.[15] It is this train of thought that underlies much of the work in musicology that uses a semiotic basis, most importantly for our purposes that of Philip Tagg. Before I come to that, there is more to say on the issue of the arbitrary.

Semiotics (of one sort or another, and most often not rigorously theorized) is regarded outside musicology almost unproblematically as the means to investigate musical meaning. However, Christian Kennett[16] argues that this should not be the case. Kennett's criticism takes as its starting-point the observation that a particular meaning posited for a track by Philip Tagg was not one that was picked up by Kennett's own students, in spite of the fact that Tagg's reading was very well anchored in details of the track concerned. What are we to make of this disparity? A normative reading of semiotics would assert that the meaning of an artistic expression has become encoded within it, such that the role of a culturally competent spectator, or listener, is to decode that meaning. This model is strongly implied in an early essay of Tagg's, in which the music is described

---

[13]   See David Sless, *In search of semiotics* (London, 1986).

[14]   Cumming, *The sonic self*.

[15]   This is a gross simplification of Peirce's complex thinking, but is the most useful set of concepts for the discussion of how this repertory refers outside itself.

[16]   Kennett, 'Is anybody listening?', in Allan F. Moore (ed.), *Analyzing Popular Music* (Cambridge, 2003). I use Kennett here partly because he has regarded my own work as semiotic (ibid, pp. 199–200), a position I shall depart from below.

as a 'channel' situated between its 'emitter' and its 'receiver'.[17] Tagg analyses the theme to the TV series *Kojak* and finds, for example, 'the music was found to reinforce a basically monocentric view of the world and to emphasize affectively the fallacy that the negative experience of a hostile urban environment can be overcome solely by means of an individualist attitude of strength and go-it-alone heroism'.[18] And what of the listener who simply cannot hear these values in that conglomeration of sounds (despite the magisterial presentation of the evidence)? This is Kennett's concern. Elsewhere, commentators are more explicit about the use of such an information theory model. This encoding is partly the result of the intentions of the 'emitter', and partly an accretion of meanings from similar (or dissimilar) examples that form part of the listener's cultural competence. Kennett offers, instead, a model in which the meaning is not considered encoded at all, but is entirely created by listeners, on the basis of his or her own experience, and he offers a thought experiment to suggest some possibilities. This model certainly helps to suggest reasons why not all listeners extract the same meaning from a listening experience – their role is simply not to extract such a meaning but to impose one. With an information theory model, one can only note a listener's 'incompetence' if they 'fail' to pick up the 'correct' meaning and, of course, it is a political issue as to who takes the right to determine what that right meaning might be. So, Kennett's dissatisfaction is perhaps well-placed. However, if we take seriously his cure, then we can only address the individual listener. In other words, we become powerless in the face of music, a situation Tagg (rightly, to my mind) initially set out to address in developing the method he has employed and refined ever since this early essay. The problem, I believe, lies not in Tagg's aim, nor in Kennett's critique, but in the assumption of the initial arbitrariness in semiotic meaning, an arbitrariness that then becomes (sometimes) fixed through practice. It is only the least interesting meanings that bear an arbitrary relationship with the sounds of music, and the fixity of meanings that is taken to ensue is illusory.

Kennett regards Tagg's methodology as semiotic. Tagg also discusses his methodology in terms of semiotics, but with one important proviso, that *arbitrariness* of relation between a sign and its referent does not obtain, as in its development from Peirce's icon and index. Kennett's model, paradoxically, is closer to the semiotics he dislikes precisely because the meanings he suggests listeners may make in his thought experiment do not bear any determinant relationship to the music under discussion. I shall suggest a re-interpretation of Tagg's thought below, but first it needs to be discussed. Tagg and his associate, Bob Clarida, developed what they call a *sign typology*, relating particular musical features to the external world.[19] According to this schema, some (by no means all) musical sounds are taken to *represent* non-musical states. Tagg identifies four different

---

[17]   Philip Tagg, 'Analysing popular music: theory, method, and practice' (originally 1982), reprinted in Middleton (ed.), *Reading Pop* (Oxford, 2000), p. 81.

[18]   Tagg, 'Analysing popular music', p. 97.

[19]   Philip Tagg and Bob Clarida, *Ten little title tunes* (New York NY, 2003), pp. 99–103.

categories of sign, of which the most complex is the *anaphone*. This is a musical impulse that appears to translate a sound, a visual sensation, or the way something feels, into musical detail. The sound-world of Maire (Moya) Brennan's 'To the water', for example, is smooth, enveloping, with heavy reverberation, but without any dramatic attacks, seeming to give a musical analogue to the feel of gently flowing water. The percussion that later joins the track is a stylistic necessity, and does not contribute to the anaphone; the reference has already been made. Loreena McKennitt's 'Prospero's speech' is another clear example – quintessential 'music without sharp edges'.[20] The sound-world of King Crimson's 'Coda: I have a dream' is very different. The production on Adrian Belew's voice is heavily compressed, giving the impression of his being squeezed out of the textural space. The full string pad, the incessant drumming, and the never-ending harmonic sequence all conspire to create an aural analogue of a claustrophobic space. Both these are examples of *tactile* anaphones, in that one aspect of the music seems to convey what water, or what claustrophobia, feels like. Such analogues can also be momentary. In Chapter 7 I wrote about the Yes track 'Heart of the sunrise', and about the crisp attacks that accompany the word 'sharp' in the lyrics. These attacks are tactile anaphones for the word. And there's the sound of the piccolo trumpet in the Beatles' 'Penny Lane' which contrasts with the lower brass elsewhere, and appears immediately after the description of the 'clean machine' – the sound of this trumpet is, perhaps, a particularly clean one.[21] *Sonic* anaphones work in a similar way, except that it is non-musical sound that is turned into musical detail. The sounds of screams, sirens and overhead aero engines evoked by Jimi Hendrix's Woodstock performance of the 'Star spangled banner' constitute a *locus classicus* of this technique, but there are many other examples. Lee Dorsey's 'Working in a coalmine' includes, as well as an offbeat snare drum, an offbeat metallic hammer sound, clearly a sonic analogue for the regular strokes of hacking away at a seam. Jethro Tull's 'Rock island' evokes India with the sound of (what sounds like) a svarmandal, as 'Bombay' is mentioned. A moment in Genesis' 'Supper's ready' ('Willow Farm'), although sonically simple, is significantly richer. At 12' 30", a change of texture is marked by the call 'all change', the blowing of a station master's whistle, and the slamming of (pre-1990s) train doors. The following section of 'Willow Farm' is all about transformation. Returning to the opening, at 13'32", the lyric ends 'end with a whistle and end with a bang', at which point the train whistle and door banging are repeated, sonically transformed. The lyrics have not been about trains, but the sounds parade a secondary plot, one that refers to old trains, and adds another layer of (non-verbal) meaning. Sonic anaphones shade into matters of intertextuality, which I shall broach in Chapter 9. XTC's 'Summer's cauldron' actually combines two types of anaphone; it provides an

---

[20]   That both these examples might be categorized as 'Celtic' is no accident, and such textures are partly responsible for the 'New Age' connotations of some 'Celtic' music, for reasons to be explained below.

[21]   See Cumming, *The sonic self*, pp. 108–10.

aural analogue to midsummer heat through the synthesized sound of crickets in a meadow, and of birdsong. It also uses a string pad, whose pitches use a mechanized slow vibrato that acts as a *visual* anaphone for the shimmer created when heat rises from a flat surface. 'You've got the style' by Athlete uses slow vibrato and a heavy, claustrophobic texture, to a less precise end, but the signification is given by the repeating lyric 'it's getting hot in here'. Visual anaphones are perhaps harder to identify, but include the menacing guitar sound to Steppenwolf's 'Born to be wild'. Explaining this is not straightforward. Recall the rigid smile, teeth bared, of a menacing face. This is the mouth shape that we use to pronounce the vowel 'ee', a vowel that is full of upper partials. That characteristic tone is shared with the guitar sound of 'Born to be wild', hence that sound acts as a visual anaphone for such a mouth.

So much for anaphones. Tagg's remaining categories more subtly concern representation of the external world in music. The *episodic marker* works to position us within the discourse of a particular track. The opening drum figure to the Beatles' 'She loves you', for instance, serves to mark the return of the chorus, for instance at 1'03". Not all such drum figures in the track serve this function though – that under the title (51"), for instance, simply draws attention to that title. There is a heavy dose of the arbitrary here. The Troggs' 'Wild thing' contains two very obvious examples. At the end of the chorus, the guitar rhythm changes to emphasize the beginning of the bar (24"), indicating a change of section. Subsequently, the entry of the rather strange recorder, at 1'13", just before the chorus has ended, signals that an instrumental break is about to follow. Some episodic markers seem trivial, but that does not prevent their functioning (and perhaps, the more trivial they seem, the more effective they are). The crescendo at the end of the introduction to Dusty Springfield's 'You don't have to say you love me' simply marks the end of that section, although it also signals that we are in for a dramatic monologue. This latter function is another of Tagg's categories, that of the *style marker,* where a particular musical detail tells us what sort of style we are listening to, or how to relate this particular listening to other listenings – what sorts of norms to bring into play. Most aspects of music serve as style markers, in addition to whatever else they do (and many will do nothing else). The sound of particular instruments (overdriven guitar, drum machine), of particular harmonic patterns (a two-chord loop, a 12-bar blues sequence), of particular rhythms (a ska groove, or that of acid house), of vocal delivery (the growling metal voice, that of the diva), all give information about how to 'prepare our ears', that is, how to recognize the style, in addition to their functioning as part of a track's discourse. Tagg's fourth category is that of the *genre synecdoche*. This is perhaps rarer, and it also shades into questions of intertextuality. One interesting set of examples concerns the use of gospel choirs by a range of musicians, in order to convey something of the assured belief endemic to mainstream gospel: Nick Cave's 'O children' and Melanie Safka's overt 'Do you believe?' are good examples. Andy Stewart's 'Donald, where's your troosers' works differently. The entire arrangement positions the track in its time, that of 1960, and its location, that of polite Scots society (I have discussed this in more detail in Chapter 7). The function of the guitar that breaks into the texture at 1'55" is simply to indicate 'rock'n'roll', simultaneously (according to Tagg's argument), bringing into play for an audience a whole set of connotations that attach to the style label 'rock'n'roll'. And it seems this is exactly right for 'Donald', since the connotations of 'rock'n'roll' become immediately foregrounded in the track, in order to be dismissed for ideological reasons. The references of Wolfstone's 'Tinnie Run' are a little more complex, although the track occupies a similar stylistic space, albeit some decades later. It opens with an overdriven hard rock electric guitar, but as early as 15" in, this is joined by a fiddle and whistle playing what sounds like a fast dance tune, and the rest of a rock band. Which sound is acting as the synecdoche for a foreign style here? Once the Scots pipes enter at 1'41", the guitar has been placed more as the outsider, particularly as the form of the track will be recognized by a style-competent listener as a dance tune set, and as the guitar itself has doubled the tune (at 1'12"). However, the issue is important both because the opposition is only tentatively resolved (the guitar's aggressive tone is not modified), and also historically, since it is emblematic of the way Scots rock has changed over the past couple of decades.

Tagg's full methodology includes two other important ideas. I shall raise them here, although I shall not use them explicitly. The first is *interobjective comparison*, and it belongs with discussions of intertextuality. The second is *hypothetical substitution*. Here, we imagine altering one parameter of music we are listening to in order to estimate how its effect changes. What if the rock'n'roll guitar in 'Donald' had been a boogie piano? What if the drum figures of 'She loves you' had been absent? What if the trumpet on 'Penny Lane' had been a flute? or an organ? or had been played an octave lower? What if Dusty Springfield's track had been 20 per cent faster? The number of such substitutions we can think through is limited only by our imaginations, but each will tell us something about what is properly effective in the track, for us, even if only minimally so.

Reading Music: Theory

It should be clear from this discussion of Tagg's ideas that only some elements of musical detail contribute to such readings. On 'Tinnie Run', for instance, does the observation that it has a shuffle, rather than a straight, rhythm contribute to what it represents? Or the fact that it moves from minor to major mode? Are these more than simply stylistic features? That they are stylistic features is clear, but such details frequently do not contribute further to the signification of the track. So, which details do? This topic is particularly difficult, since it is not underpinned by any serious research, but it does seem important enough to endeavour to develop a set of conceivable correspondences, to which I shall return in the later stages of this chapter. What is the significance, the meaningfulness, of the actual notes employed? Syntactical elements of music, like syntactical elements of language, normally permit communication, rather than entering into the act of it. However, some elements seem to do both jobs.

The common modes in use (lydian, ionian, mixolydian, dorian, aeolian, phrygian) are not affectively equivalent. Take a common sequence of chords: I, VI, IV, V. Assume a tonic of D. The sequence of chord labels provides the following harmonic sequences:

Table 8.1   Modal versions of a common harmonic sequence

lydian	D	b	$g\sharp^0$	A
ionian	D	b	G	A
mixolydian	D	b	G	a
dorian	d	b^0	G	a
aeolian	d	B♭	g	a
phrygian	d	B♭	g	a^0

As Table 8.1 demonstrates, each of these sequences is different (and in practice, they are likely to be amended to turn the diminished triads into minor, or into dominant sevenths with a new root a major third below). Most prominent perhaps is the change from major to minor triads for I and V, but the others can be seen – the change from minor to major for VI is in some cases no less significant. As a working premise, in the abstract, it would appear that a major triad carries connotations of positive emotional states (to put it no more strongly than that), and the minor triad connotations of negative states. One problem is that music is not 'in the abstract' – as soon as triads are put together, possible meanings are compounded. Is, for example, an ionian I–iii–vi–ii–I (i.e. D–f♯–b–e–D) sequence more positive than a dorian i–IV–V–VII–I (i.e. d–G–A–C–d)? Both sequences are musically plausible, and we would have to take into account at least lyrics and instrumentation. But, the force of the triad that we identify as 'tonic' (i.e. one identified through persistence, laterality and emphasis – see Chapter 3) is such that, as a starting-point, I would identify the first sequence above as more affectively positive than the second. And we need a starting-point, provided we are willing to modify it in the case of actual examples. From this, I would suggest that the mode in which a particular sequence of harmonies is couched does have an effect on the signification of those harmonies. As I suggested in Chapter 3, put most clearly, as a mode increases the number of minor intervals above the tonic (i.e. as we move downward in the list given in Table 8.1), then either the greater the degree of negative emotional quality that sequence will connote, or the lower its energy level will seem to be. Whereas lydian mode patterns can tend toward elation (the effect of that 'sharpened' $\hat{4}$), phrygian can appear rather lethargic (the $\hat{2}$ being constantly 'pulled' down to the tonic, the $\hat{6}$ rising 'with difficulty' through successive whole tones to reach the upper tonic). This is very rough and ready, but represents a real starting-point. (Indeed, 'negative emotional quality' is itself probably too simplistic a notion, as Robert Solomon[22] explores, but in discussing the effect of harmony, it does at least provide an initial anchor.) Many examples could be given: I–VI–IV–VII as it moves from ionian (Talking Heads' 'This must be the place') through mixolydian (Jam's 'That's entertainment') to aeolian (Def Leppard's 'Love bites'); I–VI–IV–V as it moves from ionian (Four Seasons' 'Sherry') to aeolian (All About Eve's 'The dreamer'); VI–IV–I as it moves from ionian (Police's 'Truth hits everybody') to aeolian (Bob Dylan's 'Slow train coming'); I–II as it moves from dorian (Stevie Wonder's 'Visions') to phrygian (Pink Floyd's 'The trial'); I–II–III–IV as it moves from ionian (Beatles' 'Here, there and everywhere') to dorian (Deacon Blue's 'The world is lit by lightning'). Related to this are shifts of key. How are these read? Is the shift sliding (surreptitious?), blatant, does it intensify (sharpwards) or go the opposite way? Take the Beatles' 'Good day, sunshine' as an example of intensification. The chorus is in ionian C (I–V–IV), but the IV becomes reinterpreted as V of B♭, and the verse is in lydian B♭. This lydian nature, which is reinforced by the slide up from chords of B♭ to C at the end of the verse, seems to enrich the 'Good' of the chorus, to make it sound even 'better' because it is reached for (that sharpened $\hat{4}$) and achieved (and note that the song changes key sharpwards too). Simon and Garfunkel's 'Mrs Robinson' seems to work the same way, shifting from the mixolydian G of the verse (and introduction), with its B natural in the melody, which moves via the cycle of fifths to the chorus' ionian B♭, which sounds perhaps more comfortable – the G, despite its length at the opening, seeming slightly unstable because of its mixolydian nature, emphasized by the melody opening on $\hat{9}$. Diana Ross and the Supremes' 'The happening' shifts chromatically, from G ionian to A♭ ionian (at 1'54"). The change of harmony is blatantly unprepared, what some musicians therefore call the 'truck driver's shift'. However, unlike many such shifts, it does not sound forced, perhaps because the end of the verse includes a quasi-cyclic sequence moving through B♭ to E♭ to A♭, then back to D and G. The verse of Neneh Cherry's 'Manchild' begins fairly stably in D, but appears to shift to E♭ around 35". I say 'appears', because the E♭ is immediately followed by chords of F, D♭ and again E♭, shifting suddenly to b (which acts rather like a tonic) at the beginning of the chorus. These changes appear rather arbitrary, but could be taken as illustrating the disorientation described for the 'Manchild' of the title. More examples could be given, of course, and I suspect each has to be read in context, as above. These readings would usually be considered semiotic, but is the relation between 'sharpness' and 'intensification' or 'affectively positive' an arbitrary one? Is the relation between 'major' and 'positive', and between 'minor' and 'negative' also arbitrary? They have become solidified by practice, certainly, but it is worth noting at this point that we frequently express positive states with expansive (larger) arm movements, and negative states with being 'closed in' (smaller), that is, with particular embodied gestures (matching the 'larger' third of the major triad). More on this below.

---

[22]   Solomon, *True to our feelings*, pp. 170ff.

What might we say of melody? I have already suggested that the register in which a voice is singing can carry particular connotations (of effort, of comfort, of eagerness or laziness), but the details of a particular melody can carry more specific signification. Allen Forte[23] suggests that, within the repertory of Tin Pan Alley (and there is no particular reason to restrict his comments simply to that repertory), particular melodic details mark out the lyric that coincides with that detail for special importance – such prevalences as the lowest, highest, longest, most repeated notes of a melody. Take the Love Affair's 'Wake me I am dreaming'. The fast rising initial sweep of the melody (to the title lyrics) emphasizes the dreaming from which he needs to awake (Example 8.1), because "I am not myself", as he sings.

Example 8.1   Love Affair: 'Wake me I am dreaming'; opening melodic phrase

The force of this can be determined by trying Tagg's hypothetical substitution. Imagine turning that opening phase of the melody around (Example 8.2), so that it now falls. The line is plausible, and works equally well against the prevailing harmony, but that change now puts emphasis on the 'wake' rather than the 'dreaming', in other words on the agency of another, rather than on how his protagonist is acting.

Example 8.2   Love Affair: 'Wake me I am dreaming'; hypothetical opening melodic phrase

That change of sense is palpable, even if hard to put into words. On the Move's 'Blackberry Way', the melodic apex is found on the word 'I', emphasizing the song's being about the progatonist's own concerns, as opposed to the Beatles' 'She loves you', which is about this protagonist providing succour. In Oasis' 'Don't look back in anger', the apex occurring on the first word carries a particular tinge – think about the same song, but with the melodic emphasis on 'back' (the metrical emphasis already coincides with this word) or on 'anger'. Stasis can indicate a lack of interest, while excessive melismas can suggest fussiness. Take Mariah Carey's

23   Forte, *American popular ballad.*

version of 'Without you'. As Harry Nilsson sang it, the song remains unadorned, offering a direct glimpse of his heartache (which is extreme, as we reach the final chorus). But in her version, the virtuosic melisma at 35", for instance, seems to distance the listener, to force focus on her ability rather than her expression (which is not to deny the power of the performance, particularly in its measured, unfussy pace and gospel choir interjections in the playout). Similar analogies can easily be found for other melodic movements. What about a melody where the contour is dominant? How fast is it traversed? By step or by leap? The melody of Frank and Nancy Sinatra's 'Something stupid' (taken by Frank), moves by step throughout, perhaps signifying distance especially as it moves against upper pedal notes sung by Nancy. Everything is kept melodically under control, nothing is extravagant. But then the refrain ('I love you') is marked by a (risk-taking) leap, which she joins by singing in thirds, rather than with a pedal (to which the strings respond by a comically eyebrow-raising ♭VI⁷). Perhaps it's not so stupid after all?

In a text that is now rather outmoded,[24] Deryck Cooke once offered an entire lexicon of melodic intervallic movements, and their supposed expressive force. This work has been heavily criticized over the years, partly on the grounds that it confused the evocation of emotion with its expression, and partly for its supposed universality, whereby it regarded these qualities as inherent in the music. If we refuse to think of this in theoretical terms, however, and view it as a set of invitations, as a set of possibilities, to hear particular intervals *as if* they make likely particular readings, some of them are very inviting. The difference between the leap of an octave, for example, and chromatic motion by semitone. One would not choose the latter to accompany the expression of striding, nor the former to accompany the expression of slithering, unless one was being ironic. (The reasons for this will be addressed below.) Other writers sometimes offer similar suggestions. Richard Middleton, for example, in a passage contrasting the blues, African melodic practices and Beethoven, says '[the minor third] seems to suggest acceptance, resignation, and stability [while the major third suggests] a widening of horizons, a challenge and an assertion of Self'.[25] This is akin to the point I made above, concerning the differences between modes. *Why* such a suggestion is plausible will, again, be addressed below. Treated tentatively in this way, it seems to me that some of Cooke's possibilities should be borne in mind. For example, he suggests that an ascending $\hat{1}$–$\hat{3}$–$\hat{5}$ progression in the minor (i.e. dorian, aeolian or phrygian) should result in a phrase 'expressive of an outgoing feeling of pain – an assertion of sorrow, a complaint, a protest against misfortune'.[26] Such a phrase opens the Beatles' 'I want you', where Lennon's expressed need for 'you' is palpable. The same phrase underlies expressions of love in Slade's 'Coz I luv you'. At first this seems strange, but perhaps the line 'You make me out a clown then you put me down' suggests a certain masochistic intensity to the lyric,

---

[24]   Deryck Cooke, *The language of music* (Oxford, 1959).

[25]   Middleton, *Pop music and the blues*, p. 38.

[26]   Cooke, *The language of music*, p. 122.

which the phrase underlines. Cooke also suggests that the major $\hat{6}-\hat{5}$ produces 'the effect of a burst of pleasurable longing',[27] as in the dominant motif of the Archies' 'Sugar sugar', which later becomes 'you got me wanting you'. Admittedly the nondescript backing adds a layer of sentiment to this expression, but the phrase is apposite. Cooke gives as an example of this a phrase in Irving Berlin's 'Cheek to cheek' ('Heaven, I'm in heaven'). The same melodic outline is present in Elvis Costello's 'Alison'. Here, though, the melody's first note is harmonized differently, and the expression is anything but joyful, as Costello's vocal timbre makes clear. I would suggest, then, that Cooke's lexicon cannot simply be imported wholesale into popular song – melodies are tempered by harmony, by timbre and by other elements – but that it can form the basis for further consideration in any particular case.

It is common practice to speak metaphorically of 'punctuation' in terms of syntax. The cadence, for example, in common-practice music, marks the end of a phrase, and the degree of closure is harmonically controlled. I have already broached this issue in terms of harmony. But how do we read such closure?[28] When it accompanies a particular lyric, a number of possibilities seem to be open. It can be read as affirmation of, or agreement with, the view expressed. It can be read processually as arriving at a particular point, or it can be read as the completion of a particular idea. In Doris Day's 'Que sera sera', the melody seems almost formulaic. It rises questioningly, and refuses to close as the protagonist looks at various life possibilities. But her mother, taking control of the chorus, has the answer, closing securely at the end of the verse. And what is that answer? To accept the vagaries of fate. Note how the melody drops unexpectedly to the tonic in the chorus the second time we hear the lyric '*will*' that is, offering unequivocation (at the end of the second line – see Example 8.3).

Example 8.3   Doris Day: 'Que sera sera'; opening of the chorus

In the Beatles' 'I'll get you', a melodic tonic is constantly evaded until the 'oh *yeah*'. This evasion (the fact that previous points of closure are inconclusive) enacts the 'in the end' of the lyric – it is not a speedy conquest. But conquest it seems to be for, as the melody falls to 'yeah', it does not have the thrill of

---

27   Cooke, *The language of music*, p. 146.

28   Cumming argues that the conventionality of something like the perfect cadence can be understood semiotically, that 'a conventionally ordered aspect of the world ... can be viewed as having its own emerging qualities' in a manner related to iconicity (*The sonic self*, p. 103). This is a suggestion I follow subsequently, although without resorting fully to her semiotic position.

'She loves you', sounding instead rather tired. In the chorus of Kate Bush's 'Wuthering heights', the melody reaches the tonic as she announces 'I've come *home*', but refuses to close – the melody moves on as she tries to gain entrance. And, correspondingly, a smaller degree of closure, particularly if unexpected, could mark an openness. The Yardbirds' 'For your love' adopts a common strategy. Although the accompaniment finally comes to a close, the vocal melody does not – the protagonist's promises of what he will do 'for your love' are open to endless continuation. All of these comments could apply separately to melody and harmony, but there is an additional range of possibilities, when melodic and harmonic closure fail to coincide. John Lennon's 'Imagine' provides a fine example. The melody consistently (four times) reaches for an upper tonic, failing to achieve it. By the time it succeeds, the harmony has moved away from the tonic. The two do not coincide until the phrase 'You may say I'm a dreamer', and on the last word, suggesting that it is this quality of dreaming that received greatest attention in the song, and that is supported by its production values (see Chapter 7). And melody and harmony work together in other ways to amplify the affect. On Mott the Hoople's 'All the young dudes', the melodic apex coincides with the word 'nudes', in the second line of the chorus. This itself is a striking image, but as the harmony at that point turns from ionian (specified by the bass line) to mixolydian (Example 8.4), this acquires a particularly bittersweet tone as the melodic A clashes with the harmonic g.

Example 8.4 Mott the Hoople: 'All the young dudes'; opening of the chorus

One particularly important feature of these readings is their provenance. In part, they originate in 'common-sense' notions of what musical syntax is doing (and I shall return to this point later in the chapter). Closure in one domain, for example, is linked to closure in another domain and read accordingly. The fact that such readings appear to be 'second nature' is often a sure sign that they are semiotic. The reason why we attend to the lowest or highest pitch of a line, for example, is because it is the highest or lowest pitch, because of its marked *difference* from all other pitches and semiotic meaning is 'caused' by attendance to difference. A semiotic reading, for instance, would not distinguish between the importance of the highest pitch of a melody and the importance of the lowest. But sometimes this distinction matters, and that 'matters' is not a matter of semiotics. I shall discuss the theoretical justification that operates in such cases below.

In another part, these readings originate in other songs, or at least in other listening experiences, to create a chain of meanings. I shall approach this topic more fully in Chapter 9, but I want to include one particular set of examples here. Deep Purple's 'Child in time' is one of a body of songs reliant for its effect on the aeolian cadence, the cadential pattern moving VI–VII–i (i.e. F–G–a in a aeolian). This cadence in rock is, more often than not, associated with achievement in the face of high odds, what we might identify as its 'nonetheless' quality. This is the realm of its signification. The underlying pattern to 'Child in time' is formed of the sequence i–VII–i; VI–VII; VII–i. The impending, and ultimately realized, disaster apparent in the lyrics is matched by this constant reiteration, demonstrating an undesired actualization of the inevitable outcome. This sense of the inevitability of an unwanted outcome is crucial to understanding the Coverdale Page track 'Take me for a little while'. The verse begins by decorating harmonies of E, moves to a pattern dominated by a, but then sinks back. A short pre-chorus reiterates the importance of a, such that the chorus takes up the sequence a-F–G–G. Failure to resolve to chord I (or here, i), in this example to resolve to a at the end of the a–F–G–G pattern, implies the subversion of an inevitable outcome. Now the subject matter of the song's lyric concerns the inevitability of failure – at the crucial moment, the singer tells his lover to take him just 'for a little while'. Their relationship cannot remain stable, because he's 'growing older'. The harmony, in other words (being read as an aspect of the personic environment), indicates that 'taking him for a little while' is an attempt to subvert the inevitable, that is, the inevitability of failure, a failure that will come about once the final chord i is reached and closure is achieved. For this reason, the track's fade-out, without that happening, is a suitable ending. The Darkness track 'Holding my own' uses the same pattern to energize an avoidance of the inevitable. It is less marked: the analogous a–G–F–G chord sequence accompanies the song's title, asserting that the persona is 'holding his own' in the face of enormous odds; because it is less marked, the sequence functions harmonically as ionian vi–V–IV–V rather than aeolian i–VII–VI–VII. The realm of its signification is nonetheless the same. Note that any substantial substitution of these harmonies would affect their reading, even if it remained stylistically plausible (iv–v–i for 'Child in time', for example). This is but one example of such a chain of references, where the import of a pattern depends on its modification of a previous pattern.

If it is plausible to suggest that particular harmonic and melodic details call forth specific connotations, then it should be much more likely that timbre would do so. After all, timbre is a feature of all sound, whether music or not, and we react to timbre 'in real life'. Particular timbres have indeed taken on the quality of clichés. Held chords on an organ, or a string pad, are often taken to signify serenity, presumably on the grounds that they exemplify a minimum of activity. A virtuosic guitar solo likewise is taken to signify self-indulgence (whether or not this is seen as a value). I shall return to these matter-of-fact readings. Research by Serge Lacasse has supported the notion that particular modifications of timbre imply common readings. He undertook a series of listener tests, comparing eight types of timbral modification with eight types of connotation. The results are reproduced in Table 8.2.[29]

Table 8.2   Lacasse's timbral modification qualities

	Benevolence	Potency	Naturalness	Temporality	Stability	Distance	Religiosity	Happiness
Normal	2	0	3	0	2	-2	0	0
Reverb	1	1	-1.5	-1	-0.5	2	2	0
Echo	1	1	-1.5	-1	-1	3	1	0
Slap	0	1	-1	0.25	-1	1	0	0
Telephone	-0.5	0	-1	-0.75	0	3	-1	-1
Flanging	-1	0	-2	1.5	-1.25	-1	0	0
Harmonizer	-2	0.5	-3	1.5	-2.5	1	-2	-1
Distortion	-3	0.5	-2	0	02.5	2	-1	0

In this table, the higher the figure, the stronger the effect, negative figures giving negative effects. Thus, slap echo sounded slightly futuristic to Lacasse's respondents, echo a little more dated. Distortion sounded highly malevolent, reverb strongly religious, telephone compression slightly sad, and so on. Such findings as this again represent a useful starting-point, but need to be read in context. For example, distortion has become a fundamental stylistic sign of metal – within that style, it no longer carries the disruptive function it once had for all styles. So, at the end (3'37") of Trivium's 'Ignition', a song that simplistically expresses anger at the duplicity of a social establishment, distortion is somewhat impotent simply as a means of expression, and so they resort to the effective gradual detuning of a synthesized guitar arpeggio to convey a similar affect. Lacasse's list is useful, but what is perhaps surprising about it is that it is self-evident; his respondents feel about these forms of distortion pretty well exactly how one might imagine. This is not the place for an extended discussion about the value (or otherwise) of lengthy reception tests, but it seems to me that the result of work like this (and also, for example, the much more extensive work reported in Ten little title tunes) tends to be somewhat superfluous in that it simply confirms what competent musicology assumes anyway. Such confirmation is of course welcome and initially necessary, but does not necessarily repay anything like the effort required to discover it.

What is important is to recognize that not every element partakes of this sort of meaning. The model of communication developed by Roman Jacobson

---

29   The original table can be found in Lacasse, *'Listen to my voice'*, p. 161.

is useful.[30] Jacobson addresses the six functions that he regards communication as sedimenting: the referential; the aesthetic; the emotive; the conative; the phatic; and the metalingual. This chapter broadly covers his referential, aesthetic and emotive functions. The conative was covered in Chapter 7. The phatic and metalingual are often overlooked. The phatic refers to material whose function is to check that the 'channel' is working, that is, merely to check that communication is taking place. Tagg's episodic markers largely belong to this category, certainly at least in their reference to beginnings and endings. The metalingual refers to material whose function is to check that the 'code' is working, that is, that we recognize the style limits within which we're interpreting. Tagg's style markers belong in this category. And so, while it seems that every musical detail could be labelled functionally, it is only some details that work referentially, aesthetically or emotively.

Reading Music: Examples

So far, I have said that this methodology consists of asking questions of tracks in order to elucidate their signification. As this approach becomes naturalized, you will discover that it begins to be the track that appears to pose the questions, rather than having them imposed by the listener. Take Lou Reed's 'Perfect day'. There is much one could say about this, but I shall restrict myself to a question set by the opening harmonies. It opens with an introduction, using what sounds like I–iv in F. However, as the verse opens, that iv is reinterpreted as i in b♭. The sequence that then underlies the verse is dorian i–IV–VII–III–♭VI–iv–V♯. Why is that first chord minor? It could easily have been major – the melody leaps from $\hat{1}$ to $\hat{5}$, missing the third degree entirely. It could be understood (without further ado) as 'ironic' I suppose, but that's just too easy. Focus closely on the end of the first line: '… and then *home*. Just a *per*-fect day.' 'Home' coincides with the dominant, and the first syllable of 'perfect' with the major subdominant. 'Just' seems less significant, although in its sense as 'only' perhaps it highlights the unexpected nature of that perfection. The effect of the (absent) D♮ in what could be chord I, and the presence of the lower D♭ in what is chord i seems to drag the emotive effect downward – whereas the rest of the sequence has a lightness to it, there is a dark tinge to that opening chord that adds a slight negativity to the perfection of the day (as if, perhaps, it is unlikely to be repeated).[31] Perhaps this hints at the otherwise hard to understand repeated 'you're going to reap just what you sow' with which the song ends? Wild Turkey's 'Gentle rain' moves in the opposite direction. Example 8.5 shows the opening of the verse.

---

[30]   See Middleton, *Studying popular music*, p. 241.

[31]   A similar stomach-dropping effect is achieved in the final aeolian ii[7]–vi–i cadence to Grand Funk Railroad's 'Mean mistreater'.

Example 8.5 Wild Turkey: 'Gentle rain'; opening of the verse

The flattened sixth and seventh degrees (in relation to the ionian) mean that to reach $\hat{3}$ (which would perhaps 'normally' be flattened in this context) implies a stretch, an expansiveness of gesture that is so beautifully appropriate to the expression of love in the lyric.

Or, take Elton John's 'I've seen that movie too'. It seems to me that the speed of this track is just slightly too slow to be comfortable, and this is most telling in the downward complex piano blues scale that acts as to lead into the verse, a scale that wanders fractionally out of time. What could be signified by such awkwardness? The only link I can make is to observe that in everyday existence, we encounter instances of speaking just slower than is comfortable, and one notable case where this happens is when someone is expressing a high degree of anger, but is just able to keep things 'under control'. This is a tone that is easy to hear in this song; it amplifies the protagonist's anger at his interlocutor's inauthenticity, whose emotions are simply borrowed from an unspecified film. In Garbage's 'A stroke of luck', it is the texture rather than the speed that calls for attention. Why does it seem so effective? It is full of reverberation, it is dense, and the string pad implies a cocooning context. The lyrics speak of cold 'closing in', they speak of constantly 'falling', they speak of a refusal to change, to escape from this texture. And indeed, from the fade-in with its repeated mechanical grinding sound, it is a texture that seems to offer no alternative, no moments of respite. This is a common set of feelings to express, but the texture of this track matches that expression. A very different example is provided by Dory Previn's 'The altruist and the needy case'. Here, the question is just who is the needy case? The track contrasts a man who is concerned about an almost infinite number of 'good causes' with the singer, who asks why it is that 'he' can't stretch his concern to a concern for her. He is clearly the altruist, and she needs him. However, by the end of the song, the lyrics hint that he is at least as much in need of the intimacy she also lacks. What is interesting is that the setting does nothing to suggest this alternative reading – it does not contribute to the sense of the song in this way. And that's fine, it is a strategy clearly open to musicians, to leave an ambiguity unresolved, to leave that up to the listener.

It is time that some of these varied ideas were put together in the service of individual tracks: separating features out is necessary in order to give them proper consideration, but this process is only useful if they are put together again. Natalie Merchant conventionally sings with a powerful, resonant voice low in tessitura and with the air being forced into the upper palate – a voice hard to forget once encountered. However, on the track 'The ballad of Henry Darger', she chooses to adopt a very different voice, less forceful, almost childlike, and perhaps this implies the key question the track raises – how does she present him (for Henry Darger was a real individual)? Her voice, in the context of her output, suggests a sympathetic portrayal, but why, and with what effect? The song is cast in a very straightforward fashion – four short interrogative verses interrupted by a bridge – but each verse is immediately ambiguous. Is Merchant addressing Henry, asking who it is who will act for the "poor little girl", or is she asserting that Henry himself will? Perhaps Merchant is embodying the subject of the song, namely two young girls (Merchant's voice is openly double-tracked)? Merchant encountered Darger only through a posthumous exhibition of his work;[32] Darger, a recluse, spent a lifetime writing and illustrating an enormous fantasy in which two young sisters were the leading characters, enslaved (as were countless others) and in need of rescue. The lyric hints at suggestions that Darger's perspective on this work was not entirely innocent (the 'patron saint of girls' is a somewhat nauseating title to be accorded), and yet the song is in no way condemnatory – the final verse, asking who will 'love a poor orphan child', in its answer 'Henry' could almost be asserting that Merchant sees Darger himself as that child. So how is this sympathetic portrayal effected? Instrumentation is one means – the chamber orchestra creates a sense of friction with Merchant's more normal backing – there is nothing aggressive in this setting. The horn line conveys a wistfulness with which it has been associated in recent times, partly because it is holding back just ever so slightly (think Neil Young's 'After the goldrush'), the harp-like gentle acoustic guitar arpeggios imply a pastoral setting, and the fragile clarinet opening statement lacks any self-assurance. These characteristics imply both Merchant's persona's delivery and also the imputed state of mind of Darger. Note how the enveloping sound of the band in the first part of the song slims down after the bridge to provide the barest accompaniment to that final verse, throwing it into relief. The song is cast in the aeolian mode, meaning the cadence (VII–i or F–g) avoids the assertive sharpened leading-note. An unambiguous V (D) appears in the midst of the verse, but each time it is answered with 'Henry, Henry, oh Henry …', reasserting the sympathetic tone. And the final tag is surprisingly long – it is easy to hear this as mourning for the man (Darger) she (Merchant) never knew until after his death. So, a number of characteristics of the song encourage us to a positive posthumous encounter with this strange individual (Darger), an attitude perhaps rather different from that we might have adopted in simply encountering his work unmediated. None of these is conclusive, of course, we can still adopt whatever position we wish, but we now do so in contrast to this presentation.[33]

Queen's 'Bicycle race' is an altogether different example. The title sets a key question – in what sense is this about a race? The key line of lyric seems to be

---

[32]   'Natalie Merchant biography' (http://www.sing365.com/music/lyric.nsf/Natalie-Merchant-Biography/3CEA058C189748B248256926002783A9, no date).

[33]   Note that if, as a result of this track, we approach Darger's work through its perspective, we are making a second-order interpretation of Darger's work.

'I want to ride my bicycle', and ride it 'where I like', which is precisely what a race is not about. Indeed, there is a strong assertion of Freddie Mercury's own individuality here. This is overt in the verse, where he simply contradicts whatever opinion is presented: 'you say black, I say white', etc. Although this may be read as simply an argumentative pose, there is certainly a refusal to be pinned down here – he appears secure in his identity, withstanding external assaults. As a result, this passage can be read as competitive, that is, as implying a race. It would be possible to read the song's harmonic language as an argumentative assertion of individuality too, its almost ridiculous waywardness suggesting a devil-may-care attitude. Although the track centres on an implied tonic A♭ ('I *want* to ride …'), it is reached very unusually (via chords of D and B[34]), and it appears almost incidental. The track interpolates a reference to Queen's own 'Fat-bottomed girls', and this appears as a moment of relaxation, certainly in terms of tempo, although whether it could be read ironically is unclear, since it is unsupported in the accompaniment in any way. The track also interpolates a sequence of ringing bells. These are not a sonic anaphone, since they are actual bells, but the way they intrude on each other implies perhaps a multiple ride through the park (although, again, this is hardly a race, where one would not expect to hear bicycle bells). The bell sequence is followed by a passage of guitar scales chasing each other, at ever closer distances, and here the image of a race is actually brought to the fore.[35] Perhaps the key feature of the track is the way that it overcomes certain dualities. It is an example of stadium rock, and it has something of the anthemic tone common to much of Queen's output, made particularly apparent in the downward phrase[36] to which the opening 'Bicycle' is sung, encouraging participation (after all, it's a bike ride we're all invited to, as the massed bells also make plain), and yet it deals with such a prosaic activity as 'ridin' me bike'.

The Madness track 'Our house' is another example rich in signification. Again, the question seems to be one of presentation. What view of 'our house' are we being presented with? A feature of much of Madness' early music is their chromatic approach to harmony,[37] and this track is no different. The basic pattern is a mixolydian I–v–ii–iv˜, which hints at the aeolian in the last chord (indeed it could, slightly less easily, be read as aeolian I'–v–ii˜–iv). This is pretty familiar and unchallenging, if tinged with melancholy. It is how the pattern is used that is

---

[34]   Chords whose roots are separated by a minor third form a chromatic sequence often used by King Crimson (and much less often by other musicians) in the sense of a cycle of events that needs to be escaped from but cannot be.

[35]   One of my students (Mark Claydon) has suggested that the relationship between these ringing bells and the ensuing guitar 'race' is akin to the relationship between the revving up of racing cars and their ensuing race. This seems to me at least plausible.

[36]   'Rock anthems' tend to focus on short downward phrases for collective singing. See Ruth Dockwray, *Deconstructing the Rock Anthem: Textual Form, Participation, and Collectivity* (PhD thesis, University of Liverpool, 2005).

[37]   Moore, *Rock: the primary text*, pp. 139–42.

interesting. The verse consists of two repeats of this pattern, in C mixolydian. The first chorus doubles the speed – we again hear the pattern twice (but it lasts for only two rather than four bars) and is transposed up to D mixolydian. The chorus that follows the second verse then adds a further two hearings of the pattern, but now transposed to B mixolydian. Following a strident saxophone solo, the third verse doubles the speed at which the lyric passes – verbal space is, all of a sudden, compressed. And then, after a repeat of the first verse, the final chorus repeats the pattern at all three transpositional levels (beginning on D, B, C and back to D to fade). The lyric fondly recalls a busy, conventional, mid-century working-class childhood: dad off to work early, mum doing the ironing and cooking (and 'so house-proud'), and kids gently running riot, a general busyness that finds expression in the texture. Perhaps it is not going too far to hear the backwards guitar chord with which the track opens as a very palpable return to the past. The repeat of the first verse perhaps suggests that the protagonist is stuck in his nostalgia, especially as it follows the double-speed verse, in which the perspective changes from one of the idealized present to one of the past, a definite looking back from a subsequent vantage-point. It is as if black and white footage suddenly becomes colour at this point, before shifting back. So, again, this is a rather sympathetic presentation, but with a slightly uneasy nostalgia to the fore.

What is the status of these readings? They are only partial of course, but they develop from details of the track as presented to us: they are exploratory forays into the relationship between what we hear and the significance we might place on it. For some writers, they would be classed unequivocally as semiotic. Time and time again, however, I have referred details to the way something would appear 'in real life' as an aspect of our experience outside the world of these particular tracks. For me this is absolutely crucial. In Chapter 1, in the section on 'theory', I made brief reference to the fields of ecological perception and embodied cognition, which I suggested formed the theoretical basis of my methodology. It is time for me to explore these in more detail. I begin with the latter.

Embodied Cognition

What I am calling 'embodied cognition' is an aspect of the super-field known as cognitive science, which has infiltrated many areas of scholarship, and has even extended to the humanities.[38] It has entered musicological discourse,[39] but its use tends to remain at rather an abstract level.[40] My interest was particularly sparked

---

[38] Lakoff and Johnson, *Metaphors we live by*.

[39] Zbikowski, *Conceptualising music*.

[40] For example, Janna Saslaw: 'Forces, containers, and paths: the role of body-derived image schemas in the conceptualization of music', *Journal of Music Theory* 40/2 (1996).

by work by Susan Fast and William Echard,[41] but I have taken it in a different direction. Embodied cognition has resonated most strongly, perhaps, in linguistics, psychology, philosophy and aspects of neuroscience.[42] Perhaps a key idea is the notion of *conceptual metaphor*, initially theorized by Lakoff and Johnson. Rather than seeing metaphor as a rather minor aspect of language usage, they reposition it as a dominant feature of cognition, whereby we develop new knowledge by conceiving new experiences in terms of understanding we already have, a process that is often termed *cross-modal*, whereby discreet modes of understanding are thereby linked. Johnson[43] introduces the concept of the *image schema*. The *schema* is an important, and exceedingly rich, concept in psychology that can be traced back to Kant. Johnson himself says: 'A schema is a recurrent pattern, shape and regularity in, or of, these ongoing ordering activities [of our experiences]'.[44] An alternative description I find useful suggests that schemata are 'mental representations of the properties that concepts usually have'.[45] Daniel Levitin brings the concept closer to home: for him, schemata 'frame our understanding; they're the system into which we place the elements and interpretation of an aesthetic object'.[46] Johnson argues that it is our embodied experience of the world that forms the basis for all abstract thought and language, and that this experience is processed, cognitively, as *image schemata*. These are highly abstract things, both simple and very general. It is this generality that enables them to serve as the basis for understanding concepts related to objects, to actions and to abstract thought, in the way that images themselves cannot. In their simplicity, they contain just a small number of parts and their relations: 'their most important feature is that they have a few basic elements or components that are related by definite structures, and they have a certain flexibility. As a result of this simple structure, they are a chief means for achieving order in our experience so that we can comprehend and reason about it'.[47] They can, perhaps, be identified as stereotypes of underlying pattern translatable from one sense-domain (or medium, or mode of understanding) to another, but

---

[41]   Susan Fast, *In the houses of the holy: Led Zeppelin and the power of rock music* (Oxford, 2001), pp. 132ff. and William Echard, 'An analysis of Neil Young's "Powderfinger" based on Mark Johnson's image schemata', *Popular Music* 18/1 (1999).

[42]   I acknowledge the severe doubts that remain in some circles regarding its claims, doubts that are well served by Leonard Shapiro, *Embodied cognition* (London, 2011). While I believe that the possibilities this field opens up for a meta-understanding of music are worth the risk, their status as *explanation* (of the sort I offer below) has to remain open to uncertainty.

[43]   Johnson, *The body in the mind*. See also Lakoff and Turner, *More than cool reason*, pp. 90ff.

[44]   Johnson, *The body in the mind*, p. 29.

[45]   Mike Rinck, 'Spatial Situation Models', in Priti Shah and Akira Miyake (eds.), *Cambridge Handbook of Visuospatial Thinking* (New York NY: 2005), p. 337.

[46]   Daniel J. Levitin, *This is your brain on music* (London, 2006), p. 234.

[47]   Johnson, *The body in the mind*, p. 28.

originating in bodily experience of the world. It is by means of metaphorical extension that these schemata act as the basis for rational thought, and they serve as the pre-conceptual ground for the process of *cross-domain mapping*, which will become important below. By connecting propositional thought to pre-conceptual schemata, Johnson extends what is commonly meant by 'reasoning' to include activities of the body, a bodily knowing that is intimately and inherently linked with rational processes, rather than separate from them: 'Logical inferences, I am claiming, are not just inexplicable structures of rationality (of pure reason). On the contrary, they can be seen to emerge from our embodied, concrete experience and our problem solving in our most mundane affairs. The patterns of our rationality are tied, in part, to the preconceptual schemata that give comprehensible order and connectedness to our experience'.[48]

An understanding of musical experience as embodied would not, of course, be new, but embodied meaning is not discussed uniformly, even within thinking about music. For Louis Arnaud Reid, for example, a musical work's meaning was provided by an appreciation of aesthetic embodiment. This is how perceived objects convey meaning they do not literally possess.[49] For the perceiver, Reid argued that this comes down to 'the actual presence of what we are sensibly aware of and attending to …'.[50] More recently, Judith Becker describes three, interlinked, modes of consideration of embodied experience: 'the body as a physical structure in which emotion and cognition happen … the body as the site of first-person, unique, inner life … the body as involved with other bodies in the phenomenal world, that is, as being-in-the-world'.[51] In other recent work Naomi Cumming has developed David Lidov's theory of gesture, arguing that 'the music creates a bodily possibility that listeners may entertain, as freeing them from known limitations';[52] she opposes 'feel' to structure, following the work of Charles Keil.[53] My approach, however, is not to seek such escapism (not to accept such a duality), but to observe the grounds of embodied meaning that pay heed to our limitations, which approach calls for the ecological approach I develop below. The mode of cognition which has developed from cognitive science is described as embodied because Johnson sees the body as structural to many, if not most, image schemata, both as a foundational point of experience upon which schemata are built, and also as providing a viewpoint inherent to the structural relations of many image schemata.[54] In addition, he argues for the culturally-determined and -maintained

---

[48]   Johnson, *The body in the mind*, pp. 99–100.

[49]   Louis Arnaud Reid, *Meaning in the Arts* (New York NY, 1969).

[50]   John T. Langfeld, 'Louis Arnaud Reid' in Bennett Reimer & Jeffrey E. Wright (eds.), *On the nature of musical experience* (Niwot CO, 1992).

[51]   Becker, *Deep listeners*, p. 8.

[52]   Cumming, *The sonic self*, p. 193.

[53]   Particularly Keil and Feld, *Music grooves*.

[54]   Johnson, *The body in the mind*, pp. 33–4, 36–7.

nature of most schemata;[55] these positions are developed variously by Damasio, Gibbs, Kövecses and others.[56]

So, how does this relate to a discussion of song? Johnson's pioneering study refers to an extensive list of schemata, including: containment; path; blockage; centre/periphery; cycle; compulsion; counterforce; diversion; removal of restraint; enablement; attraction; link; scale; balance; contact; surface; full/empty; merging; matching; near/far; mass/count; iteration; object; splitting; part/whole; superimposition; process; collection. The linguistic usage of some of these has been developed by others, and there is no reason why this list should be exhaustive. Nor is there any reason why they should all relate to music. But some very clearly do. Two of the more useful schemata are the 'containment' schema[57] and what Johnson calls the 'twin-pan' version of the 'balance' schema (as in a pair of weighing scales). They come together to enable a powerful exegesis of the song 'All along the watchtower'. The lyric to Bob Dylan's original song has troubled many in its interpretation. The first two verses record a highly allusive conversation between two figures, 'the joker' and 'the thief', while a third narrates an observation from 'the watchtower' of what might be encroaching menace.[58] The key line is the very first: 'There must be some kind of way out of here'. Where is 'here'?[59] A likely supposition is that it identifies some sort of dungeon. Such a room could easily appear in the vicinity of a (historically unspecified) watchtower. The menacing 'two riders' could be seen as offering a 'way out' for the joker and the thief, as mounting an escape. In Dylan's original recording, it is left simply as that. His voice is central in the mix, smothering the guitar except at the points shown in Example 8.6.

Example 8.6   Bob Dylan: 'All along the watchtower'; basic groove

---

[55]   Johnson, *The body in the mind*, p. 30.

[56]   Antonio Damasio, *The feeling of what happens: Body and emotion in the making of consciousness* (New York NY, 1999); Gibbs, *Embodiment and cognitive science*; Zoltán Kövecses, *Metaphor in culture: universality and variation* (Cambridge, 2005).

[57]   Johnson, *The body in the mind*, pp. 21–3.

[58]   As far as I am aware, nobody has ever thought to comment that 'along the watchtower' is a barely possible position to be able to take up, a watchtower being, in the biblical times which are so often the source of reference of Dylan's obscure lyrics, tall and very narrow. Of course, 'all along the battlement', despite having the right number of syllables, doesn't quite convey the same necessity for acute observation of the environment.

[59]   I explore this (to me, fascinating) question extensively in Moore, 'Where is "here"?' from the same theoretical perspective that I develop across this book.

Harmonica to the left and drums to the right balance the bass, which is also in the centre. Jimi Hendrix's cover is dissimilar in terms of the soundbox. The kit is now to the left, with a second guitar to the right, but Hendrix's voice and lead guitar, and Noel Redding's bass, are all central. The harmonic pattern is identical, but is articulated very differently, as shown in Example 8.7.

Example 8.7 Jimi Hendrix: 'All along the watchtower'; basic groove

The upbeat was introduced by Hendrix to this song, and it means that the grouping and phrase boundaries do not coincide at the very opening to the track. Rather than the pattern dropping from the tonic and then returning, as in Dylan's version (aeolian: i–(VII–)VI–VII–), the pattern as performed now contains both a rise and a fall from VII (aeolian: VII–i–VII–VI–). The pivot, the centre of the pattern, has now become VII, as result of the empty third beat, which demarcates the pattern. The harmony moves to both sides of this VII, but is unable to escape, throughout the entire song. I suggest that the force of this harmonic reformulation can be best understood as an example of a schema we might term 'pendulum'. The key features of this schema are that it swings from side to side in an arc, but never exceeds the reaches of that arc, and that the arc is symmetrically extended about a central axis. The schema does not appear in Johnson, but has been introduced by Christopher Schmidt.[60] Schmidt does not offer an analysis, but it seems that 'pendulum' combines the two characteristics I mentioned above, a version of the 'balance' schema, and the 'containment' schema. The sense is of the harmonic motion swinging one way (to i) and then the other (to VI), but without being able to break free (of the boundary set by i and VI as extremes), constantly returning to VII. The harmonic motion, then, implies that the joker is wrong, that there is indeed no 'way out of here'. Neither the versions of the song by Richie Havens, nor U2, incorporate Hendrix's upbeat; this implies a different reading of the song, one that fails to use Hendrix's rhythmic rethinking to energize the metaphor that enables us to feel that, for the joker and the thief, 'here' is not somewhere that can be escaped from. The i–VII–VI sequence crucial in this case also coincides with the word 'here' on the Sparklehorse track 'Eyepennies'. There is no overt intertextual reference made – the style of the latter is most often described as 'alt. country': gentle, laid back, disturbingly surreal. In 'Eyepennies', 'here' appears

---

[60]   Christopher Schmidt, 'Metaphor and cognition: a cross-cultural study of indigenous and universal constructs in stock exchange reports', *Intercultural Communication* 5 (http://www.immi.se/intercultural/, 2002).

to refer to the grave, to which the narrator will 'return someday' to retrieve an assortment of buried items. It is surely coincidental that a grave is also an enclosed space, although the rigidity of both the soundbox positions and the groove do accord with this interpretation. Mark Linkous' voice is very far forward in the mix, with other sound-sources statically behind him and to each side, while the very slow $^{12}_{8}$ shuffle metre is only rarely decorated with short upbeats; otherwise, everything is very much 'on the beat'. The same image operates in Queen's 'Now I'm here'. The track is a standard glam rock boogie with voices covering a wide arc in the centre of the stereo field. In the song's introduction, Freddie Mercury's persona takes up four separate positions – hard left and hard right, mid left and mid right. From the outer two positions, we hear 'now I'm here'; at the inner two 'now I'm there'. Toward the end of the track, this 'now I'm here' is recovered, and followed by the declaration 'think I'll stay around', which switches from side to side, perhaps providing an approximate image of 'aroundness'. The annoying inability of music to move backwards in time is a perennial problem in the specification of circular features: what is circular in space can only be cyclical,[61] or pendular in time (depending on the presence, or not, of a definable point of rest towards which a cycle tends).

A second image schema that is particularly explanatory is that of the 'path'. Often this is used (without reference to the concept) of the harmonic language of a great deal of music, where the normative assumption is that a harmonic sequence leads *from* somewhere *to* somewhere else, and that 'leading' is the essential component of the path schema.[62] Here, though, I observe some other uses. In the Beatles' 'Here comes the sun', the sun's arrival (whether at sunrise, or from behind clouds, is left unclear) is marked at 45", as Harrison's guitar leaps momentarily to the fore. At the second appearance of this moment (in the chorus at 1'16"), an organ doubles the guitar's four-note lick. This is clearly an important moment for, repeated at 2'30" and 2'42", the guitar clearly crescendos through its four notes. And during the $^3_8$ bridge (from 1'30"–2'4": 'sun, sun, sun, here it comes') the texture grows both in weight and in range, as a synthesizer line is repeated but each time in a higher octave, while the bass remains registrally stable. It is this regularity of directional growth that implies Johnson's 'path' schema, which has three components. Johnson's 'source' is the lowest register in which the synthesizer line appears, his 'sequence of contiguous locations' is the octave transpositions, while his 'goal' is the effective top of the synthesizer range, although it could also be understood as the moment of escape from the consistent aeolian III–VII–IV–I sequence, achieving a dominant V preparing the retrieval of the verse. The chorus of the Beach Boys' 'Here today' opens with the phrase 'love is here'; to emphasize its presence, the whole band enters on 'here'. However, this had been preceded by a pre-chorus with stepwise ascending harmonic roots, over which Carol Kaye's bass alights on each downbeat with great delicacy, in its upper range. This rising

---

[61]   Johnson, *The body in the mind*, pp. 119–21.
[62]   Johnson, *The body in the mind*, pp. 113–17.

bass line is another instance of the path schema, with a focus on the point of arrival (above, it was arrival of the sun – here it refers to the arrival of 'love'). The 'presence' of the bass is unmistakeable. The transience of love, which is the real content of the lyric, seems supported nowhere in the environment – indeed, finally realizing the sphere of reference of the lyric comes as quite a shock after the glittery timbres of the track.

In Chapter 4 I made some small use of Leonard Talmy's cognitive semantics, a close relative to this line of thought. I shall return to further features of embodied cognition below but, before I do, I need to turn to an exploration of an equally valuable perspective, that of ecological perception.

Ecological Perception

At first sight, the field of ecological perception may appear to proceed according to very different principles. It was initially formulated by James J. Gibson.[63] It has been long utilized for the discussion of music by Eric Clarke and a handful of others.[64] In semiotic terms, this work can be understood as reformulating the Peircean concepts of iconicity and indexicality in terms of everyday perception.[65] A key argument in Clarke is that the assumption of static, or fixed, interpretations of signs is misleading. (Naomi Cumming's *The sonic self*, a thoroughgoing exploration of the consequences of Peirce's work for an understanding of some music, is in line with Gibson in her assumption 'that it is a basic psychological proclivity *not* to hear sound as an uninterpreted quality, but to hear it as bearing information that is adaptively useful'.[66]) The key process in Clarke's work is threefold, and can be summarized in the phrase: invariants afford through specifications. An ecological approach identifies *invariants* that are perceived in the environment, constants such as the flowing of water (which we identify as a river), a bounded slab of metal with a sharp edge (which we identify as a knife), or a high-pitched squeak. It observes what actions these invariants *afford*. A river, for example, affords both swimming and drowning. A knife affords both cutting and stabbing. A high-pitched squeak is more complex, without identifying precisely what invariants it has, but such a squeak might afford flight, if it sounds like a mouse, inquiry, if it sounds like a squeaking door, or contemplation if it sounds like (or even is) the opening to a piece of electroacoustic music. The action that an invariant affords may consist of no more than a decision to make sense of that sound in relation to others.

---

[63]   Gibson, *The senses considered*; *The ecological approach*.

[64]   Clarke, *Ways of listening*; Nicola Dibben, 'Musical materials, perception, and listening', in Martin Clayton, Trevor Herbert and Richard Middleton (eds.), *The cultural study of music: a critical introduction* (New York NY, 2003); Luke Windsor, 'An ecological approach to semiotics', *Journal for the Theory of Social Behaviour* 34/2 (2004).

[65]   See Moore, 'Interpretation: So what?'.

[66]   Cumming, *The sonic self*, p. 118.

Whichever of these responses we choose will depend on the particular source, for us, that the sound *specifies*. These affordances arise, as can be seen, not only from the environment, but also from the perceiver operating within a particular cultural environment. It is for the perceiver to either swim or drown, for example; that specific environment does not determine their swimming abilities. Bearing the example of the squeak in mind: '[the ecological perspective on musical meaning discusses how] sounds specify their sources and in so doing afford actions for the perceiver …'.[67] Although cognition plays a part in this field, the main emphasis is on the perception of facets of our bodily environment that lead to action without the need for their cognitive interpretation – such action is thus considered *direct*. And this, surely, is how Tagg's anaphones work – rather than consider them part of a non-arbitrary semiotic, it seems they specify sound-sources in the environment, in very much the way ecological perception describes.[68]

Invariants operate at different levels. In music, it is certainly possible to identify those constants that remain necessary to the performance of a particular song, and that remain present from one performance to another. Distinguishing again *song*, *track* and *performance*, at one extreme invariants seem to be those very characteristics that define a particular *song*. At the opposite extreme,[69] the binary metre of both 'Henry Darger' and 'All along the watchtower', or their tonal centres, operate as invariants against which the constant change of individual durations, or of individual pitches, creates meaning, so that invariance can work both externally, and internally, to a track. Most of my discussion here concentrates on its external operation. The importance of this approach is that it necessitates the restraint upon free interpretation that I addressed in Chapter 1 by way of Ricoeur and Johnson. Nicola Dibben, like Clarke elsewhere, conflates this with the concept of subject-position: 'The performance limits its possible readings by encouraging the listener to adopt a particular subject position towards it, which, while not identical to the listener's own subject position (which is due to their [*sic*] personal biography, and therefore differs from person to person), is necessarily at work with or against it.'[70] While I do not directly employ the concept of subject position here, the implication that a track can suggest a possible reading is there throughout.

Before demonstrating the value of the theory in discussion of songs, I need to explore the relationship between ecological perception and embodied cognition, because I argue that they are not contradictory. The relationship between ecological perception and that linguistic aspect of embodied cognition represented in the work of George Lakoff has been addressed indeed by Lakoff. He briefly refers to Gibson's theoretical position in his study of principles of categorization.[71] He

---

[67]   Clarke, *Ways of listening*, p. 126.

[68]   I'm grateful to Eric Clarke for our discussions, which, in part, led to this realization.

[69]   Again, my thanks to Eric Clarke on this point.

[70]   Nicola Dibben, 'Representations of femininity in popular music', *Popular Music* 18/3 (1999), p. 336.

[71]   Lakoff, *Women, fire*.

acknowledges the importance of Gibson's work in 'the importance [it makes] of the constant interaction of human beings with, and as an inseparable part of, their environments'.[72] However, Lakoff believes their two positions, as he characterizes them, are not fully compatible. Lakoff's criticism of Gibson's work lies in what he considers to be Gibson's objectivism (the belief that the environment is the same for all who experience it), and in Gibson's failure to deal with '*categories* of phenomena'.[73] While this may be a pertinent response to Gibson's own work, at least from the perspective of a study of categorization, subsequent developments in the field of ecological psychology[74] have markedly developed the theory (and countered any notion of such 'objectivism'), work that Lakoff in 1987 could not of course reference. Clarke makes two important observations: that other writers have made criticisms similar to those of Lakoff; and that Gibson did indeed also imply that 'affordances are the product both of objective properties and the capacities and needs of the organism that encounters them'.[75] In other words, affordances are not *just* present in the environment, as Lakoff (understandably) takes Gibson as believing (it is invariants that are found unambiguously in the environment). *Affordance* is a key term, which Gibson defines thus:

> When the constant properties [i.e. the invariants] of constant objects are perceived (the shape, size, color, texture, composition, motion, animation and position relative to other objects), the observer can go on to detect their affordances. I have coined this word as a substitute for values, a term which carries an old burden of philosophical meaning. I mean simply what things furnish, for good or ill.[76]

Other cognitive scientists and linguists, writing more recently, such as Gibbs, Kövecses and, arguably, Coulson,[77] in the reliance in their work on environmental affordances, clearly see no such contradiction. Lakoff's partial rejection of Gibson reads, perhaps, as a somewhat marginal point, for Lakoff's deeper criticism is of the 'ecological realism [which] cannot make sense of experiential or cultural categories',[78] an 'ecological realism' that, as Lakoff describes, has been erected by others, not by Gibson. Clarke's book, if nothing else, supports Lakoff in this criticism: he cites various other writers, arguing that 'cultural regularities are as much a part of the environment as natural forces, and they exert their influence

---

[72]   Lakoff, *Women, fire*, p. 215.

[73]   Lakoff, *Women, fire*, p. 216.

[74]   For example, Reed, *Encountering the world*.

[75]   Clarke, *Ways of listening*, p. 37.

[76]   Gibson, *The senses considered*, p. 285.

[77]   Gibbs, *Embodiment and cognitive science*, pp. 43–4; Kövecses, *Metaphor in culture*, p. 19; Seana Coulson, *Semantic leaps: frame-shifting and conceptual blending in meaning construction* (New York NY, 2001), p 121.

[78]   Lakoff, *Women, fire*, p. 216.

on the invariants of the world in just the same way',[79] a definite development of Gibson's original position.

So, Lakoff's explicit criticism of Gibson's work does not in itself entail a contradiction between these cognitive and ecological positions. Both Clarke and Mark Johnson have addressed a specific issue in music, the notion of *musical motion*, and a detailed comparison of their perspectives[80] demonstrates that their positions do, indeed, seem to be congruent. My reason for choosing to use the topic of musical motion to this end, other than that it is addressed from both positions, will become clear subsequently. Towards the end of Johnson's study of embodied meaning to which I have already referred, he argues that 'we are not merely mirrors of a nature that determines our concepts in one and only one way. Instead, our structured experience is an organism–environment interaction in which both poles are altered and transformed through an ongoing historical process. In other words, the environment is structured in ways that limit the possibilities for our categorizations of it.'[81] The terms of this assertion are strikingly similar to the line Eric Clarke takes: 'Perception is the awareness of, and continuous adaption to, the environment … Ecology is the study of organisms in relation to their environment' and thus Clarke's approach is 'ecological because it takes as its central principle the relationship between a perceiver and its environment'.[82] The first specific point to note is that Johnson and Larson had access to a draft of Clarke's argument, and explicitly regard Clarke's perspective as supporting theirs.[83] They make this claim in the context of their contention that 'musical motion is just as real as temporal motion and just as completely defined by metaphor'.[84] Compare Clarke, discussing recordings of auditory sequences of events: they 'are not heard as specifying apparent or metaphorical events: they specify perceptually real events that happen not to be present'.[85] In this argument, Clarke uses Stephen McAdams' notion of a 'virtual source', coined by analogy with the 'virtual object' of optics, a concept that identifies the 'object' seen in a mirror or a painting.[86] Both Clarke's and Johnson's theoretical stances admit ambiguity over 'what' is moving in music. Johnson and Larson set out two possible viewpoints, that of the participant in musical motion, and that of the observer of music that is in motion, depending on whether 'you are travelling over the path that defines a particular music piece'

---

[79] Clarke, *Ways of listening*, p. 40.

[80] As found in Johnson and Larson, '"Something in the way she moves"', later refined in Johnson, *The meaning of the body*, and Clarke, *Ways of listening*, pp. 62–90.

[81] Johnson, *The body in the mind*, p. 207.

[82] Clarke, *Ways of listening*, pp. 4–5.

[83] Johnson and Larson, '"Something in the way she moves"', p. 77 fn 9.

[84] Johnson and Larson, '"Something in the way she moves"', p. 77.

[85] Clarke, *Ways of listening*, p. 71.

[86] Clarke, *Ways of listening*, pp. 71–2. Stephen McAdams, 'Recognition of sound sources and events', in Stephen McAdams and Emmanuel Bigand (eds.), *Thinking in sound: the cognitive psychology of human audition* (Oxford, 1993).

or you are at 'a distant standpoint from which you can observe the path through a musical landscape that defines a particular work'.[87] Indeed, Johnson argues unapologetically that such ambiguities are 'typical of a vast range of abstract concepts, including causation, morality, mind, self, love, ideas, thought and knowledge'[88] and are thereby intrinsic to our everyday experience. Clarke also acknowledges this duality, describing the alternatives as the movement of musical objects (a perception more common with polyphonic textures) and as self-motion (more common with homophonic textures – 'movement of the listener in relation to the environment'[89]). He notes, though, that the viewpoint(s) specified by the motions of particular sequences of sounds can be left open and do not require resolution; music is thus 'underdetermined'.[90] As Johnson suggests, this duality is important beyond the discussion of motion in music, since the possibility of aligning one's identity as a listener with that of the track's persona, or with the track's observer, is a point I made in Chapter 7.

Clarke approvingly notes a comment by Watt and Ash that 'loosely speaking, music creates a virtual person'. In this sense, Watt and Ash's virtual reality is reality itself, but at one remove. Mark Johnson focuses also on what we might call 'reality at one remove', insisting that if 'concepts of musical motion ... turn out, under scrutiny, to be anything but clear, literal, and unproblematic' then 'Musical motion must be some kind of metaphorical motion'.[91] At the very least, Clarke offers an alternative to this insistence, this *must*, but both his 'virtual', or non-present reality, and Johnson's metaphorical reality, exist at equivalent distances from experienced 'reality' – an equivalence that, as Johnson and Larson state, Clarke's position supports. So is the difference between these two positions material? I argue that it is not. Johnson and Larson insist that the process of making sense is not one of 'experience first, understanding second', just as Clarke insists the process is not one of 'perception first, cognition second'.[92] Johnson and Larson:

> We do not merely experience a musical work and then understand it. There is not experience first, followed by our grasp of the meaning of that experience. Rather, our understanding is woven into the fabric of our experience. Our understanding is our way of being in and making sense of our experience.[93]

---

[87] Johnson and Larson, '"Something in the way she moves"', pp. 72, 73.

[88] Johnson, *The meaning of the body*, p. 259.

[89] Clarke, *Ways of listening*, p. 76.

[90] Clarke, *Ways of listening*, p. 88.

[91] Johnson, *The meaning of the body*, p. 246.

[92] It seems to me unproblematic to effectively equate perception and experience (see Reed, *Encountering the world*); cognition and understanding.

[93] Johnson and Larson, '"Something in the way she moves"', p. 78.

Clarke:

> the standard cognitive approach is to regard perception as simply the starting-point for a series of cognitive processes ... the ecological approach presents the situation entirely differently ... perceiving organisms seek out and respond to perceptual information that specifies objects and events in the environment, and this perceiving is a continuous process that is both initiated by, and results in, action ... while mainstream psychology presents the temporal aspect of perception as a stream of discrete stimuli, processed separately and 'glued together' by memory, an ecological approach sees it as a perceptual flow ... Ideologies and discourses, however powerful or persuasive they may seem to be, cannot simply impose themselves arbitrarily on the perceptual sensitivities of human beings, which are rooted in (though not defined by) the common ground of immediate experience.[94]

For me, the important point here is the congruence between descriptions of the same process as on the one hand 'woven' (Johnson and Larson) and on the other 'continuous' (Clarke). The way to move between *conceptual metaphor* and *ecological perception* is perhaps to suggest that the ecological experience generates schematic structures (structures that Johnson would argue *extend* our perceptual experience), and that underlying what we may want to call the 'truly' perceptual is metaphorical abstraction, even if only primitive:[95] in Johnson's earlier words, 'I now want to pursue this claim more thoroughly by focusing chiefly on the nature and operation of "image-schematic" structures of meaning. This requires an exploration of the way in which our perceptual interactions and bodily movements within our environment generate these schematic structures that make it possible for us to experience, understand, and reason about our world.'[96] If we accept that there is general congruence between the position Johnson takes up and those of other theorists of embodied cognition to whom I shall refer, then on the basis of this comparison of understandings of musical motion, I contend that there is no less congruence between principles of embodied cognition and ecological perception and, thus, that the hermeneutic perspective I adopt here is not self-contradictory in utilizing variously the languages and findings of both.

So, how does this enable fruitful understandings of songs? I observe a few tracks from this perspective, returning first to 'Good vibrations'. Aside from the semiotic 'meaning as difference' discovered in the transpositions of the track's closing hook, what else can be said? The opening to the track is unusually assertive. There is no introduction, simply the announcement of the singer's almost breathless identity, 'I', followed by an empty bar before we find out what this 'I' is about.

---

[94]   Clarke, *Ways of listening*, pp. 41–3.

[95]   I am very grateful to Patricia Schmidt for this particular characterization of the relationship, far more elegant than I was able to come up with.

[96]   Johnson, *The body in the mind*, p. 19.

The 'I' specifies a source, an individual speaker, whom we encounter unplanned (that lack of introduction), suddenly, in a way (I would suggest) that will always be with some apprehension; the immediacy of the encounter is dependent on the metaphorical space that surrounds the 'I'. What about that opening descending sequence? Perhaps its most immediate function is intertextual (see Chapter 9), in the reminiscence it permits of stylistically similar tracks such as the Turtles' 'Happy together', a track whose lyric takes up a similar (although less nuanced) position; the tracks resemble each other in their bass lines, but without imposing a necessity of interpretation on the act of recognition. The delicacy of the bass line also acts intertextually, reminding us as it does of Paul McCartney's upper register playing. Here, the historical location of 'Good vibrations', as part of the attempt to upstage the Beatles' *Sgt. Pepper* is inescapable. The theremin line, on which some of the track's notoriety is based, is perhaps best understood via Tagg's category of *genre synecdoche*, whereby the pure, slightly ethereal, quality of its tone calls to mind the entire genre of science fiction movies, although whether it brings with it (as Tagg would suggest) the connotations of B-movie status (cheap effects, poor plots, the emphasis on wonder) attendant on the sound-world is moot.[97] Various other aspects of the track ask for this sort of treatment – in the competing melodic lines at the end, for example, we are given a choice as to which to identify with. Perhaps most importantly, we can choose to switch our identification from one time to another. Do we exult in the vibrations ('good, good, good vibrations'), or do we keep an eye on the relationship ('she's giving me …')? And this is where the bridge works so well since, in jettisoning everything from the texture (at about 2'15"), an important stage in the plot is reached – this is surely preparation for a greater level of attention that we are asked to give, and it is in that moment that the change happens. The sequence that becomes reversed, though, and that is key to my interpretation of the track, seems peculiarly inert. Many another sequence, and an alternative set of transposition levels, would have signified in the same way, since it is only the relative levels, conjoined as they are to the lyric, that carry the signification. This would suggest that an ecological perspective is not all-explanatory, but that where conscious interpretation is necessary, we do need to talk in terms of symbolic reference.

This is only one among very many examples I could cite. Take the Beatles' 'With a little help from my friends' and, in particular, the use on this track of the tambourine. I have recently realized why this is so effective, and it is to do with the strange pacing of its shuffle rhythm. Because of the speed at which one needs to move a tambourine to get a decent rattle of the jingles 'in real life', the particular speed of this tambourine sounds just too slow (particularly in the chorus preceding the final bridge). It seems to me this helps to portray Ringo Starr's awkwardness, perhaps reluctance, to admit his dependence in that final bridge, and I note that

---

[97]   I am grateful to Milton Mermikides for reminding me that for some contemporaneous listeners, the theremin's electronic nature adequately represented the idea of 'pickin' up' vibrations from the ether, particularly since it is sounded without physically touching it.

this realization is dependent on the way this sound specifies the movement of a tambourine in natural surroundings – the speed with which a tambourine moves in reality is an invariant feature of its construction.

I have already referred to John Lennon's 'Imagine', and the moment at which melodic tonic and harmonic tonic first coincide, after a number of near-misses, on the word 'dreamer'. This observation seems to back up Lennon's uncertain ideology – the oft-noted position that he was 'all talk and no action'. However, it is harder to suggest that harmonic/melodic closure specifies closure in some other realm. Here, I'm taking it as specifying secure affirmation, specifically of the stance occupied by 'dreaming' rather than 'doing', taking the accompanying lyric as key. It may be that we can only understand this move through Peirce's symbolic category, rather than directly ecologically, and here I'm reminded of two other positions. The first is Luke Windsor's argument that even using the ecological model, 'thirdness' is always necessary, that the symbolic 'interpretation' of a sign is a necessary stage, is what we engage in.[98] The second is David Sless' insistence, in his critique of semiotics, that interpretation is not simply, or even mostly, the decoding of a message, but is marked initially by a quality Sless calls 'letness' – one begins from the creative act of allowing something, in one's own experience, to stand for something else.[99] Both of these critiques imply that at the root of interpretation is a creative act, but it is not an act built out of nothing. It is this bounded position that seems so well-addressed in an ecological manner – the meanings I discuss here, and have put forward throughout, are not encoded in the music in such a way that they permit only one 'decoding', but nor are they simply flights of fancy, in that they all start from sources specified in the recordings.

I have previously noted that 'Good vibrations' is unusual as songs go, in that its course maps out a change of position on the part of the persona. Cilla Black's singing of the Bacharach/David classic 'Alfie' is also, as we have seen, a song that marks a change of position. I recapitulate some of its details, but take the argument further. Black's persona is at first rather cowed by this Alfie, a man who holds it 'wise to be cruel', a position that corresponds to the way she pronounces his name, with the stress always on the first syllable, as if she were pleading with him to come to an accommodation. However, after a bridge that threatens to challenge the harmonic world of the opening, her enquiries become an assertion: 'I believe in love'. A chromatic bass line moves us into what is formally a new area – what started as the third verse veers off somewhere new – an area where she insists that 'without true love we just exist, A*lfie*', stressing for the first time the last syllable of his name. Against the invariant of her approach to her lover, this moment specifies our perception of her inner change, a change that in everyday life is often marked by a difference of facial expression, and that is modelled here by the shift in harmonic language and the transgression of normative formal practice. It thus affords us the possibility of extending our understanding of how

---

[98]   Windsor, 'An ecological approach'.

[99]   Sless, *In search*.

an individual may respond under the pressures her persona is portrayed to have endured. Indeed, we can now see that the major argument of Chapter 7 can be reformulated thus. The environment in which the persona moves is specified (to use ecological language) by three musical domains: the textural matters normally considered under the heading 'accompaniment'; the harmonic setting, including the modal/tonal vocabulary; and the formal setting or narrative structure, that is, the order in which its events take place, and the patterns of repetition within this order.

Billy Bragg's recording of 'The Home Front' relies for its force on a bald presentation of detail, which seems particularly notable for a character like Bragg whose name is founded on his integrity, on his live performance. Bragg sings this rather equivocal song about English identity, accompanying himself on electric guitar, with a full brass band behind him. The band, however, is bathed in reverberation. At one point, Bragg sings of nostalgia being the opium of the age. Bearing in mind that the production on the band sounds so strongly reminiscent of David Bedford's similar writing behind a track such as Roy Harper's 'When an old cricketer leaves the crease', and bearing in mind also the association such bands have with a then almost-past, and now dead, mining culture, it seems to me that the sound of these glorious cornets and flugelhorns reeks of that very nostalgia. Perhaps this is why Bragg's vocal is so dry; the visual image is perhaps akin to the contemporary use of black and white newsreel footage, as a backdrop to a talking head. Bragg isn't part of that world, they live in separate spaces; one resonant, one dry. So what of the track's strange ending, as a heavily compressed recording of 'Jerusalem' intrudes on the band's gentle exit. Surely to sing 'Jerusalem' is simply to evoke that very nostalgia Bragg is uncomfortable with? But that was not his intention: '*Jerusalem*, I think, should be the national anthem. I think it's the most powerful statement of pride in what the socialist tradition in Britain is about.'[100] In the article he does move on to offer an explanation, but what is important here is, first, the way that this ultimate expression is treated. It does not sound as if it is coming from either Bragg's, or the brass band's, world. At first appearance, it sounds as if it might be coming from under water, enacting the sinking that Jerusalem, that is, Britain, appeared to the left to have endured under Thatcher. Simultaneously, it situates the narrative somewhere in the 1940s, since this sonic modulation also specifies the typical sound of interference as on a contemporaneous radio broadcast. And yet 'Jerusalem' is not swamped by the sound-world it finds itself in – it remains recognizable – perhaps the possibility of survival is made apparent. Bragg is also actually demonstrating the necessity of interpretation in that he himself offers an interpretation that was certainly at odds with what was the 'normative' (jingoistic) reading of 'Jerusalem' in 1986. Can he, though, escape from the nostalgia that hearing such a song inevitably brings to so many minds? And, in presenting it to us so problematically, is he not implicating

---

[100]   Billy Bragg and Ian A. Anderson, 'The taxman's poet', *Folk Roots* 42 (December 1986), p. 27.

us in that nostalgia too? These thoughts, to which there is no unequivocal answer, only arise from noticing what sound sources appear specified in the last half minute of the track.

Tori Amos' 'Hey Jupiter' serves to bring together an ecological perspective with a discussion based on proxemics (Chapter 7). In Chapter 4, I suggested that the intimacy of the song is, at least in part, given from its excess of pronouns. We can now add to that understanding. Nothing intervenes between Amos and the listener; we can clearly hear her intakes of breath; the piano is far in the distance and has little width even though, if we think about it, we will probably presume she is playing it simultaneously with singing: her voice has greater width, although she does not cover the entire space. This intimacy is an aspect of our everyday experience – we respond by coming close to someone speaking to us softly and in a low voice. The intimacy is particularly clear in her vocalise at 2'20", a moment of unself-consciousness that is particularly affecting, and a response to the introduction of an electric piano that increases the sense of environmental width. It is reinforced by the constant addressing of 'Jupiter' as 'you', and we are invited to take on the persona of Jupiter. However, the repeated line 'no-one's picking up the phone' makes better sense if the song is understood as an interior monologue, to which we are made party. Recognition of this (and other similar lines) keeps us uncertain of our position, enabling the maintenance of a certain interest.

What about tracks that do not have such an overt reference to the world? Is it even possible to read melodic and harmonic patterns ecologically? The Vapors' 'News at Ten' suggests that it might be. What is specified by the opening bass line? First of all, of course, a guitar itself. The harmonic sequence is G–D/F♯–C/E–D/F♯. The descending bass line cannot continue further because of the (normal) tuning of an electric guitar, bass string E. The line thus returns on itself. The best way of conceiving the import of this is actually, I think, through the image schemata for the balance and the cycle:[101] the line is beautifully balanced between its outer points (G and E), swinging constantly via the F♯; but it also cycles around this unending sequence, each time a little further into the narrative of the song, but not having gained any wisdom from the encounter the lyrics narrate, until much later in the song (as noted below). But then, second, there is the treble-rich modulation, as if the line is partially hidden, an awkwardness picked up by the subsequent continuation of the sequence to root position C (the F♯–C move executed quite unself-consciously, it seems). The song concerns generational non-communication ('still I can't hear you' repeated *ad infinitum* to the end) and leads to a climax (which in the context of these lyrics, in most adults' experience will specify one or more adolescent arguments). The tension grows over that initial sequence and, when the high point is reached, a bass guitar G–F♯–E–D comes to the fore (it had been heard earlier, but not in a prominent position). This finally completes its path down through C–B–A–G, this downward scale neatly signalling the close of the track (acting as both an 'episodic marker' and the conclusion to a

---

[101]   Johnson, *The body in the mind*, pp. 74–96; 119–21.

'path' schema). The attraction of this line is such as to encourage desire for such non-communication, for the communality offered by such overt opposition; the environment outlined here is a historical one, but a probably inevitable aspect of adolescent experience in UK culture.

Seth Lakeman's 'The charmer', to which I referred in Chapter 5, is perhaps more perplexing. Over the opening strummed guitar, with extreme width, we hear a compressed, and narrower, vocal vowel approaching at speed and stopping abruptly, but with no reverb. The verse continues with the same intimate presence, and an underplayed guitar and bass. The accompaniment grows in power for the chorus, and Lakeman's voice is double-tracked with a little more reverb. Such double-tracking is perhaps problematic from an ecological standpoint, although its purpose is to thicken the voice, to provide a greater sense of projection as if emanating from a more resonant space, and in this it is an able mimic of reality. Lakeman's persona recounts a narrative of the past, and the sense is of the details being private, but the general tenor (the chorus) being available to the public. The listener is in a privileged position. But then, in the final verse, at 1'56", the line 'she has two hearts, I have none' is doubled at the third by Lakeman. This simple word-painting ruins the illusion of intimacy, and we realize that the tale is not being vouchsafed to us personally. This use of self-doubling is now commonplace, and it is a moot point whether this destroys an ecologically valid response or not. Does it perhaps increase his sense of authority as teller of the tale, achieving a mode of delivery that we cannot?

Finally, here, I take a single track which illustrates a number of these perspectives. Example 8.8 outlines the two-bar groove that is so definitional of Annie Lennox's 'Walking on broken glass'.

Example 8.8 Annie Lennox: 'Walking on broken glass'; bars 1-4

It has a hard-edged quality, which is intensified by its being doubled at the octave (and with a prominent harmonic a further octave higher). It seems unproblematic to describe this timbre as a sonic anaphone: the actual sound is reminiscent of the sound of shattered glass. It is not an exact reproduction, of course, it doesn't quite specify that sound source, but in the timbre's crunchiness it is a musically coherent representation of that sound. The actual sound chosen is possibly the best representation one could get from a sound-source with a precise pitch (unlike the actual sound of shattered glass). Note, also, the string portion of the groove. Because the attack is so precise across this timbre, I suspect it is a synthesizer patch rather than actual strings, but the difference is not material to my argument – I shall continue to identify them simply as 'strings'. The most obvious feature of these two lines, those of the keyboard and the strings, is the nature of their interlocking. After an opening in which they threaten to work across each other (both the strings' first two rests are masked by the keyboard line), they coincide on no less than four successive offbeats. The precision of this coinciding, while easy to achieve through quantizing, is nonetheless striking because it avoids the obvious downbeats. It is as if the two dare not get out of alignment until the end of second bar. Even if one has not experienced the sensation, it is easy to creatively imagine walking across a floor, reaching broken glass, treading very carefully so as not to injure oneself, and then reaching the other side and walking normally again. That process seems to me to be rendered into music by these two bars: what is represented needs to be contextualized, as this is by the song's title, which Lennox announces immediately after we have heard these four bars, but once this is done, the potential link in the listener's mind is made. On two counts, then, we have a potential experience from everyday life (the sound of broken glass, and the experience of walking across it) rendered into music. A great deal more could be said even about this tiny moment of one particular track, but I restrict myself to just one further comment. At the end of bar 3 of Example 8.8, the two instrumental strands offer alternative harmonic realizations of the underlying I–IV–V process. The keyboard inserts a potential I (giving I–IV–I–V), while the strings are more fussy, perhaps a further illustration of the care one must take walking across such a terrain: the result of these two separate realizations is that on the second half of the third and fourth beats of bar 3, the two strands disagree – we twice have an F against an E, and the fact that neither ever gives way (the two are, of course, dissonant, even if the second has a lower level of dissonance) intensifies both the carefulness and the hardness already referred to.

As I have mentioned, at 8″ Annie Lennox's voice enters the track with the title. She repeats the first two words, and then on 'broken', a second Annie can be heard in the distance, and slightly to the right, doubling the line an octave higher (thereby conforming to a pattern already set by the keyboard). At the end of the verse, just as she heads into the repeated refrain (at 54″), a second Annie offers a contrapuntal ornamentation of the main melody. This device, of vocal self-accompaniment, we have already encountered in the Seth Lakeman example. At 17″ into the track, a drum kit enters. It is situated in the centre of the stereo space, behind Lennox's voice, but with the offbeat marked simultaneously by the snare and a handclap slightly to her right. At 42″ we have the entry of a guitar, but now slightly to her left. At 1′38″, three cymbal crashes to the extreme right illustrate the sung phrase 'windows smash' (another example of a sonic anaphone – in such carefully produced work as this, it seems very difficult for producers to avoid these illustrative anaphones), but the first of these subtly echoes on the left. During the bridge section (from 1'58"), a subtle piano arpeggio figuration that is situated to the left issues in a string arpeggiation that climaxes to the right; the piano repeats but this time is answered by a repeated two-note guitar figuration to the right (c.2'10"), and then an electronic perturbation, pulsing at the rate of a semiquaver, moves around the stereo space from side to side, from 2'12". This is simply a description of some of the textural events that can be heard in the track, behind Annie Lennox's central voice. It can be seen (and heard) that there is a concern to match what is happening on one side of the stereo space with what is happening on the other side; and this is by no means unusual.[102] This idea we have already encountered – it is a temporal extension of the balance image schema. Note that this series of balances, between left and right, are not symmetries: Johnson is clear that symmetry is only a limiting case of balance operating in the visual domain;[103] perhaps the key idea is that what happens on either side of an axis does not provide *equality* but *equivalence*. It is a norm, then, for sound-sources to be balanced in the stereo field, either side of a central axis that is normally occupied by the lead voice, the persona. The question is, why should this be? Johnson encourages us to start from the body; Clarke, too, suggests beginning from the observation of the organism in the environment. When hearing a new sound in an environment, we are able to judge its location by the subtle difference in time between the sound-waves reaching first one, and then the other, of our ears. We will then frequently turn our heads towards it, so that the sound-waves set in motion by the sound-source reach both ears simultaneously. Achieving this orientation, we are able visually to identify the source of the sound (which is to be understood as an environmental invariant, in ecological terms) and thus to determine what action to take. The seeking of balance is thus endemic to our acting as aural beings; rather than having to determine why it should be that we prefer the soundbox to be balanced, it would require determining how we would cope were the soundbox not to be balanced. Indeed, as I have argued elsewhere,[104] we are struck by the strangeness of an orientation that does not operate this way: Such an orientation is the marked term of the pair and requires addressing. So much for these small portions of one song. One thing remains, and for this I return to the opening groove, which so aptly encapsulates the experience Lennox refers to by way of the track's title. Having heard the track, we realize that those elements that remain firmly in place, both in terms of stereo and in terms of their distance from the listener, are Lennox's voice and persona, and the groove that represents the placing of the protagonist's feet on broken glass. Neither have moved from their central position. Or, rather, they

---

[102]   I chose to write about this track purely because of the opening groove – such balancing details are ubiquitous.

[103]   Johnson, *The body in the mind*, pp. 81–2.

[104]   Allan F. Moore and Ruth Dockwray, 'The establishment of the virtual performance space in rock', *twentieth-century music* 5/2 (2008).

have moved but in one dimension only, that of time. And, again, this is what we would expect of our own actions if we were walking, carefully, on broken glass. No sudden shifts of direction or speed, everything careful, considered and poised.

This discussion of a range of individual tracks has raised three particular problems for an ecological approach. If you did not recognize them as problems, this simply serves to reinforce their ubiquity: I refer specifically to the spatial divorce between Tori Amos' voice and her piano; to the double-voicedness of the climax to Seth Lakeman's performance, which is also found in Annie Lennox's chorus; and to the association between everyday events (walking across broken glass) and their representation in music.

To deal with the last issue first: having made such an association, accounts of the understanding of music normally leave it at that and move on. But we should not be so hasty. What is it that permits us to make such analogies? We take them for granted in respect of language – that is, after all, the primary purpose of language, as a communicative medium. Music, however, is not universally recognized as such a medium, and so additional evidence is necessary to enable us to make such a link. Such evidence, it seems, is found within embodied cognition, and specifically in the concept of *cross-domain mapping*. 'Cross-domain mapping is a process through which we structure our understanding of one domain (which is typically unfamiliar or abstract) in terms of another (which is most often familiar and concrete).'[105] Zbikowski illustrates the concept by suggesting we understand electrical conductance through a hydraulic model – we talk of electricity flowing, for example. In this case, I argue that two specific aspects of the music at this point (the timbre of the keyboard; the delicate avoidance of downbeats in both sound-sources) are telling us how to cognize particular features of our interaction with broken glass. Such an understanding would seem to me to lie behind possibly all attributions of extra-musical meaning to specifically musical processes, and this is an awareness worth achieving. Compare the compartive paucity of a semiotic understanding, in which the relationship between these two things is accepted merely because they have become linked through association over a period of time.

The double-voicedness that I have isolated in Lennox and Lakeman presents a different problem. What are we to make of these aural events that it is impossible to encounter outside the virtual word of the recording? Embodied cognition offers a relative to cross-domain mapping in *conceptual blending*. According to Fauconnier and Turner, conceptual blending is a 'basic mental operation' that is 'an invisible, unconscious activity involved in every aspect of human life'.[106] Conceptual blends occur through 'integrating partial structures from two separate domains [*mental spaces*] into a single structure with emergent properties within a

---

[105]   Zbikowski, *Conceptualising music*, p. 13.
[106]   Fauconnier and Turner, *The way we think*, p. 18.

third domain'.[107] Two or more 'input' mental spaces[108] are compressed into a single output 'blended' space, while 'the structure that inputs seem to share is captured in a generic space'.[109] A subordinate category, of particular use to the examples posed by those features of Amos' and Lakeman's performances I have referred to is that of the *mirror network*, which they define as an 'integration network in which all spaces – inputs, generic, and blend – share an organizing frame'.[110] Among the examples they give to clarify is their report of an article from the *New York Times* from July 1999, which notes that the Egyptian runner Hicham el-Guerrouj had broken the world mile record. The article included an illustration that portrayed el-Guerrouj together with mile record holders from each of the five previous decades, illustrating the distance behind el-Guerrouj that each would have been, had they all raced together. Such an illustration, or even just a description, they claim, prompts a reader unconsciously to construct a blended space. Input spaces consist of aspects of the six individual races concerned; in the blended space we will find some elements of those races (the individual winners and their relative times, the presence of a finishing line in each race) but not others (the actual location of the individual tracks, the identities of the losing runners in each race, etc.). While Fauconnier and Turner describe such a blend as 'immediately intelligible and persuasive', its construction is 'remarkably complicated'.[111] To return to Annie Lennox's double-voicedness, I would suggest this appears as an *unreal realism*. It is realistic in that it is presented matter-of-factly, and the voices are not manipulated in any way beyond the ordinary. And yet it is unreal in that the manner of presentation can only exist in the artificial environment of the recording. It seems that this unreal realism is an example of just such a blend. In the case of Tori Amos, her vocal performance takes place in one input space, and her piano accompaniment in another (after all, anecdotally, most listeners are aware that different elements of a recording are recorded at different times, and even perhaps in different locations, whatever may have been the actual case here). Our hearing of the track prompts both this construction and the creation of a blended space in which her voice (and hence her persona) is in an intimate zone relative to us, but her fingers (and thus, again, her body) are further distant. The same explanation lies behind Lakeman's self-accompaniment. Here, there is no doubt that his voice is recorded twice at separate times since one cannot produce two vocal lines simultaneously. Each of these lines takes place in an input space, and we understand the resultant recording within a blended space. In this sense, the reason we find these effects so unremarkable (although they cannot be experienced without the aid of recorded media) is that we make such blends so very frequently

---

[107] Fauconnier, *Mappings*, p. 22.

[108] 'Mental spaces are small conceptual packets constructed as we think and talk, for purposes of local understanding and action'. Fauconnier and Turner, *The way we think*, p. 40.

[109] Fauconnier and Turner, *The way we think*, p. 47.

[110] Fauconnier and Turner, *The way we think*, p. 122.

[111] Fauconnier and Turner, *The way we think*, p. 124.

in our everyday lives. Thus, we readily create two or more 'Lennoxes', two or more 'Amoses' or 'Lakemans',[112] as we create six race-tracks, and superimpose them in blended mental spaces. Explanations of such phenomena have, of course, been offered, particularly in relation to Bakhtinian double-voicing (de-constructing the idea that an individual's subjectivity is embedded in their physical voice), but such explanations do not address why their very presence passes uncommented, and has done so ever since Les Paul began experimenting with double-tracking in the early 1950s. This may seem like a laborious explanation for such common features of recordings. However, their commonality should not deafen us to their impossibility outside the virtual space created in the recording, and it is because we create such blended spaces all the time in our understandings of aspects of the world we encounter, that these devices appear inevitable, 'natural'.

So, what the larger part of this chapter has undertaken is to suggest that an explanation that follows the assumptions of ecological perception and relevant findings from embodied cognition is at least adequate to a discussion of iconicity and indexicality; indeed, in its refusal of an arbitrary basis to such meanings, I find it preferable. I have elsewhere undertaken an exhaustive study of the Kinks' 'See my friend', endeavouring to demonstrate the greater explanatory power that an ecological approach offers over a semiotic one.[113] However, if a semiotic approach via iconicity and indexicality is preferred, that does not negate the force of my interpretations here. My necessary assumption is that my approach will act congruently for readers, insofar as I am a normal listener. This perspective makes sense of the realist position I have adopted thus far, and provides it with a firm theoretical underpinning. But it is important to note that in this perspective, in Clarke's, in Tagg's, in Johnson's, one-to-one correspondences are being observed between musical details and life experience. In the case of the ecological explanation, this is overt, since such experiences are by definition the matter of our experiential reality. If invariants specify sources, they are not inventions of fantasy: as Cornelia Fales, says, 'the inclination to hear sources in sound constitutes a perceptual schema',[114] before arguing that in ambient music, such an inclination is overridden. And it can only be overridden because it is there in the first place.

To conclude, I return to a further point that originates with both Johnson and Turner, that there is no perspectiveless position from which to develop an understanding (of anything). This aspect has remained implicit in what I have written so far – in the next and final chapters it becomes more central.

---

[112]   Lakemen?

[113]   Moore, 'Interpretation: So what?'

[114]   Cornelia Fales, 'Short-circuiting perceptual systems: timbre in ambient and techno music' in Paul D. Greene and Thomas Porcello (eds.), *Wired for sound* (Hanover NH, 2004), p. 165.

Chapter 9
Belonging

Authenticity

The ecological approach that I developed in Chapter 8 can be taken one step further. When we listen ecologically, we inevitably note the inevitability of the relationship between musicians and the sounds they make (whether voices, instruments, or electronic boxes). When we listen to a recording, of course, there is no visual element. The development of music video may be seen as a corrective to this 'deficiency', but there is an imperative to question the relationship between the sound and from whom it issues, an imperative that will again bring into play the relationship between the persona and the performer. Two questions come to the fore, and will partially drive this chapter. First, to what extent does the sound that the musician makes belong to that musician? And second, with a nod back to my opening quotation from Ricoeur, can this be determined from within the text itself?

I suspect that the most damning descriptor to throw at any popular musicians is that they are derivative, that their material derives from some other source, which carries the implication that all they are fit for is to reproduce that other source. This assertion is meant to apply across the entire range of popular song for, even where singers perform material written by others, in a style that is already a part of the mainstream, unless they add something that is demonstrably, or can be argued as being, of themselves, then what they are doing is frequently seen to have no value. In other words, what is prized is, in some sense, to be valued as original. Now this concept is problematic, for it can be understood in two distinctly opposed ways. On the one hand, to exhibit originality (to be valued as original) is to offer something that is (at least slightly) different from anything that has been offered before. One's voice must be different, one's way of actualizing particular harmonic or rhythmic patterns must be different, one's imagery must in some measure be different, the vision one offers listeners must be different. This originality can be manifested in different degree (from minimal to extensive, although we should notice that a strong measure of familiarity must be retained – there is such a thing as being 'too original'), and can be manifested in a large range of different domains (in terms of musical detail, of lyric message, of image, of assumed identity, of representation). On the other hand, to be valued as original (to exhibit originality) is to be true to the origins of a practice, to retain some of the magic accruing to those few musicians who are capable of transporting listeners into the proper world of that practice. Both these senses of originality intersect with the two terms that are key to this chapter, namely *authenticity* and *intertextuality*. I shall deal with them in turn, but at all times retain one eye on these notions of originality. The importance of these ideas for interpretation relates to two observations. In terms of *authenticity*, the relationship between *persona* and *performer* matters for listeners: listeners make commitment to the music to which they listen, and it is important to know what sort of commitment is made by the music's producers. In terms of *intertextuality*, meaning is a relational term, and listeners do not make interpretive judgements without reference to other music. In both these senses, listeners approach the music from a specific perspective, their own: there can be no external judgement of the relationship they themselves develop with the music.

'Authenticity' is an unavoidably loaded term, for it carries an ethical charge: in some circumstances, to be declared inauthentic is, somehow, to be less than fully human. As Coyle and Dolan demonstrate,[1] the question of authenticity arose from deeply intellectual objections to consumer culture, even if it has now been both appropriated and subsumed by that culture. Debates surround not only whether authenticity in music *is* found, but also whether it *can be* found, that is, whether the search itself is meaningful, or is one of illusion. Under modernism, with the autonomous striving of the individual, it is a value to be sought, even if the sites of its achievement are contested. Under postmodernism, with its questioning of essences, the very possibility of authenticity's being sought is doubted or denied, but I maintain that the issue remains pertinent, even under that very postmodernism. Some while ago Born and Hesmondhalgh suggested that the concept 'has been consigned to the intellectual dust-heap',[2] since, in that postmodern world where sampling and associated practices have become normative, it no longer carries its originary force. They are by no means alone in making such a declaration. Before considering assenting to so damning a judgement, it is necessary to rehearse some of the history of the idea, for we shall find that there is not a single authenticity.

Lawrence Grossberg's analysis[3] may be seen as a key initial theoretical intervention. He argued that the distinction between music that is 'authentic' and music that is not (he uses both 'entertainment' and 'commercial' to oppose 'authentic', but other terms are also sometimes counterposed) underpins the history of popular music from the time of Elvis Presley onwards. I believe it can be traced back further, and suggest five key moments. The first is marked by an ideological view that underpinned the English folk revival, and that was voiced by Hubert Parry, a key figure in the emergence of a British concert music in the late nineteenth century. A fundamental part of this process was the drive to escape the hegemony of continental (largely Austro-German, French and Italian) musics and to develop a music that was felt to be intrinsically British, or even English. In order to do so, some leading musicians (among them Ralph Vaughan Williams)

---

[1]   Michael Coyle and Jon Dolan, 'Modelling Authenticity, Authenticating Commercial Models', in Kevin Dettmar and William Richey (eds.), *Reading Rock and Roll* (New York NY, 1999).

[2]   Georgina Born and David Hesmondhalgh (eds.), *Western music and its others* (Berkeley CA, 2000), p. 30.

[3]   Grossberg, *We gotta get out of this place*.

and educators (most prominently Cecil Sharp) went about collecting what they felt to be examples of a dying art, that of folk singing, in rural locations and, most importantly, put it to new use. Parry praised this music of which established culture had been largely unaware, comparing it to music hall and declaring that folk songs had 'no sham, no got-up glitter, and no vulgarity'.[4] By denying 'sham' he was in effect validating their integrity, considering them as exactly what they appeared to be. We have access to very little recorded material from this phase of the collection of folk songs, but the voice of folk singer Joseph Taylor, collected by Percy Grainger in 1908 (and the first such singer to be recorded), sounds far from the stereotypical image of the folk-singing yokel. His was a considered, and probably (to some extent) trained, voice, clear in diction and pitching, and regular in phrasing. The opposition here was between *integrity* and *sham*, but it was an opposition as much created as observed, when we note that the repertory of such singers was happy to include items of music hall (and other sources). The second moment is found in an argument that took place in the UK music press in the late 1920s. It concerns Bert Ambrose, a notable society bandleader, and a younger, jazz-oriented bandleader, Fred Elizalde.[5] Elizalde, much lauded in the music press and winner of readers' polls, declared in a 1929 article that the future of popular music (which at the time was the same thing as saying the future of jazz) lay in the development of new and interesting rhythms, in escape from verse–chorus structures, and in positing a secondary role for melody, presumably in relation to rhythm and harmony (i.e. he actually predicted the near future of jazz). Ambrose's response declared that this could never happen, because the floor would empty in a minute. He once pointed out, when playing in Monte Carlo, that 'if I couldn't hear the surf, I knew we were playing too loud'.[6] The opposition characterized here was between what musicians wanted to play, what was 'good for music', and what the audience apparently wanted to hear, in which the musicians' integrity, of finding a place for their self-expression, was simply not an issue, an opposition between *autonomy* and overt *function*. A third moment arises in the wake of rock'n'roll, that style that had changed the face of Anglophone popular song. Pat Boone, who had already gained a reputation for singing slow ballads, was used by his label Dot to record covers of early rhythm'n'blues songs in 1955. Charlie Gillett is generous in noting that Boone's covers may have generated some interest in the original singers of this material, for 'he was important to rock'n'roll only in the role he played bringing a little conservative respectability to the music's image'.[7] The opposition here was more complex, for both of Boone's personae were overtly commercial, but whereas the first *responded* to a market need, the second attempted to *annex* one. A fourth moment, now famed, occurred in 1965

---

[4]   Quoted in Boyes, *The imagined village*, p. 26.

[5]   Mark Hustwitt, 'Caught in a whirlpool of aching sound: the production of dance music in the 1920s', *Popular Music* 3 (1983), pp. 25–7.

[6]   Albert McCarthy, *The dance band era* (London, 1974), p. 49.

[7]   Charlie Gillett, *The sound of the city* (London, 1983), p. 125.

when Bob Dylan, hitherto darling of the Left, and writer of serious lyrics, began performing with electric guitar. The accusations of 'selling out', to which many subsequent singers have been subjected for similar reasons, were to do with his transgression of the image that, with his connivance, had been created around him. The opposition here was between Dylan's *accepted* persona, and one that was received as *transgressive*, although, as Lee Marshall argues,[8] the issue's repercussions are complex. A fifth moment can be represented by the writer Iain Chambers, writing in 1985 on progressive rock, which he denigrates by means of the word 'calculated', in opposition to dance music, whose migration to the social margins served to 'intensify its significance'.[9] The opposition here is a critical one, between the apparent dominance of *mind* or *body*.[10]

For all the differences between these examples, the oppositions they maintain can be aligned. On the one hand, an expression is valued because its production appears to rest on the integrity of the performer, an integrity that is read as secure, as in some sense comfortable. On the other hand, an expression is denigrated because that integrity appears, from the viewpoint of the critic, to have been compromised (whether by the unacceptable face of capitalism, or just by too much thinking). What is fascinating, first of all, is that the notion of personal integrity still has such power to address listeners. After all, it is a value that has little sway in so many parts of contemporary life, where petty theft, the dominance of pragmatic values, infidelity in relationships, the pursuit of individualist goals, and the like, are positively condoned. Does it represent an ideal to which people aspire, because it has no strong presence elsewhere in our experience? But this is to separate out this part of life from the rest of life, and this runs against the value system of popular music, which is to deny such separation. Second, the issue of 'appearance' is fundamental. To address first that integrity, what does it sound like? Nearly two decades ago, Roy Shuker declared 'that using authenticity to distinguish between rock and pop is no longer valid, though it continues to serve an important ideological function'.[11] Even earlier, and before Grossberg's intervention, Michael Pickering had argued that '"authenticity" is a relative concept which is generally used in absolutist terms',[12] while Johan Fornäs argued later that a 'realist' approach to the question is far too limiting in aesthetic discourses.[13] In each of these accounts, there is a sense in which different understandings of authenticity

[8]   Lee Marshall, *Bob Dylan: the never ending star* (Cambridge, 2007).

[9]   Iain Chambers, *Urban rhythms* (London: MacMillan, 1985), pp. 108, 118. see also Moore, *Rock: the primary text*, pp. 73–5, 93–4.

[10]   On which, in popular music scholarship, see Tagg and Clarida, *Ten little title tunes*, pp. 66–78.

[11]   Shuker, *Understanding popular music*, p. 8.

[12]   Michael Pickering, 'The dogma of authenticity in the experience of popular music', in McGregor, G. and White, R. S. (eds.), *The art of listening* (Beckenham, 1986), p. 213.

[13]   Johan Fornäs, *Cultural theory and late modernity* (London, 1995).

are conflated in the presence of this fundamental paradigm, a view supported in Shuker's later discussion.[14]

So, on what does this integrity rest? A first view might be to suppose that authenticity is assured at the point where the identities of *persona* and *performer* are co-extensive. At that point, there is no gap between the identity presented 'on stage', and that presented 'in real life'. Nicola Dibben argues that the details of Björk's working methods make it possible for her fans and supportive critics to come to such a judgement, and this is something they desire to do.[15] This is not, however, what the term is usually taken to mean. David Bowie would fail the authenticity test on these grounds, while Girls Aloud would (conceivably) pass it. And, while there is perhaps value in arguing for one understanding of authenticity along these lines, in doing so we must acknowledge that there is no single authenticity. No, the commonest attribution of the term 'authentic' in relation to music refers to the maintenance of the origins of a performance practice – an authentic musician is true to such a practice: 'authentic blues' perhaps, or 'authentic folk'. The first finds expression in Bob Brunning's study of British blues,[16] wherein a hagiographic narrative is constructed whereby a host of musicians discover this blessed 'other' music (the blues), and by Brunning rendering such a move unproblematic, it becomes naturalized. For Philip Bohlman, identification of the 'authentic' requires '[the] consistent representation of the origins of a ... style', such that 'When the presence of the unauthentic [*sic*] exhibits imbalance with the authentic, pieces cease to be folk music, crossing the border into popular music instead'.[17] While the latter comment is jaundiced, the former is key. A related example can be found in the case of the punk movement of the 1970s. In its direct opposition to the growth of disco, it was read as an authentic expression.[18] Here, authenticity is assured by recovering an earlier authentic practice (that of various 1950s and 1960s musicians), founded on musicians whose technique and means of expression were unsophisticated. Bohlman's identification has found its way into rock discourse, in that proximity to origins entails unmediated contact with those origins: 'Real instruments were seen to go along with real feelings in Springsteen's rise: a certain sort of musical and artistic purity going hand in hand with a sincere message'.[19] The importance of retaining a point of origin is also exemplified in Paul Gilroy's conceptualization of the equation for black listeners of local ('original') expressions of culture with authenticity, and more global manifestations with cultural dilution

---

[14]   Roy Shuker, *Key concepts in popular music* (London, 1998).

[15]   Nicola Dibben, *Björk* (Bloomington IN, 2009), pp. 131–9.

[16]   Bob Brunning, *Blues: the British connection* (Poole, 1986).

[17]   Philip V. Bohlman, *The study of folk music in the modern world* (Indiana University Press, 1988), pp. 10–11.

[18]   Laing, *One chord wonders*, pp. 14–17; Reebee Garofalo: 'How autonomous is relative: popular music, the social formation and cultural struggle', *Popular Music* 6/1 (1987), pp. 89–90.

[19]   Steve Redhead, *The end-of-the-century party* (Manchester, 1990), p. 52.

(or lack of aesthetic value[20]). The current popularity of the 'tribute' band provides another, markedly different, example. There is no single ethos that underlies the activities of this mass of everyday musicians, but that of faithful reproduction in order to recover the reality of originary performances can be widely found. Thus, the Portsmouth-based Silver Beatles are lauded because they 'purvey a far more natural feel to their performance' – Cynthia Lennon is reported as claiming that they 'look alike, sound alike and even think alike'.[21] The US Rolling Stones cover band Sticky Fingers draw attention to the trustworthiness of their approach, in declaring themselves 'not just a band playing covers', but a real 'tribute' to the Stones.[22] The leading Genesis tribute band, ReGenesis, for a February 2001 gig went as far as attempting to reconstitute the 'vintage' keyboard rig played by Genesis' Peter Banks c.1973 as a way of strengthening their ability to give people access to an experience (that of a particular live performance) otherwise denied them by Genesis' demise (and this gig they then reproduced extensively). They play their repertory 'because Genesis don't play it any more … some of us like to hear "Supper's Ready" or "Return of the Giant Hogweed" live once in a while'.[23]

Whereas for Bohlman, authenticity was identified by a *purity of practice*, for Grossberg, it was more clearly identified by an *honesty to experience*. According to Grossberg, the authentic rock singer requires '[the] ability to articulate private but common desires, feelings and experiences into a shared public language. It demands that the performer have a real relation to his or her audience'[24] in terms of shared, or at least analogous, experiences. The music needs both to transcend that experience in some way (in order to be presented as an idealized, i.e. artistic, statement rather than through everyday conversation), but also to authenticate it by expressing it in a way particular to that singer. Middleton argues for a similar honesty to experience when he suggests that 'honesty (truth to cultural experience) becomes the validating criterion of musical value'.[25] Starting from a very different point, Steven Feld develops a similar line, arguing that 'authenticity only emerges when it is counter to forces that are trying to screw it up, transform it, dominate it, mess with it …',[26] equating authenticity to a concept of genuine culture. Theodore Gracyk finds the concept of rock authenticity bound up with rock's association with the project of liberalism (citing in particular U2), founded as it is on the identification of a pre-existent subjectivity.[27] As such, he argues against Grossberg's view that authenticity has become increasingly irrelevant in the

---

[20]   Paul Gilroy, *The Black Atlantic* (London, 1993), p. 96.

[21]   Silver   Beatles   (http://www.beatles-tribute-band-uk.co.uk/actinfo.asp?actid=
%7B09796A64–1D52–4B3C-9F54-D59E730BCDA1%7D, no date).

[22]   Sticky Fingers (http://www.stickyfingersband.com, no date).

[23]   ReGenesis (http://www.regenesis-music.com/, no date).

[24]   Grossberg, *We gotta get out of this place*, p. 207.

[25]   Middleton, *Studying Popular Music*, p. 127.

[26]   Keil and Feld, *Music grooves*, p. 296.

[27]   Gracyk, *Rhythm and noise*, pp. 221–3.

face of postmodernism, in the process equating authenticity to self-expression.[28] Redhead's analysis of Springsteen (above) has something of this sense. So here, we have two possible understandings of the way musicians parade their integrity. One is through the maintenance of a performance practice associated with a particular tradition, the other through a maintenance of their own performance practice.

Although these readings may be dominant, there are other ways to conceptualize authenticity, including: the accuracy of reporting of events or the views of others; the capturing and expression of universal (extra-cultural) aspects of the human condition; fitness for purpose; lack of sophistication (the intimacy and immediacy of expression); and antipathy towards commercial gain.[29] In each of these cases, the determining factor appears to be that the expression is being received as if it is unmediated, unchanged by any transmitting medium. We can thus see that although the notion of an original expression is key to understanding authenticity, it is not sufficient. In Toynbee's account of performance, authenticity appears to be only one available mode. He argues that, partly as a result of the inevitable distance between performers and listeners erected by the practice of recording, performers now take up one (or more) of four possible positions. The *expressionist* mode is entirely unmediated, wherein the performer insists on a direct expression of their emotional world. For Toynbee this is entirely unreflective and, ultimately, 'anti-creative ... because it denies that creativity consists in an *encounter* between the musician-subject and objects ... it proposes a kind of subjective supremacism'.[30] Its opposite, the *transformative* mode, identifies a mode of conscious working within a tradition, although without slavish adherence to its characteristics. This relates to the concept of signifyin(g), which I address below. Between these lie the *direct* mode, wherein a performer performs with perceived sincerity, and the *reflexive* mode that is marked by self-awareness, by a recognition that belief in a 'direct' mode is naïve.[31] As Toynbee's discussion of the Velvet Underground makes clear, these modes are not mutually exclusive: he finds in their work clear presences of 'expressionist' and 'reflexive' modes. The distinctions Toynbee draws are useful, although they can be mapped on to others I shall discuss. While they clarify the scope of the twin topics of this chapter, in the way they are explored, they are hard to disinter from issues of intention, which makes them of limited use in my context.

So, what might be problematic about this range of understandings of authenticity? In previous chapters, I have argued that meaning is not embedded in the music listened to, but is discovered in the act of listening, and I can see no reason why attributions of authenticity that are, after all, an aspect of meaning, should fall into a different class. This means that any analysis that claims that a particular song, or a particular performance, *is* authentic must be regarded

---

[28]   Gracyk, *Rhythm and noise*, pp. 224–5.

[29]   My thanks for my former student Alan Little for some of these.

[30]   Jason Toynbee, *Making popular music* (London, 2000), p. 63.

[31]   Toynbee, *Making popular music*, pp. 58–66.

with suspicion. In its stead, we should observe how (if at all) a track expresses authenticity, and for what particular audience (of one or more, taking into account the difficulties with predicting an audience's understanding raised in previous chapters). The analytical issue, then, becomes how it should do this. If authenticity is a property of the listening experience rather than simply of the track listened to, if it is not inherent in the music, it follows that it cannot be taken for granted, that it needs to be carefully considered. Indeed, as the critiques cited above imply (but rarely state explicitly), 'authenticity' is a matter of interpretation that is made and fought for from within a particular cultural and, thus, historicized position. Like all meanings, it is *ascribed*, not *inscribed*. As Sarah Rubidge has it: 'authenticity is … not a property *of*, but something we ascribe *to* a performance'.[32] David Brackett critiques Hank Williams' authenticity along these lines, by insisting on a distinction between the 'authentic *effects*' his music created with an audience and Williams' own position of resistance within the field of commercial country music.[33] Richard Middleton's approach to the construction of authenticity is useful here; he argues that this conceptualization builds a refuge of meaning within the bourgeois romantic critique of industrial society. And yet, within this manœuvre, there do hide real processes – he focuses on what he calls 'continuity' and 'active use' (which combine as 'tradition') and which suggests that 'from the debris of "authenticity"'[34] we may rescue the notion of 'appropriation'. He then argues that such a move is universally available; it is not tied to any particular stylistic formulations. 'Authenticity', therefore, carries meanings that, while they coalesce around particular poles, are redefined according to the writer, and are necessarily constructed in the listening act, rather than being discovered. Let me explore this briefly with respect to one particular example, that of John Lee Hooker's 'I'm in the mood'. His style, that of relatively unsophisticated bluesman, is one frequently associated with authenticity, since the blues has long been a vehicle for the expression of difficult emotions, as an outlet where no other was possible; it is also a stylistic tradition that Hooker appropriated from the inside – socially and geographically, it is his, but to assure ourselves of the authenticity of his expression, we would want to know this of his personal history. We would also want to know whether he has ever been 'in the mood' and, thus, whether his report of what it was like could be trusted. For some listeners, it may even matter whether he was 'in the mood' at the moment he expressed himself as being so (either in the recording studio, or even whenever he first made the decision to sing these lyrics), although that moment will always already be past before we as listeners can enter into it. And we would ask whether the song accurately portrays the situation Hooker found himself in when he realized he was 'in the mood'. Perhaps he is able to

---

[32]   Sarah Rubidge, 'Does authenticity matter? The case for and against authenticity in the performing arts' in Patrick Campbell (ed.), *Analysing performance* (Manchester, 1996), p. 219.

[33]   Brackett, *Interpreting Popular Music*, pp. 85–9.

[34]   Middleton, *Studying Popular Music*, p. 139.

convince his listeners not only that this is what being 'in the mood' is like, and that this is what it's like for you, as a listener, but this is what it's like for everyone, that this is a universal condition. Perhaps, in wishing to feel 'in the mood', or recall what it was like, we play this recording to remind us (and it succeeds). Perhaps our observation that the recording does not carry lots of overdubs, of studio trickery, convinces us of its authenticity, or Hooker's disdain for singing 'what his public wants' (i.e. being driven by the commercial imperative), rather simply allowing them to 'overhear' what he wants to sing. It is highly unlikely that a listener would require that all these conditions were met, although I suggest that if as few as one were, it is unlikely that the track would be perceived as having much authenticity. Some criteria carry more value than others, some rely on the projection of our own listeners' desires, since they are unanswerable. This rich range of meanings is not normally considered, but there are some writers, such as Toynbee, who have acknowledged that authenticity is not a monolithic concept, that it must be understood in different ways, and that these ways relate in such a fashion that they can be articulated.

Robert Walser insists that there are two clear types of 'authenticity' that can be observed, specifically in rock music.[35] The first is upheld by critics who have equated commercial mediation with ideological compromise, and who have thus decried the reliance on recording contracts with major record companies and the ensuing big distribution deals; to follow this path is to court inauthenticity. The second is in terms of the Romantic vision of the artist as hero, an identification that is frequently overplayed, and thus compromised, by the phenomenon of heavy metal as visual spectacle; to rely too strongly on spectacle is, again, to appear inauthentic. This is the position satirized so clearly in the film *This is Spinal Tap* (1984) and represented (in real life) by the sound of a band such as Europe ('The final countdown'). A more usual analysis is tripartite. In opposition to Middleton's perspective, Grossberg argued for three different understandings of authenticity, each relevant to a specific genre.[36] Thus he discussed rock authenticity as founded on the romanticized ideology of the rock community, where the musicians 'tell it like it is', in as direct a manner as possible (rather like the first of Walser's categories). We might find this authenticity expressed in a track like the Who's 'I'm a boy'; the Who of course problematized this very notion early in the history of the concept, with *The Who sell out*. Grossberg identifies an authenticity of black genres, founded on the rhythmicized and sexual body. We might find this authenticity expressed in James Brown's 'Soul power'. Grossberg also posits an authenticity of self-conscious postmodernity, demonstrating honesty in the acceptance of cynical self-knowledge, a move we might find expressed in Madonna's constant recrafting of her own identity. This latter is a bold move on Grossberg's part, rehabilitating the notion in a postmodern context. However, he

---

[35]   Walser, *Running with the devil: power, gender, and madness in heavy metal music* (Hanover NH, 1993).

[36]   Grossberg, *We gotta get out of this place*.

argues that such a history proceeds as a pendulum, swinging from one extreme to the other, frequently with much disagreement among fans and critics as to which term to apply to which music; such attributions, such interpretations, are to be debated rather than simply perceived. It is this realization that seems to have led Johan Fornäs to generalize Grossberg's typology of authenticity, producing three distinct authenticities: *social authenticity*, *subjective authenticity* and *meta-authenticity*, each of which has both conservative and progressive variants.[37] Thus, 'social authenticity' is ensured in an act of judgement legitimate within a particular community, and relevant particularly to the mass of indie music: Nirvana come to mind. 'Subjective authenticity', on the other hand, is validated by the individual. 'Cultural or meta-authenticity' is a more recent development, validating 'synthetic' texts through the evidenced meta-reflexivity of their authors (a position developed in Redhead,[38] and an alternative formulation of Toynbee's *reflexive* mode), as in the work of the Pet Shop Boys. The third of these is particularly marked as an authentication of the author, although this aspect is also strong in Fornäs' first two categories. Moreover, Fornäs argues that authenticity is not directly opposed to artificiality since authenticity is, after all, necessarily a construction we place upon what we perceive.[39]

Timothy Taylor has also developed a tri-partite analytic scheme, but growing from his work in world musics. He argues that these various authenticities share a base assumption about 'essential(ized), real, actual, essence',[40] and identifies authenticities of *primality*, *positionality* and *emotionality*. Authenticity of primality we have already encountered in the guise of the maintenance of original practice. Taylor argues that an expression is perceived to be authentic if it can be traced to an initiatory instance, if it 'has some discernible connection to the timeless, the ancient',[41] noting that such a connection is constructed. Although he exemplifies this through marketing strategies, the sound of the Blind Boys of Alabama's recent unaccompanied 'The last time' has the potential to convey such a sense. Authenticity of positionality we have also encountered: it relates to musicians who have refused to sell out to commercial interests.[42] For many 'world' musicians, such selling-out equates to the adoption of style codes of the industrial West (those of pop and rock), and is not marked by the adoption of non-indigenous style codes *per se* – within Anglophone popular song, this corresponds to the first of Walser's categories, above, but can also be exemplified by a singer like Eliza Carthy, who has recently alternated the encounter with big labels and self-written material (*Angels and cigarettes*; *Dreams of breathing underwater*) with returns to tradition (*Anglicana*; *Rough music*) in order, presumably, to revivify her own practice.

---

[37]   Fornäs, *Cultural theory*, pp. 276–7.
[38]   Redhead, *End-of-the-century party*.
[39]   Fornäs, *Cultural theory*, p. 275.
[40]   Taylor, *Global Pop*, p. 21.
[41]   Taylor, *Global Pop*, pp. 26–8.
[42]   Taylor, *Global Pop*, pp. 22–3.

Authenticity of emotionality we have encountered also (it relates to that vision of the musician as explorer, returning to his or her community with the results of that inner exploration), but Taylor glosses it differently, seeing it as a capturing of the spiritual origin of the music-making impulse,[43] a position identified by many listeners with the singer Jeff Buckley (and typically with his cover of Leonard Cohen's 'Hallelujah'). Each of these descriptions adds something to what we have already discovered, and it is important that Taylor views them operating with some independence, but always relating back to that notion of 'actual essence', a relationship that argues that such authenticities are inherent, an argument I have already discounted. My own tri-partite scheme[44] is rather different in that, rather than asking what it is about the music that appears authentic, I ask who it is that a performance authenticates. In this sense, there can be only three possibilities. The performance can authenticate the musician(s), can articulate on their behalf 'this is what it's like to be me'. This authenticity I call *authenticity of expression*, or *first person authenticity*, and it is a similar formulation to Toynbee's *direct* mode. The intimacy of a late period Johnny Cash ('Solitary man', say), combined with the aura of his own history, is a likely candidate to make such an expression convincing. The recorded performance can also authenticate the experience of the audience, can articulate on their behalf 'this is what it is like to be you'. This authenticity I call *authenticity of experience*, or *second person authenticity*. In most cases, of course, this will not be found without first person authenticity, since musicians are far more likely to try and articulate 'this is what it means to be us', to include themselves in such an articulation. When Mike Skinner of the Streets tells his interlocutor (and vicariously his audience) to 'Dry your eyes', this works because the experience he describes so intimately is one his listeners are likely to be only too familiar with. Finally, a performance can authenticate the experience of absent others. This is an alternative formulation of *authenticity of primality*, or authenticity as truth to the origins of a practice, as it articulates 'this is what it is/ was like to be him/her'. This authenticity I call *authenticity of execution*, or *third person authenticity*, and is exemplified by revivals of all sorts – Teenage Fanclub's recreation of the world of the Byrds, for instance, on a track like 'Sparky's dream'. This formulation I believe to be particularly useful for the latter part of this chapter, for it maintains that there is no necessary contradiction between singing another's material and convincing listeners of your authenticity in so doing. Richard Middleton has argued that we need to consider authenticity as both inscribed and ascribed, for '… we also wonder if music expresses or represents us … in an honest way… Authenticity is a quality of selves and of cultures; and they construct each other …'.[45] And yet, as I have argued throughout, it is people who express; both

---

[43]   Taylor, *Global Pop*, pp. 28–30.

[44]   Allan F. Moore, 'Authenticity as authentication', in Moore (ed.), *Critical essays in popular musicology*, (Aldershot, 2007). This article contains a fuller discussion and exemplification, from a wider range of sources, of these various authenticities.

[45]   Middleton, *Voicing the popular*, p. 206.

listeners and musicians find themselves represented in music, but it is not 'music' that is active, intentional, in expressing or representing – music is medium, not agent. Were this not the case, its meanings could inhere, and would not have the contingency the final paragraphs of Middleton's book[46] celebrate.

So, far from consigning authenticity to the dust-heap of history, it seems to remain of permanent importance, for questions of the integrity of those with whom we relate is pertinent to every generation. For three reasons, then, I believe we cannot ignore the issue. First, 'authenticity' is too often simply aligned with questions of originality and the maintenance of original practice. This is too simplistic, as I have argued, and does not actually bear out the practice of how listeners find in song an authentic expression. Second, the notion of appropriation (of sonic experiences by perceivers), which I move on to below, remains foundational to processes of authentication, and thus the idea of sampling someone else's work is itself no bar to authentic expression. Ulf Poschardt discusses a range of theorists on sampling, only to conclude that 'however much quoting, sampling and stealing is done – in the end it is the old subjects that undertake their own modernization. Even an examination of technology and the conditions of production does not rescue aesthetics from finally having to believe in the author. He just looks different.'[47] For the third reason, I refer again to Grossberg's analysis, wherein the growth in the 1950s of new structures of technological, economic, and social practices tended to deny many (most particularly working-class, adolescent males) access to the heady, future-oriented, post-war social enterprise. This rejection engendered an alienation that was nurtured by a spirit of optimistic liberalism that in turn repressed social and cultural differences, and that was articulated by the emergence of the lascivious hips, the narcissistic gaze and the analgesic beat of rock'n'roll. For Grossberg this was a key moment: the 'authenticity' that its fans found in this music was defined not by its anchorage in the past, nor by the integrity of its performers, but by its ability to articulate for its listeners a place of belonging, an ability that distinguished it from other cultural forms, particularly those that promised 'mere entertainment' (in which they invested nothing more than cash), or those belonging to hegemonic groupings (in which they could not invest). In an early article, I follow an argument of George Allan[48] in defining this 'place of belonging' as a 'centredness', calling attention to the experience that this cultural product offered an affirmation, a cultural identity in the face of accelerating social change, in large part because it itself had no history apparent to its participants. This 'centredness' implies an active lifting of oneself from an unstable experiential ground and depositing oneself within an experience to be trusted, an experience that centres the listener. Here, it seems to me, is the most pressing contemporary understanding of authenticity. In acknowledging that

---

46   Middleton, *Voicing the popular*, pp. 245–6.

47   Poschardt, *DJ culture*, p. 284.

48   Moore, 'U2 and the myth of authenticity'; George Allan, *The importances of the past* (New York NY, 1986).

authenticity is ascribed to, rather than inscribed in, a performance, it is beneficial to ask who, rather than what, is being authenticated by that performance. Three types of response are possible, according to whether it is the performer herself, the performer's audience, or an (absent) other who is being authenticated. Siting authenticity within the ascription carries the corollary that every music, and every example, can conceivably be found authentic by a particular group of perceivers and that it is the *success* with which a particular performance conveys its impression that counts, a success that depends in some part on the explicitly musical decisions performers make, and that is open to judgement by all listeners collectively and, ultimately, individually. Whether such perceivers are necessarily fooled by doing so is beside the point, since we may learn as much from creative misunderstanding as from understanding. I close with a trenchant admission from Michael Frayn, asking the same question of novelists: 'You have to believe, with even the trashiest writers, that they are offering you some genuine personal vision of the world, however trite, that they are in some sense transmuting their own experience and appealing to yours. If you begin to suspect that the author is simply manipulating a formula then the situation changes at once'.[49] It is this unerring belief, even in such a careful study of subjectivity as his, that makes any simple rejection of the idea of authenticity *per se* forever wrong.

Intertextuality

If originality is deeply intertwined with authenticity and its synonyms, it would initially seem to be entirely antithetical to *intertextuality*. Intertextuality is a concept borrowed from literary studies, where it is closely related to theorizations of the postmodern. Intertextuality is fundamentally about borrowing, about transgressing the unity, the self-containedness, of the utterance, and about the opening of it to other utterances. As such, it seems to challenge the notion of an utterance as an authentic expression of the self, unmediated by other factors. As we have seen, this notion of unmediated expression cannot be supported in actuality, although the desire to find it remains strong. What a focus on intertextuality does do is to challenge the notion of original creation, of inventing music *ex nihilo*, or inventing out of pure genius. In postmodern theory, a focus on intertextual presence is commensurate with the downgrading of the importance of the author as the inscriber of meaning, and thus it finds a ready place in the theoretical perspective of this book.

To address intertextuality is to acknowledge the presence within a text of other texts. There are two important components to this assertion. The first is the focus on *text*. A text, effectively, is something that is read, recognizing that the activity of reading encompasses not only the perception of marks on paper, but their necessary interpretation. The word 'text' has expanded its meaning in recent years to cover

---

[49]   Michael Frayn, *The human touch*, p. 415.

not only written objects, but objects heard (thus an item of music can be considered a text if it is interpreted – this says nothing about whether it is represented on paper or not) and other objects seen (a landscape can be 'read', or a house, or even a face); effectively, anything that is perceived can be considered a text, placing the accent on the necessary process of interpretation. The 'presence within a text of other texts' is a recognition that music is self-similar. A particular melodic phrase in one track can sound like another, and so call the other to mind for a particular listener, thereby 'interfering' with the simple attention given to the former track. The openings to both the chorus to Bob Dylan's 'Idiot wind' and the verse of Derek & the Dominos' 'Keep on rollin'' share a striking melodic phrase – $\hat{5}$–$\hat{3}$–$\hat{1}$–$\hat{6}$–$\hat{5}$ – but is it difficult to see how to 'read' that melody – there is no obvious correlation between the sets of lyrics, for instance. It has a generally falling (depressive) contour, but it also reaches out to its starting-point and exceeds it ($\hat{6}$) before retrieving it ($\hat{5}$). That much can be said, but in the absence of any correlative features, such a phrase is simply part of the 'common stock' that contemporary musicians use; since it is hard to see how to 'read' it, it does not function as a text; its function is rather metalingual. The same goes for the $\hat{4}$–$\hat{5}$–$\hat{3}$–$\hat{1}$, which appears under the eponymous heroes of the Beatles' 'Sexy Sadie' and the Damned's 'Grimly Fiendish'. A less obvious example is the melody shared between Chuck Berry's 'Sweet little sixteen' and the Beach Boys' 'Surfin' USA', which I referred to in Chapter 7. Here, it appears the latter melody was modelled on the former, and this requires a reading: the copying appears overt. And it need not be a melodic phrase: a particular instrumental timbre; a chord sequence; a few words of lyric; the tone of a singer's voice; all these elements can act in this way, such that the meaning of a particular track can never entirely be removed from its context, a context whose horizon is the listening history of any particular listener to it.

In popular music studies, intertextuality has long been recognized as a crucial theoretical construct. Scholars from outside musicology who began to apply this theory to popular music made the unfortunate assumption that, because it is a characteristic of postmodernism in other fields of cultural expression, it was necessarily also a characteristic of postmodernism in music. I say 'unfortunate', since it is a necessary constituent of the invention of music itself – in the sixteenth century, for instance (a period that is yet to be analysed as postmodern), the device was behind the construction of parody and paraphrase masses, dominant features of the established musical landscape, and it has always been an integral feature of all music. Anyhow, we do not need to worry about the inaccuracy of the attribution of the terminology. What is important is the recognition that intertextuality remains an important part of the invention of music, and that it needs to receive a focus that it rarely does.

There is a multitude of different ways in which one text may resemble another. Serge Lacasse distinguishes between pairs of oppositional terms, a number of which are particularly useful. Crucial for him is the distinction between *intertextuality* and *hypertextuality*.[50] He uses 'intertextuality' to cover categories of *quotation* and *allusion*, that is, instances where some *actual* musical material is re-used in a new context – this issue becomes important with the rise of *sampling*. 'Hypertextuality', on the other hand, is used to cover instances where a text is transformed, renewed, or otherwise modified, and he discusses the differences between *parody*, *remix*, *pastiche*, *copy*, *cover* and *travesty* (as well as a few less useful categories). Hypertextuality, therefore, creates a new text out of an earlier one; these two texts bear the relation of *hypotext* (the earlier manifestation) to *hypertext* (the subsequent one). He makes an additional important distinction, between *allosonic* and *autosonic* instances. An autosonic quotation is created when part of a track is sampled and inserted into a new track (and although Lacasse avoids using the terms hypotext and hypertext in this particular instance, it is quite useful to do so), whereas an allosonic quotation creates the relevant part anew. For example, an allosonic quotation is created when Elvis Presley sings 'I wish I was in a land of cotton' (on 'American trilogy'), taking his melody from Mickey Newbury's original (which of course took its melody from earlier versions, creating a chain of allosonic quotations right back to its earliest performance). With these terms in play, then, the distinction between intertextuality and hypertextuality becomes less important – what are interpretively important are hypertexts and hypotexts, and allosonic and autosonic references.

Lacasse's other categories are distinguished by the difference between *style* and *content*. Quotations and parodies (whether allosonic or autosonic) tend to retain style constants, but alter the content. Thus, Amy Winehouse's 'Tears dry on their own' quotes its accompaniment from Marvin Gaye and Tammi Terrell's 'Ain't no mountain high enough'. (Indeed, whether it works allosonically or autosonically is very hard to pin down, and mired in the details of record company licensing.) Another example is provided by Cheap Trick's cover of 'California man'. The song was originally written by Roy Wood and recorded by his Birmingham-based band The Move in 1970. Cheap Trick's cover is just that, made by a band from Illinois, so perhaps embodying an equal degree of desire to situate themselves on the West Coast. However, the cover also interpolates (at 2'1") the (heavy, lumbering) riff from the Move hit 'Brontosaurus'. The fascinating aspect of this cover is how authentically the vocal and the boogie guitar are re-created, for not only were the Move far from being California men, but Wood was an adept mimic of 1960s/1970s styles. Can one make an authentic cover of an inauthentic performance? The idea of allusion I cover below, in talking about harmony. For parody, we need look no further than the work of Neil Innes, Eric Idle and the Rutles, whose entire *raison d'être* was to rework the music of the Beatles.[51]

---

[50]   Serge Lacasse, 'Intertextuality and hypertextuality in recorded popular music', in Moore, *Critical essays in popular musicology* (Aldershot, 2007).

[51]   As discussed in John Covach, 'The Rutles and the use of specific models in musical satire', in Moore (ed.), *Critical essays in popular musicology*, (Aldershot, 2007). It is worth noting that Neil Innes successfully sued Oasis for plagiarism for their song 'Whatever'.

On the other hand, remixes, covers and pastiches retain the same (or very similar) content, but make alterations in terms of style. Covers I shall discuss below, while it is worth noting that remixes are rare (and not desperately consequential) in terms of song – in a remix, the relationship between lyric, the projection of the persona and aspects of the track tend to remain constant by definition. If such a practice seems to be too easy (and to retain no element of originality), we would do well to recall the Adornian concept of pseudo-individuation, to describe the re-clothing of a cultural product where its content is simply recycled, adding nothing by way of significance. Pastiche is perhaps more interesting in that it gives rise to issues of plagiarism. I have already raised the case of 'Surfin' USA' and 'Sweet little sixteen'; another example concerns Steps' 'One for sorrow' and Abba's 'Winner takes it all'. Both songs employ a striking melodic figuration, of a leap of a seventh followed by a stepwise descent, repeated in sequence. What differs is the rhythmic placement – whether the dissonant seventh falls on the strong beat, or precedes it (compare Example 9.1 with Example 9.2, which is transposed down a semitone).

Example 9.1   Abba: 'The winner takes it all'; chorus

Example 9.2   Steps: 'One for sorrow'; chorus

Technically, Doves' 'M62 song' seems to count as a pastiche of King Crimson's 'Moonchild', but the reference is explicitly made on the album sleeve. Whereas a parody has ironic intent, a pastiche[52] is transparent as to intent. But this is not the case with Doves – we need to recognize here the quality of *homage* that 'M62 song' carries, a quality that relates strongly to issues of signifyin(g), covered below.

Space does not permit an exhaustive discussion of these different categories, but I will rather illustrate the extremes with particular examples. It is not difficult to develop this line of thinking. The 'cover' exists at one extreme. Here, an entire hypotext is transformed into a hypertext. This does not necessarily mean every element of the hypotext is re-employed, but sufficient to convey the sense of identity between the two. Many critics have written on details of covers. Byrnside noted that in rock'n'roll covers, 'a performer (usually white) offered a vocally softer and textually less objectionable version of a song previously recorded by a black rhythm and blues performer.'[53] Dave Headlam observes the way that specific blues have been covered, have undergone change in the hands, respectively, of Led Zeppelin and Cream.[54] Deena Weinstein suggests that particular eras of rock have been typified by the values inherent in the covers made during the period[55] (values respectively of domestication, of authenticity, of romanticism, of parody, and of the archival approach). Dai Griffiths observes the ways that the field of reference of a track changes when it is covered by someone of a different gender, race, or place.[56] A particularly rich example is the 'American trilogy' I referred to earlier. Mickey Newbury's original was released in 1971; Elvis Presley picked it up very quickly, releasing his version in 1972. According to anecdote, country singer Newbury dreamed up the combination almost on the spur of the moment[57] in live performance, and the studio version retains something of the intimacy one imagines that original performance contained. This is partly a function of the bare guitar opening, partly a quality of his voice, sad with a touch of yearning, and

[52]   Certainly in Fredric Jameson's well-known distinction. Fredric Jameson, 'Post-modernism and consumer society' in Hal Foster (ed.), *Postmodern culture* (London, 1985), pp. 113–14.

[53]   Ronald Byrnside, 'The formation of a musical style: early rock', in Moore (ed.), *Critical essays in popular musicology* (Aldershot, 2007), p. 242.

[54]   Dave Headlam, 'Does the song remain the same? Questions of authorship and identification in the music of Led Zeppelin', in Elizabeth West Marvin and Richard Hermann (eds.), *Concert music, rock, and jazz since 1945: essays and analytical studies* (Rochester NY, 1995); 'Blues transformations in the music of Cream' in John Covach and Graeme M. Boone (eds.), *Understanding Rock* (New York NY, 1997).

[55]   Deena Weinstein, 'The history of rock's pasts through rock covers', in Thomas Swiss et al., *Mapping the Beat* (Malden MA, 1998.).

[56]   Dai Griffiths, 'Cover versions and the sound of identity in motion', in David Hesmondhalgh and Keith Negus (eds.), *Popular Music Studies* (London, 2002).

[57]   'Mickey Newbury biography' (http://www.musicianguide.com/biographies/1608003817/Mickey-Newbury.html, no date).

partly a function of the string backing, which sounds synthesized (there's just too much treble there), and therefore potentially also under the hands of Newbury. He is almost singing to himself of his sadness. He is in a resonant space for his voice and, though not interrupted by any other objects, this seems to be a public, but empty, location. Even the later harpsichord and harmonica are 'tasteful' and don't intrude on him (even though the harmonica may conjure up a camp-fire setting, which the other instruments must counter). For Presley, on the other hand, notwithstanding the live performance, the immediate introduction of kit drums and backing voices makes this a public occasion. Sentimentality is hard to define, but this performance seems to exemplify it. The vocals are overblown, perhaps because of the backing (the big orchestra intervention at 1'30" seems in bad taste compared to Newbury's). The effect of running the first two lines of the third song straight together fails to leave time for the performance to breathe, while the bluesy flute (of all things) towards the end, and Presley's return for the 'big finish' seem to epitomize his showmanship. Sometimes, it can be demonstrably difficult to carve out one's own expressive space within a cover. In order to take on 'Piece of my heart', so familiar to audiences from Janis Joplin's singing, Nazareth make three particular changes. First, the chorus is signalled (under the repeated 'come on') very clearly by an episodic marker; the downward bass scale, which lends a greater continuity to this part of the song than can be heard in Joplin's. Second, the power chord downbeats of the chorus itself permit silence to creep through under Dan McCafferty's entreaties, separating out his vocal projection from the rest of the band. Finally, the tempo fluctuations that allow Joplin to sing her heart out are not indulged in by Nazareth. The result is, perhaps, that McCafferty's persona's disintegration appears more inevitable than Joplin's, and somewhat more understated.[58]

Covers thus offer rich interpretive pickings. What about self-covers? I have already discussed some features of the Beach Boys' 'Good vibrations' in Chapter 8, and here make a comparison between this original and the recording issued by Brain Wilson in his finally completed *Smile* project. The first obvious difference lies in the main voice, now Wilson's own. It is of course older than Carl Wilson's (singer of most of the original) had been. It is more worn. With our knowledge of Brian Wilson's personal history, it is hard not to hear in this voice the scars of that history. One consequence of this is that the protagonist in this version (played by BW) is not the young ingénu (CW) of the Beach Boys' version. In that version, CW realizes the necessity of becoming active in the relationship (during the bridge) where hitherto he had simply picked up 'good vibrations', been on the end of her 'excitations'. But can we believe someone with the experience that seems to show in BW's voice could be that naïve? The lyrics of the first verse have been re-written. BW (the protagonist) now moves away from simply observing 'her' to

---

[58]   An uncharitable reading would hear this as simply going through the motions, and bearing in mind their cover of the Rolling Stones' 'Ruby Tuesday'; such an uncharitable reading could be made persuasive.

observing the effect she has on him. Does this suggest greater maturity; greater self-absorption; or both? The second verse continues the self-absorption theme, but this does permit BW to ask 'I wonder what she's pickin' up from me?'. This is a question which only occurred to the singer (actually Mike Love, at this point) much later in the course of the original version of the song (during that bridge). Here, one wonders whether it will promote an earlier change in the course of this version, but it doesn't. Indeed, that it is immediately followed by the 'And I'm pickin' up' pick-up, absent in the original version, does seem to be a lamentable inattention to detail – switching back to this needless observation gives the lie to his asserted sense of 'wonder'.[59] But this is offset by a new interpolation ('dum be dah', at around 3') before the final section, which puts off the resolution. This seems masterly; in a track of this sort of length (only 4½ minutes), almost any delay of final resolution will intensify its effect, and where it literally enacts the words 'gotta keep those vibrations happening', its presence is almost too good to be true.

'Good vibrations' is a song that enables a rich reading, and I have only delved some way into it at this point. Such richness makes it hard for other musicians to cover, but I do want to refer to one such here, that by the Troggs, which appeared very soon after the original, at a period when covers were legion, when the drive towards authorial authenticity was still inchoate. The differences are many; let me point to a few key ones. First, Reg Presley speaks the words rather than sings them, at a pace a little too slow for speech, and with heightened emotion. Can one hear a touch of irony here (especially since the lyric now praises the 'clothes she *almost* wears', and later Presley says 'gotta keep those vib---rations …')? The opening harmonic sequence is re-thought – it maintains a descending bass, but under a different chord sequence. And of course all the timbres are different, although there are still some ethereal backing voices. Most importantly, though, the chord sequence of the chorus, which undergoes the crucial transformation in the Beach Boys' version, remains steadfastly the same in the Troggs', turning the song from one in which the protagonist learns something of himself, to one that simply recounts how great it is to have other people turn one on.

What happens at the other end of the scale? In a cover, the hypotext is commensurate with an entire track, but what about where the hypotext is minimal? Hatch and Millward utilize (not altogether successfully) the folk concept of 'blues families' to get at the way styles changed in the rock'n'roll era.[60] This topic has

---

[59] This alone appears as evidence that the interpretation I have developed here is not one that occurred to Wilson, despite the many thousands of hours he must have spent with this material over the years. For some readers, to be sure, this will invalidate my interpretation. For others, it will simply confirm that we are not the authors of the consequences of our actions (and of course I find myself in this latter group).

[60] David Hatch and Stephen Millward, *From blues to rock: an analytical history of pop music* (Manchester, 1987). Incidentally, whatever the 'analytical' refers to in their title, it is not the analysis of individual examples of music.

fascinated many, not least Byrnside.[61] But whereas Hatch and Millward lose touch with detail in describing style change, Byrnside focuses particularly on rhythmic detail. To explore the minimal hypotext, I shall take a standard harmonic sequence and observe something of its history. The pattern I have in mind is the I–vi–IV–V sequence, although similar points could be made, I believe, with other standard sequences. This sequence qualifies as a text because it calls forth interpretation, as I shall demonstrate, as an aspect of Philip Tagg's method of interobjective comparison. Tagg's methodology here[62] entails the collection of a large variety of segments of music that share a dominant feature, and then to observe similarities in the signification of these. Such features may be melodic (the combination of a particular pitch and syncopation, for example), instrumental, harmonic, or found in any particular domain. The need is to secure one or more appearances with a specific lyric, or in a key interpretive move. What follows is just such a discussion, based on this harmonic sequence. A starting-point for this discussion is represented by Hoagy Carmichael's 1938 song 'Heart and soul' (I have in mind Al Bowlly's late recording), the first part of whose verse uses this harmonic pattern. (Its cultural ubiquity, and perhaps that of the pattern, can be gleaned from its key position in the repertoire of so many piano-playing non-musicians.[63]) During the 1950s, it becomes a staple of popular song. The Penguins' 'Earth angel' (1955) is frequently cited as a key instance, but there are others from the same style and period: Frankie Lymon & the Teenagers' 'Why do fools fall in love?' (1956); the Diamonds' 'Little darlin'' (1957); the Platters' 'Smoke gets in your eyes' (1958); Dion & the Belmonts' 'Where or when' (1959). It is from recordings such as these that the pattern becomes known as the 'doo-wop progression'.[64] A little later, we can also find it underpinning the Viscounts' 'Who put the bomp' (1961) and the Marcels' version of 'Blue moon' (1961) although by the time both these latter were released, it appears to have attained such a degree of currency as to permit a hint of irony in its use (which may have been present as early as 1957, in Frankie Lymon and the Teenagers' 'I'm not a juvenile delinquent'). And yet, although it clearly signifies 'doo-wop' both for contemporary and later audiences, it can signify more widely: 1950s; innocence; Eisenhower; 'senior prom', perhaps.[65] It does this through its use in stylistically different examples: Pete Seeger's 'If I had a hammer' (1949) and 'Where have all the flowers gone?', Buddy Holly's 'Everyday' (1957) and 'Maybe baby' (1958), Eddie Cochran's 'I remember' (1959), and the Marvelettes' 'Please Mr Postman' (1961). There is no mistaking that it is this harmonic pattern that gives rise to these significations. When musicians working in the early 1970s

---

[61]   Byrnside, 'The formation of a musical style'.

[62]   See Tagg and Clarida, *Ten little title tunes*, pp. 94–9.

[63]   People whose most likely other repertoire item tends to be 'Chopsticks'.

[64]   For instance, on http://www.angelfire.com/fl4/moneychords/rockballadlesson.html (no date).

[65]   My thanks to Stephen Rumph for these suggestions, in the midst of an email conversation over whether or not this sequence counted as a semiotic 'topic'.

(beginning with the so-called rock'n'roll revival associated with glitter rock) wanted to evoke that earlier era, one specific way they did so was through this pattern (articulated as it was by other domains): Elton John's 'Crocodile rock', and Roxy Music's Noel-Cowardesque 'Bitters end' (both 1972), 10cc's 'Johnny don't do it' (1973), Mud's 'Lonely this Christmas' and even the chorus to Slade's 'Far far away' (both 1974). (Ralph McTell's 'Streets of London' (1969) uses the same strategy to refer to the Seeger songs.) And they do it with irony, too – Led Zeppelin's 'D'yer mak'er' (1973), the Village People's 'Y.M.C.A' (1979) – and even with menace as the pleasure derived from the pattern is turned on its head (it is presumably enjoyed by the song's protagonist) in the Police's 'Every breath you take' (1983). In all these examples, the harmonic pattern could not be excised from the track without a loss of this referential chain, but it raises interesting questions over the sense of where the pattern belongs. An authentic performance creates the sense of the pattern belonging either to the performer, to the audience, or to an unnamed other. How does this pattern belong? It could clearly be said to belong to the doo-wop style, partly definitional of it as it is, but it could also be said to belong to its earliest exemplars, thereby suggesting that later examples acquire a third person authenticity (and is this still the case for the ironic glam rockers?). Then again, in a very material sense it belongs to each of these tracks themselves, otherwise they would be different tracks.

Close listening will at this point reveal that the pattern is evolving. In the Slade and McTell examples, passing chords are inserted between each pair of chords in the pattern, producing a stepwise descending bass line that demonstrates the pattern's affinity for that of Procol Harum's 'A whiter shade of pale' (1967). Perhaps this means we should find an evocation of 1950s innocence in that example, too. Such evolutions are normative. Other doo-wop tracks, for example, modify our I–vi–IV–V to create a first-generation variant: I–vi–ii–V, by means of which (speaking with concern for chronology) this family of progressions moved into doo-wop. This I–vi–ii–V appears in the Moonglows' 'Sincerely', the Crew-Cuts' 'Sh-boom' (both 1954), and as far back as 1951 in the jazz-inflected introduction to the Dominoes' 'Sixty-minute man'. Indeed, Buddy Holly's 'Everyday' is more correctly described by means of this later progression, but it is not a material difference in this case. It may be in order briefly to explain the grounds for the assumed equivalence of these invariants. The most stable harmonies in this family of patterns are the I and the V. The other harmonies are, in practice, frequently inflected, thus the IV will often contain an added sixth (IV^6), while a ii will as frequently contain an added seventh (ii^7). IV^6 and ii^7 contain identical pitches, and thus function almost equivalently[66] – it is but a short step (one easily made as a result of hours of listening) to hearing IV and ii as also *functionally* equivalent. Similarly, vi^7 often elides into iii.

---

[66] In the key of C, thus: F,A,C,D and D,F,A,C, reading from the bass upwards. The difference lies in the pitch which appears in the bass of the texture, discussion of the aesthetics of which I omit here in order to simplify the argument.

This pattern, however, has yet another set of significations. These may start from the same point, in that 'Earth angel', 'Why do fools fall in love?' and 'Little darlin'' are not only doo-wop songs, but are also immature ('teen') love songs. It is this latter aspect that is perhaps uppermost in its use for Ben E. King's 'Stand by me' (1961), Sam Cooke's 'Wonderful world' (1958) and the latter's 'Cupid' (1961).[67] It becomes particularly potent in 'Unchained melody' (first recorded in 1955, but best known in the Righteous Brothers'[68] 1965 recording). By this point, the signification begins to narrow – not only immature love, but almost transcendent, all-forsaking love, with a sense of abandoned delivery. It is this particular signification that I think is picked up in the chorus to the Small Faces' 'All or nothing' (1966),[69] and certainly develops into Whitney Houston's somewhat nostalgic rendition of Dolly Parton's 'I will always love you' (1992). The context for these tracks, with their gradual distanciation from doo-wop, is created by tracks such as 'Sherry' (1962) and 'Big girls don't cry' (1963) by the Four Seasons, Unit 4+2's 'Concrete and clay' (1965) the Beatles' 'Tell me why' (1964) and 'Girl' (1965), and Bob Dylan's (more particularly Manfred Mann's contemporaneous recording of) 'Just like a woman' (1966) – love songs all, and all founded on this pattern, but just without the same passionate desperation, the same abandonment. It is also possible that some of its significations are less easy to observe. I have already mentioned two Beatles tracks where it appears,[70] and there are others: 'I call your name'; 'I will'; 'I'm so tired'; 'Octopus' Garden'; 'Penny Lane'; 'You're going to lose that girl'. It also appears as a near-relation, with one chord dramatically altered: 'Hello goodbye'; 'Her majesty'; 'I should have known better'; 'Like dreamers do';[71] 'This boy'. The originary signification for all these is, clearly, not identical. In 'Penny Lane' (1968), the pattern only begins the verse, thereafter becoming lost, and the chords are connected via the same falling bass as in Slade's 'Far far away'. Indeed, from this range of examples, perhaps it acquires another, less precise, meaning, functioning as an idiolectal expression of the music of Lennon and McCartney (and Starr) themselves.

So, it dominates the 1950s, is present to a lesser extent in the 1960s, and recurs with clear referential intent in the 1970s. Thereafter, it has tended to lie low, such that more recent employment becomes highly noticeable and, therefore, significant. Let me point to two such appearances. In 1994, the sequence appeared

---

[67]   Another variant this - after each chord of the pattern, the harmony returns to I, producing this subtle alternative: I–vi–I–IV–I–V–I.

[68]   Strictly, Bobby Hatfield's.

[69]   The song's basic pattern is I–vi–IV–I. It is only at the most impassioned point that the variant I–vi–IV–V is introduced.

[70]   'Tell me why' actually uses the I–vi–ii–V variant already encountered, and 'Girl' the I–iii–ii–V also mentioned above, although disguised by the bass.

[71]   Written by Lennon-McCartney, recorded by the Applejacks in 1964.

cadentially in Green Day's 'In the end',[72] while in 2004 the same pattern turned up as the chorus to the McFly hit 'Colours in her hair'. For McFly, if one pays attention also to matters of texture and timbre, the pattern is perhaps best understood as connoting the era of the Beatles, as making use of the general signification I suggested in the previous paragraph. But what of the Green Day? The song appears not to have ironic intent, and surely evocation of the entire world the pattern has conjured up so far would be decidedly strange here? It is in a highly prominent (because cadential) musical position, as if marked for attention. So, is the pattern being misused? Are Green Day ignorant of its connotations, and therefore is this particular track misjudged? Not necessarily. In 1969, the radical English Edgar Broughton Band used precisely that sequence, for ironic intent, on their 'American Boy Soldier'. In this track, it overtly conjures up an earlier more innocent era, but its meaning is transformed into such a powerful statement of opposition to American military might (and established values) that, for listeners familiar with it (the live version is even more powerful), the pattern can probably never recover the aura of innocence on which so many earlier tracks depend. An earlier, if less potent, example of the same appropriation is Frank Zappa's parody 'Go cry on somebody else's shoulder' (1966). In the context of these two tracks, perhaps, Green Day's use makes sense, although whether it is necessary to demonstrate that band's consciousness of the prior models I leave to others to determine. Throughout, what I have not endeavoured to suggest is that this usage is conscious, that it is a matter of intention. Tricia Rose has argued that, with respect to hip-hop, producers consciously 'use samples as a point of reference, as a means by which the process of repetition and recontextualization can be highlighted and privileged'.[73] That is by no means the case with all forms of intertextuality, and I shall return to this issue below.

As I have suggested here, though, the identity of the pattern is not rigorous – it is in some sense contiguous to related patterns, and on this could be developed another layer of intertextual meaning. Take the equally common pattern I–V–vi–IV, familiar from tracks like Bob Marley's 'No woman no cry', Police's 'Roxanne', McGuinness Flint's jugband 'When I'm dead and gone' or Dire Straits' 'Romeo and Juliet'. The two patterns differ, you will note, only in the position of chord V. However, in containing a IV–I rather than an V–I sequence, this second pattern may be likely to be heard as less assertive. In the first two of these tracks the reggae/ska presence is unmistakeable, while it also lurks beneath 'When I'm dead and gone'. A possible historical location for this pattern is suggested by the I–vi—IV–V of Millie Small's 'My boy Lollipop', itself originally a ska hit. But to move to this new pattern: because of its implied cadence its frame of reference appears to have something to do with providing comfort, on the basis of these examples.

---

[72] This is not entirely a foreign importation, as it also appears in their track 'Basket case'.

[73] Tricia Rose, *Black noise: rap music and black culture in contemporary America* (Hanover, NH, 1994), p. 73.

A second case is founded on David Bowie's 'Five years'. This track is based on the related pattern I–vi–II–IV, although the course of the song demonstrates its proximity to I–vi–II–V, which is also implicit in the way it is presented. Bowie himself uses variants on this elsewhere, as on 'The prettiest star', whose founding pattern is I–(vi–I^7–)III–V. The I–vi opening, continuing to a four-chord loop, is as indicative of the doo-wop progression as is the turn to IV half, or a third of the way through, a progression indicative of a blues. When My Chemical Romance open *The black parade* with I–vi, and with a song about the end of existence ('The end'), the link back to Bowie's 'Five years' is implicit, and enhances the track. The I–vi–♯iv^0–iv pattern of 'The end' is strongly related to that of 'Five years' (each of the subsequent two chords shares two common-tones with that in the same position in 'Five years'), and the track contains an overt, if momentary, reference to doo-wop styling in the lower neighbour-chord to I employed at the end of the tag between the first two verses. The argument could go much further, of course, tracing these into neighbouring patterns in a rigorous way, but I think enough has been done here to make my point. Intertextuality operates on both the large and the small scale and, while a taxonomy of the sort Lacasse offers is useful, practice is not yet sufficiently rigid for it to be prescriptive – each intertextual relation needs to be developed on the basis of what is actually present.

I referred above to Tricia Rose's comment on the intentional nature of reference within the hip-hop community. This intentionality cannot be assumed for all popular music, but it is a reasonable assumption within African American cultural practice, and may well be suitably found in other African diasporic contexts. The context for such a statement is found in the literature on 'signifyin(g)'. The term covers a range of rhetorical practices, of which intertextuality is only a part,[74] but a very significant part. At the minimum, it refers to the appropriation of others' material, but with an additional layer of meaning. Thus one 'signifies on' someone else's utterance, in so doing praising it, undermining it, twisting it, expanding it, and so on. This transforms the use of others' material into a creative one, a use in which it is quite possible to intervene originally. Thus, a jazz musician's improvisation on a particular tune will not only be an improvisation on that tune, but will also be (and be understood as) a commentary on other improvisations on that tune. In talking of the lyrics to James Brown's 'Super bad', Brackett notes that '[the emphasis] is on reusing and recombining stock phrases in an original way from one context to another rather than on creating phrases that are strikingly original in themselves'.[75] Here, then, there is no necessary antithesis between authenticity and intertextuality. Samuel Floyd offers the following definition:

> African Americans have their favourite tunes, but it is what is done with and inside those tunes that listeners look forward to, not the mere playing of them. The hearing of an old or a favorite [*sic*] tune may carry pleasant memories, but

---

74   Brackett, *Interpreting Popular Music*, p. 122.
75   Brackett, *Interpreting Popular Music*, p. 123.

those memories and their quality – absent inquiry – are based in preference and nostalgia. With the *musical* experience, the expectation is that something musical will *happen* in the playing of the music, and it is the *something* that fascinates, that elevates the expectation and places the hearer in a critical mode.[76]

From such a discussion, it seems eminently plausible to extend the use of the term (as others have) beyond the African American experience (particularly since such musicians not only signify on African American music – think only of Nina Simone's exploration of Bach within 'Love me or leave me' – there is little doubt that she was signifyin(g) on Bach's intricate, contrapuntal keyboard style), and align the reuse of material *per se* with the notion of signifyin(g). However, Floyd is equally clear that the origins of this practice are historically circumscribed; they lie in experiences of alienation undergone by African Americans in the period between the Emancipation and the First World War: 'The resulting black cynicism was accompanied by psychological self-defense [*sic*] and self-empowering strategies, one of which was Signifyin(g).'[77] This practice Floyd traces back to African models, as have parallel discussions on African American literary arts. The question, then, is whether this means that the use of such practices itself implies that users are alienated, and is an argument parallel to that which asked whether white blues musicians would ever 'properly' sing the blues. For instance, in Albin Zak's discussion of 'All along the watchtower', he argues that Bob Dylan's original clearly signifies on both the blues, and on British ballads.[78] Neither Dylan, nor British ballads, could be seen as African American except by way of the most tenuous chain of links. By way of such extension, the key link between signifyin(g) and alienation is lost, which seems unfortunate since Dylan's practice can be described in other ways. This seems to be an instance of making the concept do just too much work.

So, this chapter has addressed two key questions in the interpretation of popular song, two questions that are often taken to be entirely antithetical. I hope to have shown, however, that both address, in their different ways, questions of to whom the virtual performance of the track, or the material of that virtual performance, belongs. In this way, they can be seen to be very different ways of answering the same question.

With this chapter, I have completed my discussion of the means by which recorded songs mean. The discussion, extended as it is, is not exhaustive, for my focus throughout has been on the ways open to individual listeners to make sense of the objects of their listening. Many will complain, and not without justification, that I have ignored a great deal of literature on the supposed 'social' meanings of popular song. In response, I simply return to a point I have made earlier, that whatever meaning may be felt to be attached to specific patterns, specific tracks,

---

[76] Floyd, *The Power of Black Music*, p. 97.

[77] Floyd, *The Power of Black Music*, p. 92.

[78] Zak, 'Bob Dylan and Jimi Hendrix', p. 623.

Chapter 10
Syntheses

So What?

Having read this far, it would be natural to have turned the previous page expecting to find those 'complete analyses' that usually act as the culmination to a book such as this.[1] I cannot tell whether their absence here will be a cause of joy or frustration, but a few words on that absence cannot be avoided. My focus throughout has been on how, as a listener, you can discover meaning in the act of listening to the popular song you listen to. The reason for this approach is worth reiterating. Much detailed writing on music contents itself with sophisticated description, and analysis. This is a worthwhile activity in its own right, but it is also worth keeping an eye on pragmatic reality. As an academic, part of my responsibility is to produce the results of my work in a form that is usable by others. For my own peace of mind, if nothing else, I need to be able to answer the question that should follow all such enquiry: so what? The second part of this book is a series of direct attempts on this most difficult of questions. I have been publishing analytically informed work on popular song for nearly 20 years now, and have constantly worried about how well it passes what I call this *so what?* test, that is how well it moves from analysis to useful, and usable, interpretation. At first, I was content that the analysis of large areas of the repertory, if necessarily somewhat superficial because of its scope, brought important understandings in terms of common practices[2] or 'style', helping to reinstate that concept as one worthy of consideration – indeed, I maintain that without an understanding of the style that *organizes* a particular performance, we cannot properly understand the details of that performance, hence my extended focus in Chapter 5. More recently, I discovered that other key questions, particularly for me those explored in Chapters 8 and 9, could be addressed by analytic means. But if the focus is on the means by which meaning is found, to present my own understandings of a range of songs would be to re-erect the *results* of such questioning as more important than the *process* of questioning, or at least as more important, more valid somehow, than yours. That will not do. If you are curious, then my little study of the Jethro Tull album *Aqualung*[3] will demonstrate how some of the essential features of this methodology work in relation to complete songs (and an entire album), but that is

---

[1]   For example, Everett, *Foundations of rock*; Stephenson, *What to listen for in rock*.

[2]   Allan F. Moore: 'The textures of rock'; 'Patterns of harmony'; *Rock: the primary text* (first edition); 'The so-called "flattened seventh"'.

[3]   Allan F. Moore, *Aqualung*.

not the focus of this particular book. There is an additional reason for avoiding the presentation of complete songs, which is that I am suspicious of the (modernist) assumption of coherence, that is, the idea that a song represents a whole in itself, an entirety that can be interpreted consistently. One reason for restricting myself to commenting on parts of songs is that this is the approach that so many songs encourage. But that is a minor point and not one I shall develop here.

The *so what?* question is one that I believe needs to be asked of every piece of work, of the results of every piece of thinking, and the test is in how it is made available for others to use. Much could be written on possible uses, but for me there is an overriding practice. There are many possible answers to the question of why we bother with the issue of interpreting music. Why bother with the lengthy (even if interesting) set of questions on which this study is based? Why not just listen? Well, if the ensuing has not convinced you, it is unlikely that anything I say here will do so, but for me there is one overriding reason why 'just listening' is ultimately unsatisfactory. From a good song, we learn about ourselves. From finding out what we make of the song, we make that learning conscious, and that seems to me to be of inestimable value. The most important question, then, to which those of the next chapter are in a sense an addendum, is this: as a listener, what does the track you are listening to teach you about your own actions or responses, or your proposed actions or responses?[4] This is, perhaps, worth demonstrating and that, finally, is the purpose of this chapter.

The tactic I shall use is one that allows me to demonstrate how some of the techniques I have introduced can combine together to address particular tracks. My choices of material here will be highly idiosyncratic and necessarily grow out of music to which I listen by choice, rather than in order to develop a rounded methodology; others' choices would be equally idiosyncratic, and they would differ markedly in detail. My organizing frame is very simple, and is intentionally associative – I focus on how one track, in my experience, suggests thinking about another (although I have also focused on tracks that allow me to discuss pertinent issues that do not readily fit the structure of the rest of the book). Thus, intertextuality is an initial means of focus but, as you will see, that is merely a presentational device. There is an important reason for this: work in embodied cognition has strongly discredited the traditional, Kantian, notion of how we categorize our knowledge. Rather than erect categories in terms of a list of specific features, and assign items of knowledge to such categories, work initiated by Eleanor Rosch has demonstrated that we actually categorize according to

---

[4]   Bearing in mind that even the simple decision to think is a most valid response. I have never really understood Dai Griffiths' categorization of my work but having begun to write this footnote, I now perhaps think I possibly do. Dai Griffiths, 'The high analysis of low music', in Moore, *Critical Essays in Popular Musicology* (Aldershot, 2007), p. 398 (original pagination).

non-canonic principles[5] – only think how difficult it is to operate the category *genre* unambiguously within the field of popular song.[6]

If Six was Nine

It is, perhaps, difficult to pin down the dominant principles of any social movement that finds expression in music. For the musicians of the 'Woodstock generation', we can perhaps cite a mix of attempts to arrest processes of alienation, the development of a 'new consciousness' founded on personal responsibility and the embedding of the individual within the community, and an avoidance of uniformity.[7] In more specifically musical terms, we find that musical ambition, the use of up-to-date technology, virtuosity, big ideas and interest in conceptualization[8] are key. It is perhaps the idea of a new consciousness (itself a very 'big idea') that is paramount in the work of Jimi Hendrix, and specifically so in his track 'If six was nine' (as in Chapter 5). This much has to be gleaned from external sources: to what extent is this determinable from the track itself? It depends for its understanding on its very title, perhaps to a greater extent than do many songs. That title posits the ludicrous suggestion that our very understanding of reality is based on an insecure foundation (something is wrong with the number system). As such, it insists on a very definite distinction between what appears to us as 'real' and what constitutes 'reality', a distinction that might suggest Platonic idealism. And, insofar as it is realized musically, it is perhaps that final freak-out (the last minute and a half or so, i.e. from 3'54") that is most representative. Each of the three musicians goes his own way, we lose a sense of the beat, and we lose a sense of harmony although bassist Noel Redding sticks resolutely to the tonic. This can be read, by way of cross-domain mapping, as an instantiation of personal responsibility on behalf of the musicians to explore themselves, but in that all three sound together, that self-exploration is nonetheless embedded within a community. Would it matter, if the three lines moved entirely out of alignment? Of course it would, if only because this particular virtual performance has its own identity.

Much has happened in the track by this point. Perhaps a key aspect to note is its origin in the blues, apparent at least in the first two verses. These have the

---

[5]   See particularly Lakoff, *Women, fire*.

[6]   See Fabbri, 'Browsing music spaces'.

[7]   Allan F. Moore, 'The contradictory aesthetics of Woodstock' in Andy Bennett (ed.), *Remembering Woodstock* (Aldershot, 2004), drawing particularly on Charles Reich, *The greening of America* (Toronto, 1971) and Theodor Roszak: *The making of a counter culture: reflections on the technocratic society and its youthful opposition* (London, 1969).

[8]   John Covach. 'The hippie aesthetic: cultural positioning and musical ambition in early progressive rock', in *Proceedings of the International Conference Composition and Experimentation in British Rock 1966–1976* (http://www-3.unipv.it/britishrock1966-1976/testien/cov1en.htm, 2005).

conventional three-part 12-bar blues structure, which appears as two pairs of lines in each verse, followed by a two-line refrain, repeated each time. Harmonically and texturally, the 'verse' is sparse, empty and unchanging (a minimal riff over a tonic pedal), while the 'refrain' is texturally dense and rich (complex guitar chords and an unspecific harmonic pattern based on phrygian iii, phrygian ii and ionian II). A blues (minor) pentatonic is undeniably behind the verse's vocal, while the refrain carries a greater sense of heightened speech. And the lyric tells us how to interpret this difference. The refrain's 'I *got* my own world to live through, and I *ain't* gonna copy you' emphasize Hendrix's difference ('ain't gonna copy'), while the stresses apparent in the way Hendrix delivers the lyric (italicized) distinguish his persona through self-assertion and self-distinction. Since the blues is a pattern shared *par excellence*, it is an ideal choice as vehicle to demonstrate what Hendrix is not going to 'copy'.

The opening texture is very striking, consisting simply of a minimal riff through the first beat, and then a cymbal through the next four. When Hendrix's voice enters, there is a sense of thickening texture because he doubles his vocal line on the guitar, but there is still a great sense of space surrounding what we hear – the scene is wide. This is compounded by the vocal delivery – there is a high degree of vocal space, with lengthy gaps after every three or four syllables, as if these are either very difficult to articulate, or of supreme importance. This massive spaciousness is manifested later in extreme echo, specifically at 2'49", where two percussive strikes on the guitar are allowed to rebound. How should we hear this? One, very effective, context is formed by the Bonzo Dog Doo-Dah Band's 'Canyons of your mind'. Although this particular song is ludicrously ironic (although is it more ludicrous than confusing six for nine?), it closes with a chorus (c. 2'15") of extreme echo, providing a return to the song's title with which the lyric had begun, thereby suggesting this extreme echo represent some inner space. Fillmore's discussion of frame semantics argues that we cannot understand any word without understanding its conceptual context: 'the word's meaning cannot be truly understood by someone who is unaware of those human concerns and problems that provide the reason for the category's existence'.[9] I bring this to bear on Hendrix's complete lack of concern for a sun that 'refuse to shine' and mountains that 'fall in the sea' or a six which 'turns out to be nine' for, or course, these categories of natural objects simply don't act in that way. They are stable, in our experience (and even mountains, should they begin to crumble, don't usually reach the sea). This only serves to highlight the following image, that of hippies who might 'cut off all their hair' for, of course, in the later 1970s, that is what so many of them did.

Although the track opens with some nod toward convention in the blues reference, it does not stay there. Indeed, although the lyric simply serves to focus in on the individuality of Hendrix's persona, musically we have a PATH schema operating. This starts right from the introduction, which divides into four brief

---

[9]   Fillmore, 'Frame semantics', p. 382.

phrases. Each of these phrases is marked by four cymbal strokes, each successively louder, with the fourth allowed to ring undamped. This minimal PATH (four times traversed) operates also over a longer scale. The relevant stages of this PATH are:

1. the introduction, marked by the bare riff and cymbal;
2. the first verse (13″), with its minimal texture and blues delivery giving way to a more idiosyncratic refrain;
3. the second verse (54″), with the texture now thickened by the bass and by a fuller riff that 'fills in' the space left empty by the riff in the first verse (compare Examples 10.1 and 10.2, where the crossed head represents a snare drum beat), and with a more agitated delivery of the lyric;

Example 10.1   Jimi Hendrix Experience: 'If six was nine'; verse 1 riff

Example 10.2   Jimi Hendrix Experience: 'If six was nine'; verse 2 riff

4. an escape from the regular presentation of verses (1′32″), with a yet busier guitar role in the texture, into what appears almost as sermonizing (his voice moves to a slightly less extreme position on the right), through four lines with a decaying sense of structure due largely to the loss of the riff;
5. a free section (1′48″) that alternates phrygian II with I (thereby, possibly, being seen as an expansion of the sense of the refrain);
6. a texturally abrupt return (2′52″) to what sounds like it may be 'just another' verse, but that turns out to be the expressive climax to the track, due first to the expansive kit, and second to Hendrix's lyric; this represents thereby a spiralic rather than a circular return to the riff (I shall return to this section below);
7. the final freak-out (3′53″).

The song, thus, has seven phases through which it passes, while all but the beginning of the sixth are marked by an increasing density and energy of texture. This is an extremely common pattern (i.e. a process broken only to return renewed), and it may be considered a particularly musical rendition of the PATH schema. Note that although the seventh section generally picks up where the fifth section concluded, the bass has moved from alternating $\hat{5}$ an octave apart to alternating $\hat{1}$ and $\hat{5}$ – a clear telegraphing of the track's coming closure.

Just as a sense of growth was apparent through the first few sections, there is another such in the sixth section, although this is manifested through the soundbox rather than by way of the track's instrumental textures. The stage for this has been set in the introduction where what sounds like Noel Redding's whispers give way to Hendrix's initial melodic line. Note that that line is delivered from a fairly extreme space to the right of the soundbox (I have noted the unusual placement here in Chapter 2). This serves to balance his guitar, which sounds correspondingly to the left and, as to the extent that we hear this persona as an expression of Hendrix the performer, then we must operate a blended space here (as discussed in Chapter 8). Proxemics and ecology combine to gives us a perspective on how his vocal performance develops. Through the first three sections (above), Hendrix's voice has been getting gradually louder, to cut across the growing busyness of the texture, and has been situated in a social space. At 1'32", he suddenly changes attitude. Vocal space becomes immediately compressed ('white-collar conservatives ...') as the guitar covers what vocal space remains, and he adopts a more personal space (the compression of vocal space is indicative of urgency in getting his 'message' across). This sharing with his listener(s) more particular details of his experience gives way to a moment when he waves his 'freak flag high' (1'44"), simultaneously declaring his individuality and membership of the counter-culture. As we slip into the fifth (wordless) section, the guitar shoots from one side of the soundbox to the other, but notably exchanges its Gs for G♯s (the tonic is E), a turn to the positive that, in combination with the growing virtuosity of his guitar playing, seems to express the exultation of newly discovered freedom, a freedom curbed by the arrival on chord V and that stunning echo. As we enter section 6, drummer Mitch Mitchell gradually explores his own version of Hendrix's display. At first we hear Hendrix's persona command 'fall, mountains', suggesting that the earlier understanding of this 'frame' (his lack of concern at the possibility of such an eventuality) may have been superseded (as, in his exultation, he assumes the Godlike ability to create such an eventuality by fiat). Mitchell runs wild, masking what a very softly spoken Hendrix continues to say, specifying his own psyched-out space. Initially, Hendrix no longer needs to raise his voice over the kit, because we (his listeners) have become tuned in to his intimate space, but I think not tuned in enough, as he vanishes behind the kit. This relationship is turned on its head at 3'35" when, astonishingly, it is almost as if Hendrix has swallowed the microphone – 'when it's time for me to die' (how more intimate a declaration could you get?) is delivered almost from inside the listener's space. This, clearly, is as much as one can handle, for the only response is the wordless freak out.[10]

As an adolescent, this was on the only Hendrix album I knew (a situation that lasted decades). While for many fans it represents the least typical in his output, for me the opposite is the case (this represents a reality all listeners will encounter in some respect, and one that should never be ignored). Perhaps because I got to

---

[10] I develop this analysis in a different direction in Allan F. Moore, 'Addressing the persona' in Dietrich Helms and Thomas Phleps (ed.), *Black Box Pop* (details to follow).

know it so well, every moment seems special but, for some reason, none quite as much as a little throwaway guitar gesture that occurs at 52″. Just as the second verse is about to begin (and in preparation for the track's growing intensity), Hendrix plays the short tag that appears as Example 10.3.

Example 10.3 Jimi Hendrix Experience: 'If six was nine'; guitar tag

Example 10.4 Jimi Hendrix Experience: 'If six was nine'; guitar tag (tablature)

Example 10.4 reproduces this as guitar tablature. This indicates how very simple it is to play this phrase – in turn, the open A, D and G strings are struck (the '0' sign), and then stopped at the second fret without being re-plucked. Insofar as this phrase has a function, it is to set off the PATH. It represents a very basic finger movement on the guitar, and its 'offhand' nature is made clear by its diminishing dynamic (the D and G strings are barely plucked, Hendrix relying on the vibrations already set in motion on the guitar). This very simply constructed upward pattern itself has characteristics of a PATH schema (the upward rise) but, in the regularity of the finger movement required to execute it, it seems to me to have characteristics of a ladder, and thus I shall term it here. As a basic, almost involuntary movement for a guitarist, it enables intertextual links, a few of which I shall raise.

Do You Want Me

It was when I first heard the (double) B side to Slade's single 'Coz I luv you', in my late teens, that I first gained a glimpse of the richness which intertextual practice offered music, where Hendrix's tag is transmuted into the main riff of 'Do you want me'. This riff is slightly more developed, as transcribed in Examples 10.5 and 10.6. Note that the 'G' is stopped, rather than open, befitting its emphasis (it is often played with a brief upward bend in the track). The riff points back, in its way, to the Hendrix track and, thus, would be a candidate for third person authenticity. Its change of function (ornamental in the Hendrix, main riff in the Slade) makes it difficult to hear in this way, but there are a couple of factors that make such an interpretation plausible. First, there is the locational space of the Slade track – the guitar sounds in a strongly reverberant space, which recalls the spaciousness of the Hendrix. Second, this resonates with other aspects of Slade's idiolect.

Example 10.5   Slade: 'Do you want me'; main riff

Guitar

Example 10.6   Slade: 'Do you want me'; main riff (tablature)

In their early years, a phase of trying to develop that idiolect, we find covers of Steppenwolf ('Born to be wild'), Frank Zappa ('Ain't got no heart'), Janis Joplin ('Move over'), the Beatles ('Martha my dear'), Ten Years After ('Hear me calling') and even the Lovin' Spoonful ('Darling be home soon'). 'Hear me calling' coincidentally employs the reverse of our tag – similar hand position, opposite contour (see Example 10.7).

Example 10.7   Slade: 'Hear me calling'; main riff

Guitar

(It is there in Ten Years After's original, but without the final 'E'). The end of Slade's live recording of 'Born to be wild' sounds like an attempt at the sort of freak out with which 'If six was nine' ends, but in 1973, in the UK, and with far less technical ability (made up for by feedback-fuelled pyrotechnics). These, however, are all straightforward examples of covers. As far as I am aware, Slade never covered Hendrix (both were managed by Chas Chandler, which might be a pertinent observation). Indeed, the search for an idiolect is perhaps one of the most instructive aspects of Slade's long career. A track like 'Kill 'em at the Hot Club tonite' has a 1920s vaudeville feel, but executed with Noddy Holder's trademark rasp. This is perhaps pastiche rather than parody. Elsewhere, musical details are reiterated. The climax to 'Gospel according to Rasputin' (1971) employs what I suspect is quite a common filler pattern (transcribed in Example 10.8, from 4'01").

Example 10.8   Slade: 'Gospel according to Rasputin'; guitar at 4'01"

Guitar

It appears also, from 2'55", in Stray's contemporaneous 'Leave it out', where it has the same function, as a motif that marks the culmination of a period of increasing instrumental excitement. Different sources give the date of release of the Stray album as 1971 and 1972, so it is by no means clear which came first, or whether the motif was independently arrived at. Slade's 'Sweet box' is full of hints at Jethro Tull's early 'Sweet dream'. The underlying sequence (dorian i–III–VII–IV) is shared with the bridge of the Tull track, together with the crisply struck two-beat upbeat to the verse and a direct quote at 1'56" (taken from 'Sweet dream' at 1'03" and also appearing subsequently). Then there's the guitar's chromatic downward scale, in mid-range at the close (3'08") which also appears so prominently in 'Sweet dream' (first heard at 1"). Alone, these are all trivial but, appearing together as they do, they conjure up a reminiscence of 'Sweet dream' without actually seeming to imitate it.

A few words are perhaps in order on Jethro Tull's 'Sweet dream' itself since it is based on what remains to me the most startling, even daring, basic groove, shown in Example 10.9.

Example 10.9   Jethro Tull: 'Sweet dream'; basic groove

That first beat, with the triplet, sounds as if it ought to be an upbeat, but it's not – it appears countless times through the track, and every time on the downbeat. This refusal to conform to such a basic norm is redolent with menace, and particularly because a shuffle beat carries a lazy connotation in comparison to a straight beat (and also, I think, because the tonic – E – arrives so inauspiciously). Thus I have always heard the 'sweet dream' as ironic, as pertaining to a nightmare, a nightmare full of familiar, but just unrelated images typical of Ian Anderson: 'you'll hear me calling'; 'all wrapped up tightly'; 'the place of resting'; and then, a sudden moment of waking, perhaps: 'don't hear you leave to start the car' (for me as an adolescent, a car was still an exotic, beyond-your-means, thing). So powerful this that after 40 years of listening, it is one of few tracks I cannot ever tire of.[11]

Back, though, to 'Do you want me'. The speed – perhaps slightly too slow to be comfortable – ecologically suggests a certain uneasy awkwardness, particularly when combined at the opening with a kit that has no kick drum, and a deep, brooding bass playing the main riff. The reverberant space is clearly demarcated twice. First, as the guitar joins with the riff far to the left, and is then repeated, doubled (with a slightly richer tone) far to the right. Second, as Noddy Holder begins the

---

[11]   The other is Slade's 'Shape of things to come', but I forebear to write about this here, except to note that this was the track that taught me the expressive power of simple contrary motion.

first verse, reverberant but dead centre, accompanied only by the kick drum and bass simply on the beat. His line is based around the $\hat{7}$–$\hat{1}$–$\hat{3}$ of the end of the riff and, like the riff, he bends the G ($\hat{3}$), which finishes the phrase tortuously sharp. I think the fundamental interpretive question relates to where the listener is in the track. Holder is addressing a female ('do you want me', etc.), characterized by her 'stockings black and slender', who strokes his 'palm', and in whose company he struggles to 'keep control', but 'don't need no other'. Words of command (such as this 'control') are everywhere evident – 'just *look*' for instance, or in the chorus where the title is followed by '*take* me, here I *come*'. But who is controlling who? The difference between the spacious verse and the more conventional chorus (with the guitar thickening the texture) perhaps characterizes this question. Me, though? I'm clearly on the outside, looking in. I'm not his object of address, and neither can I coincide with Holder's protagonist, since in the chorus he's fairly bellowing at me, but addressing her.

Offering

As an adolescent I somehow missed Spooky Tooth. There's no explanation: I caught Quintessence; I caught Tractor, Stray, Edgar Broughton and Spirogyra, but not Spooky Tooth. It is only in the last year or so that I have caught up on their notorious *Ceremony*, notorious because it effectively finished them as a band. In a pre-'progressive' atmosphere of cross-genre explorations that produced such things as the Nice's *Five bridges* suite, Curved Air's 'Vivaldi', Deep Purple's *Concerto for Group and Orchestra* (which still moves me, I have to say) and the Electric Prunes' *Mass*, Spooky Tooth (then a band poised for great success) were persuaded by their label to work with ('collaborate' is far too strong a word for what actually happened) the French electroacoustic composer Pierre Henry on a rock/electronic 'mass'. The album was not well received and Spooky Tooth disintegrated as a result. One track on that album, 'Offering', is relevant to the current discussion because it is based on the very riff I have identified in 'Do you want me', although played at about twice the speed.[12] This raises an important question about historical priority. Clearly, Spooky Tooth recorded this riff before Slade did (although there is no way of knowing who conceived it first). It is possible, therefore, that Slade were influenced by Spooky Tooth in using it, although the opposite is almost certainly impossible (unless Spooky Tooth were aware of live performances of 'Do you want me' prior to their working on *Ceremony*: there is no evidence of this being the case.) Had a listener heard them at the time, he or she would have heard Slade in terms of Spooky Tooth. However if, like me, one's experience was reversed, then there is a strong chance (again, like me), that 'Offering' is heard *in terms of* 'Do you want me'. There is no way to pretend otherwise. The 'objective'

---

[12]   This doesn't exhaust its appearances – the second bar of the riff is used, more than two decades later, on World Party's 'Sunshine'.

view that a historian (of these or any other things) is expected to present can only ever be a subsequent construction. I could write about 'Do you want me' as if I had already known 'Offering', but to do so would be to deny my actual experience. E.H. Carr offers a valuable (historian's) perspective:

> We sometimes speak of the course of history as a 'moving procession'. The metaphor is fair enough, provided it does not tempt the historian to think of himself [*sic, et seq.*] as an eagle surveying the scene from a lonely crag ... . The historian is just another dim figure trudging along in another part of the procession. And as the procession winds along, swerving now to the right and now to the left, and sometimes doubling back on itself, the relative positions of different parts of the procession are constantly changing ... . The point in the procession at which [the historian] ... finds himself determines his angle of vision over the past.[13]

One might put this alongside a notable moment of historical paradigm change, the so-called quarrel between the ancients and the moderns, also known as the 'Battle of the Books', which took place across Western Europe at the time of the reign of Elizabeth I. Francis Bacon developed an unusual line of argument within this debate: he argued that, not only are we 'the moderns', not dwarfs sitting on the shoulders of giants (this was the accepted, self-deprecatory argument for our superiority over the thinkers and actors of classical antiquity) but we are, in fact, the 'real ancients'. In the words of literary theorist Matei Calinescu:

> Bacon constructs a paradox involving the inexperience of boyhood and the wisdom of old age. From the vantage point proposed by the philosopher there is little doubt that it is we, the moderns, who are the real ancients, the ancients having been, when they lived, young and 'modern'. For those whom we call ancients are only with respect to ourselves ancient and elder, *being clearly younger than we with respect to the world.*[14]

Placing this reading of history into Carr's procession, it is clearly our perspective that is dominant, and needs to be recognized as such. The procession may be there, but we cannot construct what it 'really' looks like, any more than we can determine the point at which we enter it.

Back to 'Offering'. Unlike Slade, Spooky Tooth take the riff (Example 10.5) in two parts – the first bar provides a vocal line doubling the guitar, the second acts as a response. This is matched by instrumentation, in that the bass doubles the first bar, but not always the second.

Like the Slade track entering the chorus, 'Offering' moves from riff straight into a chord (is that a lack of invention, perhaps?), but whereas Slade move to IV,

---

[13] E.H. Carr, *What is history?* (Harmondsworth, 1987), pp. 35–6.

[14] Matei Calinescu, *Five faces of modernity* (Durham, NC, 1987): p. 24, my emphasis.

Spooky Tooth move to V. This provides a strongly affirmative cadence for the line 'bring us sal-*va*-tion', coinciding with the second syllable (51"), with a straining voice suggesting there is effort involved, perhaps in recognition of need. The song's bridge deals with affirmation of the act of communion. The chord sequence used, IV–I–IV–V is found elsewhere as a bridge sequence, providing an aside before a return to the main narrative (as in Led Zeppelin's 'Livin' lovin' maid'). Strange, then, that a mixolydian IV–I–IV(–I–VII) also happens to underpin the chorus to 'Do you want me'. Pierre Henry's electronic track was added to the masters after Spooky Tooth had finished recording – no attempt is made to make the two musical worlds work together, they simply collide. And, because it is generally mixed higher, Henry's sounds make the rest of the track (and the entire album) recede from the listener, totally destroying any sense in which Gary Wright's persona can act as it, presumably, should as an intercessory priest. This really causes questions over the 'us' in the line above – there is no way that the persona acts for us, no way that it embodies an authenticity of experience. Perhaps this also contributed to its poor reception, in an era when the authenticity paraded by rock bands was barely challenged.

The track's other particularly interesting idea appears first at 1'21" – a simple gradually rising chromatic line over a tonic pedal. Such a line activates the SCALE schema, and its smoothness implies inexorability. We can say that its rising implies an increase of emotion, since it specifies a tapering of space, a greater tautening; to produce such a line in the voice requires a tightening of the vocal cords, and to produce it on a guitar requires a gradual constriction of the body (as the left hand moves towards the right), and so on. The lack of lyrics at this point draws attention to the one sound-source I have not yet mentioned – a constant gasping for breath, an incessant series of intakes of breath disorienting because there is no exhalation. It sounds as if this is more part of Henry's contribution rather than of Spooky Tooth, largely because it is equally in the foreground (it actually remains present throughout the track, although it is not always equally apparent). Whose breath does it appear to be? It is clearly not that of the persona while singing, since it cuts across that singing, but it could suggest an inner world, perhaps, or it may simply serve to unite the worlds of the electronic score and the rock band. It certainly adds to the sense of distanciation already noted. What it does resemble, for me, is a passage from Arthur Brown's 'Fire' (from 1'49") where an increasingly hysterical screaming of the word 'burn' is underpinned by a chromatic rising line. 'Fire' preceded 'Offering' by a couple of years, and the opposition of fire to communion bread is striking in these two examples. Thus, 'Do you want me' can be seen as a secularization of a musical idea originally generated in what is (putatively, at least) a sacred context.

Cold Turkey

Gasping for breath and hysterical shouting at a steadily rising pitch are both means of expression in which the human body is audible, and the embodiment of that expression is undeniable. They are not symbolic, they are directly communicative. And, although the perspective in 'Offering' is one of distanciation, these sounds appear generally closer to us, in that they so easily inhabit us – closer, in truth, than the singing voice, for ours is always different from the one we're hearing. Such vocal expressions are symptomatic of extreme emotion (as in Led Zeppelin's 'Whole lotta love' – the passage from 2'02") and dominate John Lennon's 'Cold turkey'. Never having been in a position to suffer this myself, it is necessary to rely on Lennon's evocations. They extend to almost half of the track, and they move through a number of clearly differentiated phases, in the way that complaints such as flu, or vomiting, change. Their arrangement could nonetheless be seen as artful, and so while we may be encouraged to read this as authentic of Lennon's expression, there is room for disagreement. The track's melody, while minimal, is also artfully contrived (see Example 10.10). Each verse contains eight short phrases. The first falls from E♭ to D; the second repeats this, returning via C to E♭. The third and fourth repeat this move, except that the fourth falls to the tonic (A). The fifth to eighth repeat the same move except that the final note rises, sometimes to an E♭, sometimes to an E♮. (There are small changes to this plan in subsequent verses, but the structure remains in place.)

Example 10.10   John Lennon: 'Cold turkey'; melodic contour of verse

Such a small degree of movement (and the observation that it is 'even' smaller since the basic span is a diminished, rather than a perfect, fifth) is exactly what one might expect in suffering from acute pain, and so this melody may be felt to specify the degree of movement one makes in such a situation – this is what gives it some authenticity. The guitar 'riff' that is repeated identically after every phrase has the same limited movement, with a fall, from G to E. This may be felt to be echoed by Lennon who, in the chorus, harmonizes his line with upper thirds. While that repeated riff (and harmonic drone) ensures Lennon's positioning remains static, it is also expressive of a line such as 'can't see no future'. Perhaps the lack of surprise in the track, the way everything (melodically, rhythmically, registrally) is so firmly in place cocoons Lennon's protagonist in a way that, under the circumstances, is probably comforting. While the kit occasionally alters its pattern (from 3'47", for instance) this is akin to a slight shift of the body having become stuck in one shape for too long (the upbeat into the refrain at 1'32" is a purely conventional episodic marker, as are the measured downward guitar thirds that immediately precede each verse). The only moment of surprise, melodically, comes at the end of the final verse (of 3), at 2'49" when he sings 'promise you *anything* to get me out of this hell'. The end of the last verse is perhaps the right place for any sort of unexpected climax, but here it is not on the word 'hell' that the line climaxes (that simply rises, as normal, towards the E♮), but on 'anything', which rises to a high G – totally out of the (minimal) range already set. It is interesting that, in a song in which the protagonist is otherwise so completely self-absorbed, the climax comes on the offer of a commitment (although perhaps a commitment that, in the absence of agony, might be less generously offered), rather than on 'get me out of this *hell*', which is what one might expect.

The final two minutes display the protagonist's pain, as I have suggested, in fairly convincing terms. This passage begins at around 3'14". Hitherto, the structure of the track has been based on Lennon's melodic phrases (each a bar in length) being answered by that guitar riff (again a bar in length). As the final verse closes, the pace of repetition of the riff doubles – we hear it every bar. On the end of the first hearing comes Lennon's first gasp, and the relationship has changed – it is now as if the never changing riff is causing Lennon to gasp in response (and so we may read the riff as symbolizing the addiction his lyric tells us that, in its unsatisfying repetition, he wants to escape). This series of gasps first begins to get hysterical, then comes 'down to earth' ('oh no, no, no' etc. at 4'04"), before rising again (at 4'14") coinciding with the introduction of a second guitar (about which more below). This is certainly an aesthetically pleasing trajectory.[15]

These guitars, though, require more to be said about them. What I have identified as the 'second' guitar, which can be heard from 4'14", had already made an appearance at 1'50", in a short break that comes after the second verse (it is clearly distinguished from the first guitar by its different position in the soundbox). On both entries, it sounds as if some sort of guitar solo will ensue, but it never does. Both times, the guitar simply plays single, long held notes, filling in time but without giving the ear anything, really, to focus on. This absence could be read in a number of ways but purely as a sonic gesture, while it conventionally avoids monotony in the song (this is 1969, after all, rather than a decade later), it refuses to take the focus away from Lennon's protestations. Finally, I return to the first guitar, the sound that opens the track. This is a remarkably potent riff, extremely difficult to fix in terms of exactly what is being played. Perhaps this is why it bears so very much repetition (we hear it more than 80[16] times in all). Part of its potency, though, surely comes from its sense of space. While we hear it, it seems full of reverberation. As soon as it stops, it stops dead (conforming to the very dead acoustic within which the kit and bass are situated). It lasts through 3½ beats and is then silent through 4½ beats. It is thus doubly thrown into relief. One

---

[15]   I suspect that the track's final gesture, which seems to come from a different world entirely, is a guitar recorded on tape and played backward, rather than the harmonium whose sound it resembles. Perhaps it is part of that riff, although I can't really turn that sound backwards in my head to work it out.

[16]   82, I (usually) count.

could also talk about that slight edge to its timbre. All of these features contribute to its tremendous potency but it is, I think, the spaciousness that surrounds it at the beginning, and that is gradually encroached upon as we get to the end of the track, which is most telling.

Bridge of Sighs

The two uses of guitar which I have identified in 'Cold turkey' effectively come together in Robin Trower's 'Bridge of Sighs'. Trower's guitar eschews obvious virtuosity, remaining for much of the time with long notes but played, in the words of Robert Fripp, by a man 'who hung himself on the details: the quality of sound, nuances of each inflection and tearing bend'.[17] It also has that particular quality of sound, that particular indescribable *quale* that Fripp implies. Unlike the 'Cold turkey' riff, though, it brings its space with it as held notes remain just that. Example 10.11 sketches the riff (in the studio recording, the bracketed lower D in bar 1 is omitted: in the many live versions available on YouTube, it is the bracketed low E in the third beat which is usually omitted; the inflection on the C♯–A is a momentary upward double string bend). I have left the fourth bar empty, since Trower fills it in many different ways, but the first 1½ bars remain pretty constant. One of the aspects of this that so interest me is that held fourth (G and D). Of course, I really have no words to talk about it as a *quale*, to talk about its very thisness, other than to use an adjective like 'searing', because it sounds to me rather how that sort of heat feels (and while this might identify it as a potential anaphone, it is hard to insist that the sound *specifies* such heat – it no more than hints at it). What is particular about it is its refusal to move – few if any riffs are so identified by their relative stasis. What does it indicate? For that, I think I have to return to the title.

Example 10.11   Robin Trower: 'Bridge of Sighs'; main guitar riff

It is commonly believed (as judged by various fan postings, or the relevant Wikipedia article) that the title, 'Bridge of Sighs' refers back to its appearance in the Small Faces' 'Itchycoo Park'. There, it is associated with 'shades of green' and 'dreaming spires', suggesting that the reference is not the enclosed bridge in Venice that passes over the Rio di Palazzo, but the enclosed bridge that links two

---

[17]   Robert Fripp, Sleevenote to Robin Trower, *Bridge of Sighs* (Beat Goes On, 1974).

parts of Hertford College in Oxford.[18] No particular bridge seems to be referenced by Trower's track, however. It is a drawn-out blues with very limited lyrics. The persona spends what feels like an eternity crossing this bridge, an eternity that is perhaps referenced by the extremely slow pace of the track. There is bitterness and despair here. Neither the sun nor the moon are portrayed as acting as they ought (as they do in everyday experience), while 'the gods look down in anger' and a 'cold wind blows'. This despair is appropriate to the common assumption that condemned prisoners in Venice passed over the bridge prior to their execution, this being their last glimpse of the outside. While this may be merely myth, the (architecturally far more minimal) Bridge of Sighs in Chester does seem to have served that function. Anyhow, in a case such as this it is what people believe to be true that seems important, and such a denotation would at least make some sense of the descriptions of an unnamed something as 'so unforgiving' in the chorus. Over the riff prior to each of the (two) verses, can be heard what sounds like the boss of the cymbal being struck, fairly randomly, and the pitch of this then being manipulated (generally downwards) – an eerie sound indeed, specifying immense space through a high degree of reverb. At 2'30" in the track, that is, a third of the way through the second verse, this sound gives way to the sound of a whistling wind, fast-moving and pretty constant. During the playout (nearly 2' of this 5'02" track), we can hear both sounds beneath a new repeated riff (Example 10.12) together with a circling little guitar pattern. And then, at 3'56", a listener can just hear a spoken monologue, but without it being sufficiently distinct to make out the words. The extended nature of that playout, over a riff and chord sequence (VI–i) that do not change, also specifies that 'long time crossing'. The wind is so powerful that it does not die until more than 20" into the ensuing track, 'In this place', which could, just, be heard as answering the questions posed by this track. But I take a different route.

Example 10.12   Robin Trower: 'Bridge of Sighs'; guitar exit riff

The overwhelming sense that I take from this track is one of resistance. Leonard Talmy presents a careful analysis of how causation is rendered into the English language, a structure that he calls *force dynamics*.[19] His analysis details some 20 possible relationships between two forces (with differing degrees of strength and change) and a series of nine very clear limitations to such a concept. His interest is linguistic, and is bound up with the role of such words as 'make, 'let', 'have',

---

[18]   There are a number of other bridges, worldwide, that can be identified by the same name.

[19]   Talmy, *Toward a cognitive semantics*, pp. 409–70.

'help', 'stay', 'leave', 'hold', 'keep', and so on, but the reconceptualization of causation as a relationship between two forces is instructive, and of value here. The track presents a number of possible sources of force: the sun, the moon, the tides, gods, 'this poor child'. None of these, however, seem to enter into a causative relationship. The two that seem to me active are the cold wind, which 'blows', and the track's persona, who spends time 'crossing'. Is there a relationship between these two? When a wind 'blows', its activity can only be observed by the movement of objects that are subject to that activity – clouds, leaves, kites, stationary trees, pedestrians, and so on. Whereas clouds and leaves are entirely subject to the movement of the wind, the movement of a kite can be guided to an extent by whoever is flying it (depending on their degree of competence). Trees are necessarily resistant to the movement of the wind, a resistance rooted in their roots, but the flexibility of their branches is necessary to withstand the strength of a forceful wind. Pedestrians have more flexibility still. If the wind is powerful enough to blow you off your feet then presumably you stay indoors. If it is less powerful then you either move with it, or in some way you withstand it. In order to withstand it, you lean into it. Here you will walk *despite* the action of the wind,[20] and this action is one of resistance. But how does this relate to listening to the track?

I have an abiding memory of the band's bassist/vocalist James Dewar singing the song in a television broadcast from around 1974, but dressed in tuareg headgear. This memory is so strong that it has always coloured my understanding of the song. Strange, then, that in trying to unearth that memory, I have been unable to source it – there are YouTube clips aplenty of him singing, but neither there, nor in any extant still, is he so dressed. I am forced to the conclusion that I may well have invented this image, but why should it seem so appropriate that it has stayed with me? I have never been in a desert, but believe it to be potentially assayed by the strongest winds, particularly at night, when such a wind would indeed be 'cold'. Experience of being on a sandy beach in winter is enough to confirm that trudging in sand in the face of a wind requires more effort than trudging across solid land. Then there is the design on the album's original sleeve that, in terms both of its shape and colour, can easily be seen as a pair of stylized sand dunes. On such a beach, even more, one seriously has to walk into the wind to make any headway. One's body leans into the wind. It is that sense of leaning that is so crucial, that *specifies* the action of walking in the wind, and it is that action that, it seems to me, is captured by Trower's opening riff that subsequently is heard through (i.e. despite) the whirling wind. It works thus. Recall looking at someone leaning into the wind, but observing them from the side. The incline is clear – the back foot is to one side (from your vantage point) of the body, which is to the same side of the head. It is that shape that is picked up by Trower's riff, as it grows slowly from the feet (the low E) up to the head (the high G). Such an 'explanation' may be entirely personal but is an example of how such specification may work. Whether or not it is transferable is beside the point. My feel for the track depends on my

---

[20]   Talmy, *Toward a cognitive semantics*, p. 416.

own prior experience and the combination of that experience and my listening. Such a response is open to all, as is the response anyone else may make. What is crucial is the process. In this case, I begin with what is objectively present in the music. I then move to my own response, so ingrained that I am unable to trace its actual development. I then, by means of one or other aspects of the methodology I have introduced, proceed to try to link the two. It is that linking, personal as it may be, that provides the instruction as to *what the track I am listening to teaches me about my own actions and responses*. (Of course, my wandering into this byway regarding deserts and beaches is entirely superfluous to the general experience of resistance to the wind, but it is crucial to my own understanding of my own experience of such resistance, which listening to this track awakens.) It is interesting to note that Opeth's recent cover of this song,[21] aside from being slightly faster (which is to me a crucial change that somehow lessens its power), introduces the wind right at the beginning. I'm yet to work out the consequences, for me, of that realization (let alone of the other, even subtler, differences).

Me to the Future of You

What is the point of those inaudible words at the end of Robin Trower's original? (They are replaced in Opeth's cover by a 'proper' guitar solo.) In the Trower, their presence lasts from 3'56" to 4'54", the exact moment the guitar is cut dead. It sounds from their timbre as if the words issue from a single voice, speaking from three distinct positions – near left, near right and dead centre. (It is therefore possible to hear it as a three-way conversation.) The voice appears to be in a personal space – there is no sense of projection such as would be expected of greater distance, and the tone appears to be conversational, although because the level is very low, it is impossible to hear any intakes of breath, any smacking of the lips or equivalent. The level is clearly lower than that of any other sound-source in the track (expect, possibly, that of the wind, but of course this has very different characteristics – unchanging continuity, for one thing). Were nothing else going on, their enunciation carries the sense that the conversation would be untangled – therefore what is happening is that the 'conversation' is masked by the instruments, purpose unknown.

By observing similar occasions in other tracks we may come to understand the possible force of such masking. At 11'30" of King Crimson's 'Larks' tongues in aspic, part one', we hear the return of an extended violin passage that had originally appeared at 3', bridging the gap between the track's atmospheric opening and its

---

[21]   There is much worthwhile work to be done on tracks like this that cross generations, where front rank contemporary musicians take on difficult, front rank music by musicians of earlier generations. 34 years divide these two. A comparison of King Crimson's 'Larks tongues in aspic, part II' (1973) with Dream Theater's recent cover (2009) would be equally valuable.

first large climax. On its return at 11'30", however, it is accompanied by a female voice speaking. Whereas the band appears to be in a social space (this is hard to determine since the track has no persona as such, although the violin effectively approaches this role because of its prominence), the voice appears more distant. As the music rises in pitch (generating tension within this context), her voice appears to become more and more animated. At 12'06", the violin retrieves its opening idea (but now one octave higher) and the female voice is replaced by a male voice, equally indistinguishable, but in a subtly different acoustic (its reverberation quality seems deeper). As the track reaches its final climax at 12'27", the voice becomes ever more agitated, and louder, but still its words are indistinct. The function here appears to be to increase the level of tension of the track (as we have already heard this violin music, it intensifies the increasing tension heard at its first occurrence), since it seems hard to hear speech without trying to decode it. That difficulty is precisely what is specified by the spoken voices in this track.

The voices that appear in XTC's 'There is no language in our lungs' work rather differently. They first appear at 2'45" during a break between verses – various voices, sounding as if taken from other media (perhaps film or radio) and situated at mid-left and mid-right of the soundbox, as if taking part in a multi-voice conversation – and return for the last 20" under the cymbal coda. They are far back in the mix, but it is perhaps possible to pick out the odd word – the consonants are more audible than in the King Crimson example. The poetics of their use is also more overt, since the topic of the track appears to be the impossibility (from the perspective of the persona) of communicating how we actually feel, through words. This impossibility is then neatly illustrated for us, as listeners.

The indistinct voices in Living Colour's 'Postman' also illustrate the track's topic but rather than addressing us, they seem to illustrate vocalist Corey Glover's persona's state of mind. They seem to move swiftly in and out of focus but are overlapped and distorted so that individual words are not audible. The persona's difficulty is portrayed not only by the aggressive style and use of guitar, but also by his troubled assertiveness, found in lines such as 'chaos and carnage around me, well I hear their shouts and cries'. However, because he's an 'invisible angel' clearly these voices can't be directed at him, and can only really come from him. This strikes me as perhaps an obvious usage of such a sound source.

In Mary Hampton's 'Meanwhile …', we are presented with a large number of voices talking across each other, as if at a party. There is no distortion here, it is simply the sheer numbers that prevent any particular words from coming across. Their level increases toward the end of the track, and yet this does not seem to equate to their coming closer to the listener; there is therefore a disjunction between their sound and their authenticity. The only other element in the track is some elegant eighteenth-century sounding keyboard counterpoint, which one would perhaps not ordinarily expect to be masked by voices (except perhaps at an after-concert party or some similar occasion) and which, being foregrounded, possibly acts as a persona. This unusual juxtaposition therefore raises tension, although it is hard to interpret this increase in terms of the album tracks on either side of this interlude.

In all these cases, then, whatever significance these difficult voices seem to have, it is that very difficulty that is involved in the creation of tension. I can think of only one example where this is clearly not the case, Roxy Music's 'Bitters end', where the evocation of a polite party simply underscores the rather regretful lyric. But there are examples where such voices are not pitted against some sort of persona, as in Knifeworld's 'Me to the future of you', where they actually represent the persona. The style of this track is perhaps best described as angular progressive metal, but with some of the stylistic features of some math metal, particularly the guitar line with its awkward contour and large intervals prevalent in the first couple of minutes or so. The track consists of three verses with a 'solo' after the second, and then a simple playout. The only strange thing about this is that the playout lasts for more than 6' of an 8'40" track (it may be that the best way to hear it is as a playout to the entire album). In the opening verse, a female voice is embedded in the texture, but no sound source intervenes between her persona and the listener. She is not singing with any noticeable effort until the vocal line rises high, when her voice gets harsher, or at least more emotional, as if the words here are meaningful. She is presumably in a social space, but a space just too busy for us to pick up her words. Some syllables are identifiable ('losing you this time' appears twice), but not much is definite. A second verse gives way to an awkward 'solo', consisting of long held guitar notes over spiky arpeggios, somewhat reminiscent of the introduction. After a third verse, the playout begins, presenting a chord sequence that we hear four times prior to an atmospheric, noise-ridden last 40" or so that closes out the album.

During this extended playout, the bass is very far forward in the mix, the drums less so, although there is a very prominent crash cymbal on the left-hand side. A heavily overdriven guitar holds the chordal sequence dead centre, and there is an uncomplicated-sounding synthesizer line that sticks to single pitches of the harmony, but that dramatically leaps a couple of octaves back and forth every beat. The lead female voice is doubled, but without giving it any real bulk, perhaps intensifying its fragility in the context of the band. The third time through this playout sequence, a double-tracked compressed male voice offers a line in counterpoint, with much faster movement (and weakly doubled at the octave), but still with indistinct words. The lyric is clearly meaningful – the line 'like a whip, aah, aah' is audible at one point – but only in giving the impression of a certain anguish. The fourth time through this sequence, the kit gets more and more frantic, as if raising the tension in the most straightforward way possible (the Beatles' 'Helter skelter' comes to mind). No subtlety here. I think it is about time I spoke about that chord sequence I've been referring to. Example 10.13 presents a four-voice analysis.

It is a curious sequence, of course, consisting of perfectly understandable chords but without any real underlying sense of direction. It starts suggesting a tonic of E, shifts semitonally from vi after four bars to suggest C, and then another

Example 10.13   Knifeworld: 'Me to the future of you'; closing sequence

semitonal shift after four bars suggests B♭, after which the movement back to E sounds curiously light-headed. Throughout, words are indistinct. The move to B♭ is accompanied by words that sound like 'beautiful' and 'angel', implying a serenity that belies the energy of the band. That is matched by a couple of magical moves, the hinted aeolian VI–VIId–i of the fifth bar, and the implied IV–Vd–Ib of bars 9–10. I say implied, because of course the bass is in root position; but there is a very prominent E♭–D motion in the lowest upper (human) voice that, because of its timbre, carries through the texture. The very final (male) words, which one might presume to be important, sound something like 'foiled again', 'called again', 'told again', 'sold again' or 'unfold again'. Both the indistinct words, and the chord sequence that doesn't make orthodox sense, imply a meaningfulness without meaning, and this incredible experience is matched by the track's exhausting play of textures. I am reminded of that strange experience of seeing people, almost certainly at some distance, engaged in an activity clearly purposive to them, but without being able to make out what that purpose is. It's akin to a certain feeling of awe, a recognition that one is in the presence of *meaningfulness* rather than of identifiable *meaning*.

I've just read this short passage through. The outcome is rather disappointing, perhaps, as an evocation of the feeling the track produces. I am reminded of my own insistence on the importance of communicating a track's meaning, of not being content simply to bask in its meaningfulness and yet, despite my blundering attempts at pinning down its power, that seems to be all I am doing. I suspect this is because of the lack of words to anchor a reading – the persona here is veiled (both because of her embeddedness in the texture and her refusal to *present* herself, through words, for our interpretation). And this makes some sense. I encounter a similar failure to interpret when listening to the strongly inflected Spanish of Marina Rossell's 'Ha llovido' with its almost endless, joyous alliterations (which work whether one understands the language or not), or of Kadril's Flemish in their beautifully measured 'Martelen', although in both cases the homely textures problematize that wonder. A key question here, of course, is whether the issues of interpretation caused by indistinctness of words are acceptable, or whether, because words carry ostensible meaning, that meaning has to be tracked down in order to make the fullest available interpretation. I have, so far, been writing as if the words are unavailable. But they are printed on the CD insert. This does not help a great deal, since while they are highly allusive, they simply circumscribe a kind of wonder that escapes being pinned down. This is intensified by their indistinctness, which is clearly not accidental, because it results from decisions made by the musicians in the act of putting together the recording. I guess one simply makes the best of what results and, if that is meaningfulness in the absence of meaning, then so be it.[22]

I suspect, despite all this, that it is the power of Knifeworld's harmonic sequence that makes the result palatable, that unusual combination of very usual harmonies. It is worth dwelling on a few similarly affective and effective patterns. The first is a track I have already talked about, in Chapter 4, the Feeling's 'Blue Piccadilly'. The key sequence underpins the entire track and is sketched in Example 10.14.

Example 10.14   The Feeling: 'Blue Piccadilly'; harmonic pattern

It consists of three elements. The initial four-chord loop forms the verse, then a six-chord open period forms the pre-chorus, implying a resolution to C at the start of the chorus. However, this is side-stepped, producing a sequence of three chords transposed from IV to V to iv, returning to end on V. From here, the track moves in two different directions at different times. It moves back to the verse, without having stated the I towards which the track might be felt as leading. It also moves back to the beginning of the chorus in an extended loop (effectively IV–V–vi–V– etc.). This is made clear at 3'24" where we have a 30" halt on an alternating V–IV motion, swinging between the last and first chords of the loop, as if this is a moment of indecision. Finally the chorus get underway again (as if the indecision has finally been resolved), only finally winding down at 4'48", where we hear for the first and only time an unambiguous chord I, and the track can end. One of the reasons for the track's interest, aside from its intoxicating sequence, is the combination of its narrative, the protagonist's proxemic positioning, and the soundbox. The initial, declarative, lines are presented with a voice very close to the listener, but it is not conventionally intimate, since the subject matter is not, at this point, interpersonal. A piano is just off to one side, simply outlining the block harmonies; a second voice, much compressed and deeper in the mix, echoes the

---

22   Terry Eagleton is rather good on this question, as on so many others. See Terry Eagleton, *The meaning of life: a very short introduction* (Oxford, 2007), pp. 44ff.

description of why '*he* gave it all', before coming in time with the last line of the section. The verse proper is marked by an offbeat ride cymbal to the left of singer Dan Gillespie Sells, matching the piano on the right, and initially by a regularity in the vocal line, a regularity that indicates a step away from the free tempo of the introduction. The protagonist's relationship with 'her' is only very briefly sketched – he begins to list for us things that he did for her, and refers to her ability to 'make' him do things that others could not (specifically, to 'run'). She clearly has some sort of hold over him. A second verse is texturally richer, as befits the PATH schema that is activated by the tortuous harmonic progress. An arpeggiating guitar adds textural density, and rhythmic motion, to the harmonic scheme, while the bass and kit are also present. All are pretty central in the mix, although there is width to the ensemble, as they unite behind Sells. His tentative declaration of love ('I think that I love ya') is accompanied by smooth upper vocal lines, a generic device common since the 1960s, betokening a solidarity we are almost invited to feel. The thick texture vanishes at 3'24", a point I have already marked, while the chorus fails to conclude, on the line 'I think I'll go home'. From this it becomes clear that the protagonist has not been at home, but is presumably on the train heading north from Leicester Square (12 stops away from Bounds Green where Sells himself once lived – the album is entitled *Twelve stops and home*). Since neither chord in the IV–V motion is in root position, they still promise some other finish, as Sells sings the album's title, answered by 'there is no better friend'. His addressee is unresolved at this point, although one could hear the friend either as the underground train (which takes him home), or even as the (comforting) pub to which the action will move in a moment.[23] The 'why are you here again?' sung by the backing voices is presumably asking why Sells is not, preferably, at home. A final thinning of the texture at 3'53" (piano alone, low and to the right) leads to the big finale at 3'57", but the backing singers have receded from private to social space – a clinking of glasses at 3'52" (the first intrusion into the track of a diegetic sound-source) eases their move to that of a large pub chorus. The lilting waltz tempo, with strong drum on the second beat and bass on the final shuffled upbeat, has now taken over the mood of the song and created one of a wordless 'singalong' into which it is hard not to be drawn. Sells re-enters at the end of the chorus with 'you take me down', this time presumably addressing his mode of transport rather than his friend. A final time through this same pattern his voice is replaced by the ringing guitar arpeggio, with the location having moved entirely to the pub (identified by the banging of glasses and calls of 'time's up'). We then finally achieve the root position tonic and the goal of the PATH is achieved, that achievement signalled in part by the kit's ecstatic hemiola at 4'32". I shall return to this memorable track at the conclusion to this chapter.

Example 10.15 sketches the opening to Genesis' 'Watcher of the skies', a comparably rich sequence. I simply want to draw attention to its succession of perfectly ordinary harmonies and gradual thinning of texture (which is appropriate

---

23 My thanks to an unnamed reader for these plausible suggestions.

to the negative tone of the lyrics) but its constant shifting of 'tonic' – initially implying F♯ (*1) without stating it, it moves towards A♭ (*2) before cadencing successively in C (*3) and b (*4). It then finally seems to settle on g♯ (*5), moving upward by step in confirmation, but then downward by step as any sense of tonic dissipates, before without preparation, the opening F♯ is suggestion reasserted (eventually, as the rest of the band enter, F♯ is confirmed). Not only does this set the tone for the track. but also for the entire album.

Example 10.15   Genesis: 'Watcher of the skies'; opening sequence

Example 10.16 sketches in four voices the harmonic sequence that, with the exception of a central bridge, underlies the entirety of George Harrison's 'Beware of darkness'. It seems equally unorthodox, in that each part of the sequence is perfectly unproblematic. The whole, however, is rather convoluted. G is a tonic in that it both begins and ends the sequence proper, but it is quitted and reached chromatically (to g♯ and from B, via a brief A). The remainder of the sequence then coalesces around it furthest neighbour, c♯. One can easily read this metaphorically, as representing 'you', as the song's addressee, and the darkness, or sadness or maya (or mires), you are urged to avoid at all costs (and this 'message' develops directly from Harrison's Hindu faith). But that is hardly satisfactory, for these two 'centres' are presented successively, whereas you encounter that darkness simultaneously. Rather it is the precariousness of that sequence that so aptly captures the ease with which one falls into darkness, or sadness, and so on.

The sequence in Example 10.17, Steve Hackett's 'Shadow of the hierophant', is another closing sequence, repeated endlessly (and extending to more than 11' in one recording). Its very ponderousness serves to convey a dark atmosphere, intensified when it just refuses to finish. Again, it both suggests and avoids confirmation of firm tonics – it moves from f♯ to b almost diatonically (the switch between G♯ and G being crucial) over the course of eight bars, suggesting a further eight to complete a return. However, the 'second half' returns to bar 5, twice moves chromatically (bars 10–11, 13–14) and then returns almost unprepared to the

Example 10.16   George Harrison: 'Beware of darkness'; basic sequence

Example 10.17   Steve Hackett: 'Shadow of the hierophant'; closing sequence

beginning of the sequence. It seems that no matter how many times this is heard, the effect of the strange foreshortening of the second half never quite convinces, which is surely the point. Also notable here is the prominent avoidance of root position chords in two places (bars 7 and 14, strangely enough), an aesthetic that was crucial in the Knifeworld track. Indeed, I think that some of the most powerful such sequences gain their effectiveness precisely because of the bass's insistence on avoiding the root.

Both my final two examples of harmonic sequences come from Van der Graaf Generator. They do not work quite as some of the above: the sequence from 'Pilgrims' (Example 10.18) underlies the chorus, while that for 'Childlike faith' (Example 10.19) underpins the final stanzas of a very complex song. Both songs take as their subject indomitable persistence in the face of despair, so suited it seems to sequences where the bass simply refuses the easy path of sticking on root positions. The bass shown at the end of Example 10.18 (in the last four bars) only actually appears right at the end of the track, but its persistence is perfectly positioned against the harmonic sequence. 'Childlike faith in childhood's end' envisions the

Example 10.18   Van der Graaf Generator: 'Pilgrims'; chorus sequence

Example 10.19   Van der Graaf Generator: 'Childlike faith in childhood's end';
                 closing sequence

end of ordinary humanity in the real beginning of the race's superseders. Less
the übermensch of Nietzsche via David Bowie, this is more the simple world-
weariness of sci-fi; while the plot is a fleshed-out version of that of 'Watcher of the
skies', it seems to have migrated here from Arthur C. Clarke's novel with a similar
name.[24] Whether a listener considers its message as utopian or as dystopic depends
on the point from which it is viewed, perhaps on whether the plot or the music

---

[24]   Arthur C. Clarke: *Childhood's end* (London, 1956).

dominates for each listener. It ends with Peter Hammill's hysterical declaration that 'in the death of mere humans, life shall start', delivered nonetheless from a human perspective. What, to me, makes these last two examples so extraordinary is that their sense (and particularly that of 'Childlike faith') is so dire, and yet the sequence that underpins them is so forcefully, richly, diatonic. No doubts here about key centre, even if those centres are not exactly points of rest. I suspect the best reading of these concerns the relationship of diatonicism (no notes that do not 'belong') to the directness of motive of the persona, who is not to be swayed in whatever declaration he makes. (The simplicity of Example 10.19, on paper, only demonstrates how crucial is the force of Hammill's actual delivery.)

It is worth reiterating, I think, the basis for such a reading, since it is so attractive (and almost inevitable) a move to make. Such a reading implies a congruence of relationship between real life and what happens in the world of the track, a congruence I discussed in Chapter 8 in terms of cross-domain mapping. Here, I am reading the harmonic world of these two sequences as specifying directness, lack of contamination, or contact with disruptive elements, and the world particularly of the persona in 'Childlike faith' as one in which uncertainty is banished, and in finding the two congruent, suspect that they amplify 'each other's' meaning. What unites all these varied sequences is their relative interminability; they are sequences in which to get lost, and where the sense of being lost is comfortable because the sequence will repeat. 'Getting lost' in such a sequence is made easier if the sequence's tonality and voice-leading are unconventional. One important lesson to learn from them is of course the limitations of the methodological perspective I put forward in Chapter 3. There is little that is periodic about them ('Childlike faith' perhaps excepted) and, though they consist of repeating patterns, they are a long way away from the triadic loops to which I counterposed periodic structures. They work almost by trial and error, perhaps, as a songwriter may feel his or her way from one chord to another to see whether the combination works, trying to avoid the influence of memory. They are rare, which is why the methodology is still effective (as in all domains, it represents a starting-point), but demonstrate that the unusual always has to remain a possibility at the corner of one's ear, as it were.

Teenage Dirtbag

Harmonic diversion over: the other particularly effective feature of 'Me to the fortune of you', which I largely passed over, is its noisy textural world. Such textures have been part of the possibilities of popular song since the punk era, and are often associated with genres of metal (although much metal aims at textural clarity, despite its extreme volumes and liking for distorted individual timbres). An altogether less hectic production of a noisy soundbox comes with the work of a band like Garbage, particularly in the arresting opening track of their debut album, 'Supervixen'. The band's debt to Nirvana and, further back, the Pixies, is made clear by the alternation of loud, brash pre-choruses and choruses with more restrained verses. Among their timbral resources we can hear Shirley Manson's persona, together with at least two separate backing vocal lines, a prominent bass, a kit that sounds as if it has added echo at the rate of a semiquaver (although possibly this is simply highly energetic drumming), an overdriven guitar holding the harmonic filler (and, I suspect, a rather cleaner sounding guitar doing the same), together with a solo guitar holding the dominant riff, and at least three separate solo lines in the section at 2'16". In the verses, although everybody plays down, the textures are still rich: in addition to voice, bass and kit there is the 'cleaner' harmonic filler guitar, a solo line in call and response mode with the voice, and some rich synthesizer timbres. Throughout, the textures seem to be driven by twin aims: first, a sense of confusion, of a great deal of busy playing going on; but second, placement within the soundbox such that, although the scene width is both wide and deep, everything is identifiable on subsequent listenings. We have a combination, then, of both waywardness and dangerous precision.

I suspect, though, that the track's most striking gesture is the reiterated swallowing up of everything into silence. The track seems to take a common theme, that of control in the face of obsession. Shirley Manson voices her perception of her own power, possibly over an individual – at least, something that can be said to have a 'mouth' – determining what s/he/it can or cannot do in the course of their interaction. And she demonstrates that power most convincingly, by turning on and off the environment in which she is perceived. Note the way the powerful attack of bass, guitars and kit is sucked away, almost like air escaping a dying planet. But, once her control is demonstrated in all its nakedness – the constant demand at the end to 'bow down to me' – the full texture gradually creeps back in. Since it is we as listeners who are potentially placed in the position of obsessing, here, is this not an image of sexual teasing? I'm suggesting, then, that the silence does not communicate in its own right, but acts as a signal of the persona's control, and it is that control that is significant.

Momentary silences are not, of course, unusual. The first track on the Arctic Monkey's debut album provides something of a catalogue of them, whether they involve all or just part of the band. An indication of what is to come might be heard in the absence of the bass through most of the first verse. Beneath the break between first and second verses, the guitar is left alone for half a bar every two bars, to throw it into relief (I'll call this 'a'). The second verse effectively repeats the first but now two guitars, separated in the soundbox, appear heterophonically to throw chords between each other (from 1'01" – 'b'), each lapsing into silence as the other strikes a chord. At 1'28", the upbeat to the chorus leaves Alex Turner alone ('c'), making the entry of the chorus more striking. The final phase of the chorus, from 1'42", is marked by offbeat stop time ('d') across the whole band, beneath Turner's vocal. All four of these ideas repeat, in turn, but with some slight variation. Idea 'a' now dies into total silence, leading into a repeat of 'b' but now with strong syncopation, sounding (until the whole band enters) as if the track has somehow gone wrong. Idea 'c' repeats, but now accompanied by the kit, as does idea 'd'. Two of these ideas, then ('a' and 'b') serve to throw aspects of the texture into relief, providing a means of focus for the listener, while the other two are means of increasing the track's momentum.

The moments of total silence in 'Supervixen' comprise a very rare gesture. It could be heard as the texture vacating its place (a negative absence), or as the silence intruding (a positive erasure). I suspect the latter is closer to the effect created. In Super Furry Animals' 'Mountain people', the melodic line dips out of the texture momentarily as, in playing the part of these mountain people, the band erects small sonic barriers between themselves and an unspecified but dominant 'they', with their 'hand-me down culture', barriers that occupy the spaces between their snatched lyrics. The mountain people's presence remains audible, however, spilling over into those gaps. The function of these gaps is very different to those of 'Supervixen' though – it is evasion that the 'mountain people' are after, and perhaps because they leave their trace, they finally succumb to 'nets and cages' as the track's characteristic three quaver-quaver-rest rhythm, which symbolizes them, is overwhelmed.

I want to return for a moment to what I identified as idea 'c' in the Arctic Monkeys' track. Bars are grouped pretty regularly throughout the track, in 4s and then 8s. But at that moment, as the chorus is about to enter and the syllabic emphasis changes (as shown in Examples 10.20 and 10.21), we find an extra bar.

Example 10.20   Arctic Monkeys: 'The view from the afternoon'; opening melodic
                 phrase

Example 10.20 shows that in the verse the downbeat tends to coincide with a line's opening stress (it may occur slightly later, or slightly earlier, but the emphasis is on the beginning of the line). For the chorus, however, this changes, and the emphasis moves to the end of the line.

Example 10.21   Arctic Monkeys: 'The view from the afternoon'; opening chorus
                 phrase

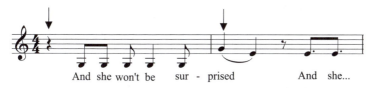

This is effected by the addition of an extra bar. Immediately prior to what is transcribed in Example 10.21, we have had an 8-bar group, such that the beginning of the example may appear to mark the beginning of the next group. However, the absence of the band at this point, and their re-entry one bar later (the second bar of the example) demonstrates that this point (on the syllable '-prised') is the real beginning of the next group. (In Chapter 3 I drew attention to a similar shift in the Casuals' 'Jesamine').

Such grouping extensions are not at all unusual, but sometimes their effect is far more marked than in this example: I have in particular mind the one-bar extension to the chorus in 'Teenage dirtbag', the one-off hit by Wheatus. In fact, both verse and chorus are interesting from a grouping point of view. The verse (beginning at 14') starts with one bar, which is slightly altered to provide the second bar of a 2-bar phrase. This is immediately repeated. This is followed by a 1-bar phrase whose melodic contour is immediately repeated (approximately a third below), and then by a 2-bar phrase that is immediately repeated. The verse, then, is 10 bars long, but I think it supports two alternative readings. The first follows the patterns of repetitions as I have given them, thus: 2 + 2; 1 + 1; 2 + 2. The second observes how clearly the opening 8 bars recall, in compressed form, the AABA of 32-bar song form, where the 'B' consists of the two 1-bar phrases. In this hearing, the last two bars are an extension of the 8-bar verse, raising the level of expectation for the chorus. This hearing, then, represents the verse as 2 + 2; 1 + 1 + 2; (+2).

It is the chorus, though, that is particularly interesting. If you follow the guitar part, you'll hear a 2-bar pattern repeated four times, together with an extra half-bar. I have sketched the repeating pattern as Example 10.22. I don't think there's a realistic alternative to hearing it this way.

Example 10.22   Wheatus: 'Teenage dirtbag'; guitar chorus pattern

The opening power chord follows, as I, from the V of the end of the verse; the texture changes at exactly this point (in a Nirvana-esque switch from gentle verse to powerful chorus), while the end of the pattern is marked by an increase of density on the c♯ and g♯ (vi and iii) chords. There are a number of reasons to hear this increase as a localized point of closure. For one, it acts as an episodic marker, in the same way that a drummer will frequently fill the space during an upbeat, increasing the felt emphasis on the ensuing downbeat. A similar thing happens in a lot of Western concert music, where the approach to a cadence (a point of local closure) is marked by an increase of density, that is, an increase in the rate of harmonic motion. And we experience similar increases of density of action in everyday life, whether it is the momentary acceleration to breast the tape in a middle-distance race, the larger breath one takes as one is about to dive into water, or the slight increase of adrenalin as one puts one's foot down on the accelerator in order to enter a roundabout ahead of a driver entering from your right. These are all local increases of density which mark the closure of one phase of activity and the beginning of another.[25] The fourth 2-bar group would thus be heard as in Example 10.23.

Example 10.23   Wheatus: 'Teenage dirtbag'; guitar chorus pattern, final occurrence

So far, so good. The lyrics, however, suggest an entirely different reading. The first verse is an interior monologue in which the persona positions himself as protagonist in respect to 'Noelle' who acts as his antagonist. In the chorus, he simultaneously bemoans and exults in his outsider status. In terms of setting, it is rather reminiscent of the Shangri-Las' 'Leader of the pack', brought 40 years up to date. Each melodic line of the verse is marked by a short, 1-quaver upbeat. At first hearing, that pattern continues into the chorus, so that we hear Example 10.24.

Example 10.24   Wheatus: 'Teenage dirtbag'; opening of chorus

The emphasis, however, seems all wrong. Surely, the persona is trying to get across *what* his protagonist is, rather than *who* it is that fulfils a description ('teenage dirtbag') that the track has yet to give us. It is for this reason, principally, that I hear the link from the verse into the chorus as in Example 10.25, with the emphasis on '*teen*-age' rather than on '*I'm* just a'. The guitar, then, suggests an additional half-bar at the end of the chorus, while the melody/lyrics suggest an extra half-bar at the beginning of the chorus. How might we read this disparity? One way will come as no surprise by now. By reading the guitar as the protagonist's external

---

[25]   I feel this is likely to be a very common experience and, thus, should be describable via an image schema, although nothing in the relevant literature quite captures this experience. It is, I suspect, a particular class of PATH schema, combined with the SCALE schema, since that provides a clear recognition of stages.

environment (a high school in which he seems not to fit) via cross-domain mapping, the confusion between the guitar and the persona itself conveys that failure to fit.

Example 10.25   Wheatus: 'Teenage dirtbag'; link from verse into chorus

Consideration of the track's frame semantics reveals the highly deft way the narrative setting is handled. The first verse is about 'Noelle' who never notices the 'teenage dirtbag'. The high school setting is conveyed by the simple line 'got gym class in half an hour' which interrupts his mooning. The second verse focuses on her boyfriend, a 'dick [who] brings a gun to school'. Again, this odd line interspersed with the protagonist's recounting of his feelings is filled in with numerous mental images brought from shows on American media (for me, I think everything from *Malcolm in the Middle* through *High School Musical* to episodes of *CSI*). I think the setting is crucial in enabling a listener to position the realm of the protagonist's 'failure' – a realm in which it is possibly cool to fail, and by no means prevents his 'getting the girl'. In the third verse, he cannot believe she's 'walking over to me', which leads to the transformative final chorus, in which 'she' *becomes* the protagonist, inviting him to an Iron Maiden concert (whereas in previous verses he's only 'dreamt' about her accompanying him). The only substantial marker of this transformation is the paired down texture of the final chorus, in which vocalist Brendan Brown voices Noelle.

Pretty Woman

Such a transformation is comparatively rare in popular song. Perhaps one of the best-known examples is Roy Orbison's 'Oh pretty woman' and a comparison would seem to be instructive. This song consists, essentially, of three verses and an extended bridge. In the first verse, the protagonist observes the 'pretty woman' in the street. In the second he appears to engage her in interaction. The ensuing bridge, however, seems to take place outside the narrative of the song, for he returns to an internal monologue imagining such an encounter and its successful outcome. In the third verse, the protagonist recognizes that his approach has been unsuccessful until, suddenly, he realizes that she is 'walking back to me'. The key musical elements are perhaps threefold: the I–vi–IV–V sequence that underpins the verses and the second part of the bridge; the vi-ii-V-I sequence that underpins the first half of the bridge, and the song's hook, a 12-string guitar arpeggiation of V that appears in two versions (Examples 10.26 and 10.27).

Example 10.26   Roy Orbison: 'Oh pretty woman'; guitar hook (i)

Example 10.27   Roy Orbison: 'Oh pretty woman'; guitar hook (ii)

At the song's opening, it appears as in Example 10.26. It is as if the song is building up momentum prior to launch – the drummer simply attacks snare and kick drums on the beat. This shifts into Example 10.27, where the blatant flattened seventh (D) can be understood as part of either a blues scale on the tonic, or a dominant preparation. It turns out to be the latter, as the song moves into A for the first verse. I–vi–I–vi–IV takes us to V and a return of this introduction, preparing for the second verse. The opening of the bridge shifts unceremoniously to ii in C. This change of key marks the removal of this section from the narrative course of the song, and after circling around the cycle of fifths, it shifts smoothly back to A for two hearings of the I–vi–IV–V sequence, dwelling on the final V as does every other section of the song. It is because the melody line here is different to that of the verse that I feel this part (from 1'36'') belongs as part of the bridge.

The song's proportions seem somewhat unusual. 2'56'' is made up as detailed in Table 10.1 (to the nearest second).

Table 10.1   Roy Orbison: 'Oh pretty woman'; proportions

Intro	Verse 1	Break	Verse 2	Break	Bridge	Break	Verse 3	Final 'break'
15''	18''	8''	18''	8''	42''	8''	32''	27''
8.5%	10.2%	4.7%	10.2%	4.7%	23.7%	4.7%	18.1%	15.3%

The main part of the action, where the protagonist sees and then interacts with 'pretty woman' takes up merely the first third of the track. The bridge, whose role in the narrative is problematic as I have suggested, takes up almost a quarter of the track, while the final part of the action, where the protagonist accepts with resignation his failure to attract her, and then his surprise as she turns back towards him, takes about the last quarter of the track. I suspect that the re-launch of the track's introduction at 2'29", announced by the phrase 'there'll be tomorrow night – but wait!' is crucial in creating the effectiveness with which her apparent change of mind is conveyed. That initial hearing of the hook (Example 10.26) was strongly associated with the song getting into gear, prior to the entry of the lyrics, and it is here re-employed to reclaim that 'gearing up' in the service of his wonder at her about turn.

There are some strange groupings in 'Oh pretty woman', and the piano is instructive in leading us through them. First, of course, there is the opening riff, which shifts from ⅜ to ¼ as I have suggested. Once it becomes Example 10.27, we hear four unambiguous bars of introduction and at this point the opening ⅜ may seem simply a momentary aberration. The verse, though, fails to maintain this regularity. Table 10.2 maps the 18" of the verse.

Table 10.2   Roy Orbison: 'Oh pretty woman'; pacing of the verse

Chord	I	vi	I	vi	IV	V
Beats	4	4	4	4	4 + 2	4 + 4 + 4 + 4

During a simple 4-beat bar, the piano regularly keeps to the following reverse habanera rhythm (Example 10.28).

Example 10.28   Roy Orbison: 'Oh pretty woman'; characteristic piano rhythm

During the extra half-bar of chord IV, it plays on the offbeat, returning to the above pattern for chord V, thereby confirming the grouping. Because this verse is then followed by a further 16 beats of 'break', that means that from the start of the verse, we hear 22 beats of changing chords, followed by 32 beats of V. The immense anticipation this builds up will need dissipating somewhere. The second verse only intensifies the issue, while the bridge sidesteps, as I have noted above. The piano confirms this sidestep by breaking into a regular arpeggio pattern, rather than playing its offbeat chords. The third verse begins in the same way, but from the arrival of V at the end of the verse, we have a total of 100 beats, before the final resolution onto chord I. That represents fully a quarter of the song spent on that V, ever growing in intensity, with the kit retreating to its opening stop-time attacks. That final resolution is insufficient to dissipate the immense tension built up, and so it is as if Orbison's protagonist's exhilaration at seeing her returning to him spills over, cannot be contained by the track, but continues into the silence that follows it. It is this, I think, that finally conveys that immense relief.

The additional half-bars and irregular groupings that I have noted in 'Oh pretty woman' might almost be regarded as common practice in some styles – they certainly seem to be a feature of Orbison's idiolect (I have in mind 'Blue bayou', 'Cryin'' and the extraordinary 'It's over' and 'Only the lonely' for instance). Frequently they will occur in songs that otherwise seem so unproblematic and straightforward. The Beatles' 'We can work it out' is one such, but here the irregularities seem to arise directly from the lyrics. Sometimes, the virtues of what we do hear can best be judged by pitting them against a 'normalized' version. That is what I present in Examples 10.29 and 10.30 – first two possible 'normalized' versions of the first half-verse of the track (creating regular 4-bar phrases), followed by the Beatles' actual version.

Example 10.29   Beatles: 'We can work it out'; first verse 'normalized'

Example 10.30   Beatles: 'We can work it out'; first verse actual

It would seem to me that Example 10.30 is so much better than either of the 4-bar versions because it retains a generally regular pacing of syllables – with the exception of the very last syllable, we three times perceive a pattern of faster movement slowing, while the most important word ('my', opposed to 'your' in the next half-verse) is the first hearing of the highest pitch. Both versions of Example 10.29 fail to keep 'my way' distinct in terms of length. In addition, the poetic quality of having to talk 'till I can't go on' seems to be beautifully portrayed by a line in which syllables are squashed together, as opposed to one in which they are allowed to trip out of the mouth at an agreeable pace.

The other key metrical aspect of 'We can work it out' has already been raised, in Chapter 3, but it bears re-investigation here. The first three bars are notable for the syncopated rhythm in the second half, anticipating both the fourth beat and the ensuing downbeat. The repetitions of this pattern secure its identity as 'normal' for the context of the bridge (see Example 10.31).

Example 10.31   Beatles: 'We can work it out'; bridge melody

Its absence in the second half of the bridge is then very noticeable. It is replaced by triplets as shown. The effect of these triplets is to 'smooth out' the earlier line, enabling an interpretation whereby the triplets demonstrate the (less ruffled) situation that would follow an absence of fussing and fighting. If it is true, as many have supposed, that the songwriting of the Beatles can be held to be superior to that of so many other songwriters, then that may be because we find appealing such clever expressions of lyric detail in music. I do not think anyone has ever seriously addressed the question from this perspective (and indeed, it would be a mammoth task not only to analyse their oeuvre from this hermeneutic perspective, but to analyse a sufficiently large number of other songs in order to demonstrate a difference), but I think it is a hypothesis well worth pursuing.

Focus

When I focused on triplet shifts in Chapter 3, I ignored one of the most impressive instances, and I want to address it now, in order to compare the function of the triplets with that of 'We can work it out'. I have in mind Genesis' 'Your own special way'. The track comes from their post-Gabriel period when Genesis were rediscovering the simplicity of conventional song structures. This track consists of three verses/choruses, with a short keyboard break after the second. Example 10.32 summarizes the end of the first verse and the passage into the chorus (beginning at 1'12"). The verse is in a regular § which suits the rather intimate, gentle song they create. In the verse, the melody is accompanied only by 12-string guitar and a keyboard line, so that the pace of the beat remains implicit. At the end of the verse the relationship of the quaver to the beat changes. The guitar stops on the first beat of the fourth bar of the excerpt, while the keyboard dies away. When the whole band enters on the downbeat C chord, the beat has been re-thought. This

Example 10.32   Genesis: 'Your own special way'; from verse into chorus

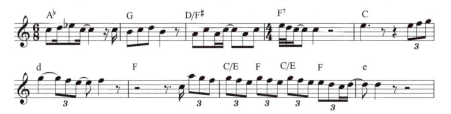

change is simple enough, but then in the chorus, the threefold division of the beat returns, but now as what I have written as triplets. These are of course faster than the quavers of (for instance) the second bar but, matched as they are by the kit, they seem to capture a delicacy of communal nuance, which perhaps illustrates 'your own special way', a way that seems quite out of the ordinary. The recovery of the § at 2'10" (for the second verse) is simply achieved by the kit dropping out, and the 12-string guitar picking up the pace of the quaver.

The hook, which is sung to the song's title, can be seen to be an elaboration of a much simpler structure, sketched in Example 10.33. The compound thirds between melody and bass are a not uncommon occurrence, although they are disguised by surface melodic movement.

Example 10.33   Genesis: 'Your own special way'; structure of hook

Example 10.34   Focus: 'Focus ...'; structure of opening hook

For long I was struck by the audible similarity between this and a far earlier track, the eponymous track by the band Focus. Example 10.34 sketches the structure of the opening hook (transposed from E♭ to aid comparison). The similarity is, however, somewhat illusory as can be seen by looking at the function of the various parts of the hook. Both have that rise from the $\hat{3}$ to $\hat{5}$, followed by a fall to $\hat{2}$ and then a steep rise to $\hat{6}$, after which they fall back towards the tonic (in 'Your own special way', this is only reached after the end of the hook). However, the underlying structure seems quite different, and the bass line is crucial here. In 'Your own special way', $\hat{5}$ (the G) becomes dissonant, falling to $\hat{4}$ (the F). In 'Focus …', the $\hat{5}$ is never dissonant, and $\hat{4}$ is only a step along the way to $\hat{2}$. In 'Focus …', the $\hat{6}$ is dissonant, and the leap sets up momentum used in the following fall, which is arrested at $\hat{3}$ before continuing. In 'Your own special way', the $\hat{6}$ is consonant and simply falls by step coordinated with the bass, and where $\hat{3}$, although emphasized, is simply a step on the fall down to $\hat{2}$.

In the instrumental version of the Focus track, this hook is followed by another (at 1'06''), which is sketched in Example 10.35, again transposed to C. It is clear that, again, movement by compound thirds between melody and bass dominates this passage, in contrast to the contrary motion that directed the first hook. And, just as the first hook was called to mind by the Genesis track, so to this latter hook points back to the hook of a far earlier track.

Example 10.35   Focus: 'Focus (instrumental)'; structure of secondary hook

Example 10.36   Kathy Kirby: 'Secret love'; structure of hook

Example 10.36 sketches the main melody from Kathy Kirby's showstopper 'Secret love'. Again, while the audible similarity is striking, it is achieved with different means. Here, the melody and bass are generally in contrary motion. In addition, the melody can be seen to occupy a chromatic descent from C to G, a motion that is interrupted in 'Focus …' after only three steps (C to B♭). This short chain of melodic references could easily be continued and I suspect that differences between melodic surface and structure would be no less common than

I have identified in this short segment. It is worth noting that each of these three tracks operates closer to the period structure end of the continuum I set up in Chapter 3 – whether the same conclusion could be drawn from melodies at the other end of the continuum is a different matter entirely. It is worth reiterating that the similarities here, while they rest partly on the relationship between melody and bass, are of the same order as those I raised in Chapter 9 that indicate uses of a common fund of material, rather than intertextuality proper.

The Night Watch

Lulu's version of Harry Nilsson's standard 'Without her' represents a different approach again to common material: here, it is the chord sequence. The structure of the opening of (as she sings it) 'Without him' is reproduced in Example 10.37. The expected tonic is avoided – the sequence runs: III'–VI'–ii–V, and it is the successive fifths in the bass that define it. In 'Secret love', the equivalent pattern is vi–II'–V–I. Again, then, a similarity of pattern (here, in the bass) belies a difference of function.

Example 10.37   Lulu: 'Without him'; structure of opening

In both cases, note that there is a single melodic pitch that dominates each harmony, combined with a small number of passing notes. In 'Secret love', however, this passage lasts for 18 syllables, and 18 pitches, and this includes the V repeated as chord v, and the IV that completes the pattern. In 'Without him', the four chords underlie 19 or more syllables (depending on the verse), but only eight pitches. 'Without him' contains many repeated melodic pitches that, rather than creating a line full of passionate outpouring, creates a line in which the persona appears to rest on each pitch, taking stock, before moving on. This also means that the word that appears after a number of repeated pitches, and in each case after a largish downward leap, receives unusual stress: 'I spend the *night* on the chair thinking he'll be there but he *never* comes.' The effect of this is related to Griffiths' notion of verbal space, introduced in Chapter 4.

Although the speed of Lulu's melody is not much greater than that of Kathy Kirby, the effect is of the melody being generally compressed, and relieved by those large leaps that simply emphasize how compressed the line is, by contrast.

This reading is strengthened by observing Lulu's supporting texture. The spaces between her sung lines are taken up by essentially two elements. First, there is Lulu herself, vocalizing with great reverb, perhaps symbolizing her emptiness, although this is not a particularly elegant reading, and there is no other obvious connotation for this. Second, though, there is a fiddle line, playing regular quavers with an almost baroque feel in the way it traverses its melodic compass. This complete filling of melodic space makes for strong support for the sense of limited verbal space in her sung melody, and it gradually impinges on the song, such that the line is sometimes worked contrapuntally with other strings and an oboe. Strangely enough, other versions of this same tune appear to find the same need for incessant movement against the melody. In Herb Alpert's 'Without her', flute and brass tend to echo the melody, or to play long held lines, while a Mexican-style guitar plays fast arpeggios throughout. In the version by Blood Sweat and Tears, the kit is extremely busy except where Al Kooper takes the main verse, when nothing else is going on.

Reading this compressed verbal space ecologically, one would surely note that it specifies time literally being filled, the negation of self-reflection, those moments when the reality of a situation needs to be placed at one remove. Extremes of stress precede such moments, as when a lover dies, perhaps or, as here, when they have vanished never to return. So such textures as these versions present make sense, do not strike the listener as false (although the Italian baroque feel of Lulu and the Mexican feel of Alpert certainly place their respective narratives in very different geographical locations, which will have a bearing on how effective they may seem to be to a particular listener).

Compression of verbal space can be a very effective marker of a protagonist's attitude as portrayed in a song. A very opposite effect is achieved by the Broughtons' 'Waiting for you'. The verse works at between two and four syllables per (slow) beat, which seems pretty normal. The chorus is very different – four syllables stretch across the first six beats, with a further 10 across the remaining 10 beats. Example 10.38 sketches the melody of the chorus, which begins at 2'41", at about 72 bpm.

Example 10.38   Broughtons: 'Waiting for you'; chorus

Edgar Broughton's persona sings of disenchantment with love, over that I–vi–IV–V sequence that sounds so tired at the speed at which they take it. This tiredness, and also his perpetual waiting, are both illustrated by the immense verbal space both in the first bar, and in the first half of the second and third bars. This is not a waiting enjoyed or spent with equanimity, then, but a waiting endured. As such, it represents the opposite pole from that explored in King Crimson's 'The night watch'.

Rembrandt executed the painting known as the 'Night Watch' in the mid seventeenth century.[26] King Crimson's song, with lyrics by Richard Palmer-James and a setting by Robert Fripp with John Wetton, represents an astonishing attempt to understand the scene from the perspective of its actors. In the song's three verses, Wetton's persona first addresses a viewer of the painting, then the subjects in the painting, and finally takes the part of those subjects. The track, which appears on *Starless and bible black*, is a combination of live performance and studio recording. It has four distinct phases. After an improvisatory introduction that introduces the first vocal theme, Wetton (1'25") enters with a handful of lines that briefly describe key aspects of the painting (the shining light, the group of soldiers, and the centuries'-worth of dirt that have accumulated on the painting's surface). The 'song proper' takes from 1'59"–4'18" (two verses, a solo of chilling Frippery, and a final half verse and coda) before the melody of the opening handful of lines returns to round the song off rather abruptly. The section that interests me particularly, from two viewpoints, is what I've called the 'song proper'. During the verses, Wetton's verbal space is at an absolute minimum. The speed is around 132 bpm (fast, then), and the lines are delivered at the speed of two syllables per beat. This only relaxes right at the end of each verse. There is no space for breathing, no space for rounding the tone of his voice, there is simply space to get across these very rich lyrics, with their different perspectives and their rich descriptions. Indeed, I would suggest it is that sense of richness that is the dominant attribute. It took me many listenings to work out exactly what was being sung about, and more re-working my understanding once I had seen the Rembrandt painting. Indeed, I think I constantly put this moment off, preferring to let my mind dwell on individual words: 'creditors', 'guild', 'blunderbuss', 'respectability', 'wife', 'posterity'. 'Understanding', in this song, seems to me more about recognizing the importance of that speed of delivery, in conjunction with its curious harmonic profile (which I shall come to in a moment). While the lyrics suggest that, with the wars over, there is now time to settle back into a preferred mode of existence, the speed of their delivery suggests that things are not quite so easy, and that suggestion is perhaps what lies behind the song's final line, as the 'little men', these 'burghers', as rendered by the artist, 'request you all to understand'.

I said that the curious harmonies are equally important. Beneath the verses, the predominant harmonies are i, iv and v, while VI is also apparent. I, IV and V are the principal triads from which tonal systems are built, and that still applies to the modal harmonic system I outlined in Chapter 3, although triadic modifications are necessary. To hear all three of them in a major context is very common. i–IV–V is not uncommon, and is perhaps best conceived in terms of the ascending 'melodic

---

[26]   Rembrandt's own title was *The Militia Company of Captain Frans Banning Cocq* and, far from being a night-time scene, once the painting was cleaned (very soon after the close of the Second World War), it was seen to depict a daylight procession.

minor' scale (i.e. the natural minor, or aeolian, with sharpened sixth and seventh degrees). I–iv–V can even be encountered, and this is equates to the 'harmonic minor' scale (i.e. natural minor simply with raised seventh). Pretty unusual is i–iv–v, which equates to the descending 'melodic minor' (directly equivalent to the aeolian). It is certainly the case that, for many listeners, preceding a tonic by V appears to strengthen that point of arrival. In 'The night watch', then, that arrival is necessarily weak. Indeed, that weakness extends to the texture, at least of the opening verse, which consists only of what appear to be guitar harmonics (and, a little later, individual pitches with a similarly languid timbre) and minimal bass. Because I, IV and V are so 'normative', the sense of this music is of something accepting a norm, but in turning all the chords to minor, subverting it *from the inside* (rather than openly opposing it with alternative chords). It is this subversion, I think, that creates the possibility of experiencing this music as so intensely sad and that, in combination with the uncertainty suggested by the verbal space, and with the acknowledged failed attempt (to judge by that final line) of Palmer-James to retrieve that experience of the 1640s, explains its extreme effectiveness.

King Crimson are not alone in trying to explore the power of this particular sequence. Much more recently, the band Hard-Fi have made something of a habit of it – it acts almost as an idiolectal feature of their debut album. The opening track, 'Cash machine', bemoans a state of constant penury and it is as if the aeolian mode, and hence the i–iv–v sequence particularly of the chorus, is constantly dragging down any possibility of Richard Archer's persona responding positively, constructively perhaps, to his situation. Even the comparative beauty of the little melismas at the end of the verse only result in a reinforced tonic minor at the beginning of the chorus. And one could search further for key usages: the Electric Light Orchestra, for instance (think only 'Turn to stone' and 'Showdown').

Closure

There would be a number of ways to invent a 'neat' closure to this distended discussion. I had thought of focusing on the banality of the Hard-Fi track's closing repetition of the phrase 'there's a hole in my pocket', with its unmistakeable reminiscence of 'There's a hole in my bucket (dear Liza ...)', to take me back to the banality of the little guitar phrase in Jimi Hendrix's 'If six was nine', and declare the circle closed. But I shall not do that. Instead, I shall simply bring this set of open-ended gestures to a forced conclusion, since there is no natural, logical, nor inevitable end to this chain of links. To close both the chapter and the book, I want to return explicitly to the end of Chapter 8, and the insistence I made there that there is no perspectiveless position from which to make an interpretation. And it will surely be clear to you that my perspective in this chapter has been, necessarily, that of myself as a listener. I have not raised the possibility of taking on an imaginary perspective simply because I both doubt that it is possible to do so effectively (and consistently), and also because to attempt to do so would cloud the issue too far. So, I want to do a little more to specify what that perspective is (in order to enable you to bear this in mind when returning to any portion of this tome), and I shall do so by returning to the Feeling's 'Blue Piccadilly', which I discussed particularly in terms of harmony earlier in this chapter. I could focus on any particular track and develop the same general argument, but this particular track brings certain points into relief.

You will recall that I identified the track's persona by naming him 'Dan Gillespie Sells', and indeed, throughout the book I have identified a persona with the name of that persona's performer, while maintaining that the two are distinct. Who, though, is this 'Dan Gillespie Sells' that I construct? Years of indoctrination by the texts of critical theory make me comfortable with, and almost unaware of, the consequences (the 'so what?') of such a question, but a strict ecological approach would, I suspect, rule such a question out of court.[27] How we act, according to an ecological position, is to encounter the invariants of an environment that already has its own topography, its own morphology; we do not construct internal models of the world we encounter and respond vicariously to that world by interpreting those models (this latter description might be held to characterize a more frequently held belief, at least in academic circles). And yet, in this case, I suspect something more is given. I have not encountered Dan Gillespie Sells, the flesh-and-blood human being, but I have encountered a recorded voice to which that name can conveniently be given (provided I recognize that the name identifies a *persona* rather than an actual *performer*). But, as Ricoeur[28] tells me, the text cannot itself be so construed as to fill in any gaps that my interpretation of it encounters, and so I necessarily have recourse to inference on the basis of the recording I do encounter. So, who is this *persona* that I construct? He is male, adult and British-sounding, and so there is an immediate, easy, almost unthinking possibility of my identifying myself with him. As with the fundamentally important discussion of musical motion in Chapter 8, we observe two possibilities, of participation in the narrative of the track, or of observation of it. I am not the 'you' who acts as Sells' antagonist, not only in this track, but in other love songs on the album. This is particularly pertinent when he is in the intimate zone. However, if I am disposed to read his performance as authentic, I will want to ensure parity between Sells as the performer who I can discover outside the text, and Sells the persona within the text (and, hence, Sells as protagonist). For such a reading I must necessarily go beyond the text, for Sells the performer exists only there. Internet evidence aplenty (not least, his own words), tells us Sells is gay. An authentic reading, then, will see his protagonist as gay. In such a case, I can identify myself with neither the protagonist nor his antagonist (recall that I am not interested in taking on an imaginary perspective). I think it is worth noting that there appears to me to be nothing in Sells' vocal delivery that marks him out as gay, camp or queer, just as I might expect from hearing that in his upbringing, Sells was never presented 'with

---

27   Reed, *Encountering the world*.

28   Ricoeur, *Interpretation theory*.

a closet to come out of',[29] and his masculinity is not presented as being in crisis.[30] Indeed, the language of 'Blue Piccadilly' seems clearly gendered. 'He ' and 'she' are coupled at the opening, and the verse proper takes on the same chord sequence, such that it seems inevitable to superimpose on this pairing the 'I' and 'you' who inhabit the rest of the track. Sells' vocal timbre, to my ears, resembles nobody's as strongly as Glenn Frey's. I cannot but rehearse my experience of hearing the latter (and hence hearing the Eagles), and of the connotations I thereby bring to that experience, in encountering the former (and the historically attested behaviour of the *performer* Frey is 'notoriously' heterosexual).

In terms of gendering, then, the nearest to a definitive subject position developed here is of Sells as in a relationship with 'her' (although the nature of the relationship, while intimate, is properly left unexplored). Bearing in mind the sexuality of Sells the performer, listeners are generally free to construe the position as they wish (or as they are inclined to do). If I should decide I wish to hear Sells' performance as authentic, I would have to take up a position as observer of the actions described. But this would also be very difficult for me, since I am made party to information I could not acquire, ecologically speaking, in a realist manner (although I might observe, perhaps over the fence, that he 'put[s] the dog out', I could not know his motive for doing so, 'for you', from such an observation). Therefore I cannot, myself, hear Sells' performance as authentic. This is not a problem (I actually have no desire to do so), but the process of clarifying the reasoning is, I think, valuable. The most likely position for me to adopt, then, is to treat his protagonist as a strongly fictional construct,[31] a construct who is not gay, and with whom I can then identify (since I cannot identify with his addressees without becoming fictional myself). My assumption is that you, and other listeners, will go through an analogous process to this (although you may be very unlikely to have either the patience, or the need, to spell out to yourself clearly the reasons why). But I am, perhaps, making invalid assumptions of other listeners: I am perhaps ignoring certain listener specificities. I must come clean about these.

The embodied perspective that I have tried to develop as an underpinning to this book's hermeneutic method rests, as should be clear if you have persevered this far, not only on some positions inherited from ecological perception, but on some very similar positions from embodied cognition. This perspective is strongly cognate with the operation of metaphor at a deep, structural level of our experience

---

[29]   Adrian Thrills, 'It's not over for crowd-pleasing band The Feeling as they return with a new single', (http://www.dailymail.co.uk/tvshowbiz/article-507614/Its-crowd-pleasing-band-The-Feeling-return-new-single.html, 2008); Beverley D'Silva, 'Relative values: Dan Gillespie Sells and his mother, Kath', (http://women.timesonline.co.uk/tol/life_and_style/women/the_way_we_live/article3931402.ece, 2008).

[30]   Jason Lee Oakes, '"I'm a man"; masculinities in popular music', in Derek B. Scott (ed.): *The Ashgate Research Companion to Popular Musicology* (Farnham, 2009).

[31]   This is the position I would reach from an extended analysis of the majority of the material I discuss in this book.

of the world.[32] I have no problem in making sense of this observation. Some writers have criticized the work of Johnson from a feminist perspective[33] and, despite work by others addressing the universality of operation of this structural understanding of metaphor,[34] the degree of universality of explanation throughout the field remains an open question at present. However, the literature also maintains that 'we' (i.e. normal human beings) operate this way at the neural level (this is the force of the evidence in favour of a universalist position): the findings of embodied cognition are operative because they are cognate with the way our 'brains are wired' (to use a common metaphor); culture does not determine the fact of the operation of cognitive metaphor, only its particular manifestations. As a result, we all instantiate metaphor (we operate schemata, we map across domains) as we act and as we think, in practice. The evidence from neuroscience offered by leading writers[35] makes me unwilling to reject this proposal.

And yet, I can and will not avoid my own identity, my own specificity, one dominant aspect of which is that I write as someone with an autistic spectrum disorder. One consequence of this is that some of my neural processes work differently from those of the majority of the population.[36] For instance, I find it all but impossible to invent explanatory analogies in everyday conversation. Unless I actively take time out to think, I interpret words 'literally' (which may account for gelidity in some of the writing here, if that's what you find). I am also deeply ignorant of so much conversational (and other) interactional 'etiquette' (as my family and colleagues will attest). Thus I appear to myself to find it exceedingly difficult to think 'metaphorically'. To the extent that this is my book (rather than simply the sedimentation of many encounters), this will clearly have affected the foregoing. My experience of others' encounters with my previous work implies that neurotypical[37] readers will find my readings tend to chime with their own experience, but I do not know the limits to such personalization. Does this mean that the application of findings of embodied cognition to music are appropriate

---

[32]   Lakoff and Johnson, *Metaphors*.

[33]   For example, Susan E. Henking, 'Review, The body in the mind', *Journal of the American Academy of Religion* 58/3 (1990), but see the rejoinder in Moore et al., 'The hermeneutics of spatialization'.

[34]   For example, Kövecses, *Metaphor in culture*.

[35]   For example, Damasio, *The feeling of what happens*; Feldman, *From molecule to metaphor*.

[36]   Aspects of this finding are explored in, e.g. Mirella Dapretto et al., 'Understanding emotions in others: mirror neuron dysfunction in children with autism spectrum disorders', *Nature Neuroscience* (http://www.fil.ion.ucl.ac.uk/SocialClub/nn1611_Mirror_Neurons_in_autism.pdf, 2005); Nicole Schmitz et al., 'Neural correlates of executive function in autistic spectrum disorders'; *Biological Psychiatry* 59/1 (2006); Gary B. Mesibov et al., *Understanding Asperger syndrome and high functioning autism* (New York NY, 2001); Tony Attwood, *The complete guide to Asperger's Syndrome* (London, 2007).

[37]   This is the way the ASD community tends to refer to those without the disorder.

only for neurotypical listeners? Perhaps only you can judge. There are as yet unanswerable questions here.

In the wake of a host of feminist and post-colonial approaches to cultural products, experiences, texts, it is now widely (and rightly) accepted that we cannot presume an objective position from which to write hermeneutically. But this is precisely why an ecological position is so important, for the theory of affordance notes what opportunities are available in an environment: it does not prescribe which of those opportunities must be taken by particular organisms. I urge you, if you encounter claims purporting to identify 'the meaning' of a particular song, or claims as to 'the way to hear' something, with the implication 'the only way…' or 'the right way…', *disbelieve them*. I, and any other writer, can only write from my/ our own individual perspective; a perspectiveless perspective is impossible. Yours is for you to choose, and I hope this book acts as sufficient invitation.

Chapter 11

Questions

The purpose of this chapter, very simply, is to present the series of questions on which the methodology of the book is based, together with a list of the key theoretical terms introduced in each chapter. These can be used as a guide when working on a particular track, while the details to which they refer will be found in the relevant chapter. While it may well be best to begin at the beginning, of course you can begin anywhere. Indeed, I'm sure these questions can usefully be extended; they are not an exhaustive list, but simply the questions I tend to use. What is taken for granted here, is that you have already worked out what happens, that is, identified the melody, its harmonies and lyrics, its form, its instrumentation, and so on. Remember that a negative answer to a question is often as useful as a positive answer, and that by no means every question has to be asked, let alone answered. However, all the tracks I have ever encountered will yield up something of interest in response to some of these questions.

Chapter 1   Methodology
1.1   Are the distinctive features of 'song' and 'performance' clear?
          methodology; musica practica; song; performance; track

Chapter 2   Shape
2.1   Are all the functional layers employed? How are they constituted?
2.2   Does the instrumentation that makes the functional layers explicit alter during the course of the track?
2.3   Are any instruments involved in more than one layer? With what effect?
2.4   How is the harmonic layer filled out? How dominant is this layer?
2.5   Does the way layers are disposed help define the track's style?
2.6   How is the soundbox disposed throughout the track?
2.7   Does the way the soundbox is inhabited vary during the track's course?
2.8   Does the soundbox consist of blocks of sound, of discrete points, or of some mixture?
2.9   Are holes opened up within the soundbox?
2.10   Are some sounds masked? When are they unmasked, and with what effect?
2.11   Does the voice's position (or that of any other source) wander across the soundbox? With what effect?
2.12   What is the import of any particular effects you can identify?
2.13   Do timbres betray, or disguise, their sources?

2.14   How do the timbres line up against the oppositions of modified and natural sources?

2.15   What class of gestures is implied by the timbres?

2.16   How do timbres and gestures pair up, and with what effect?

explicit beat layer, functional bass layer, melodic layer, harmonic filler layer; strumming; boogie; riff; arpeggiations; power chords; soundbox: laterality, register, prominence; perceived performance environment; diagonal mix, cluster mix, triangular mix; reverberation; echo; double-tracking; flanging; speed modification; naturalistic/communitarian; synthesized/mechanical

Chapter 3   Form

3.1   What is the track's basic kit pattern, if it has one?

3.2   Can any part of the track be heard at half- or double-speed? Why?

3.3   Is the beat tight (a strong straight beat), loose (perhaps a shuffle) or does it vary? Where?

3.4   How do other instruments contribute to the basic groove? Does it vary?

3.5   Is the hypermetre regular?

3.6   Do any changes to the hypermetre relate to specific details of lyric?

3.7   Do any changes to the hypermetre affect the track's momentum, or flow?

3.8   How are melodic phrases structured?

3.9   How variable is the track's use of verbal space?

3.10   How thoroughgoing is syncopation within the track? Does it link up with the lyric?

3.11   Where (if at all) does the groove, or time signature, change? With what import?

3.12   Are metres superimposed? To what effect?

3.13   Are the song's modes easy to identify? Can they be related to the import of the lyrics?

3.14   Can the tonic of any harmonic loop be identified? According to what criteria?

3.15   What other tracks use any of the harmonic patterns found? Are there lyric similarities?

3.16   Where open-ended patterns are employed, is the junction between repeats smooth, or not? Why?

3.17   How does the bass move? Is its character consistent?

3.18   What is the track's outline form?

3.19   Does the track use blues, ballad, or any other clearly defined formal pattern you recognize from another track?

3.20   How does the track sit on the continuum between open-ended gestures and period structure?

3.21   How do formal and harmonic patterns inter-relate?

standard rock beat; backbeat; fill; straight; shuffle; groove; hypermetre; phrase; AABA form, 32-bar song form; cut, elision, extension; end-

accented, 2 + 2 model, extension-overlap model, first-downbeat model, 1+1 model; verbal space; syncopation; re-grooving; 3 + 3 + 2 pattern; tihai; harmonic modal system; harmonic loops; open-ended repetitive gestures; blues structures; loose verse/tight chorus model; regular/ variety; static/mobile bass; verse, pre-chorus, chorus, bridge, refrain, introduction, break, playout, tag; period structure; ballad structure

Chapter 4   Delivery

4.1   Does the melody use an unambiguous contour? What are its essential elements?

4.2   Is a contour model employed? How would you describe it?

4.3   Does the tessitura change gradually or suddenly, radically or minimally?

4.4   If the melody has a period structure, what is its main movement?

4.5   Where are the melody's focal pitches? Are the lyrics that fall thereon linked?

4.6   Do contour and open-endedness (or period structure harmony and melody) align?

4.7   How does the sung rhythm differ from a normative spoken rhythm?

4.8   How is the voice located in terms of its positional aspects?

4.9   How is the voice located in terms of Jungr's categories?

4.10   Is the performer conforming to the sense of the lyric by his or her articulation?

4.11   Does the singer have his or her utterance under control? Are the expressed emotions to be trusted?

4.12   Is the singer singing in a recognizable style?

4.13   What does the song address: interpersonal relations and/or some other subject matter?

4.14   How does the song address its subject matter?

4.15   Does the song make any use of euphonics, clichés, or other sonic parallelisms?

4.16   How else is the song's ordinary language made to glow?

4.17   Who is being addressed, and in what manner? Does this change?

4.18   Does the manner of address conform to social expectation?
       contour: falling, rising, flat, undulating, chant, axial, oscillating, terraced; focal pitch; tenor principle; positional aspects: register, resonating cavity, heard attitude to rhythm/pitch; embellishment; vocal width; melismas; rubato; glissando; opera, twang, belt, speech, falsetto, sob; sonic parallelisms; rhyme types; euphonics; clichés

Chapter 5   Style

5.1   What factors in the song define it with respect to style?

5.2   In which phase of the style did the song appear?

5.3   Does the song reinforce, or undermine, particular style characteristics?

5.4   Does the track use production techniques unusual in the style?

5.5   Does the track represent a conscious effort to be 'different'? Why?
5.6   Is the track involved in the development of a taste culture?
5.7   Does the track encourage a particular mode of reception?
5.8   Does the track respond, stylistically, to external agencies?
5.9   Does the track use musical techniques novel for the style?
5.10   Are any of the factors underpinning style change apparent in the track?
         *emergent/dominant/residual; everyday/auratic/critical listening; style
         label*

Chapter 6   Friction
6.1   How apparent is the track's meaning?
6.2   How deeply is the track coded?
6.3   What order of interpretation are you making? Is it self-evident?
6.4   Is the track's style likely to be self-defining?
6.5   Does it perform a style in which you have sufficient competence?
6.6   What features define the idiolect found in the track?
6.7   Does the track's opening or close make use of an unusual texture?
6.8   Are any of the key instrumental-functional relationships challenged or
         dispensed with during the course of the track? With what effect?
6.9   Is the diagonal mix tampered with in any way?
6.10   Do harmony or melody move in an unexpected direction?
6.11   Are there any intimations of arch, bolero, or medley forms? With what
         effect?
6.12   Does the track work against the connotations of its style?
         *over-/under-coding; inherent meaning; competence; delineation;
         subject-position; idiolect*

Chapter 7   Persona
7.1   How far is the distance between the track's performer, persona and
         protagonist?
7.2   What sort of persona is adopted by the performer?
7.3   To what extent does the protagonist narrate the song? Is he or she involved
         or observing?
7.4   What is the overall quality of the production (and, indeed, of the
         performance)? Is it constructed or realist, or does it show aspects of both?
7.5   How would you situate the timespan and the tense of the song?
7.6   Does the production seem to work within the limits of the technology
         available at the time, or does it extend/challenge these?
7.7   How does it relate to his or her identity as performer and protagonist?
7.8   What proxemic positions does the persona take up?
7.9   Do any of these transgress a more appropriate position for delivering the
         lyrics?
7.10   What sort of narrative is traced by the track?
7.11   How does the persona relate to the narrative of the track?

7.12	How does the environment relate to the persona? With what consequences?
7.13	Which musical domains activate the environment?
7.14	Is the environment monolithic, or is it in any way problematic?
7.15	Does the track appear to have a 'normative' reading, in terms of subculture or scene?
7.16	If an intention lying behind the track can be discovered, what relationship does that have to an interpretation?
7.17	Who wrote and produced it?
7.18	Who (else) performed on it?
7.19	What other work have these individuals been involved in?
7.20	What differences (in any domain) might be observed between these individuals?
7.21	Was it intended for a particular market? Did it cross over?
7.22	What label is it for? Is it an unusual choice for that label?

performer, persona, protagonist; realistic/fictional persona; realistic/ fictional narrative; involved/observer; address: protagonist/observer/ antagonist; temporality; timespan; bedrock persona; proxemics; realist/ romanticist aesthetic; environmental support, amplification, explanation, undermining; media pairing: conformity, complementation, contest; subculture; scene; intentional fallacy; market

Chapter 8 Reference

8.1	To what do particular parts of the track make reference?
8.2	What anaphones can be identified?
8.3	What details function as episodic markers and genre synecdoches?
8.4	How pervasive are Tagg's categories in the track?
8.5	How does the mode contribute to the track's meaning?
8.6	What lyrics coincide with melodic peaks? To what end?
8.7	In substituting alternative melodic details, what stands out as significant?
8.8	How is the contour traversed? With what effect?
8.9	Does the melody incorporate key motions shared with other melodies?
8.10	What connotations attach to any timbral modification?
8.11	In substituting alternative harmonic details, what stands out as significant?
8.12	What image schemata are energized by the track?
8.13	From what invariants is the track built?
8.14	What sound sources are specified by these invariants?
8.15	What affordances arise from the sound sources specified?

signifier/signified; icon, index, symbol; anaphone: tactile, sonic, visual; episodic marker; style marker; genre synecdoche; hypothetical substitution; melodic apex; melisma; communication functions: referential, aesthetic, emotive, conative, phatic, meta-lingual; invariants, affordance, specification; image schema; cross-domain mapping

Chapter 9   Belonging

9.1   Can the track be understood as expressive of an authenticity? Which? By means of what devices/strategies?

9.2   Who has an investment in so understanding the track?

9.3   What other performance mode(s) does the performer take up?

9.4   Does the track explicity or implicitly refer to others?

9.5   How extensive is such reference?

9.6   In what domains do such references take place?

9.7   Is there any relationship between such references and the lyrics?

9.8   What effect do such references have on an interpretation?

9.9   What are the consequences of an interpretation that fails to acknowledge such references?

9.10   Is there evidence that such a reference is consciously designed?

authenticity: purity of practice, honesty to experience; performance modes: expressionist, transformative, direct, reflexive; social authenticity; subjective authenticity; meta-authenticity; authenticities of primality, positionality, emotionality; authenticities of expression, experience, execution; intertextuality, hypertextuality: hypertext, hypotext; quotation; allusion; sampling; parody, remix; pastiche, copy; cover; travesty; allosonic; autosonic; interobjective comparison; signifyin(g)

Chapter 10   Syntheses

10.1   As a listener, what does the track you are listening to teach you about your own actions or responses, or your proposed actions or responses?

10.2   What elements of other tracks are brought to mind by the track you are listening to? How idiosyncratic might such a 'calling to mind' be? Can you gather any evidence for your answer?

10.3   Are any of the methodological assumptions of earlier chapters proved false? How, and with what effect?

Bibliography

Adorno, Theodor, *Introduction to the Sociology of Music* (New York NY: Seabury, 1976).

Allan, George, *The importances of the past* (New York NY: State University of New York Press, 1986).

Anon, (http://www.mp3-easy.com/mp3blog/2006/11/watch-amy-winehouse-rehab-music-video.html, 2006), accessed 13 May 2008.

—, 'Amy Winehouse's rehab advice' (http://www.femalefirst.co.uk/celebrity/Amy+Winehouse-20753.html, 2008), accessed 13 May 2008.

—, 'Natalie Merchant biography' (http://www.sing365.com/music/lyric.nsf/Natalie-Merchant-Biography/3CEA058C189748B248256926002783A9, no date), accessed 7 May 2008.

—, 'Mickey Newbury biography' (http://www.musicianguide.com/biographies/1608003817/Mickey-Newbury.html, no date), accessed 4 April 2008.

—, (http://www.angelfire.com/fl4/moneychords/rockballadlesson.html, no date), accessed 7 May 2008).

Attridge, Derek, *The rhythms of English poetry* (London: Longman, 1982).

Attwood, Tony, *The complete guide to Asperger's Syndrome* (London, Jessica Kingsley, 2007)

Auslander, Philip, 'Musical persona: the physical performance of popular music', in Derek B. Scott (ed.), *The Ashgate Research Companion to Popular Musicology* (Farnham: Ashgate, 2009): 303–15.

Ballinger, Robin, 'Politics', in Bruce Horner and Thomas Swiss (eds.), *Key terms in popular music and culture* (Oxford: Blackwell, 1999): 57–70.

Bane, Michael, *White boy singin' the blues* (New York NY: Da Capo, 1992).

Barthes, Roland, *Image–Music–Text*, tr. S. Heath (London: Fontana/Collins, 1977).

—, 'The grain of the voice', in *Image–Music–Text*: 179–89.

—, 'Musica practica', in *Image–Music–Text*: 149–54.

Bateson, Gregory, *Mind and Nature: a necessary unity* (London: Wildwood House, 1979).

Becker, Judith, *Deep listeners* (Bloomington IN: Indiana University Press, 2004).

deBellis, Mark, *Music and Conceptualization* (Cambridge: Cambridge University Press, 1995).

Bennett, Andy and Peterson, Richard A. (eds.), *Music scenes: local, translocal, and virtual* (Nashville TN: Vanderbilt University Press, 2004).

Bjornberg, Alf, 'On Aeolian Harmony in Contemporary Popular Music' (originally 1989), in Allan F. Moore (ed.), *Critical essays in popular musicology* (Aldershot: Ashgate, 2007): 275–82.

Bohlman, Philip V., *The study of folk music in the modern world* (Bloomington IN: Indiana University Press, 1988).

Boone, Graeme M., 'Tonal and expressive ambiguity in "Dark star"', in John Covach and Graeme M. Boone (eds.), *Understanding Rock* (New York NY: Oxford University Press, 1997): 171–210.

Born, Georgina, and Hesmondhalgh, David (eds.), *Western music and its others* (Berkeley CA: University of California Press, 2000).

Boyes, Georgina, *The imagined village: culture, ideology and the English Folk Revival* (Manchester: Manchester University Press, 1993).

Brackett, David, *Interpreting Popular Music* (2nd edn., Berkeley CA: University of California Press, 2000).

Bradley, Dick, *Understanding Rock'n'roll* (Buckingham: Open University Press, 1992).

Bragg, Billy, and Anderson, Ian A., 'The taxman's poet', *Folk Roots* 42 (December 1986): 26–9.

Bright, Spencer, *Peter Gabriel* (London: Headline, 1990).

Brunning, Bob, *Blues: the British connection* (Poole: Blandford Press, 1986).

Burns, Robert, *Transforming folk: innovation and tradition in English Folk-Rock* (PhD thesis, University of Otago, 2008).

Byrnside, Ronald, 'The formation of a musical style: early rock' (originally 1975), in Allan F. Moore (ed.), *Critical essays in popular musicology* (Aldershot: Ashgate, 2007): 217–50.

Calinescu, Matei, *Five faces of modernity* (Durham, NC: Duke University Press, 1987).

Camilleri, Lelio, *Il Peso del Suono* (Milan: Apogeo, 2005).

—, 'Shaping sounds, shaping spaces', *Popular Music* 29/2 (2010): 199–211.

Capuzzo, Guy, 'Neo-Riemannian theory and the analysis of pop-rock music', *Music Theory Spectrum* 26/2 (2004): 177–99.

Carr, E.H., *What is history?* (Harmondsworth: Pelican 1987, originally 1961).

Chambers, Iain, *Urban rhythms* (London: MacMillan, 1985).

Chanan, Michael, *Musica practica* (London: Verso, 1994).

Clarke, Arthur C., *Childhood's End* (London: Pan, 1956).

Clarke, David, 'Elvis and Darmstadt, or: Twentieth-Century Music and the politics of cultural pluralism', *twentieth-century music* 4/1 (2007): 3–45.

Clarke, Eric, 'Subject-Position and the Specification of Invariants in music by Frank Zappa and P.J.Harvey', *Music Analysis* 18/3 (1999): 347–74.

—, *Ways of listening* (Oxford: Oxford University Press, 2005).

Clarke, Paul, '"A magic science": rock music as a recording art', *Popular Music* 3 (1983): 195–213.

Cone, Edward T., *The composer's voice* (Berkeley CA: California University Press, 1974).

Cook, Nicholas, *Music, imagination, and culture* (Oxford: Clarendon, 1990).

—, *Analysing Musical Multimedia* (Oxford: Clarendon, 1998).

Cooke, Deryck, *The language of music* (Oxford: Oxford University Press, 1959).

Coulson, Seana, *Semantic leaps: frame-shifting and conceptual blending in meaning construction* (New York NY: Cambridge University Press, 2001).

Covach, John, 'We won't get fooled again: rock music and musical analysis', in David Schwarz et al. (eds.), *Keeping Score: Music, Disciplinarity, Culture* (Charlottesville VA: Virginia University Press, 1997): 75–89.

—, 'Form in rock music: a primer', in Deborah Stein (ed.), *Engaging music: essays in music analysis* (New York NY: Oxford University Press, 2005): 65–76.

—, 'The hippie aesthetic: cultural positioning and musical ambition in early progressive rock', in *Proceedings of the International Conference Composition and Experimentation in British Rock 1966–1976* (http://www-3.unipv.it/britishrock1966–1976/testien/cov1en.htm, 2005), accessed 13 November 2010.

—, 'From "craft" to "art": formal structure in the music of the Beatles', in Kenneth Womack and Todd F. Davis (eds.), *Reading the Beatles* (New York NY: State University of New York Press, 2006): 37–53.

—, 'The Rutles and the use of specific models in musical satire' (originally 1991), in Allan F. Moore (ed.), *Critical essays in popular musicology*, (Aldershot: Ashgate, 2007): 417–42.

—, *What's that sound? An introduction to rock and its history* (2nd edn, New York NY: Norton, 2009).

Covach, John, and Boone, Graeme M., *Understanding Rock* (New York NY: Oxford University Press, 1997).

Coyle, Michael, and Dolan, Jon, 'Modelling Authenticity, Authenticating Commercial Models', in Kevin Dettmar and William Richey (eds.), *Reading Rock and Roll* (New York NY: Columbia University Press, 1999): 17–35.

Cubitt, Sean, '"Maybellene": meaning and the listening subject' *Popular Music* 4 (1984): 207–24.

Cumming, Naomi, *The sonic self* (Bloomington IN: Indiana University Press, 2000).

D'Silva, Beverley, 'Relative values: Dan Gillespie Sells and his mother, Kath' (http://women.timesonline.co.uk/tol/life_and_style/women/the_way_we_live/article3931402.ece, 2008), accessed 15 January 2010.

Daley, Mike, 'Patti Smith's "Gloria": intertextual play in a rock vocal performance', *Popular Music* 16/3 (1997): 235–53.

Dalmonte, Rosanna, and Baroni, Mario (eds.), *Secondo Convegno Europeo di Analisi Musicale* (Trento: Università degli Studi di Trento, 1992).

Damasio, Antonio, *The feeling of what happens: Body and emotion in the making of consciousness* (New York NY: Harcourt Brace, 1999).

Dapretto, Mirella, et al., 'Understanding emotions in others: mirror neuron dysfunction in children with autism spectrum disorders'; *Nature Neuroscience* (http://www.fil.ion.ucl.ac.uk/SocialClub/nn1611_Mirror_Neurons_in_autism.pdf, 2005), accessed 21 January 2010.

Dibben, Nicola, 'Representations of femininity in popular music', *Popular Music* 18/3 (1999): 331–55.

—, 'Musical materials, perception, and listening', in Martin Clayton, Trevor Herbert and Richard Middleton (eds.), *The cultural study of music: a critical introduction* (New York NY: Routledge, 2003): 193–203.

—, *Björk* (Bloomington IN: Indiana University Press, 2009).

—, 'Vocal performance and the projection of emotional authenticity', in Derek B. Scott (ed.), *Research Companion to Popular Musicology* (Farnham: Ashgate, 2009): 318–33.

Dockwray, Ruth, *Deconstructing the Rock Anthem: Textual Form, Participation, and Collectivity* (PhD thesis, University of Liverpool, 2005).

Dockwray, Ruth, and Allan F. Moore, 'Configuring the sound-box 1965–72'; *Popular Music* 29/2 (2010): 181–97.

Doll, Christopher, 'Transformation in rock harmony: an explanatory strategy' *Gamut* 2/1 (2009): 1–44.

Doyle, Peter, *Echo and reverb: fabricating space in popular music recordings 1900–1960* (Middletown CT: Wesleyan University Press, 2005).

Durant, Alan, *Conditions of music*, (London: Macmillan, 1984).

Eagleton, Terry, *The meaning of life: a very short introduction* (Oxford: Oxford University Press, 2007).

Echard, William, 'An analysis of Neil Young's "Powderfinger" based on Mark Johnson's image schemata', *Popular Music* 18/1 (1999): 133–44.

Elliott, David, *Music Matters* (Oxford: Oxford University Press, 1995).

Evans, Vyvyan, and Green, Melanie, *Cognitive linguistics: an introduction* (Edinburgh: Edinburgh University Press, 2006).

Everett, Walter, , 'Fantastic remembrance in John Lennon's "Strawberry Fields Forever" and "Julia"' (originally 1986), in Allan F. Moore (ed.), *Critical essays in popular musicology* (Aldershot: Ashgate, 2007): 391–416.

—, *The Beatles as Musicians*: Revolver *through the* Anthology (Oxford: Oxford University Press, 1999).

—, 'Making sense of rock's tonal systems', (originally 2004), in Allan F. Moore (ed.), *Critical essays in popular musicology* (Aldershot: Ashgate, 2007): 301–35.

—, 'Pitch down the middle', in Walter Everett (ed.), *Expression in Pop-Rock Music* (rev. edn, New York: Routledge, 2008): 111–75.

—, *The foundations of rock* (New York NY: Oxford University Press, 2009).

Fabbri, Franco, 'Browsing music spaces: categories and the musical mind' (originally 1999), in Allan F. Moore (ed.), *Critical essays in popular musicology* (Aldershot: Ashgate, 2007): 49–62.

Fairley, Jan, 'The "local" and "global" in popular music', in Simon Frith et al. (eds.), *The Cambridge Companion to Pop and Rock* (Cambridge: Cambridge University Press, 2001): 272–89.

Fales, Cornelia, 'Short-circuiting perceptual systems: timbre in ambient and techno music', in Paul D. Greene and Thomas Porcello (eds.), *Wired for sound* (Hanover NH: Wesleyan University Press, 2004): 156–80.

Fast, Susan, *In the houses of the holy: Led Zeppelin and the power of rock music* (Oxford: Oxford University Press, 2001).

Fauconnier, Gilles, *Mappings in thought and language* (Cambridge: Cambridge University Press, 1997).

Fauconnier, Gilles, and Turner, Mark, *The way we think: conceptual blending and the mind's hidden complexities* (New York NY: Basic Books, 2002).

Feldman, Jerome, *From molecule to metaphor: a neural theory of language* (Cambridge MA: MIT Press, 2008).

Ferre, Rafael, 'Embodied cognition applied to timbre and musical appreciation' *British Postgraduate Musicology* 10 (http://www.bpmonline.org.uk/bpm10/, 2009), accessed 23 March 2010.

Fillmore, Charles J., 'Frame semantics' (originally 1982), in Dirk Geeraerts (ed.), *Cognitive Linguistics: basic readings* (Berlin: Mouton de Gruyter, 2006): 373–400.

Fiori, Umberto, 'Listening to Peter Gabriel's "I have the touch"', in Richard Middleton (ed.), *Reading Pop* (Oxford: Clarendon, 2000): 183–91.

Floyd, Samuel A., *The Power of Black Music* (New York NY: Oxford University Press, 1993).

Ford, Charles, 'Robert Johnson's rhythms', *Popular Music* 17/1 (1998): 71–93.

—, 'Musical presence: towards a new philosophy of music', *Contemporary Aesthetics* 8 (http://www.contempaesthetics.org/newvolume/pages/article.php?articleID=582, 2010), accessed 11 March 2010.

Fornäs, Johan, *Cultural theory and late modernity* (London: Sage, 1995).

Forte, Allan, *The American Popular Ballad of the Golden Era* (Princeton NJ: Princeton University Press, 1995).

Frayn, Michael, *The human touch* (London: Faber & Faber, 2006).

Fripp, Robert, Sleevenote to Robin Trower, *Bridge of Sighs* (Beat Goes On, 1974).

Frith, Simon, *Sound effects* (London: Constable, 1983).

—, 'Towards an aesthetic of popular music', in Richard Leppert and Susan McClary (eds.), *Music and society* (Cambridge: Cambridge University Press, 1987): 133–49.

—, 'Popular music 1950–1980', in George Martin (ed.), *Making music* (London: Barrie & Jenkins, 1988): 18–48.

—, *Performing rites* (New York NY: Oxford University Press, 1998).

Frith, Simon and Goodwin, Andrew (eds.), *On record* (London: Routledge, 1990).

Frith, Simon, and McRobbie, Angela, 'Rock and sexuality', *Screen Education* 29 (1978): 3–19. Partly reprinted in Derek B. Scott, *Music, Culture, and Society: a reader* (Oxford: Oxford University Press, 2000).

Gammon, Vic, 'Problems of method in the historical study of popular music', in Philip Tagg and David Horn (eds.), *Popular Music Perspectives* (Gotenburg: IASPM, 1982): 16–31.

Gardner, Howard, *Frames of Mind* (Cambridge MA: Harvard University Press, 1985).

Garofalo, Reebee, 'How autonomous is relative: popular music, the social formation and cultural struggle', *Popular Music* 6/1 (1987): 77–92.

Gelbart, Matthew, 'Persona and Voice in the Kinks' Songs of the Late 1960s', *Journal of the Royal Musical Association* 128 (2003): 200–41.

Gellner, Ernest, *The psychoanalytic movement* (London: Paladin, 1985).

Gibbs Jr, Raymond W., *Embodiment and cognitive science* (Cambridge: Cambridge University Press, 2006).

Gibson, David, *The Art of Mixing* (2nd edn, Boston MA: Course Technology, 2005).

Gibson, James J., *The senses considered as perceptual systems* (Boston MA: Houghton Mifflin, 1966).

—, *The ecological approach to visual perception* (London: Lawrence Erlbaum, 1979).

Gillett, Charlie, *The sound of the city* (London: Souvenir, 1983).

Gilroy, Paul, *The Black Atlantic* (London: Verso, 1993).

Goodwin, Andrew, 'Drumming and memory: scholarship, technology, and music-making', in Thomas Swiss, John Sloop and Andrew Herman (eds.), *Mapping the Beat* (Malden MA: Blackwell, 1998): 121–36.

Gracyk, Theodore, *Rhythm and noise* (London: I.B.Tauris, 1996).

—, *I wanna be me: rock music and the politics of identity* (Philadelphia PA: Temple University Press, 2001).

Gray, Louise, *The no-nonsense guide to world music* (London: New Internationalist Publications, 2009).

Green, Lucy, *Music on Deaf Ears* (Manchester: Manchester University Press, 1988).

Griffiths, Dai, 'Cover versions and the sound of identity in motion', in David Hesmondhalgh and Keith Negus (eds.), *Popular Music Studies* (London: Arnold, 2002): 51–64.

—, 'From lyric to anti-lyric: analyzing the words in pop song', in Allan F. Moore (ed.), *Analyzing Popular Music* (Cambridge: Cambridge University Press, 2003): 39–59.

—, 'The high analysis of low music' (originally 1999), in Allan F. Moore (ed.), *Critical Essays in Popular Musicology* (Aldershot: Ashgate, 2007): 63–109.

Grossberg, Lawrence, *We gotta get out of this place* (New York NY: Routledge, 1992).

Grünbaum, Adolf, *The foundations of psychoanalysis: a philosophical critique* (Berkeley CA: University of California Press, 1985).

Hall, Edward T., *The hidden dimension* (London: The Bodley Head, 1969).

Harris, Chris, 'Amy Winehouse's "Rehab", the theme song of modern-day celebrity trash culture: behind the Grammys' (http://www.mtv.com/news/articles/1580806/20080201/winehouse_amy.jhtml, 2008), accessed 13 May 2008.

Hatch, David, and Millward, Stephen, *From blues to rock: an analytical history of pop music* (Manchester; Manchester University Press, 1987).

Hawkins, Stan, 'Prince: harmonic analysis of "Anna Stesia"', reprinted in Richard Middleton (ed.), *Reading Pop* (Oxford: Clarendon, 2000): 58–70.

—, *The British pop dandy*, (Farnham: Ashgate, 2009).

Headlam, Dave, 'Does the song remain the same? Questions of authorship and identification in the music of Led Zeppelin', in Elizabeth West Marvin and

Richard Hermann (eds.), *Concert music, rock, and jazz since 1945: essays and analytical studies* (Rochester NY: University of Rochester Press, 1995): 313–63.

—, 'Blues transformations in the music of Cream', in John Covach and Graeme M. Boone (eds.), *Understanding Rock* (New York NY: Oxford University Press, 1997): 59–92.

Hebdige, Dick, *Subculture: the meaning of style* (London: Methuen, 1985).

Henking, Susan E., 'Review of Johnson, *The body in the mind*', *Journal of the American Academy of Religion* 58/3 (1990): 503–06.

Herman, Luc, and Vervaeck, Bart, *Handbook of narrative analysis* (Lincoln NE: University of Nebraska Press, 2005).

Hesmondhalgh, David, and Negus, Keith (eds.), *Popular Music Studies* (London: Arnold, 2002).

Holm-Hudson, Kevin J., 'Your guitar, it sounds so sweet and clear: semiosis in two versions of "Superstar"', *Music Theory Online* (http://www.societymusictheory.org/mto/issues/mto.02.8.4/mto.02.8.4.holm-hudson_frames.html, 2002), accessed 14 October 2005.

Horner, Bruce, and Swiss, Thomas (eds.), *Key terms in popular music and culture* (Oxford: Blackwell, 1999).

Hughes, Timothy, *Groove and flow: six analytical essays on the music of Stevie Wonder* (PhD thesis, University of Washington, 2003).

Huron, David, *Sweet anticipation: music and the psychology of expectation* (Cambridge MA: MIT Press, 2006).

Hustwitt, Mark, 'Caught in a whirlpool of aching sound: the production of dance music in the 1920s', *Popular Music* 3 (1983): 7–31.

Jameson, Fredric, 'Post-modernism and consumer society', in Hal Foster (ed.), *Postmodern culture* (London: Pluto, 1985): 111–25.

Johnson, Mark, *The body in the mind: the bodily basis of meaning, imagination, and reason* (Chicago IL: Chicago University Press, 1987).

—, *The meaning of the body* (Chicago IL: Chicago University Press, 2007).

Johnson, Mark, and Larson, Steve, '"Something in the way she moves" – metaphors of musical motion', *Metaphor and symbol* 18/2 (2003): 63–84.

Jungr, Barb, 'Vocal expression in the blues and gospel', in Allan F. Moore (ed.), *The Cambridge Companion to Blues and Gospel Music* (Cambridge: Cambridge University Press, 2002): 102–15.

Keil, Charles, and Feld, Steven, *Music grooves: essays and dialogues* (Chicago IL: Chicago University Press, 1994).

Kennett, Christian, 'Is anybody listening', in Allan F. Moore (ed.), *Analyzing Popular Music* (Cambridge: Cambridge University Press, 2003): 196–217.

Klein, Bethany, *As heard on TV: popular music in advertising* (Farnham: Ashgate, 2009).

Kövecses, Zoltán, *Metaphor in culture: universality and variation* (Cambridge: Cambridge University Press, 2005).

Krause, Bernard, Sleevenote to Beaver and Krause, *Gandharva* (Warner, 1971).

Krims, Adam, *Music and Urban Geography* (New York NY: Routledge, 2007).

Lacasse, Serge, *'Listen to my voice': the evocative power of vocal staging in recorded rock music and other forms of vocal expression* (PhD thesis, University of Liverpool, 2000).

—, 'Intertextuality and hypertextuality in recorded popular music' (originally 2000), in Allan F. Moore, *Critical essays in popular musicology* (Aldershot: Ashgate, 2007): 147–70.

—, 'The phonographic voice: paralinguistic features and phonographic staging in popular music singing', in Amanda Bayley (ed.), *Recorded music: performance, culture and technology*, (Cambridge: Cambridge University Press, 2010): 225–51.

Laing, Dave, *One chord wonders: power and meaning in punk rock* (Buckingham: Open University Press, 1985).

—, 'Listen to me' (originally 1971), in Simon Frith and Andrew Goodwin (eds.), *On record* (London: Routledge, 1990): 326–40.

Lakoff, George, *Women, fire, and dangerous things* (Chicago IL: Chicago University Press, 1987).

Lakoff, George, and Johnson, Mark, *Metaphors we live by* (Chicago IL: Chicago University Press, 1980).

—, *Philosophy in the flesh* (New York NY: Basic, 1999).

Lakoff, George, and Turner, Mark, *More than cool reason: a field guide to poetic metaphor* (Chicago IL: Chicago University Press, 1989).

Langfeld, John T., 'Louis Arnaud Reid', in Bennett Reimer and Jeffrey E. Wright (eds.), *On the nature of musical experience* (Niwot CO: Colorado University Press, 1992): 138–51.

Leppert, Richard, and McClary, Susan (eds.), *Music and society* (Cambridge: Cambridge University Press, 1987).

Lerdahl, Fred, and Jackendoff, Ray, *A generative theory of tonal music* (Cambridge MA: Massachusetts Institute of Technology Press, 1983).

Levitin, Daniel J., *This is your brain on music* (London: Plume, 2006).

Lilja, Esa, *Theory and analysis of classic heavy metal harmony* (Vantaa, Finland: IAML, 2009).

Maasø, Aarnt, 'The proxemics of the mediated voice', in Jay Beck and Tony Grajeda (eds.), *Lowering the boom: critical studies in film sound* (Urbana IL: University of Illinois Press, 2008): 36–50.

Marshall, Lee, *Bob Dylan: the never ending star* (Cambridge: Polity, 2007).

Martin, George (ed.), *Making music* (London: Barrie & Jenkins, 1988).

McAdams, Stephen, 'Recognition of sound sources and events', in Stephen McAdams and Emmanuel Bigand (eds.), *Thinking in sound: the cognitive psychology of human audition* (Oxford: Oxford University Press, 1993): 146–98.

McCarthy, Albert, *The dance band era* (London: Hamlyn, 1974).

McDonald, Chris, 'Exploring modal subversions in alternative music', *Popular Music* 19/3 (2000): 355–63.

Mehrabian, Albert, *Silent messages: implicit communication of emotions and attitudes* (Belmont CA: Wadsworth, 1981).

Mellers, Wilfrid, *Twilight of the Gods* (London: Faber, 1973).

Merwe, Peter van der, *Origins of the Popular Style* (Oxford: Clarendon, 1989).

Mesibov, Gary B., et al., *Understanding Asperger syndrome and high functioning autism* (New York NY: Kluwer Academic, 2001).

Meyer, Leonard B., *Music, the Arts and Ideas* (Chicago IL: Chicago University Press, 1967).

—, *Style and Music* (Philadelphia PA: Pennsylvania University Press, 1989).

Michell, John, *Euphonics: a poet's dictionary of sounds*, (Kirstead, Norfolk: Frontier, 1988).

Middleton, Richard, *Pop Music and the Blues* (London: Gollancz, 1972).

—, *Studying Popular Music* (Buckingham: Open University Press, 1990).

—, 'Form', in Bruce Horner and Thomas Swiss (eds.), *Key terms in popular music and culture* (Oxford: Blackwell, 1999): 141–55.

—, 'Popular Music Analysis and Musicology: bridging the Gap', in Richard Middleton (ed.), *Reading Pop* (Oxford: Clarendon, 2000): 104–21.

— (ed.), *Reading Pop* (Oxford: Clarendon, 2000).

—, *Voicing the popular* (London: Routledge, 2006).

Monelle, Raymond, *Linguistics and semiotics in music* (Chur, Switzerland: Harwood, 1992).

Moore, Allan F., 'Patterns of harmony', *Popular Music* 11/1 (1992): 73–106.

—, 'The textures of rock', in Rosanna Dalmonte and Mario Baroni (eds.), *Secondo Convegno Europeo di Analisi Musicale* (Trento: Università degli Studi di Trento, 1992): 241–44.

—, *Rock: the primary text* (Buckingham: Open University Press, 1993).

—, *The Beatles: Sgt. Pepper's Lonely Hearts Club Band* (Cambridge: Cambridge University Press, 1997).

—, 'In a big country: the portrayal of wide open spaces in the music of Big Country', in Raymond Monelle (ed.), *Musica Significans: Proceedings of the 3rd International Congress on Musical Signification* (Chur: Harwood Academic, 1998): 1–6.

—, 'U2 and the myth of authenticity in rock', *Popular Musicology* 3 (1998): 5–33 (http://www.allanfmoore.org.uk).

—, 'Categorical conventions in music-discourse: style and genre', *Music and Letters* 82/3 (2001): 432–42.

—, *Rock: the Primary Text* (2nd edn, Aldershot: Ashgate, 2001).

—, (ed.), *The Cambridge Companion to Blues and Gospel Music* (Cambridge: Cambridge University Press, 2002).

—, (ed.), *Analyzing Popular Music* (Cambridge: Cambridge University Press, 2003).

—, *Aqualung* (New York NY: Continuum, 2004).

—, 'The contradictory aesthetics of Woodstock', in Andy Bennett (ed.), *Remembering Woodstock* (Aldershot: Ashgate, 2004): 75–89.

—, 'The Persona/Environment relation in recorded song', *Music Theory Online* 11/4 (http:www.music-theory.org/mto/issues/mto.05.11.4/mto.05.11.4.moore_ frames.html, 2005), accessed 25 September 2010.

—, 'Authenticity as authentication' (originally 2002), in Allan F., Moore (ed.), *Critical essays in popular musicology* (Aldershot: Ashgate, 2007): 131–45.

—, (ed.), *Critical essays in popular musicology* (Aldershot: Ashgate, 2007).

—, 'The so-called "flattened seventh" in rock' (originally 1995), in Allan F. Moore (ed.), *Critical essays in popular musicology* (Aldershot: Ashgate, 2007): 283–99.

—, 'The act you've known for all these years: a re-encounter with Sgt. Pepper', in Olivier Julien (ed.), *Sgt. Pepper: it was forty years ago today* (Farnham: Ashgate, 2008): 139–46.

—, 'Interpretation: so what?', in Derek B. Scott (ed.), *Research Companion to Popular Musicology* (Farnham: Ashgate, 2009): 411–25.

—, 'The track', in Amanda Bayley (ed.), *Recorded Music: Society, Technology and Performance* (Cambridge: Cambridge University Press, 2010): 252–67.

—, 'Where is "here"? an issue of deictic projection in recorded song', *Journal of the Royal Musical Association* 135/1 (2010): 145–82.

—, 'One way of feeling: contextualizing a hermeneutics of spatialization', in Stan Hawkins (ed.), *Critical Musicological Reflections* (Farnham: Ashgate, forthcoming 2012).

—, 'Addressing the persona', in Dietrich Helms and Thomas Phleps (eds.), *Black Box Pop* (Beitraege zur Popular musikforschung – 38).

Moore, Allan F. and Dockwray, Ruth, 'The establishment of the virtual performance space in rock', *twentieth-century music* 5/2 (2008): 219–41.

Moore, Allan F., and Ibrahim, Anwar, 'Sounds like Teen Spirit: identifying Radiohead's idiolect', in Joseph Tate (ed.), *Strobe-Lights and Blown Speakers: essays on the music and art of Radiohead* (Aldershot: Ashgate, 2005): 139–58.

Moore, Allan F., Schmidt, Patricia, and Dockwray, Ruth, 'The hermeneutics of spatialization in recorded song', *twentieth-century music* 6/1 (2009): 81–112.

Moylan, William, *The art of recording: understanding and crafting the mix* (Boston MA: Focal Press, 2002).

—, *Understanding and crafting the mix: The art of recording* (Boston MA: Focal Press, 2007).

—, 'Considering space in music', Proceedings of the 4th Art of Record Production Conference, University of Massachusetts Lowell, *Journal of the Art of Record Production* 4 (http://www.artofrecordproduction.com/content/view/180/109/, 2008), accessed 25 September 2010.

Murphey, Tim, 'The when, where, and who of pop lyrics: the listener's prerogative', *Popular Music* 8/2 (1989): 185–93.

Narmour, Eugene, *The analysis and cognition of basic melodic structures* (Chicago IL: Chicago University Press, 1990).

—, *The analysis and cognition of melodic complexity* (Chicago IL: Chicago University Press, 1992).

Neal, Jocelyn, 'Narrative paradigms, musical signifiers, and form as function in country music', *Music Theory Spectrum* 29/1 (2007): 41–72.

Negus, Keith, *Popular Music in Theory* (Cambridge: Polity, 1996).

Negus, Keith, and Pickering, Michael, 'Creativity and musical experience', in David Hesmondhalgh and Keith Negus (eds.), *Popular Music Studies* (London: Arnold, 2002): 178–90.

Negus, Keith, and Pickering, Michael, *Creativity, Communication and Cultural Value* (London: Sage, 2004).

Nettel, Reginald, *Seven centuries of popular song: a social history of urban ditties* (London: Phoenix, 1956).

Nicholls, David, 'Narrative theory as an analytical tool in the study of popular music texts', *Music and Letters* 88/2 (2007): 297–315.

O'Donnell, Shaugn, Review of Stephenson, *What to listen for in rock*, *Music Theory Spectrum* 28/1 (2006): 132–40.

Oakes, Jason Lee, '"I'm a man"; masculinities in popular music', in Derek B. Scott (ed.), *Research Companion to Popular Musicology* (Farnham: Ashgate, 2009): 211–39.

Oliver, Paul, *The story of the blues* (London: Penguin, 1969).

—, *Songsters and saints* (Cambridge: Cambridge University Press, 1984).

Patel, Aniruddh D., *Music, language and the brain* (Oxford: Oxford University Press, 2008).

Pattie, David, *Rock music in performance* (Basingstoke: Palgrave MacMillan 2007).

Pedler, Dominic, *The Songwriting Secrets of the Beatles* (London: Omnibus, 2003).

Pickering, Michael, 'The dogma of authenticity in the experience of popular music', in McGregor, G. and White, R. S. (eds.), *The art of listening* (Beckenham: Croom Helm, 1986): 201–20.

Poschardt, Ulf, *DJ culture* (London: Quartet, 1998).

Queenan, Joe, 'Rehab is one great song', *The Guardian*, 8 Feburary (http://music.guardian.co.uk/vinylword/story/0,2254844,00.html, 2008), accessed 13 May 2008.

Redhead, Steve, *The end-of-the-century party* (Manchester: Manchester University Press, 1990).

Reed, Edward S., *Encountering the world: toward an ecological psychology* (New York NY: Oxford University Press, 1996).

ReGenesis (http://www.regenesis-music.com/, no date), accessed 16 November 2010.

Reich, Charles, *The greening of America* (Toronto: Bantam, 1971).

Reid, Louis Arnaud, *Meaning in the Arts* (New York NY: Humanities Press, 1969).

Ricoeur, Paul, *Interpretation theory: discourse and the surplus of meaning* (Fort Worth TX: Texas Christian University Press, 1979).

—, 'What is a text? Explanation and Understanding' in Ricoeur: *From text to action: Essays in Hermeneutics, II*, trans. K. Blamey & J. B. Thompson (London: Continuum, 2008).

Rinck, Mike, 'Spatial Situation Models', in Priti Shah and Akira Miyake (eds.), *Cambridge Handbook of Visuospatial Thinking* (New York NY: Cambridge University Press, 2005): 334–82.

Rose, Tricia, *Black noise: rap music and black culture in contemporary America* (Hanover, NH: Wesleyan University Press, 1994).

Roszak, Theodor, *The making of a counter culture: reflections on the technocratic society and its youthful opposition* (London: Faber, 1969).

Rothstein, William, *Phrase rhythm in tonal music* (New York: Schirmer, 1989).

Rubidge, Sarah, 'Does authenticity matter? The case for and against authenticity in the performing arts', in Patrick Campbell (ed.), *Analysing performance* (Manchester: Manchester University Press, 1996): 219–33.

Rumsey, Francis, 'Spatial Quality Evaluation for Reproduced Sound: Terminology, Meaning, and a Scene-based paradigm', *Journal of the Audio Engineering Society* 50/9 (2002): 651–66.

Said, Edward, *Orientalism* (London: Penguin, 1995).

Saslaw, Janna, 'Forces, containers, and paths: the role of body-derived image schemas in the conceptualization of music', *Journal of Music Theory* 40/2 (1996): 217–43.

Schmidt, Christopher, 'Metaphor and cognition: a cross-cultural study of indigenous and universal constructs in stock exchange reports', *Intercultural Communication* 5 (http://www.immi.se/intercultural/, 2002), accessed 22 April 2008.

Schmitz, Nicole et al., 'Neural correlates of executive function in autistic spectrum disorders', *Biological Psychiatry* 59/1 (2006): 7–16.

Schwarz, David, *Listening Subjects: Music, Psychoanalysis, Culture* (Durham, NC: Duke University Press, 1997).

Shapiro, Leonard, *Embodied cognition* (London: Routledge, 2011).

Shepherd, John, *Tin Pan Alley* (London: Routledge & Kegan Paul, 1982).

—, 'Text', in Bruce Horner and Thomas Swiss (eds.), *Key terms in popular music and culture* (Oxford: Blackwell, 1999): 156–77.

Shuker, Roy, *Understanding popular music* (London: Routledge, 1994).

—, *Key concepts in popular music* (London: Routledge, 1998).

Silver Beatles (http://www.beatles-tribute-band-uk.co.uk/actinfo.asp?actid=%7B09796A64–1D52–4B3C-9F54-D59E730BCDA1%7D, no date), accessed 16 November 2010.

Sless, David, *In search of semiotics* (London: Croom Helm, 1986).

Small, Christopher, *Music of the common tongue* (Hanover NH: Wesleyan University Press, 1998).

Solomon, Robert C., *True to our feelings* (New York NY: Oxford University Press, 2007).

Spicer, Mark, '(Ac)cumulative form in pop-rock music'; *twentieth-century music* 1/1 (2004): 29–64.

Starr, Larry, and Waterman, Christopher, *American popular music from minstrelsy to MTV* (New York NY: Oxford University Press, 2003).

Stefani, Gino, 'Melody: a popular perspective', *Popular Music* 6/1 (1987): 21–35.

—, 'A theory of musical competence' (originally 1987), reprinted in Moore (ed.), *Critical essays in popular musicology* (Aldershot: Ashgate, 2007): 19–34.

Stephenson, Ken, *What to listen for in rock: a stylistic analysis* (New Haven CT: Yale University Press, 2002).

Stewart, Alexander, '"Funky drummer": New Orleans, James Brown and the rhythmic transformation of American popular music', *Popular Music* 19/3 (2000): 293–318.

Sticky Fingers (http://www.stickyfingersband.com/, no date), accessed 16 November 2010.

Straw, Will, 'Systems of articulation, logics of change: communities and scenes in popular music', *Cultural Studies* 5/3 (1991): 368–88.

—, 'Authorship', in Bruce Horner and Thomas Swiss (eds.), *Key terms in popular music and culture* (Oxford: Blackwell, 1999): 199–208.

Swanwick, Keith, *Music, Mind and Education* (London: Routledge, 1988).

Swiss, Thomas, Sloop, John and Herman, Andrew, *Mapping the Beat* (Malden MA: Blackwell, 1998).

Tagg, Philip, *Fernando the Flute* (Liverpool: IPM, 1991).

—, 'Towards a sign typology of music', in Rosanna Dalmonte and Mario Baroni (eds.), *Secondo Convegno Europeo di Analisi Musicale* (Trento: Università degli Studi di Trento, 1992): 369–78.

—, 'Analysing popular music: theory, method, and practice' (originally 1982), in Richard Middleton (ed.), *Reading Pop* (Oxford: Clarendon, 2000): 71–103.

—, *Everyday tonality* (New York NY: Mass Media Music Scholars' Press, 2009).

—, *Introductory notes to the semiotics of music* (http://www.tagg.org/xpdfs/semiotug.pdf, no date), accessed 17 April 2008.

Tagg, Philip, and Clarida, Bob, *Ten little title tunes* (New York NY: Mass Media Music Scholars' Press, 2003).

Talmy, Leonard, *Toward a cognitive semantics, vol. 1: Concept structuring systems* (Cambridge MA: MIT Press, 2003).

Tamlyn, Gary, 'The rhythmic roots of rock'n'roll in rhythm and blues', in Tarja Hautamäki and Helmi Järviluoma (eds.), *Music on Show* (University of Tampere, Department of Folk Tradition, 1998): 330–35.

Tarasti, Eero, *A theory of musical semiotics* (Bloomington IN: Indiana University Press, 1994).

Taylor, Timothy, *Global Pop* (New York NY: Routledge, 1997).

Temperley, David, 'Syncopation in rock: a perceptual perspective', *Popular Music* 18/1 (1999): 19–40.

—, 'The melodic-harmonic "divorce" in rock', *Popular Music* 26/2 (2007): 323–42.

Théberge, Paul, *Any sound you can imagine* (Hanover NH: Wesleyan University Press, 1997).

Thrills, Adrian, 'It's not over for crowd-pleasing band The Feeling as they return with a new single' (http://www.dailymail.co.uk/tvshowbiz/article-507614/Its-crowd-pleasing-band-The-Feeling-return-new-single.html, 2008), accessed 15 January 2010.

Toynbee, Jason, *Making popular music* (London: Edward Arnold, 2000).

Turner, Mark, *The literary mind: the origins of thought and language* (New York NY: Oxford University Press, 1996).

Vernallis, Carol, 'The aesthetics of music video: an analysis of Madonna's "Cherish"' (originally 1998), in Allan F. Moore (ed.), *Critical essays in popular musicology* (Aldershot: Ashgate, 2007): 443–75.

Walser, Robert, *Running with the devil: power, gender, and madness in heavy metal music* (Hanover NH: Wesleyan University Press, 1993).

—, 'Popular music analysis: ten apothegms and four instances', in Allan F. Moore (ed.), *Analyzing Popular Music* (Cambridge: Cambridge University Press, 2003): 16–38.

Weinstein, Deena, 'The history of rock's pasts through rock covers', in Thomas Swiss et al., *Mapping the Beat* (Malden MA: Blackwell, 1998.): 37–51.

Weisethaunet, Hans, 'Is there such a thing as the "blue note"?', *Popular Music* 20/1 (2001): 99–116.

Whiteley, Sheila, *The space between the notes* (London: Routledge, 1992).

Williams, Raymond, *The long revolution* (London: Chatto & Windus, 1961).

—, *Culture* (London: Fontana, 1981).

Willis, Paul, *Profane culture* (London: Routledge and Kegan Paul, 1978).

Wimsatt, William K. and Bardsley, Monroe, 'The intentional fallacy', in William K. Wimsatt (ed.), *The verbal icon: studies in the meaning of poetry* (Lexington KY: University of Kentucky Press, 1954): 3–18.

Windsor, Luke, 'An ecological approach to semiotics', *Journal for the Theory of Social Behaviour* 34/2 (2004): 179–98.

Winkler, Peter, 'Toward a theory of popular harmony' (originally 1978), in Allan F. Moore (ed.), *Critical essays in popular musicology* (Aldershot: Ashgate, 2007): 251–74.

Young, Rob, *Electric Eden: unearthing Britian's visionary music* (London, Faber & Faber, 2010).

Zagorski-Thomas, Simon, 'The stadium in your bedroom: functional staging, authenticity and the audience-led aesthetic in record production', *Popular Music* 29/2 (2010): 251–66.

Zak III, Albin, *The poetics of rock* (Berkeley CA: California University Press, 2001).

—, 'Bob Dylan and Jimi Hendrix: juxtaposition and transformation "All along the watchtower"', *Journal of the American Musicological Society* 57/3 (2005): 599–644.

Zbikowski, Lawrence, *Conceptualising music: Cognitive Structure, Theory, and Analysis* (New York NY: Oxford University Press, 2002).

—, 'Modelling the groove: conceptual structure and popular music', *Journal of the Royal Musical Association* 129/2 (2004): 272–97.

Index of Recordings Cited

Dates cited in the following entries are the date of release of the original track – this is important in order to maintain a sense of historical location. Catalogue numbers and label names quoted are of the actual (normally, currently available) recording to which I refer in the text, not the number of the original release ([n/a] – not available – indicates that the track or album was only available on download when I completed this discography). This is in order to enable the listener to track down the precise version in those cases where multiple versions exist. Rarely will such differences be material to my argument, but precision is important in this process. Rather than compile a separate index of recordings, which would be cumbersome to use, every recording is indexed here in the discography; page numbers appear after the catalogue number.

It is nowadays comparatively easy to get access to a very wide range of material (one reason I have not fought shy of that range in my examples) – legal free sites such as www.spotify.com and www.mflow.com are an extremely valuable resource, and a large part of this discography can be accessed there.

FRANKIE LYMON & THE TEENAGERS
'I'm not a juvenile delinquent'; *Doo Wop vocal group greats*; Shout! Factory 1957 [D3K 33744]. 278
'Why do fools fall in love?'; *The golden age of rock'n'roll 1956*; Reader's Digest 1956 [RDCD2153]. 278, 280

MADNESS
'New Delhi'; *The rise and fall*; Virgin 1982 [CDOVD190]. 73
'Our house'; *The rise and fall*; Virgin 1982 [CDOVD190]. 64, 183, 236–7
MADONNA
'Material girl'; *Like a virgin*; Warner 1984 [9 47901-2]. 65, 193
MANAU
'Panique celtique'; *Panique celtique*; Polydor 1998 [557-887-2]. 155
MANFRED MANN
'Just like a woman'; *The love songs album*; Universal 1966 [541 266-2]. 280
'Pretty flamingo'; *Original hits*; Disky 1966 [BA 860092]. 170
MANSUN
'An open letter to the lyrical trainspotter'; *Attack of the grey lantern*; EMI 1997 [72438 55741 2 7]. 211
MARCELS
'Blue moon'; *The original doo-wop album*; EMI 1961 [7243 4 73808 2 2]. 278
BOB MARLEY AND THE WAILERS
'No woman no cry'; *Live!*; Island 1975 [548 896-2]. 155, 281
AL MARTINO
'Spanish eyes'; *Music to watch girls by*; Columbia 1966 [SONYTV67CD]. 65
MARVELETTES
'Please Mr Postman' *Tamla Motown Gold*; Universal 1961 [016301-2]. 278
MATCHING MOLE
'Signed curtain'; *Matching mole*; Sony 1972 [505478 2]. 211
GEORGE McCRAE
'Rock your baby'; *Disco mania* 1974 [CRIMCD89]. 147
McFLY
'Colours in her hair'; *Room on the 3rd floor*; Universal 2004 [MCSTD40389]. 281
McGUINNESS FLINT
'When I'm dead and gone'; *Goodnight Saigon*; Disky 1970 [HR 864252]. 281
LOREENA McKENNITT
'Prospero's speech'; *The mask and mirror*; Quinlan Road 1994 [QRCD105D]. 222
MALCOLM McLAREN
'House of the blue Danube'; *Waltz darling*; Epic 1989 [460736 2]. 157
BIG JAY McNEELY
'3D'; *1953–55*; Classics 1954 [CLASSICS 5170]. 132
RALPH McTELL
'Streets of London'; *Streets of London – the best of Ralph McTell*; Castle 1969 [PLS CD 164]. 279

'Wheels ain't coming down'; *We'll bring the house down*; Air Mail Archive 1979 [AIRAC1309]. 212

SLY & THE FAMILY STONE
'Luv'n'Haight'; *There's a riot goin' on*; Epic 1971 [46 70632]. 141

MILLE SMALL
'My boy lollipop'; *1959–64: Ska is the limit, vol.1*; Island 1964 [5243932]. 281

SMALL FACES
'All or nothing'; *It's all or nothing*; Spectrum 1966 [550 047-2]. 280
'Itchycoo Park'; *Best of the 60s*; Disky 1967 [SI 990782]. 47, 299
'Lazy Sunday'; *Ogden's Nut Gone Flake*; Immediate 1968 [IMSP 012]. 138

BESSIE SMITH
'Spider man blues'; *Sweet mistreater*; Blue Orchid 1928 [BLUE202CD]. 79, 126

PATTI SMITH
'Gloria'; *Horses*; Arista 1975 [88697546602]. 77, 106

SNAP
'The power'; *Pump up the volume*; Universal 1990 [584 164-2]. 48, 54

SNOW PATROL
'You could be happy'; *Eyes open*; Polydor 2006 [9852908]. 96

SONNY AND CHER
'I got you babe'; *The best sixties love album ... ever!*; Universal 1965 [VTDCD235]. 196

SONS OF THE PIONEERS
'Baby doll'; *RCA country legends: Sons of the Pioneers*; RCA 1946 [82876 60613 2]. 100

SPARKLEHORSE
'Eyepennies'; *It's a wonderful life*; Capitol 2001 [7243 5 25616 2 9]. 241–2

SPIRIT OF MEMPHIS
'God save America'; *Happy in the service of the Lord*; Acrobat 1953 [ADDCD3007]. 133
'There's no sorrow'; *Happy in the service of the Lord*; Acrobat 1952 [ADDCD3007]. 107

SPIRITUALIZED
'Cheapster'; *Amazing grace*; Sanctuary 2003 [SANCD214]. 87
'Hold on'; *Amazing grace*; Sanctuary 2003 [SANCD214]. 87
'Lay it down slow'; *Amazing grace*; Sanctuary 2003 [SANCD214]. 87

SPOOKY TOOTH
'Offering'; *Ceremony (an electronic mass)*; Minority 1969 [Minor. 271]. 294–7

DUSTY SPRINGFIELD
'You don't have to say you love me'; *Just Dusty*; Universal Music TV 1966 [5317738]. 223–4

STATUS QUO
'Caroline'; *Twelve gold bars*; Vertigo 1973 [080 062-2]. 25–6

STEELEYE SPAN
'The mooncoin jig'; *Now we are six*; Beat Goes On 1974 [BGOCD157]. 194
'Two butchers'; *Tempted and tried*; Beat Goes On 1989 [BGOCD537]. 75

STEELY DAN
'Rikki don't lose that number'; *Pretzel logic*; MCA 1974 [MCLD 19081]. 43

STEPPENWOLF
'Born to be wild'; *Best of Steppenwolf*; Universal 1968 [MCD 19386]. 148, 223

THE VERVE
'A northern soul'; *A northern soul*; VC 1995 [CDHUT 27]. 42, 44, 46
VILLAGE PEOPLE
'Y. M. C. A.'; *The best of the Village People*; Casablanca 1979 [314 522 039-2]. 279
VISCOUNTS
'Who put the bomp'; *Rock 'n 'roll – Rock Britannia*; Reader's Digest 1961 [RDCD2611]. 278

WALKER BROTHERS
'The sun ain't gonna shine any more'; *The best sixties love album ... ever*; Virgin 1966
     [VTDCD235]. 174
ANITA WARD
'Ring my bell'; *Disco mania* 1979 [CRIMCD89]. 147
DIONNE WARWICK
'I say a little prayer'; *Burt Bacharach and Hal David Songbook*; Connoisseur collection
     1968 [VSOPCD128]. 60
WEAVERS
'Wimoweh'; *The best of the Weavers*; Half Moon 1952 [HMNCD012]. 154
PAUL WELLER
Stanley Road; Go! 1995 [828 619-2]. 48
WHEATUS
'Teenage dirtbag'; *Wheatus*; Columbia 2000 [499602 2]. 314–6
WHIPPERSNAPPER
'John Gaudie'; *Promises*; WPS 1985 [WPSCD001]. 197
THE WHO
'Anyway, anyhow, anywhere'; *My Generation – the very best of the Who*; Polydor 1965
     [533 150 2]. 60
'I'm a boy'; *My Generation – the very best of the Who*; Polydor 1966 [533 150 2]. 267
'My generation'; *My Generation – the very best of the Who*; Polydor 1965 [533 150 2]. 22
The Who sell out; Polydor 1967 [527 759-2]. 267
WILD TURKEY
'Gentle rain'; *Battle hymn*; Mason 1972 [MR56422]. 234
HANK WILLIAMS
'Mind your own business'; *Famous country music makers*; Pulse 1953 [PLSCD328]. 64
ROBBIE WILLIAMS
'Angels'; *Life thru a lens*; Chrysalis 1997 [7243 8 21313 2 8]. 105
'Strong'; *The ego has landed*; Capitol 1999 [CDP 7243 4 97726 2 5]. 212
BRIAN WILSON
'Good vibrations'; *Smile*; Nonesuch 2004 [7559-79846 2]. 276–7
'Heroes and villains'; *Smile*; Nonesuch 2004 [7559-79846 2]. 216
'On a holiday'; *Smile*; Nonesuch 2004 [7559-79846 2]. 216
'Roll Plymouth Rock'; *Smile*; Nonesuch 2004 [7559-79846 2]. 216
AMY WINEHOUSE
'Rehab'; *Back to black*; Island 2007 [175 211 9]. 209
'Tears dry on their own'; *Back to black*; Island 2007 [175 211 9]. 273

Index of Names and Topics

This is an index of people (authors, musicians) and topics. Major references to topics are indexed here. References to particular recordings, and their musicians, will not be found here, but in the Index of Recordings Cited.